SUMMER OF '71

ALSO BY JOHN A. JENKINS

The Litigators: Inside the Powerful World of America's High-Stakes Trial Lawyers

Ladies' Man: The Life and Trials of Marvin Mitchelson

The Partisan: The Life of William Rehnquist

SUMMER OF '71

Five Months That Changed America

JOHN A. JENKINS

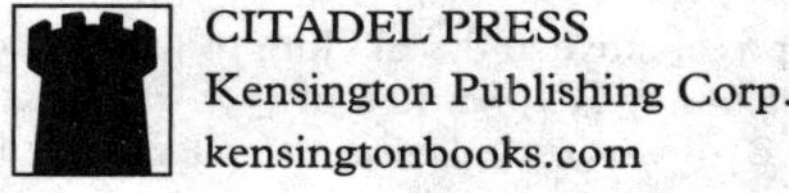

CITADEL PRESS
Kensington Publishing Corp.
kensingtonbooks.com

CITADEL PRESS BOOKS are published by

Kensington Publishing Corp.
900 Third Avenue
New York, NY 10022

All Kensington titles, imprints, and distributed lines are available at special quantity discounts for bulk purchases for sales promotions, premiums, fund-raising, educational, or institutional use. Special book excerpts or customized printings can also be created to fit specific needs. For details, write or phone the office of the Kensington sales manager: Kensington Publishing Corp., 900 Third Avenue, New York, NY 10022, attn Sales Department; phone 1-800-221-2647.

10 9 8 7 6 5 4 3 2 1

First Citadel hardcover printing: July 2026

Printed in the United States of America

ISBN: 978-0-8065-4446-5

ISBN: 978-0-8065-4448-9 (e-book)

Library of Congress Control Number: 2026935114

The authorized representative in the EU for product safety and compliance
is eucomply OU, Parnu mnt 139b-14, Apt 123,
Tallinn, Berlin 11317; hello@eucompliancepartner.com

For Susie, Jenny, Christie, Greg, Zeb, and Caroline . . .
without whom—well, you already know.

The men who shape governments and turn the course of history are prisoners of decisions made before their time, and they themselves imprison their successors by the decisions they take in office. And yet they can see behind them only dimly, and ahead of them not at all.

ABE ROSENTHAL
JOURNAL ENTRY
JULY 6, 1971

RESEARCHERS

Caitlin Doherty
Noah Feiwell
Benjamin Gilbert
Seth Kershner
Isabella Pietro

CONTENTS

A Note to Readers xi
Introduction: Why the Summer of '71 Matters xv

PART I: BACKSTORIES

1: Iconoclast 3
2: Reporter 18
3: Cowboy 38
4: Madman 61
5: Red 85
6: Revolutionary 105

PART II: SUMMER

7: Mayday 127
8: Choice 157
9: Deceit 176
10: Shadows 215
11: Secrets 230
12: Pressure 260
13: Distress 283
14: Revolution 310
15: Aftermath 346

Acknowledgments 355
Sources 357
Photographic Credits and Permissions 362
Notes 365
Bibliography 411
Index 415

America is mired in an unwinnable war, half a world away. The president and his FBI have a secret agenda for revenge against political enemies. Hundreds of thousands of demonstrators mass at the Capitol, many bent on violence. More than thirteen thousand people are rounded up and detained without charges by a police state run amok—the largest mass arrest in America's history. Press freedom is under attack. Threats from China and Russia loom. A Black activist on the run becomes a symbol of resilience and resistance for a movement. The Supreme Court takes up *Roe* v. *Wade*. All this, more than a half century ago. Events that will unalterably reshape America are unfolding. The rhythm of the past resounds today. This is the summer of '71.

A NOTE TO READERS

You are about to return to the summer of '71, a place that may seem eerily like the time you are living in right now. It's not your imagination. Seeds of turmoil and division were planted then. My objective here is to show you—through the writings and accounts of the main players—how events during the summer of '71 set up the hyperpartisanship and ideological battles of today. This is a complex, impressionistic history, but it's all here, and the present-day parallels are striking: a calculating King Lear–like president sowing chaos and bent on revenge; press freedom at risk; surging inflation; Black martyrdom; reproductive rights under attack.

I lived that summer in real time, witnessing many of the events described here. In the summer of '71, I landed a reporting job at a Washington publisher that today is part of the Bloomberg empire. After World War II, four very shrewd young men bought what was then a failing enterprise from the owner of *U.S. News & World Report* for next to nothing—a rock-bottom price of $50,000. By the time I arrived in their daily newsroom twenty-five years later, they'd struck gold. We compiled the "official text" of anything and everything the federal government did that affected American corporations, and hand-delivered those reports every business day. There was no Internet or twenty-four-hour news cycle in those days; you had to be in the room to get the official text. Our subscribers were the Fortune 500. This was like having a license to print money, and yet we flew under the radar of the big dailies, like the *New York Times* and the *Washington Post*. Which was just fine with the owners. We had our niche.

I quickly learned the importance of primary sources. That's what this book is based upon—tens of thousands of them. Memories may fade or change, but documents do not. One of the first things I was told that summer by George Cullen, a crusty seventy-one-year-old former Associated Press editor straight out of *The Front Page*, who smoked a fat cigar and wore a green eyeshade, was the importance of the primary source materials that we gathered. George was wizened and wise. He started out as a telegraph operator for the AP in Jersey City and worked his way up. (When George told me he was the telegrapher who sent the FLASH! across the AP's national wire that war had been declared, I didn't realize at first that the war he was talking about was the one from 1917, not 1941.) "Get the documents," George instructed. "You are not working for a dime newspaper." Ten cents was the newsstand price of the *Post* in 1971. The *Times* cost a nickel more. We charged thousands for a subscription.

On the morning after the biggest economic news since the Great Depression—Nixon's freezing wages and prices and abandoning the gold standard on August 15, 1971—I suddenly became the available man. Congress was in recess. Lawmakers had scattered, and the workaday press and lobbyists and others who make Washington hum were vacationing. I was thrown directly into the tumult, covering the briefings by H. R. "Bob" Haldeman and John Ehrlichman at the White House, John Connally and Paul Volcker at the Treasury, Nixon's address to the joint session of Congress, Canada's Pierre Trudeau pleading for tariff relief (yes, history repeats), and on and on—all things that mattered hugely to the economy and the world that summer.

I was hooked. I've been a journalist in the city of my birth, Washington, DC, ever since—but I've never known another summer like that one. Fifty-five years later, I can say with confidence that America hasn't, either—at least not until now.

My purpose here is to show the drama—the pain and the hope—of a summer when America faced some of its greatest challenges at home and abroad. Watergate was still one summer away. But during the summer of '71, the stage was already being set for the downfall of a president, and the ideological divide of a nation. That's the defining importance of the summer of '71.

This book tells the story of that summer through the larger-than-life stories of people who defined it, notably Daniel Ellsberg, Neil Sheehan, Henry Kissinger, Sarah Weddington, and Angela Davis. Each main character has an important backstory that sets them up for the summer to come. You'll explore that context in Part I. The intertwined threads of the *Summer of '71* begin in Part II. History didn't stop at the end of the summer; some outcomes remained unresolved. I'll tie off the characters' loose ends in Chapter 15: Aftermath.

A few other things to know: Because primary sources are essential to this book, I've relied on contemporaneous accounts where possible. Archives and collections, many of which weren't opened until recently, form the backbone of this book. I have extensively mined those, as you will see in the Acknowledgments and Notes at the end of this book.

If multiple accounts of a particular event are at odds (such as the starkly differing recollections of Ben Bradlee and Edward Bennett Williams about publishing the Pentagon Papers), I have accorded greater weight to documents created in the moment or closer to when something happened. In some instances, quoted material has been edited or condensed for style, grammar, or clarity.

I don't intend *Summer of '71* to be an exhaustive or definitive history of all the events described. I've also chosen not to recount details already thoroughly documented elsewhere by journalists and historians. For those who want to know more, consult the Bibliography. Mine is an impressionistic view of one fateful summer—told through the words of the key players themselves.

Regardless of what you think about the events unfolding in America today, in these pages you will find parallels between then and now. I'll leave it to you to decide which of the main players of the *Summer of '71* are virtuous and which deserve their fate—and to consider the many similarities with today.

John A. Jenkins
Washington, DC
July 2026

INTRODUCTION

Why the Summer of '71 Matters

INFLATION RAGES. CRIME IS RISING. China poses an existential threat. *Roe* v. *Wade* takes center stage at the Supreme Court. Black lives are under attack. Capitol rioters are on trial. Mass arrests are ordered as protesters take to the streets. A scheming, paranoid president seeking reelection battles the press and seeks to subvert not just the political order, but the rule of law itself.

This was the summer of '71.

More than a half century later, it is hard to overstate the importance of the events that defined the American experience during the fateful five months of May through September 1971. America faced upheaval. The characters in this real-life drama were complex—some virtuous, others deeply flawed, but all of them dramatic in their own ways, and each compellingly drawn.

Fifty years on, it's apparent now that the summer of '71 was a scene-setter, not an aberration. Issues and controversies that beset America today—inflation, guns, *Roe* v. *Wade*, civil rights, domestic and international terrorism, intolerance—presented themselves, front and center. A president grappled with them all. And, in that moment, solutions seemed possible, but soon would slip away amid historic scandals.

What does the summer of '71 tell us now? What can it teach us? What lessons shall we, as a republic, learn and apply to the present day? Is our democratic system preordained to repeat cycles of economic turmoil, political discord, racial mistrust, and geopolitical trauma? Was there an alternate path? Through the lives, thoughts, and actions of some of the key actors of the time as they engaged with epic events and each other, the *Summer of '71* will provide compelling insight and, perhaps, a path to answers.

Daniel Ellsberg risks his freedom to seek an end to the Vietnam War. Neil Sheehan and the *New York Times* expose the lies of a generation of American presidents. Sarah Weddington takes up the cause of reproductive rights and becomes the youngest Supreme Court advocate in history. Henry Kissinger embarks on a secret mission to start diplomatic relations with China. Angela Davis becomes an icon of Black struggle and resistance.

Those are but a few of the characters who make the *Summer of '71* such a compelling story with present-day relevance.

It was in the summer of '71 that President Nixon began taping his conversations at the White House, making even more complete the historical record of that time. Richard Nixon's White House tapes comprise 3,800 hours and 7 million pages of transcripts.

This book will certainly use those tapes and transcripts.

Nixon taped everything and everyone in his orbit. With the full availability and indexing of those tapes, his modus operandi becomes clear.

As the first president since the nineteenth century to enter the White House without his party's control of either body of Congress, Nixon necessarily had to play the role of a conciliative politician. Without strong Democratic backing, no part of his agenda could pass. Incongruously (for a president who was, until recently, without peer in his conspiratorial paranoid nature, his antipathy for the press in general, and his hatred for the *Washington Post* and the *New York Times* in particular), that pragmatic imperative actually played to Nixon's strength. And, by the summer of '71, Nixon had achieved notable successes—including major environmental and consumer protections, and the opening of diplomatic relations with China. He aspired to do much more on both the domestic and international fronts. The Watergate cover-up wasn't just his undoing; it canceled those future possibilities, and it undermined his legacy.

A generation later, historians continue to reconsider the Nixon presidency and the opportunities he seized or lost.

Through Nixon's tapes, we now know how one important event of that summer—the Pentagon Papers—fed Nixon's paranoia and became the precursor to Watergate, the biggest political scandal of the last century. Two summers later, I had a reserved seat at the press table in the Senate Caucus Room for the aftermath: the Watergate hearings.

Of course, there were several other crises brewing. What is significant is how Nixon and his team managed those crises that summer: often boldly, as in Kissinger's secret trips to China; sometimes inventively, as with Nixon's plan to replace the income tax with a European-style VAT; and once in a while with epic big plays, such as trying to halt the scourge of inflation by freezing wages and prices. Imperfect solutions. But strategies were being worked on, plans were in motion, and a bipartisan spirit held sway in Congress. It wasn't Camelot, but there was hope.

Historian Douglas Brinkley called Nixon one of the four greatest environmental presidents, along with Theodore Roosevelt, Franklin D. Roosevelt, and Lyndon B. Johnson. Whether Nixon truly cared about the environment, or was even curious about it, is a different matter. But he was a pragmatist, and after a series of environmental calamities—smog in big cities, the Santa Barbara oil spill, Cleveland's Cuyahoga River literally on fire—the public demanded action. Nixon put in the work. He had the potential to enact significant policy.

That changed one Sunday in June, with the Pentagon Papers. Nixon's paranoia, fed by ambitious underlings, got the better of him. He took actions that led inexorably to the creation of a bunch of White House villains known as "the Plumbers," and later to Watergate. Until the Pentagon Papers hit, there remained real potential for positive change from Nixon's presidency. But Nixon's reaction and the ensuing scandal ended that, and set the stage for what we're living through right now.

This is an amazing true story: an operatic summer of hope and despair that political history has ignored.

PART I

BACKSTORIES

CHAPTER 1

Iconoclast

THE IDEALISTIC YOUNG AMERICAN RETURNED to Saigon in late 1965.

Vietnam had become his problematic mistress since he first met her in 1961,[1] and he could not stay away. He'd been gone three years, including a year stuck in Washington, DC,[2] and now he was juiced all over again by the foreignness, the exoticism, the rawness. Living on the edge.

Daniel Ellsberg, thirty-four years old, was back where he wanted to be.

He began keeping a diary:

> Hard to recapture the trace of foreboding in moving through the streets and the crowds of Saigon—one's first night after a year of cable-reading in Washington. Which of the newsboys, the cyclo drivers, the soup peddlers is an enemy?

On his first night back in Saigon, Ellsberg heard an enormous thud. *What's that? Sounds like thunder. Was that lightning on the horizon?*

An old hand told him it was just "105s"—shorthand for F-105 fighter-bombers, the mainstay of the American air war against the North Vietnamese.

Just the routine evening bombing runs.

And artillery fire in the distance:

> Yet the city is not under siege. Most of the artillery firing is unregistered, unobserved. On rooftop restaurants, the steady crump crump of the firing is very plain, the flares in the distance are pretty—and the food in the restaurants is very good.
>
> As I read these notes over, I realize the prevalence of images of danger is only partly due to the fact of danger here. Also, it is because this aspect of things strikes a newcomer most: a scattered, ominous collection of impressions. But I'm hopeful, desperately glad to be here. I expect to work here a long time.[3]

Three years earlier, Ellsberg had visited Vietnam as part of a Pentagon fact-finding task force. Then he was a RAND consultant and a foreign-policy hawk. RAND, the Santa Monica–based "think tank," defined the term so much that its very name was an acronym for its defining characteristic (R & D). It specialized in top secret research for the Pentagon—especially, back then, for the Air Force. Ellsberg expected to observe how the U.S.-backed government in South Vietnam was defeating its Viet Cong adversaries. Instead, he saw the war's reality firsthand.

Ellsberg wanted to shake off the experience. Cognitive dissonance—push out the realities that bother you. He returned to Santa Monica and was soon assigned to work on the most top secret of projects. Defense Secretary Robert McNamara wanted a contingency plan for a full-scale nuclear war.[4] McNamara's Operational Plan for General Nuclear War was so secret, its existence couldn't be acknowledged, lest that lead to a Cold War provocation with Russia.[5]

While at RAND, Ellsberg wrapped up his Harvard PhD thesis about "cognitive bias" in decision-making.[6] He studied the unconscious errors in judgment that occur when people make decisions based on what they think they know (their personal beliefs, experiences, and mental shortcuts) instead of assessing the facts.[7]

Ellsberg's work as a doctoral student at Harvard was, in essence, about human foibles. He researched how and why people often made illogical choices—plainly, *bad* decisions—when faced with uncertainty. So compelling was his work that even before his thesis was accepted at Harvard, his theory about cognitive dissonance, published in a 1961 paper titled "Risk, Ambiguity, and the Savage Axioms,"[8] was given a name: Ellsberg's Paradox.

Ellsberg's Paradox explained how, when faced with a tough decision, people tend to prefer the choice with a known, quantifiable risk over other options with unknown, incalculable risks. Simply put, his theory explained decision-making in times of crisis,[9] and human nature's aversion to uncertainty. Most people are not risk-takers. They'll choose the easy yes over the hard no.

For Ellsberg, there was no better place to put his theories to use than in Robert McNamara's Pentagon. It was the ultimate laboratory for his real-world examination of high-stakes decision-making.

Ellsberg moved to DC in 1964 as a special assistant to Defense Secretary Robert McNamara.[10] Soon the Pentagon all too clearly offered him a case in point. Ellsberg, as a student of human error, slowly came to believe that McNamara and the Pentagon's top brass were getting it all wrong in Vietnam. The war was worth fighting, he thought, and was still winnable. But not the way it was being fought by the Americans. Bombs and napalm couldn't win over hearts and minds.

Perhaps his Defense bosses, mired progressively deeper in the Vietnam conflict, thought he could teach them something: Ellsberg, the glib young hotshot who could knock out policy papers.

On Ellsberg's first full day at the Pentagon,[11] President Lyndon B. Johnson ordered American warplanes to bomb North Vietnam, beginning a major escalation in the war. The pretext was retaliation for an unprovoked attack on two U.S. destroyers in the Gulf of Tonkin. But Ellsberg saw secret cable traffic that immediately belied the American cover story. There had been no attack.[12] The record is unclear as to whether Ellsberg, who was then still a hawk about the war, felt complicit in his knowledge that the Gulf of

Tonkin attack hadn't happened. Biographers, and Ellsberg himself, tell differing stories. Regardless, it was clear to Ellsberg early on that he was involved in concocting a false justification for the U.S. bombing campaign against North Vietnam.[13, 14]

After a year in Washington, Ellsberg was ready to leave.

Vietnam was calling him, that much was certain. Ellsberg wanted to get back to Vietnam, the place he saw as "the only game in town as far as adventure and risk." He could lead "the life of a soldier of fortune." And, leaving behind a broken marriage and two young children,[15] he was intrigued about the ready sexual availability of young Vietnamese women.[16]

Ellsberg thought the war fed the appetites of a certain breed of men who saw cheating death as a kind of validation of their potency, and sex as the adrenaline:

> Vietnam was staffed by divorced people. They were men who did not have strong ties to life. The thought of dying didn't disturb them. It went hand in hand with the fact that divorced men have the highest suicide rate.[17]

Ellsberg recalled watching Lucien Conein, a CIA operative who did dirty jobs in Vietnam when the Americans needed plausible deniability:

> Lou and a bunch of other guys were sitting around a table. There were girls under the table, blowing each guy. The guy who came first had to pay for the drinks.[18]

The fact that Ellsberg was heeding the war's call made him simultaneously energized and uneasy. Ellsberg's teenage life had been marked by trauma when his father fell asleep at the wheel and ran off the road, crashing into a bridge abutment and killing Ellsberg's mother and younger sister. Ellsberg and his father were badly injured; Ellsberg was hospitalized for months.[19] Why had fate spared him? Why did the trauma lead him to recklessly seek out danger? Ellsberg sought psychiatric help and confessed to having a latent desire to be killed.[20] Taking crazy risks, and surviving them, was a kind of perverse validation.

But at least he was in touch with his demons.

Ellsberg's opportunity to return to Vietnam came in the form of an offer from the State Department. He would join a small team embedded with American troops, observing the soldiers in action and making recommendations about improving their counterinsurgency efforts against the Communist guerrillas.[21]

Ellsberg was to be a neutral observer. He was seeing, firsthand, the dedication of the guerrilla forces. Although the United States had an overwhelming advantage in every possible category—weaponry, troop strength, bombs—the adversary had an enduring will to win. The curator of Ellsberg's huge trove of personal papers later explained it like this:

> Ellsberg increasingly felt like a foreign invader fighting in the enemy's backyard. Once, in the Mekong Delta, he was with a unit that was repeatedly ambushed by the Viet Cong. At the end of the day, Ellsberg turned to an American sergeant and asked, "Do you ever feel like the Redcoats?"
>
> "I've been thinking that all day," replied the sergeant.
>
> By the time Ellsberg left Vietnam in 1967, recovering from hepatitis, he had concluded that the war was an unwinnable stalemate from which the United States should try to find a face-saving exit. Over the course of the next two years, his view would grow far more radical. He would come to see the war not only as a mistaken intervention, but as an American war of aggression—unjust, immoral, and criminal, a war that must be ended immediately. What, he began asking, might he do to end the war if he were willing to risk everything—his career and even his freedom?[22]

Not long after arriving back in Vietnam, in September 1965,[23] Ellsberg sensed he'd be walking a line between President Johnson's brain trust back in Washington and the military commanders in the war zone.

LBJ's advisers at the White House wanted to improve the performance of the South Vietnamese Army by mixing South Vietnamese fighters into American platoons and battalions. But American commanders on the ground, led by General William Westmoreland, were resisting. The generals didn't have confidence in the expertise or will of the South Vietnamese fighters. They saw the directive, which came from "the highest authority,"[24] the president himself,[25] as a road to failure.

Henry Cabot Lodge Jr., the American ambassador in Saigon, agreed. Ellsberg came to perceive his own mission as a sham: *Show that it would be a bad thing to commit American troops to the delta. This was to reinforce Lodge's position.*[26] Sham or not, Ellsberg went along with the plan, traveling throughout Vietnam with the American soldiers. His frequent guide was another inveterate risk-taker, John Paul Vann.[27] Legend had it that Vann had been shot down twenty-five times on helicopter missions, including three times in a single day. He'd won every medal for military bravery, except the Congressional Medal of Honor.[28]

Vann was a muscular five-nine,[29] all swagger and cocksure. At age forty-one, seven years older than Ellsberg, Vann had already put in a full twenty years as an Army Ranger and paratrooper, retiring as a lieutenant colonel.[30] Officially, Vann was a "cadre project manager," working as a civilian for the U.S. Agency for International Development.[31] The vague title disguised his role as de facto commander of the American advisers working with the South Vietnamese Army to root out Viet Cong guerrillas in the twelve provinces north and west of Saigon.

Vann "loved his life in Vietnam," Ellsberg said.[32] Among the American expats, Vann was a legend, possessed of astonishing physical and sexual energy. As Ellsberg told it, "Vann would often screw one, two, or three women in the evening and then work until the wee hours of the morning." One time Ellsberg told Vann that he was looking tired. Vann replied that he was tired because he normally got four hours of sleep a night, and the previous night he had only gotten two hours. Ellsberg said he never knew Vann to sleep more than four hours. If Vann caught Ellsberg hanging around, just reading, he'd say, "What are you doing here? You could be out fucking!"

More than once, Vann confessed to Ellsberg that his life had been dominated by being short of stature.[33] "Classic small-man syndrome," Ellsberg called it. He thought that personality trait might be why Vann "sought out danger . . . because he felt he had already lived long enough."

Vann had once been an Army officer in Vietnam, but now he was back as a civilian adviser, ostensibly to show the Americans how they could turn South Vietnam's peasants against the Communists. Vann advocated "pacification" strategies that would appeal to the rural population. In essence, Vann was trying to tell the military that B-52s wouldn't win the war, but programs that brought prosperity and a better life for peasants might.[34] American generals were skeptical.

Vann relished playing the role of buccaneering idealist, a citizen-soldier imbued with the notion that the war was still winnable if only the Army would take his advice.[35] Vann had the run of the country by Jeep and helicopter. For Ellsberg, Vann's life on the edge was intoxicating.

And contagious.

Ellsberg carried a gun, contributed his share of the firepower, and evinced a certain amount of self-awareness, if not soul-searching, about the irony of his situation: "The idea of shooting at people who were shooting at you didn't cause any trauma. All the fighting we did over there we legitimized by calling it self-defense. We were saving our own lives. Saving American lives. Saving our friends' lives. The question we should ask ourselves is why these lives needed saving. Why were we there, saving some Vietnamese and killing others?"[36]

Laid up with a harsh case of amoebic dysentery soon after arriving, Ellsberg wrote in his diary about the sights and smells of Saigon. The writing showed his taste for danger, and his love of easy sex in the country where he would spend the next two years[37, 38]:

> "Ninety percent of the men in this town are armed," says a secretary. Some exaggeration, but the incongruous everpresence of weapons does give this French city the look of a frontier town. "All weapons must be cleared before entering," say frequent door signs. At the cashier's desk at the entrance to the PX, a modern supermarket, is a jumble of Swedish "K" submachine guns, Thompsons, grease guns, and carbines, dropped by the owners while they shop inside. Sidearms are as varied: .45s, snub-nosed .38s, huge Magnum six-shooters, back-pocket Browning .25-caliber pistolets, all in a variety of regulation or quick-draw holsters. Leaving the hotel in the morning, the next man may be covered with grenades—fragmentation, concussion, white phosphorus—and a short-stock paratrooper's submachine gun, with extra clips fastened to it with heavy adhesive tape. A jeep is waiting to take him to an operation 15 kilometers out of town; he will come back to the hotel at night.
>
> In the paper this morning: a woman is stopped for identification by a policeman. She throws a grenade, kills the policeman and injures several passersby; escapes, firing a pistol down an alley.[39]
>
> The system tends to suspect that the man who seems to love Vietnam really loves Vietnamese girls. Plausible. Yet, surprisingly, less truth to it than one would expect. For one thing, these dedicated men are great believers in (1) living out in the provinces, and (2) not getting mixed up with women in the provinces. This makes much of their life quite austere.
>
> "When I tried to extend the second time, you know what the personnel bastard said?" says the Special Forces captain who is in for the night from a western

province, where he is running a special training program with the Hoa Hao (a Buddhist sect). "He said, 'I guess you've got a Number One shack-up job!'" Great indignation followed by a rhetorical pause. At my look of reserve, suggesting I find this guess less than insulting, his friend elaborates: "Why, we spend two months in the provinces—we don't sleep with anybody in the provinces; it's deadly to your effectiveness." "That's a mistake," says Jerry,[40] (an American who has joined the Vietnamese), when I tell him how the fanatics have warned me off liaisons with Vietnamiennes. "You won't come to understand the Vietnamese that way, and they won't understand you. And do you know what you'd be missing?" (Certainly, the bar girls in their white nurses' uniforms are the prettiest whores in the world.)

"I spend most of my off hours water skiing," says the beautiful blonde secretary, "up the river at a Special Forces camp." Inevitably, the secretaries here are something of a special breed. They come from tours in Berlin, Burma, and the Congo; they don't look all that different, but they must be; they seem to have no trouble adapting to the peculiar trials of living on a bullseye.

The girls on the bicycles wear ao-dais ("ow-zai"), loose silk pajama trousers with long panels of silk fluttering down front and back, tight bodices; the rear panel butterflies behind them as they pedal. The girls in the bars wear ao-dai or white nurses' uniforms. They say: "You Number One. You buy me whicky. I love you too much?" There are men who stand around and say, "You know, I don't think you see so many of them that are really beautiful." I think you do.[41]

The lives of Ellsberg and Vann would be forever intertwined with a third man who would later tell their story: *New York Times* reporter Neil Sheehan. Although he was five years younger than Ellsberg, Sheehan was the more experienced of the two when it came to Vietnam, having arrived in 1962, at age twenty-five, as United Press International's Saigon bureau chief—one of only three American reporters assigned full-time to Saigon. David Halberstam, of the *New York Times*, and Malcolm Browne, of the Associated Press, were the other two. By the time he met Ellsberg, Sheehan, too, would be working for the *Times* in Vietnam.

Browne was the dean of what passed for the American press corps in Saigon. "Vietnam then was just a problem in counterinsurgency," recalled Peter Arnett, who later joined Browne as the AP's second man in Saigon, age twenty-seven. "You could sit at a sidewalk café with an aperitif, ogle the graceful girls strolling down the Rue Catinat"—the Champs-Élysées of the city in its heyday[42]—"and talk politics into the warm evening hours." JFK was president. "No signs that Vietnam would become a word synonymous with ugliness, horror, and butchery."

Browne had a small cubbyhole of an office and typed, in Arnett's words, "a two-fingered tattoo on his old Remington." Dispatches went via telegraph to Tokyo. Arnett remembered the first time he walked into the AP bureau:

> I surveyed the cluttered room. A withered hand hung on a wall, brought back, I learned later, by our Vietnamese photographer who had been to an ambush scene. Browne had hitched it to the wall to remind visitors that there was a war beyond the casually luxurious life of the foreign community in the Saigon of the early sixties. Hanging below the hand was a bloodied water container picked up at another ambush. I wanted to leave.[43]

Browne delighted in Arnett's queasiness. He grinned, introduced himself, and tossed across a mimeographed booklet entitled "A Short Guide to News Coverage in Vietnam."

Browne's advice to journalists new to the country was, at once, exhortative and eminently practical:

> Blaze new trails, and do it alone. The fresh story, the new angle, the hitherto unreported—these are the things we want. . . . Battle casualties often die from loss of blood. Belts, ropes and field straps make good tourniquets, and the experts recommend thinking of tourniquets first if you are bleeding heavily. Whenever flying in a helicopter, try to borrow a flak jacket from the crew—two, if possible. The second one is to sit on. You won't be considered chicken. All crew members must wear them.
>
> Carrying pistols is not condoned officially either by Vietnamese or American authorities, but American officers privately approve of the practice. Under no circumstances try to shoot it out with the Viet Cong if you are alone. They also outnumber you and generally pack Tommy guns. If you are stopped by the Viet Cong tell them truthfully who you are and what you are doing. Don't try to throw away your identification papers—identity-less suspects are regarded with great suspicion and are subject to very bad treatment. If you are American and happen to speak fluent, accentless French, you might be off with just a brief lecture.[44]

The relative idyll of those early days soon would change as Buddhist monks began a campaign of ritual self-immolation, protesting the oppression of South Vietnam's Buddhist majority by the U.S.-backed government of Ngo Dinh Diem.

After saying a short prayer, Thich Quang Duc lit a match and dropped it into his lap, instantly engulfing his body in flames. Browne got the only photos. His images of the monk's stoic self-immolation[45] sent shockwaves around the world.

Browne explained:

> While other correspondents got tired of the endless Buddhist street demonstrations that were going on all that summer, I stuck with them, because I had the sense that

> sooner or later something would happen. . . . That morning a Buddhist monk went out and sat down in a main intersection in downtown Saigon. Two of his fellow monks poured gasoline over him, and he set himself on fire and died [thirteen minutes later]. I was there, the only western correspondent present and taking pictures. I suppose I took six or eight rolls of 35-millimeter film.

In an hour, Browne had the film en route to his AP bosses in Tokyo:

> It was clearly theater staged by the Buddhists to achieve a certain political end. At the same time, there was a human element to it that was just horrifying, because the sequence of pictures showed the initial shock of the flames touching his face, and so forth. He never cried out or screamed, but you could see from his expression that he was exposed to intense agony and that he was dying on the spot. . . . I've been asked a couple times whether I could have prevented the suicide. I could not. There was a phalanx of perhaps two hundred monks and nuns who were ready to block me if I tried to move. A couple of them chucked themselves under the wheels of a fire truck that arrived.[46]

Henry Cabot Lodge Jr., about to leave for South Vietnam as the new U.S. ambassador, got a phone call from JFK the next day. The president made clear: *This sort of thing has got to stop.*[47]

Kennedy's man at the State Department, Under Secretary Averell Harriman, was in the thick of the diplomatic action in Vietnam. Not long after the first of many Buddhist immolations, Harriman approved[48] a secret cable to Ambassador Lodge:

> WE MUST FACE THE POSSIBILITY THAT DIEM HIMSELF CANNOT BE PRESERVED. . . . AMBASSADOR AND COUNTRY TEAM

> SHOULD URGENTLY EXAMINE ALL POSSIBLE ALTERNATIVE LEADERSHIP AND MAKE DETAILED PLANS AS TO HOW WE MIGHT BRING ABOUT DIEM'S REPLACEMENT IF THIS SHOULD BECOME NECESSARY.[49]

Two months later, Diem was assassinated in a CIA-backed coup.[50] Conein, the operative whom Ellsberg recalled seeing being pleasured by the girls under the table, delivered the CIA's $42,000 payoff to the plotters.[51]

By the time of Ellsberg's return, in 1965, Vietnam presented a far different quandary than just a few years earlier. LBJ and McNamara soon would send in hundreds of thousands more soldiers. The number of U.S. soldiers in the field around the time Ellsberg first arrived in 1961 was less than a thousand.[52] When Ellsberg returned in 1965, there were 184,000.[53] Ellsberg and Vann, traveling the road to American failure in Vietnam, somehow still held out hope.

From Sheehan's notes about Ellsberg and Vann:

> The two traveled by car down some roads no Americans had ever traveled before. They drove in Vann's Scout. Ellsberg said he saw some of the densest jungles he had ever seen. If he put his arms out the car window, he wouldn't have been able to get it back. The road was wide enough only for one car. They didn't drive after dark, and they were armed.
>
> [The beach town of] Vung Tau was supposed to be sure death, to travel there by road. It was one place the Vietnamese wanted to go because the beach was there. There weren't enough helicopters to take the people there on Sunday.

"We'll take the car instead," Vann said.

> There was some risk, but not enough to curtail use of the road. The people built the risk up in their minds, Ellsberg said. Vann wanted to drive there to convince the people that it was safe and also to show the [Vietnamese] that the road should be open.
>
> John [Vann] decided to take the sedan. They stopped at a garage where he was having French plates made. There was a widespread rumor that the Viet Cong didn't fire on cars that had French plates—and by the time you got past them and they realized you were an American, it was too late for them to get you.
>
> Then they stopped at Vann's house and picked up six grenades. Ellsberg was curious about this, because in the past they only took two grenades. John said it wouldn't hurt to have extra security.
>
> They came upon an ARVN (South Vietnamese Army) platoon and a long line of trucks. The platoon leader came up and started to talk to the pair in French. He said there was no way to get through. "Mille VC!"
>
> Vann doubted the word of the lieutenant who told him that there were a thousand VC on the road [ahead]. Vann said the manner of the soldiers was too relaxed. There was a plane flying very low and Vann noted that, saying that if there were VC ahead they would be shooting at it. Vann drove on, with the lieutenant literally wailing at the skies.
>
> Vann's contention was that if you don't travel the roads, you don't know what's happening. Vann was trying to get the people to drive the roads, and the best way to get them to do it was by personal example. He just wanted people to take small risks—and he was willing to demonstrate that the risks were small.[54]

Ellsberg. Vann. Sheehan. All three had their doubts about the war. For each, the risks were bigger than they knew then.

Vann, still in Vietnam, would be killed in a helicopter crash a few years later. Sheehan came back to the Washington bureau of the *New York Times* with a tapeworm,[55] in September 1966. Ellsberg contracted hepatitis—luckily, Sheehan thought, *before he [could] get himself killed*[56]—and returned to the States in May 1967.[57]

Soon Ellsberg would seek out Sheehan, giving the reporter his first big scoop about the widening Vietnam War.

CHAPTER 2

Reporter

Neil Sheehan and Daniel Ellsberg were both working in Washington by July 1967. Sheehan was a year into his stint as a reporter in the Washington bureau of the *Times*, covering the Pentagon and the occasional White House story. Ellsberg was back at the Pentagon, working on a top secret study about America's involvement in the Vietnam War.

The study was approved that summer[1] by Defense Secretary Robert McNamara. Soon a team of three dozen analysts—military officers and civilians, all promised anonymity—would be at work on the project.[2] The idea was to document the encyclopedic history of America's involvement in Vietnam, leaving a full record for historians. By the time McNamara left the Johnson Administration early the following year,[3] the project had sprawled far beyond the defense secretary's original vision for a mere compilation of documents.[4] The analysts, digging deeply, weren't just gathering documents. They were studying them and summarizing the record in excruciating detail. Their top-line findings: As America's involvement in Vietnam progressed, a succession of administrations had lied about it.

Ellsberg, assigned to study the Kennedy administration's Vietnam policy in 1961, quickly got to work, turning in a 350-page draft report. Ultimately, the full study would comprise seven thousand pages, bound into forty-seven volumes, exploring the history of U.S. involvement in Indochina from the early 1940s to 1968.

Ellsberg was disillusioned by the truth he'd found. He started thinking about how to get the story out.

A March 10, 1968, front-page bombshell in the *Times*, co-bylined by Sheehan, gave him an idea.

The piece was headlined: WESTMORELAND REQUESTS 206,000 MORE MEN, STIRRING DEBATE IN ADMINISTRATION.[5] It was a blockbuster story, based mostly on reporting by Sheehan.[6] The piece revealed, for the first time, that the Army's top general in Vietnam, William Westmoreland, was proposing a huge increase in the number of American soldiers. The military already had 510,000 troops on the ground—the highest level ever. But coordinated attacks by the North Vietnamese Army and Viet Cong guerrillas at the start of the Lunar New Year the previous January 30—the so-called Tet Offensive—had caught the Army off guard, undermined morale, and stunned Americans back home as they watched news film of the U.S. Embassy in Saigon under attack.

Westmoreland's response was to propose, once again, vastly expanding the scope of the war—and, as the leak to Sheehan and his co-author, Hedrick "Rick" Smith, showed, there was fierce opposition within the Johnson administration about it.

The leak about Westmoreland's proposal shocked and angered the Johnson administration.[7] Sheehan later got an earful about it from Walt Rostow, Johnson's national security adviser and his main war hawk. Rostow suspected the leaker to be Townsend Hoopes, a McNamara protégé who was under secretary of the Air Force. Hoopes had already made it clear that he viewed the Tet Offensive as proof of the war's futility.

Sheehan doggedly typed up his notes after speaking to Rostow. Sheehan knew that what he'd been told was a revisionist history, recounted by a Vietnam hawk who supported vastly expanding the war in order to crush the Communists[8]:

> Rostow started talking about the 206,000 troop request story. He said the story was entirely incorrect, and that [LBJ's] memoirs would show this. The story had been an "enormous disservice to the country," he

> said. The story amounted to "a traitorous act." The Times had allowed itself to be "used" by Townsend Hoopes to leak a bowdlerized version of what was going on in the White House at the highest level of decision making. Hoopes and those like him wanted to sabotage the president's policy. Because of the story—and the fact that the press misled the country by falsely interpreting the Tet Offensive as a communist victory, when actually it was "a great defeat"—"thousands of Americans" will have died in vain in Vietnam.

Rostow was at his hawkish best, lecturing Sheehan about wartime journalistic ethics and what he called "Johnson's grand design to end the war." The Tet Offensive, as Rostow explained it, had actually played right into Johnson's master plan, because, in effect, Johnson and his trusted advisers knew about it ahead of time:

> "Guerrilla experts from all over the communist world" met in 1967 "and they decided they were losing the war. They had to do something." The meeting took place in Hanoi and Moscow. The Russians then gave the North Vietnamese "a billion dollars—a billion dollars!" to stage the Tet Offensive. "It was a last resort. The Russians gave them a billion for this one great surge effort." By the time of the 206,000 story, that troop increase wasn't even under consideration. [LBJ's] memoirs would demonstrate how grossly the *Times* had been "used." [Rostow] kept emphasizing this over and over again. He said Hoopes didn't know what he was talking about because he was getting it second hand and the reporters then got it third hand. "Hoopes was hearing from [new Defense Secretary Clark] Clifford and you people were hearing from Hoopes."[9] . . . On Tet, the press had just "caved in," had been traitorous in the effect of its reporting. It was a great defeat for [the North Vietnamese and the Viet Cong]. It wasn't a victory at all.

Sheehan had seen this side of Rostow before:

> Rostow was very friendly throughout the conversation. He made these charges with his usual amiable enthusiasm. You got the feeling there was nothing personal about what he was saying about the press. It was sort of, "You poor fellows, you were so wrong and what a terrible crime you innocently committed." . . . He sounded again like the fanatic I had heard in the White House basement.* If anything, the fanaticism and the "we are right and we were always right" quality had deepened. I had the impression he is really going 'round the bend, he is the mad intellectual, following his theories to the end, hopelessly removed from reality. When reality contradicts what he thinks, he simply ignores or twists it. I also got the feeling that this is the way Johnson thinks now, and that both men are feeding each other in their bitter exile, with Rostow providing the intellectual framework for Johnson's instincts. . . . It was clear he thought Hoopes had been the source for the entire story. I did not enlighten him because I thought I and the *Times* had better keep our cards in hand. . . .
>
> Back at the hotel, he again resumed the discussion about how the *Times* had been "used" by Hoopes to get across his dovish bias at the expense of the facts. He sounded absolutely convinced. He had found the facts to justify his theory. . . . "You people were just wrong, that's all. You'll see. You'll see how you were used."

Ellsberg hadn't been the source of that leak about Westmoreland's request for 206,000 more troops—although he admired

---

*Walt Rostow served as President Lyndon B. Johnson's national security adviser from April 1, 1966, until the end of Johnson's term in 1969. He was considered a rabid hawk when it came to prolonging the Vietnam conflict. Sheehan recalled interviewing him at his office, in the White House basement, during the Johnson administration.

the audacity of whoever brought the story to Sheehan and Smith.[10] But now, for the first time, Ellsberg began strategizing about whether, and how, he could give the *Times* some of the secret documents about Vietnam that he had been compiling for McNamara's Vietnam history.

Because of his work on the Vietnam history commissioned by McNamara, Ellsberg knew that "the public had never actually heard one of the real requests [for troop increases] before. They all had been kept secret; the requests had been publicly denied and lied about by the president. Those lies had then been tacitly confirmed by Westmoreland, who had not revealed that he had made larger requests than the president had announced."[11]

Ellsberg also knew that Sheehan's reporting was as solid as it was incendiary. The story—"a very accurate account of the request for the 206,000 troops"—had revealed one of the most closely held secrets in the administration,[12] and now LBJ was boxed in.

To send another 206,000 troops to Vietnam would require a mobilization of military reserve units, increased draft calls, and a greater financial burden—clearly, not things the public would support. Ellsberg made a calculation about LBJ's likely options. "It was doubtful now, in the wake of Tet, that he was ready to give truth a chance. Under the circumstances, the idea of asking for more troops merely to continue the present strategy within South Vietnam . . . would have seemed so bizarre to the public and Congress that Johnson almost had to use secrecy and lying if he was going to get that."[13]

Ellsberg figured he could leverage the earlier leak into something broader: a scheme to induce paranoia and make it appear, to LBJ himself, that his administration had become somehow a goldfish bowl, and that there was at least one highly placed insider who was ready to break ranks and expose him to Congress.

Ellsberg's plan was to start dribbling out state secrets, "a leak a day,"[14] to create a sense of paranoia within the Johnson White House. From his work on McNamara's Vietnam history, Ellsberg had access to a raft of top secret documents. It mattered less what they were about. *The content was much less important than the leak itself.*[15] It was more important, Ellsberg believed, to show that the administration had lost the singular control over its narrative about the war. That reality would be clear to the president. "If and when he made a decision to grant most or all of the Westmoreland request, it would be known publicly."[16]

Ellsberg was firm in his resolve to keep the pressure on the Vietnam hawks inside the White House with this drip-drip-drip of state secrets, even if it put him in harm's way once the search began for the source of the leaks. But he needed a willing collaborator. Ellsberg had been impressed by Sheehan's scoop, the week before, about Westmoreland's request for the 206,000 more troops—the leak that Rostow assumed came from Townsend Hoopes.

Now Ellsberg decided to get in touch for the first time with a reporter.

Neil Sheehan would be the recipient of Ellsberg's first leak.

When Ellsberg met with Sheehan soon after, he gave Sheehan copies of cables and reports that Ellsberg had access to because of his work on McNamara's Vietnam history, which was still a work in progress. The documents, marked *Secret* and *Top Secret*, were from the Central Intelligence Agency, and they showed that CIA analysts believed that the Army's estimates of enemy troop strength in Vietnam undercounted the Viet Cong guerrillas and their North Vietnamese compatriots by as much as one hundred thousand.

Westmoreland had been citing the Army's lower estimate as evidence that enemy strength was declining, and that the United States was gaining the upper hand in the war.[17] But the CIA, while publicly silent, was secretly providing the reason why the Army had been caught off guard at the start of the Tet Offensive, six weeks earlier: The enemy was far stronger and better organized than the Army knew.

Sheehan's front-page story in the *Times* on March 19 dropped another bomb on the Johnson administration. A single-column headline, top left, said U.S. UNDERVALUED ENEMY'S STRENGTH BEFORE OFFENSIVE, with second- and third-deck heads that were enticing: CIA REPORTS FORCES WERE SIGNIFICANTLY LARGER THAN INTELLIGENCE ESTIMATES. GAP IS 50,000 TO 100,000. Appearing ten days after the revelation about Westmoreland's request for 206,000 more troops, Sheehan's story, based on Ellsberg's leak, quoted "well-placed informants" and "intelligence officials" in Washington. Sheehan's reporting knocked the legs out from under any thought that the United States might be on the way to an easy win. Instead, the United States was fighting a determined enemy. One of the main points of the CIA analysis was that the guerrillas and the North Vietnamese regulars were easily replacing their estimated fifty thousand Tet Offensive casualties with new recruits.[18]

Ellsberg's goal with the leak to Sheehan had been to create panic in the White House and the Defense Department.[19] Johnson, having eased McNamara out of the Pentagon and into the presidency of the World Bank the month before, now had his trusted adviser, Washington lawyer Clark Clifford, as his defense secretary. Ellsberg wanted them to think "that the *Times* reporters were working directly from a high-level document they had acquired from a source within the Administration."[20]

Ellsberg's plan worked. On the day that Sheehan's story appeared, Clifford received a memo from Richard Steadman, a Department of Defense deputy for international security affairs. The memo was classified as top secret:

> The figures on enemy strength contained in the New York Times this morning are precisely the same as those in the last two columns of the attached table, Top Secret, Noforn (not to be shown to foreign nationals). The CIA figures are from a March 1 memorandum prepared as part of the ongoing review of the situation in Vietnam. This document, copy attached, is classified Secret. The last column of the table was added to demonstrate the accuracy of the figures Mr.

> Sheehan quotes from the NIE (National Intelligence estimate). This document is classified Top Secret.
>
> Somewhere in the government there has obviously been a horrendous security violation, and it is my personal belief that this should be investigated, with prosecution, if appropriate.[21]

The documents from Ellsberg continued to yield more stories in the days that followed. *Times* reporter Charles Mohr had a story on March 20, datelined from Saigon[22]: ALLIED ESTIMATE ON FOE INCREASES; NORTH VIETNAMESE IN SOUTH SAID TO NUMBER 84,000.

The following day, March 21, there was another one by Sheehan, again on the front page, describing just how blindsided Westmoreland had been by the Tet Offensive: '68 GAIN WAS SEEN BY WESTMORELAND; 29 DAYS BEFORE TET ATTACKS, HE DEFINED U.S. GOALS—DID NOT EXPECT OFFENSIVE.[23]

Sheehan wrote a concise, devastating lead about Westmoreland's failure:

> In a year-end report submitted 29 days before the communist offensive against South Vietnam cities and major towns, General William C. Westmoreland predicted that the allied war gains of last year would be increased many fold in 1968.
>
> The military commander in South Vietnam sent his report to Washington on January 1. Excerpts from the classified documents have been obtained by the *New York Times*.
>
> They make clear that not only was the offensive unexpected but also that U.S. military planning did not envision the possibility of a setback on the scale of that inflicted by the enemy attacks at Tet, the Lunar New Year holiday.[24]

Inside the White House, there was more turmoil.

LBJ had a group of trusted advisers that he called the Wise Men.[25] They were men—yes, always, men—who had been, in the words of Dean Acheson (who had been Truman's secretary of state and a counselor to four presidents, and who was one of the Wise Men), "present at the creation" of the most important institutions in American Cold War hegemony: the Marshall Plan, NATO, the United Nations, the World Bank.

After three days of leaks, the last one coming on a Thursday, LBJ had the weekend to brood about what to do. He set up a meeting with his Wise Men for early the following week. The group first would receive briefings from officials of the CIA, the Pentagon, and the State Department beginning on the evening of Monday, March 25.[26] By the following afternoon, Tuesday, March 26, they would meet with LBJ.

Fourteen men would be in attendance. In addition to Acheson, there were other household names: Justice Abe Fortas, Johnson's choice to be the next chief justice of the Supreme Court, was present. Others in the group were Cyrus Vance, who'd been McNamara's deputy secretary at the Pentagon until the year before; Robert Murphy, Eisenhower's under secretary of state for political affairs; Henry Cabot Lodge Jr., the Brahmin Republican who soon would resign[27] from his second two-year stint as LBJ's ambassador to Vietnam; Douglas Dillon, the Wall Street banker and former secretary of the treasury under JFK and LBJ; renowned five-star general Omar Bradley[28]; McGeorge Bundy, who'd been the national security adviser to JFK and LBJ; Maxwell Taylor, the four-star general and former ambassador to Vietnam; Clark Clifford, newly installed as McNamara's replacement at the Pentagon; former under secretary of state George Ball; diplomat and lawyer Arthur Dean; former Army chief of staff Matthew Ridgway; and wealthy industrialist Averell Harriman, the former New York governor now serving as LBJ's ambassador-at-large, and whose diplomatic service to presidents stretched back to Franklin D. Roosevelt.

The fourteen Wise Men were Cold War tacticians, and some were battle-tested as well. Bradley had led the Allied assault on D-Day. Taylor was a D-Day paratrooper who went on to become chairman of the Joint Chiefs of Staff. Ridgway led the 82nd Airborne and jumped into Normandy the day after D-Day. Vance had seen action as a gunnery officer in the South Pacific. Murphy planned Operation Torch, the World War II Allied invasion of French North Africa. Bundy had deep involvement in JFK's Bay of Pigs invasion of Cuba and the Cuban Missile Crisis. Harriman had served successively as Roosevelt's wartime ambassador to Great Britain and Russia.

Johnson had gathered this group at the White House before. Four months earlier, he had asked their collective opinion about the Vietnam War. He'd heard, then, a consensus that he should "stay the course," in the words of Bundy, even though "public discontent with the war is now wide and deep." Now he would use them as a sounding board again.

After the Wise Men heard from officials at the CIA, the Pentagon, and the State Department, they met with Johnson. The meeting began at 3:15 p.m. on Tuesday. This time the atmosphere was one of pessimism, the tone set by Johnson himself.

"Our fiscal situation is abominable," Johnson started out.[29] The war was costing not just thousands of American lives, but billions of dollars. Johnson had already asked for a tax increase to fund the war—soon a 10 percent surcharge would be added to everyone's tax bill. Recession loomed. One of Johnson's main Vietnam critics in his own party was Ted Kennedy, the senior U.S. senator from Massachusetts who now held the seat of his assassinated older brother, John. Ted Kennedy was openly challenging the president who had succeeded the fallen JFK. Johnson spoke:

> There has been a panic in the last three weeks. It was caused by Ted Kennedy's report on corruption and the ARVN (South Vietnamese Army) and the GVN (South Vietnamese government) being no good, and now a release that Westmoreland wants 206,000 men

> and a call up of 400,000. That would cost $15 billion. That would hurt the dollar and gold. The leaks to the *New York Times* hurt us.

Ellsberg's leaks clearly had achieved their desired effect:

> The country is demoralized. I will have overwhelming disapproval in the polls and elections. I will go down the drain. I don't want the whole alliance and military pulled in with it. . . . I wouldn't be surprised if they repealed the Tonkin Gulf Resolution. Senator [Richard] Russell wants us to go in and take out Haiphong (undoing the mines the U.S. placed in North Vietnam's only major port). Senator [Eugene] McCarthy (already challenging LBJ's reelection) and Senator Kennedy and the left wing have informers in the departments. The *Times* and the *[Washington] Post* are all against us. Most of the press is against us. How can we get this job done?
>
> We need more money in an election year, more taxes in an election year, more troops in an election year, and more cuts in an election year. As yet, I cannot tell them what they expect to get in return. We have no support for the war. This is caused by the 206,000 troop request and the leaks, by Teddy Kennedy and Bobby Kennedy. I would have given Westy (Westmoreland's nickname) the 206,000 men if he said they needed them, and if we could get them.[30]

Having heard that, there was little the Wise Men could do but tell Johnson the truth. They took a vote. LBJ's twenty-six-year-old assistant, Tom Johnson (no relation to LBJ), listened and took notes.

As Tom Johnson took down their comments, the futility of LBJ's situation began to sink in. Only three men voted to keep fighting in Vietnam: two generals, Bradley and Taylor, and the hardened military strategist Murphy. Those three sided with giving Westmoreland what he wanted—in effect, unleashing the full might of the American military to crush any and all opposition. Westmoreland even had a total-victory nuclear scenario in his back pocket.

Such an all-out military solution was untenable to the others.

Bundy spoke first and summarized how the voting had played out:

> There is a very significant shift in our position. When we last met, we saw reasons for hope. We hoped then there would be slow but steady progress. Last night and today, the picture is not so hopeful, particularly in the [South Vietnam] countryside.[31]

Bundy then cut quickly to what he called the majority view, quoting Acheson by name so as to give their findings added gravitas:

> Dean Acheson summed up the majority feeling when he said that we can no longer do the job we set out to do in the time we have left and we must begin to take steps to disengage.[32] That view was shared by: George Ball, Arthur Dean, Cy Vance, Douglas Dillon and myself.
>
> We do think we should do everything possible to strengthen in a real and visible way the performance of the Government of South Vietnam.
>
> There were three of us who took a different position: General Bradley, General Taylor, and Bob Murphy. They all feel that we should not act to weaken our position and we should do what our military commanders suggest.

As to Westmoreland's request for an additional 206,000 men, Bundy tried to thread the needle—acknowledging the realities facing the battlefield commanders, while eschewing anything that would appear to support further expansion of the war:

> On troop reinforcements, the dominant sentiment was that the burden of proof rests with those who are urging the increase. Most of us think there should be a substantial escalation. We all felt there should not be an extension of the conflict. This would be against our national interest.

Most noteworthy was that he felt compelled to state the obvious:

> The use of atomic weapons is unthinkable.

The hawks weighed in next. They could only offer words of cold comfort to LBJ.

Bradley, the five-star D-Day general, was worried about showing American weakness. He supported sending in more support troops—but was willing to stop the heavy air war the United States was conducting against the North. Bradley had a condition for that: the bombing could stop only if the Americans got a neutral third party, like the pope, or the secretary general of the United Nations, to call for it. *Let's not show them that we are in any way weakening.*

Murphy, Eisenhower's former right hand, professed himself *shaken by the position of my associates. The interpretation given this action by Saigon would be bad. This is a "give-away" policy. I think it would weaken our position.*

Taylor, the four-star general and former ambassador to Saigon, added: *I am dismayed. The picture I get is a very different one from what you have. Let's not concede the home front; let's do something about it.*

But that was precisely the problem. Short of massive escalation—and, even, the "unthinkable" nuclear option—there was no clear path to victory, whatever that looked like. Dean Acheson finally spoke up:

> The issue is, can we do what we are trying to do in Vietnam? I do not think we can. Fortas said we are not try-

> ing to win a military victory. The issue is, can we by military means keep the North Vietnamese off the South Vietnamese. I do not think we can. They can slip around and end-run them, and crack them up.[33]

When LBJ finally spoke, stunned at having lost the support of his most trusted counselors, he did his best to lighten the atmosphere. He confessed that he was hearing a more dire account of America's prospects in Vietnam than from briefings he'd received firsthand. He searched in the moment, only half successfully, to find the right words to describe the discordance: *The first thing I am going to do when you all leave here is to get those briefers [from] last night.*

The room's pent-up discomfort gave way to laughter.

I want to hear what they said, because I want to see—because I want to evaluate it. I haven't heard of that kind of pictures.

Johnson thanked the Wise Men and told them he had one other request: that they keep their meeting with him a secret. *Keep it to yourself. Do not discuss it.*[34] LBJ was about to make some important decisions, and he didn't want to be second-guessed in the press. *If it does go the way of some of our intelligence documents and some of our reports that are filed with the Defense Department and State Department do, they'll wind up in print.*[35]

Five days later, there was another bombshell headline in the *New York Times*. To be sure, it was yet another direct result of Ellsberg's leaks to Sheehan. But the timing of this one was entirely LBJ's. A banner headline stretched across the front page on April 1, the morning after a stunning surprise announcement:

> JOHNSON SAYS HE WON'T RUN;
> HALTS NORTH VIETNAM RAIDS;
> BIDS HANOI JOIN PEACE MOVES[36]

A month later, Harriman would be on his way to Paris as LBJ's emissary to peace talks with the North Vietnamese. Vance would serve as Harriman's deputy.[37]

Those two Wise Men were on their next mission.

Sheehan, meanwhile, had proved himself to be a skilled investigative reporter who worked best as a lone wolf. But that also made him something of a target within the big *Times* newsrooms in New York and Washington. His close-to-the-vest style was best suited to his postings in places like Vietnam and Jakarta, where he could operate independently—slowly and methodically working up a story without the pressure of hitting a daily deadline. He produced clear, expository copy, but the act of writing was painstaking for him; getting words down on paper was never easy.

Returning to the *Times* Washington bureau after Saigon meant Sheehan was signing on for a high-pressure, internally politicized environment that he was ill-suited for. As he chafed under the daily grind of the Pentagon beat, others in the newsroom perceived him as brooding and eccentric,[38] and were annoyed that it often took him longer than most to turn out a major story.

Sheehan's protector and mentor at the *Times* was the paper's managing editor, Abe Rosenthal. The top man on the editorial side was known to play favorites, and Sheehan certainly was one. It fell to Rosenthal to mediate between Sheehan and the Washington bureau chief, Max Frankel, who perceived Sheehan as a journalistic problem child.

When Sheehan wanted to be cut loose from his regular Pentagon beat to work on a series about secret Swiss bank accounts and money laundering, it was Rosenthal who intervened and got Frankel to agree to it.

Sheehan was grateful.

Dear Abe, Sheehan wrote two days after Rosenthal had arranged the special assignment:

> In my surprise at how swiftly you had arranged things with Max, I did not adequately thank you for the opportunity to do some real investigative reporting. I'm deeply grateful. . . .

> I realize that you don't expect quick results, but I intend to do my best to fully justify the chance you're giving me. The job will certainly make my work much more meaningful for me, and I hope it will make the *Times* a better paper for you.

Sheehan's letter recalled his first meeting with Rosenthal, at the *New York Times* Tokyo bureau in 1964 while Sheehan was based in Southeast Asia for UPI. The two clicked, and when Rosenthal thereafter returned to New York as metropolitan editor, he pulled in Sheehan for the one reporting job he had available: a seven-month stint in Albany, covering state government for the *Times*. As Sheehan recalled it:

> This is the second time you've pulled me out of the water. When I needed a job and you needed an Albany reporter, not a young foreign correspondent, you hired me. Here we go again, and again my thanks.[39]

Rosenthal returned the compliment:

> Dear Neil,
>
> That was a warm and kind letter, and I do appreciate it. I remember the first time you walked into my office in Tokyo. I had a kind of hunch then that I might be seeing more of you. And I am awfully glad the hunch worked out!

But Frankel, not a party to the mutual admiration, inwardly seethed about the special preference Sheehan was afforded, and what he saw as the inordinate time that Sheehan was taking to get the story. Sheehan, pulled from the Pentagon, was chasing down all manner of financial corruption, following up on allegations from the Manhattan prosecutor that implicated the FBI's director, J. Edgar Hoover (getting rich off of secret oil-drilling ventures and freeloading on undisclosed vacations and junkets), wealthy diplomat Averell Harriman (money laundering), and Richard Nixon (investments in Mafia-run casinos, while Nixon was vice president, with his friend Bebe Rebozo, in Cuba and the Dominican Republic).

All Frankel saw was a wild-goose chase. After Sheehan had been at work on the series for two-and-a-half months, without producing anything, Frankel and his deputy at the bureau, Bob Phelps, called a meeting.

The two editors took Sheehan to task. Frankel told Sheehan how frustrated he was. The paper had "no control" over what Sheehan was up to on his "side adventures." Sheehan wasn't keeping his editors informed. "Everything is in a panic—[we're] suddenly overwhelmed with Sheehan [creating] all these problems. . . . The crisis of the moment awaits." Frankel's criticism centered on Sheehan's eccentric habits, and his penchant for secrecy.[40]

Frankel and Sheehan never got their professional relationship on track. It came down to a clash of egos, and styles, that neither man could get past. Sheehan saw himself, unabashedly, as a "non-conformist" trying mightily to adapt to the rigid culture of the *Times*. Frankel perceived him as ungovernable, insubordinate. When, two years later, Frankel finally decided he'd had enough and wanted to send Sheehan packing from the bureau, he called him "inadequate"—a "failure." The two ended whatever last vestiges remained of their professional comity with dueling letters. First came Sheehan's eight-pager, delivered at midnight to Frankel's home in Washington:

> I'm not trying to escape authority, Max, I'm trying to live with it. You may remember that I gave up general investigative reporting and tried to narrow my focus to foreign policy and defense because too many bosses telling me what to investigate and too many bosses having to clear my stories when they were finished made the end product not worth the time spent. And if you look at the best stories I have produced since leaving the White House beat in early 1969, they have been

produced on my own initiative, or by selecting one out of many directions and then swimming upstream against the tide of multi-directions. . . .

One of the frustrations of working for the *Times* is that no matter what progress you make as a reporter, unless someone decides to pull you out of writing and make you an editor, you end up being told to get back into the bullring again with everyone else. . . . I'm searching for a place on the *Times* that will satisfy me and the editors. . . . I realize that my work on the *Times* has frequently aroused irritation within the hierarchy because it has been non-conformist. I also know that if I do not someday find a place on this paper, I shall eventually become more of a liability than an asset, and I shall either force myself to leave or someone will do the forcing for me. . . .

I used to be a good soldier. I did what I was asked to do. It didn't succeed. One's life, as you so well know, is one's work. Being a good soldier often means not doing one's best work. Life is too short not to try for the best. And there it is.

Sincerely,
Neil[41]

Frankel was furious, and he let Sheehan know it in a reply to Sheehan that described the reporter's missive of the day before as "ambition" . . .

wrapped in an indictment of the way that I and other editors of the *Times* perform their responsibilities. Whatever our deficiencies, the editors of the *Times* deserved better than that in your thoughts. . . . More than any other reporter in the bureau since I have led it, those editors have indulged you in your taste of stories, in your peculiar work habits, in your outside writings and lecturing and promotion activities. Even if your assignments have been sometimes as confusing as you contend, the *Times'* adjustment to your work schedules has been vastly more difficult and troublesome still. I find your complaint about the working conditions that have allegedly hobbled your work so sad and ludicrous that I wish only to escape from the subject forever. . . .

The only irritation that your work has ever produced "within the hierarchy," as far as I know, came when it was deemed to be inadequate, not "non-conformist," as you put it. But enough of this, too.

It is plain, I think, that you do not wish to work "for" the Washington bureau chief. I am sorry about that, because now I shall not even be able to help you realize your ambitions for yourself. I shall make my other recommendations to the people that I work for. And I wish you only good fortune.

Yours,
Max[42]

Frankel next sent Rosenthal a three-page, single-spaced memo that ripped Sheehan from both ends to the middle and made it clear that he wanted Sheehan to be fired.

Sheehan's missive, Frankel wrote to Rosenthal:

> wasn't simply an immature statement by an artistic temperament, but the sad end of the affair for me. This man has lost his claim to our good will and to our long and incredibly indulgent efforts to make him productive. All this from a reporter who could not even write the lead on his own great yarn. This from a man who has consumed more editors' days, missed more deadlines, defaulted on more stories and taken more advantage of our easy personnel and scheduling policies than any reporter I have ever served with or supervised.
>
> I do not wish to belabor his petty list of complaints about the *Times'* methods of operations, except to say

> that he is fundamentally misguided and wrong from beginning to end. He has been a nightmare to manage from the day I assumed this job. . . .
>
> I enclose my memorandum to him, which I regard as the most restrained but still honest rendering of my attitude. If he is angling toward a resignation, with Technicolor coverage in the outside press, I would be proud to have him publish it. Unfortunately, it has reached [the] point where we must be mindful of such considerations.
>
> But what do we do?[43]

That was the question. Sheehan was a misfit in the hierarchical newsroom of the *Times*. But there was a second edge to that sword. Sheehan's predilection for working alone, and in secret, would provide the *Times* an incalculable advantage one day.

CHAPTER 3

Cowboy

DANIEL ELLSBERG FIRST ENCOUNTERED HENRY Kissinger at Harvard in 1957.[1] Kissinger, at age thirty-four, was eight years older than his student Ellsberg and already an academic wunderkind.

But Ellsberg, twenty-six, was showing himself to be a precocious upstart, taking cues from Kissinger and jumping into the debates in the defense studies seminar that Kissinger ran.[2]

Ellsberg had recently been discharged from the Marine Corps, having served as a rifle commander with the Sixth Fleet in the Mediterranean. He'd been accepted into Harvard's graduate program before joining the Marines, but deferred entry to get his military service out of the way. Now, upon leaving the Marines, Ellsberg was back at Harvard on a three-year fellowship to study independently at the university. Kissinger was already a brilliant academic showman.

The two would cross paths frequently in the years to come.

Kissinger was a googly-eyed policy wonk, decades before the term got traction. He made his reputation as a pop academic by writing and speaking about the one subject that the entire world was transfixed by, and troubled about in the 1950s: the A-bomb.

Kissinger hadn't yet become a full professor at Harvard when, in 1957, he published a provocative book called *Nuclear Weapons and Foreign Policy*.[3] The book expanded on his Harvard PhD dissertation,[4] *A World Restored*, which he'd turned in the same year.

Kissinger's book, a finalist for the National Book Award the following year, was a collection of three essays. Its importance didn't lie in its length, but, rather, its punch. Kissinger had smacked the world in its collective face by daring to suggest that sometimes using nuclear weapons—albeit, small ones—was the right call in wartime.

This was Kissinger's "small war" theory—in essence, that it would be "the lesser evil" for a nation to engage in limited nuclear war, if the only other options were capitulation or annihilation.[5]

Kissinger's idea got attention in a place that mattered.

A thirty-one-year-old *New York Times* reporter named Russell Baker heard about Kissinger's theory. Baker was a newcomer to the paper's bureau in Washington, DC, having jumped a few years earlier from various journeyman assignments (rewrite man, police reporter, London correspondent) at the *Baltimore Sun*.

Baker would go on to be a celebrated columnist for the *Times*, a veritable Will Rogers of his time and one of the best-known newspaper humorists ever. Later, Baker often laced his satirical columns with characters and dialogue he invented, but during a desultory late summer in Washington, slogging away at his Underwood, he typed out a story that was anything but fiction.

Baker was working the White House beat during the dog days of August. When he found out that Kissinger's book was being seriously talked about by Eisenhower's Cold War strategists, he wrote a front-page article for the Sunday *Times* that started out like one of the satires he later would be known for.

Baker's story appeared on August 11, 1957. Although the editors slotted it in the far-right bottom corner on page 1, they gave it a catchy headline: U.S. RECONSIDERING "SMALL-WAR" THEORY.

Anyone reading the first few paragraphs of Baker's story today would have wondered if it was some kind of perverse hoax, a back-to-the-future story from *The Onion*:

> For the first time since President Eisenhower took office, officials at the highest government levels are displaying interest in the theory of the "little" or "limited" war. The new thinking arises from the development of small nuclear weapons.

Baker went on to explain the prevailing theory of the time: In the new atomic age, nuclear war could never be contained; even a localized nuclear conflict would soon blow up into massive retaliation resulting in full-scale thermonuclear war. But now, Baker explained, that theory of global nuclear annihilation was being rethought. And who, the reader might ask, was behind the redo? Baker buried the payoff, deep into the story:

> The lead in this debate has not been taken up by anyone connected with the government, but by a scholar of foreign affairs, Henry A. Kissinger, in his recently published book, "Nuclear Weapons and Foreign Policy."

Kissinger's earliest writings, in other words, spelled out precisely the calculus that Ellsberg soon also would embrace: that the best world leaders were those who made rational choices from among the options in front of them, and that the most effective way to bring about the desired result in war was to make the logic of those choices clear to the enemy. Sometimes, Kissinger theorized, that meant taking things to the brink by bluffing; the existence of tactical nuclear weapons could give credence to the bluff.

Kissinger's earliest writing presaged the strategy he would bring to the Nixon administration's Vietnam policy, a decade later. Baker's story nailed Kissinger's key premise:

> The new concentration on small atomic weapons, it is now being argued, will have the effect of adjusting modern weaponry to the purposes of limited war. Thus, the argument runs, it will no longer be necessary to rely solely on the ultimate force to achieve relatively moderate policy objectives. . . .
>
> What would emerge would be a type of warfare roughly analogous to the tests of strength of the Middle Ages, with neither side committing its prestige to the utmost nor insisting upon "unconditional surrender."

This marked the beginning of Kissinger's long, symbiotic, sometimes tempestuous, and often demanding relationship with the *Times*.

Two months after Baker's article, the *New York Times Book Review* published a glowing review of his doctoral dissertation, *A World Restored*, which Kissinger had turned into a 354-page case study of the crafty Napoleonic era statesman Metternich[6]:

> One of the most promising young American experts in the field of international relations and diplomacy, Henry A. Kissinger, has skillfully applied the insight he has gained from the study of present world problems to the situation facing statesmen at the end of the Napoleonic wars.... The story is well known, but it gains in Mr. Kissinger's analysis. His often brilliantly formulated generalization shows the trained mind of the political scientist.

What impressed the reviewer was Kissinger's analysis of the compromises forged by Metternich, who used his diplomatic skills to help bring a long stretch of relative peace to Europe following the Napoleonic Wars.

> His concluding chapter on the nature of statesmanship should be carefully read and pondered by all students of international relations today.

Young Kissinger was on a roll. Mike Wallace, the hard-hitting television interviewer, had a prime-time live interview show out of New York, broadcast on ABC-TV. Kissinger was Wallace's guest on July 13, 1958.[7] Wallace brought him in to talk about the "small war" theory that Russell Baker had first written about.

Wallace interviewed in the same melodramatic style that would later be his trademark on *60 Minutes*—an edgy one-on-one interview; staccato questioning; the background nothing but a black void; camera locked in tightly on the person he was grilling, to pick up every twitch, every drop of perspiration.

Kissinger proved himself ready for prime time.

This was live television. The cameras rolled:

WALLACE: Good evening, I'm Mike Wallace. Tonight we'll tackle the immediate issue that will decide the fate of our freedom, certainly, and possibly even of our survival. We'll discuss the conflict between the United States and the Soviet Union, and the chances of war. Our guest, Professor Henry Kissinger, Associate Director of the Center for International Affairs at Harvard University, and the man whose recent proposals substantially influenced President Eisenhower's plan for military reorganization. Dr. Kissinger, last year your attack on our foreign and military policies was apparently found so disturbing that the *New York Times* carried this front-page story: They said, "For the first time since President Eisenhower took office, officials at the highest government levels are displaying interest in the theory of the 'little,' or 'limited,' war. The theory of massive retaliation is being re-examined." That was a year ago. What has come of the re-examination?

KISSINGER: I think the theory has been re-examined; the practice has not been.

WALLACE: The theory has been found wanting, then?

KISSINGER: The theory has been found wanting, but I don't think we have made the effort, or spent the money, or made the sacrifices necessary to get a capability for limited war.

WALLACE: Well, now, in order to better understand your proposal for limited war, perhaps it would be well for you to define what you understand to be our current United States' military policy. What is our military policy?

KISSINGER: Well, our current military policy is based on the doctrine of massive retaliation: that we threaten an all-out attack on the Soviet Union in case the Soviet Union engages in aggression anywhere. This means that, against almost any form of attack, we base our policy on the threat that will involve the destruction of all mankind; and this is too risky, and I think too expensive.

WALLACE: You obviously think it's wrong, dangerous to our security. I wonder if you would expand on that. Just because of, what you say, the risk and just because of the expense, it is not worthwhile?

KISSINGER: No, what it will mean is that in every crisis, an American president will have to make the choice whether a given objective is worth the destruction of American cities. The American president will have to decide whether Beirut, or whatever the issue may be, is worth about 30 million American lives. In practice, I'm afraid the American president will have to decide that it is not worth it, and it will therefore encourage the piecemeal taking-over of the world by Soviet aggression.

WALLACE: Because you believe the Soviets understand our unwillingness or inability, certainly our unwillingness, to wage an all-out war?

KISSINGER: The Soviets will understand our increasing unwillingness to engage in this kind of war, and therefore their task will be to present us with the challenge which doesn't ever seem worth taking the final jump, but which the accumulation of which is going to lead to the destruction of the free world.

WALLACE: In place of that policy, what do you believe our military and political policies should be?

KISSINGER: Well, the first thing I'd like to say is that military policy can't be a substitute for other measures. It can only be the screen behind which other measures are possible.

A good start to the interview. Kissinger was keeping it simple. But when Kissinger started to wander further afield, into his scholarly Harvard-speak about game theory in decision-making, Wallace quickly brought him back. This was prime time. Wallace obviously didn't want to hear a professorial lecture about the psychology and math behind game theory, or the realpolitik of using diplomacy to achieve practical objectives. He wanted Kissinger to get to the headline: nuclear war.

Kissinger obliged:

> KISSINGER: You say I advise a policy of limited nuclear war. I do not advise that we initiate war. The question of war will arise only if the Soviet Union attacks; then, if the Soviet Union attacks, and in fact, we are very much more afraid of total war than they are, they will gradually blackmail the free world into surrender. Everything that I say is based on the assumption that we are as willing to run risks as the Soviet Union. If this is not the case, we are lost; and I think we ought to face that fact.

Kissinger, alone, was willing to talk about the unthinkable: a nuclear war between the superpowers. That meant notoriety. And the notoriety was immense: best-selling books, network television interviews. Kissinger had a flair for showmanship. He could read people; could read an entire room. He learned early on how to please his audience, how to package the goods. His brilliance, combined with a sharp wit and dry, deadpan humor, gave him a certain ingratiating charm. Later, when he left Harvard to work in the Nixon White House, Kissinger would be not just a sought-after adviser to world leaders, but a regular in the Hollywood gossip columns. Frank Sinatra became his buddy. Henry was a captivating romantic partner for Hollywood starlets.

Oh, the starlets, and the cachet. Beginning with Kissinger's frequent trips to RAND, in Santa Monica, he'd mapped the route down Sunset Boulevard and into Hollywood.[8] But, in signing on with Nixon, Kissinger became tabloid fodder—before that was a thing.

The list of beautiful women the divorced Kissinger squired—and was photographed with—was, indeed, long. In the time before "Pics or It Didn't Happen," Kissinger gave the paparazzi the goods. Among the women Kissinger made sure he was seen and photographed with: Shirley MacLaine, Marlo Thomas, Candice Bergen, Liv Ullmann, Raquel Welch, Elizabeth Taylor, and Liza Minnelli.

"He had a weakness for young, beautiful, lesser-known types," wrote Walter Isaacson, one of Kissinger's biographers. "[They] offered, at least in the abstract, the aura of something more illicit."[9] Mamie Van Doren, a buxom B-movie blonde whose friends included Marilyn Monroe and Jayne Mansfield,[10] was one of those. While she was staying at a boyfriend's New York apartment (the boyfriend away), Kissinger showed up to take her out.[11] He also brought her as his guest to a White House state dinner, and she accepted an invitation to return to his townhouse overlooking Rock Creek Park[12] afterward—a visit interrupted by a call from the president. "In his bedroom were these piles and piles of dirty clothes," she recalled. "He apologized for the mess and said he'd been traveling. I believed him because his socks really stank. He obviously hadn't had time to change them."[13]

Barbara Howar was a Georgetown socialite during that time. Willie Morris turned her story of upward mobility into a novel, *The Last of the Southern Girls.* Howar really was that girl—"a good-looking, acid-tongued divorcee"[14] who'd slept around, been around, and seen a lot. Howar had spent enough time with Kissinger to know some things about the man she called "the super Kraut." His bachelor pad, she said, "looks like a Holiday Inn. The furniture is sort of Grand Rapids Motel. The one room that shows that somebody lives there is his library. The walls and bookshelves are lined with pictures of Henry with every world leader you've ever heard of, and some you haven't."[15]

Kissinger drove around DC in a white Mercedes. "Sex in the Nixon administration," Howar deadpanned, "consists of Henry Kissinger slowing down to thirty-five miles an hour when he drops you off at night."

Zsa Zsa Gabor had her own crazy stories about Kissinger. She told of going out to dinner with Kissinger in Beverly Hills, on one of his frequent trips to Nixon's so-called Western White House in San Clemente. Kissinger invited himself back to her place afterward, she said. But then—here we go again—Nixon phoned, and Kissinger jumped back into his sedan, only to crash into Zsa Zsa's electronic gates. Still trying, he asked to see Zsa Zsa while she was appearing on stage in Boston—she was starring in the road company of *Forty Carats*—but canceled at the last minute "because we're invading Cambodia tomorrow." It was a lame excuse, since the secret bombing had been going on for a year. But Zsa Zsa, none the wiser, included it in her autobiography. It seems Kissinger was negotiating on the world stage, but he just couldn't close those deals back home.

In Kissinger's White House heyday, the most widely read gossip columnist in the country was Lloyd Shearer, who, under the pseudonym "Walter Scott," wrote the "Personality Parade" column in *Parade*, the Sunday magazine that went out as a supplement to 129 newspapers, with a combined circulation of 29.6 million. Shearer was a schmoozer who got to know Kissinger, as well as Ellsberg. For Shearer, the Kissinger-Hollywood connection made snappy copy. Nixon, running a buttoned-down White House, got some mileage out of it, too. It gave his staid administration a humanizing touch.[16]

Publicly, Kissinger professed not to know how he got the reputation. "I didn't build it up. Others did. I find the playboy image very amusing."

The reality was different. Kissinger cared greatly about his rough edges, and he wanted the top-notch White House speechwriters to play up his reputation as a ladies' man. Among Nixon's writers, the best of the lot was William Safire, usually called the less formal "Bill" by colleagues and Nixon. Nixon's new chief of staff, H. R. "Bob" Haldeman, was a J. Walter Thompson executive, and Haldeman obviously saw something he liked in the former public relations man. Safire, at age thirty-nine, was already an old hand on the New York PR and advertising scene. He'd been a press agent for Lionel trains, Rheingold beer, Pfaff sewing machines, Good Humor, and Ex-Lax.[17] So, why not throw Kissinger into the mix?

As Safire recalled it, "[Kissinger] took me aside from time to time, to ask if this odd turn of events was a useful thing: 'Do you suppose people will think the president's national security adviser is gaga?' I said America would sleep better every night knowing their national security was in the hands of a red-blooded American boy, but he should stop saying 'gaga,' which went out with the Charleston."

Kissinger was booked to give a speech at what had previously been called the Women's Press Club, in DC. Female reporters weren't allowed into the National Press Club until 1971, so the women had formed their own. There would be no better place, no better opportunity, for Kissinger to poke fun at himself and earn some points with the all-female club.

Safire gave Kissinger a script, keyed to the news of the day, which centered on a secret visit to China, the Cold War negotiating concept of "linkage," and the eccentric, elusive billionaire Howard Hughes. Hughes had been, as Kissinger was reputed to be now, a Hollywood playboy. He owned a movie studio, RKO, and legendarily designed a "torpedo bra" for one of his stars. The aged, infirm Hughes had turned into a complete and total recluse, hadn't been seen in so long, people thought he might be dead. But when a hoaxer authored what was purported to be his autobiography, a person claiming to be the real Hughes phoned in to a news conference, with reporters on the other end of the line. There was no photographic evidence—Hughes could have been any old man, hiding in plain sight—but the phone call was confirmation enough. Hughes was alive after all. The hoaxer would end up going to prison. This was blockbuster news, and the timing was perfect for Kissinger's next speech to the female reporters.

Safire recognized the opportunity. He typed out a memo:

TO: HENRY KISSINGER
FROM: BILL SAFIRE
RE: BOFFO ROUTINE FOR WOMEN'S PRESS CLUB

. . . And now, I would like to come to the serious part of my talk to you.

Some of you may have come to the conclusion that I have an inordinate love of secrecy.

As the president put it last night, the time has come to speak out.

Many of you know me by the name of Henry Kissinger. And yet, how few of you have tried to check into whether there really is a Henry Kissinger.

I need keep my greatest secret no longer.

I am Howard Hughes.

(HENRY: AS THE PLACE BREAKS UP LAUGHING, DO NOT CRACK A SMILE.)

Some of you obviously do not grasp the enormity of my revelation.

Consider some facts you have been overlooking:

I have consistently, over the years, known a predilection for Hollywood starlets. Some of them, I admit, have some weird and far-out tastes, which is the only reason I have been called Dr. Strangelove.

Thirty years ago, I first applied the principle of linkage—in designing a brassiere for Jane Russell.

And who else but Howard Hughes, masquerading as a White House aide with a German accent, would have flown his own souped-up Piper Cub into Peking?

Some of my closest associates, of course, have had their suspicions.

Those middle-of-the-night phone calls; those refusals to permit cameras in to press briefings almost gave me away.[18]

When feminist Gloria Steinem was photographed with Kissinger and rumors started, Steinem quickly doused them—and that gave Safire the best laugh line of all to feed Kissinger for the Women's Press Club:

> As you know, I have been a somewhat controversial character lately. An example of what I have been exposed to is a Gloria Steinem remark reported in Life last week. She is quoted as having said that she is not now, and has never been, a girlfriend of Henry Kissinger. But I am not discouraged—after all, she did not say that, if nominated, she would not accept; or, if elected, she would not serve.[19]

Kissinger played coy about what was really going on—whether there was anything even remotely happening in his bachelor life—and that was also part of the act. The ladies went along with it, and Kissinger loved the attention. Among his many Hollywood girlfriends, the steadiest date was Jill St. John, the glamorous first American to play a James Bond girl, in *Diamonds Are Forever*. When a "poll" of Playboy Bunnies ranked Kissinger Number One among "men I would most like to go on a date with," he shot back with a logical explanation: "Power is the ultimate aphrodisiac."[20]

Kissinger, certainly not lacking in self-esteem, had nonetheless learned how to bridle it when the situation demanded. Safire, the keenest of observers during those early days at the White House, saw how the academic politics at Harvard prepared Kissinger for the rough stuff to come:

> To his colleagues on the senior staff, he would show the respect of a faculty member to other professors with tenure. . . . To his subordinates, he was a slave-driver. To those few who could stand the gaffe over a period of time, he built an admirable loyalty. But he

> also produced a well-strewn wayside with those who could not, or who were shocked to discover that his policy position was more hardline Nixonian than they had expected. Watching Kissinger with his staff made one add a note of caution to an assessment: He was endearing only when he wanted to be, and caused even those who were most attracted to him to wonder whether he was more respectful of position than personality.[21]

As the years went by, and Kissinger's reputation and power grew, he would describe himself as a loner who didn't need affirmation from anyone else. A cowboy—and a fearless one, at that. Riding into town to face down the outlaws at high noon. Willing to risk it all. Without a gun. Because, after all, this cowboy had a theory. The force of his presence was enough:[22]

> The main point arises from the fact that I've always acted alone. Americans like that immensely. Americans like the cowboy who leads the wagon train by riding ahead alone on his horse, the cowboy who rides all alone into the town, the village, with his horse and nothing else. Maybe even without a pistol, since he doesn't shoot. He acts, that's all, by being in the right place at the right time. In short, a Western.
>
> This cowboy doesn't have to be courageous. All he needs is to be alone, to show others that he rides into the town and does everything by himself. This amazing, romantic character suits me precisely because to be alone has always been part of my style or, if you like, my technique. Together with independence. Oh, that's very important in me, and for me. And finally, conviction. I've always been convinced that I had to do whatever I've done. And people feel it, and believe in it. And I care about the fact that they believe in me.
>
> When you sway or convince somebody, you shouldn't confuse them. Nor can you even simply calculate. Some

> people think that I carefully plan what are to be the consequences, for the public, of any of my initiatives or efforts. They think this preoccupation is always on my mind. Instead, the consequences of what I do—I mean, the public's judgment—have never bothered me.
>
> I don't ask for popularity; I'm not looking for popularity. On the contrary, if you really want to know, I care nothing about popularity. I'm not at all afraid of losing my public; I can allow myself to say what I think. I'm referring to what's genuine in me. If I were to let myself be disturbed by the reactions of the public, if I were to act solely on the basis of a calculated technique, I would accomplish nothing.

"Blackmail" had been the key word in Kissinger's answer to Mike Wallace during that early television interview:

> If we are very much more afraid of total war than the [Soviets] are, they will gradually blackmail the free world into surrender.

In his Harvard seminar, "blackmail" was Kissinger's shorthand way of explaining how, in a high-stakes negotiation, the side that appeared willing to risk everything—even if that was bluster—would invariably gain the upper hand.

Kissinger preached early on that America sometimes had no better option than one in which it hedged its bets, even if that meant threatening—or even using—small-scale nuclear weapons. There were no absolutes when world powers negotiated. Decisions would always be fraught; there would always be uncertainty. Those who favored waiting for all the facts to come in were doomed by their inaction.

For this ultimate foreign-policy realist, high-stakes policy decisions often had to be taken before all the facts were in,[23] and Kissinger used European history to make his point, and he surely could claim bona fides for his opinion: Before he was Henry Kissinger, he was Heinz Kissinger—born in northern Bavaria. He fled Nazi Germany with his family, settling in New York in 1938, and later served during World War II as a German interpreter for the U.S. Army.

In a 1963 lecture, Kissinger said[24]:

> Every statesman must choose at some point between whether he wishes certainty or whether he wishes to rely on his assessment of the situation. . . . If one wants demonstrable proof, one in a sense becomes a prisoner of events.[25]

As Kissinger biographer Niall Ferguson saw it:

> If the democracies had moved against the Nazis in 1936, Kissinger argued, "we wouldn't know today whether Hitler was a misunderstood nationalist, whether he had only limited objectives, or whether he was in fact a maniac. The democracies learned that he was in fact a maniac. They had certainty, but they had to pay for that with a few million lives." This insight had profound implications for the nuclear age, when the potential casualties of a world war could number in the hundreds of millions.[26]

Ferguson described how, as a new student at Harvard in 1948, Kissinger had written a letter home that foretold this future theory.

> "There is not only right or wrong but many shades in between," the young Kissinger wrote in a revelatory letter to his parents. "The real tragedies in life are not in choices between right and wrong," he argued, because "only the most callous of persons choose what they know to be wrong. . . . Real dilemmas are difficulties of the soul, provoking agonies." Put simply, the most diffi-

> cult choices in foreign policy are certain to be between evils, and so the truly moral act is to choose the lesser evil (even if it is politically the harder choice).[27]

A decade later, helming his prestigious Harvard seminar, authoring his seminal book on small-bore war, and even serving as a McCarthy-era informant for the FBI about possible subversive activities,[28] Kissinger styled himself as the ultimate Cold War pragmatist: *The insistence on absolutes . . . is a prescription for inaction.*

Kissinger was teaching theories about how wartime leaders could be more shrewd; how, euphemistically speaking, the savviest leaders could play poker instead of gambling at Russian roulette; how they could make "realistic" decisions based on careful assessment of the facts and options available to them.

How they could blackmail—yes, blackmail—their foes into fearing the worst by taking things to the brink, and maybe even occasionally stepping over.

This was game theory taken to a new level, with nuclear war the table stakes. Ellsberg took notes. He, too, would soon be studying, lecturing, and writing about precisely these things, which he had first heard about and debated in Kissinger's seminar.

In March 1959, Ellsberg, while a Harvard grad student, gave a series of lectures at the Boston Public Library entitled "The Art of Coercion: A Study of Threats in Economic Conflict and War."[29] Ellsberg was doing his PhD research on the topic. His opening lecture was "The Theory and Practice of Blackmail."

He sounded strikingly like Kissinger. Tom Wells, who penned *Wild Man*, an exhaustive, and highly critical, biography of Ellsberg, in 2001, described the first lecture, during which Ellsberg used tools of game theory to explain to his audience that even though threats could increase the chance of an undesired war, they could also deter Soviet aggression:

> Ellsberg also contended that if a blackmailer appeared "irrational" it might make him more effective. Ellsberg seemed, to some, a fan of blackmail. He later denied it.[30]

Ellsberg wrapped up his first lecture with a dramatic flourish, telling listeners,

> In the next lecture, we shall hear the sound of blackmail; the words that Adolf Hitler spoke, and their echoes, that won him half [of] Europe before the firing of a shot. There is the artist to study, to learn what can be hoped for, what can be done with the threat of violence.[31]

In his second lecture, Ellsberg delivered on his promise to analyze Hitler's diplomacy. He titled his second lecture "The Political Uses of Madness." Blackmail was an important diplomatic tool, Ellsberg asserted, and, when practicing blackmail, "it pays to be mad" in certain situations, or at least "convincingly mad." Hitler was "erratic, unpredictable." That, Ellsberg continued, was how Hitler made his conquests.

In his lectures about arms control, given around this time, Ellsberg cooly discussed how the United States could use nuclear threats to restrain the Soviet Union, and to end a war without surrendering. The atomic bombing of Hiroshima, he said, made such threats credible.[32]

The lectures showed just how emboldened Ellsberg was in his embrace of Kissinger's theories. And his professor was captivated. Kissinger invited Ellsberg to give the same two lectures to his Harvard seminar.[33]

Later, both men would be putting those theories into practice as they assessed U.S. options in Vietnam. Their paths would sometimes cross. But eventually they would move in radically different directions.

In October 1965, Ellsberg encountered Kissinger in Saigon. Ellsberg had only recently got there; it was the start of his two-year stint as a State Department adviser to the military.

Ellsberg's arrival in Vietnam came as President Johnson and his military strategists began the war's dramatic escalation. Although U.S. soldiers and other personnel had acted as military advisers to the South Vietnamese armed forces since about 1954, there were no American *fighters* in Vietnam at the beginning of 1965. The first combat troops arrived two months later, in March 1965. But by the time Ellsberg arrived a few months later, American troops—many of them draftees—were pouring in and dying in ever-larger numbers. There would be 184,000 American soldiers in the country by year end, up from about 23,000 noncombat advisers the prior January. And that was only the beginning of the escalation.

In his writing and lectures, Kissinger had made no secret of his feeling that the war in Vietnam wasn't worth fighting. It was, in fact, the perfect laboratory to test his theory that the optimal outcome of such a conflict was for both sides to step back from the brink and negotiate. Kissinger thought the best option for the United States was to try for what he called a "decent interval"[34] between an eventual U.S. pullout and an outright Communist takeover of the South. This was classic game theory, Kissinger's brand of dealmaking diplomacy. After all, it had worked for Metternich.

But Henry Cabot Lodge Jr., the U.S. ambassador, wanted Kissinger, a specialist in European diplomacy, not Asian, to see the war firsthand.[35] Kissinger met up with his former student Ellsberg. When Kissinger got there, Ellsberg later recalled, "he had started by asking a good question: how to inform himself quickly."

Ellsberg told Kissinger that he shouldn't waste time with official briefings, "or in talking to anyone in the presence of his boss or agency head."[36] Ellsberg believed in traveling through the provinces, talking to people in the countryside who spoke Vietnamese, or who'd been in the country a long time. That was about as close to going native as Ellsberg could get, and he was doing just as he now advised Kissinger, with John Paul Vann as his guide. "I'd been lucky enough to get that advice when I arrived, and it was working for me," Ellsberg recalled. "I gave him a list of Americans and Vietnamese to start him off."

Ellsberg told Kissinger that Defense Secretary Robert McNamara "never did any of these things on his frequent trips to Vietnam."[37] McNamara settled for elaborate briefings, never talked to lower-level commanders without their commanding generals present, and thus never heard the truth. "I was impressed that Kissinger actually acted on my advice, unlike other visitors to whom I said the same things." Kissinger did see some of the people on the list Ellsberg had given him, listening carefully and taking notes. "And in a couple of brief visits he learned a lot."

The upshot: Kissinger "became realistically skeptical and pessimistic, especially about the character and prospects of the Saigon regime."[38]

Kissinger's pessimism continued in 1967 and 1968, as Ellsberg and Kissinger occasionally found themselves at one or another seminar where the increasingly grim Vietnam situation was being discussed. Kissinger continued to espouse his "decent interval" theory—plainly unrealistic, since the North Vietnamese weren't even at the negotiating table. The U.S.-backed war continued.

With the Republican convention scheduled to be held in Miami in early August 1968, Kissinger made it clear he would not be supporting Nixon. Instead, Kissinger's choice was his longtime patron Governor Nelson Rockefeller, of New York. The two were close, and Rockefeller provided blandishments. Kissinger had an office at 50 Rockefeller Plaza when he needed it.[39] When Kissinger spirited top secret records out of the government for later personal use, Rockefeller let him use a vault at the family estate in Pocantico Hills, New York—no questions asked.[40] Rockefeller even improved Kissinger's social life: Kissinger met, dated, and would later marry a Rockefeller aide, Nancy Maginnes, eleven years his junior.

Rockefeller, like his Democratic predecessor as governor, Averell Harriman, coveted the White House, and he leaned on Kissinger for foreign policy advice. That summer, Kissinger's advice would have been about two things dominating American foreign policy: the Cold War with the Soviets, and Vietnam.

When it came to Vietnam, there were few who could match John Paul Vann's insights and connections. Vann was spinning a new line about American prospects in Vietnam—he was expressing more optimism—and he wanted to be heard. Before the two major-party presidential nominees were chosen, Vann used intermediaries to get to the contenders: Hubert Humphrey[41] for the Democrats; Nixon and Rockefeller for the Republicans.

Mayor Sam Yorty, of Los Angeles, was the conduit to Nixon, who replied noncommittally.[42]

Vann knew the way to effectively influence Rockefeller's foreign policy was through Kissinger. The intermediary Vann used to set up a meeting with Kissinger was a former intelligence officer and naval aviator[43] named Vincent Davis—the same man who had introduced Vann to Ellsberg, three years earlier.[44]

Davis made a tantalizing tease to get Kissinger interested. Vann, Davis said, had provided documents that could be shared with Kissinger: There were "detailed papers that John has sent to me over the past few years, and some lengthy tape-recorded conversations with him." Davis assured Kissinger that Vann's views "happily coincide with Mr. Rockefeller's brilliant statement on Vietnam as carried in the full-page ad in the *New York Times*."

That was important. A few weeks earlier, Rockefeller had bought space in the *Times* to trumpet a signed personal statement that he headlined: THE LAST VIETNAM. The ad was an indictment of the war that Johnson and his generals had been fighting. And, confirming Davis's assurance to Kissinger, Rockefeller's ad also echoed something Vann had long been preaching: America would prevail in Vietnam, only if it understood the rural provinces. Winning hearts and minds had to happen through what Vann called "pacification": providing security, arms, training, and social reform.[45]

From Rockefeller's full-page ad,[46] which Kissinger surely would have had a hand in:

> Our Vietnam policy was meant for the 1940s, for Western Europe, for the defense of democracies.

> Yet we apply it in the 1960s, in Southeast Asia, in defense of a people who do not know what democracy means.
>
> And in wrapping this policy around Vietnam, we blinded ourselves to the real Vietnam. We assumed the enemy meant to seize land. We were wrong. He meant to disrupt government.
>
> We sent troops in overwhelming number. We were wrong. We shattered a small country's sense of responsibility.
>
> We were preoccupied with the changing premiers and presidents in Saigon. We were wrong. It was in the village and countryside where governments failed. . . .
>
> I say, face the truth. Trust the people with the truth.
> I say, do not fight change. Guide change.
>
> And this is one reason why I run for President.

Despite Kissinger's interest in seeing Vann in person, the meeting got canceled. Kissinger and Vann ended up speaking by phone.[47] Still, Kissinger was intrigued at the prospect of getting copies of Vann's documents. He wrote back to Davis on July 26, from his Rockefeller Plaza office:

> First, let me say that I genuinely admire John Vann. If Governor Rockefeller should get the nomination, we shall certainly be in touch with John. . . .
>
> Also, for my own education, I would be very interested to have the papers that John Vann has sent you over recent years.[48]

The next time Kissinger heard from Davis, it was the day after the Republican convention ended in Miami Beach. Nixon had the nomination. Rockefeller, booed at the 1964 convention,[49] had lost his party's support a second time. Davis, disgusted that Nixon hadn't consulted with Rockefeller before choosing Maryland Governor Spiro Agnew as his running mate, wrote to Kissinger on August 9:

> I know that you, like all of us Rockefeller supporters, . . . are grimly disappointed (perhaps grief-stricken would be more accurate) over the events in Miami Beach. . . .[50]

Davis told Kissinger that his offer of the Vann papers still stood, but there was a condition to Kissinger's seeing everything. The "whole bundle" was so extensive—"about 500 pieces of paper at last count"—that Kissinger could only review it in person. The documents were in Denver.

> If you are ever out this way, plan to stop by and browse through it. I am sure that much of what John has had to say from Vietnam since 1961 will appear in the study that Mort Halperin has gotten the Dan Ellsberg group to undertake, although this may be under wraps for quite a while to come.[51]

A delicious bit of gossip had just been tossed Kissinger's way. Ellsberg and thirty-five other analysts had been working on McNamara's Vietnam study for a year. Although Kissinger had been briefly consulted at the beginning,[52] he wasn't actively involved now. Kissinger would have known, of course, that his former student Ellsberg was involved, and that his former Harvard colleague Morton Halperin, now at the Pentagon, was in charge of it. But Kissinger was hearing, perhaps for the first time, that Vann had a hand in things, too. Kissinger apparently wanted to know more, and soon opened what investigative reporter Seymour Hersh later told Neil Sheehan was a secret "back channel"[53] between Kissinger and Vann—an end around, possibly set up by the CIA,[54] for Kissinger to find out what was going on without relying on the generals.

Davis sent "a brief recent sample"—an exchange between Vann and Ted Kennedy—to whet Kissinger's appetite. "This is interesting," Davis told Kissinger, "for the light that it sheds on the Tet Offensive." Then he added:

> More interesting, however, is John's most recent assessment that we are now winning militarily, and that we are even achieving some progress on the political front.[55]

Kissinger replied a couple of weeks later. His brief August 20 letter left no doubt about two things. He was interested in Vann, and dismissive of Nixon:

> Now that I am beginning to dig out from the Rockefeller debacle, I shall read the Vann pieces with greatest interest.
>
> Nixon's behavior after his nomination was astounding—ungenerous, petty, and, I should have thought, against his long-term interests.[56]

Days after Richard Nixon's victory in the 1968 election, Kissinger visited RAND's Santa Monica headquarters for a previously scheduled talk. In front of an audience that included Ellsberg, Kissinger complimented his former pupil. "I have learned more from Dan Ellsberg than from any other person in Vietnam."[57] Ellsberg loved the flattering comment, in front of his colleagues, and figured Kissinger was referring to the candid advice he'd received in 1965—to travel the countryside and talk to the trusted people on Ellsberg's list.

Ellsberg related something else that he heard from Kissinger during that talk at RAND after the election:

> In his deep, somber, Germanic drawl, Kissinger stated: "Richard Nixon is not fit to be president."[58]

CHAPTER 4

Madman

ALTHOUGH KISSINGER HAD MADE CLEAR his disdain for Nixon, he was, more to the point, unabashedly pragmatic. Cold, hard realism was the essence of what Kissinger preached. So it was not altogether a surprise when, after dismissing Nixon at every opportunity, Kissinger flipped. Power really was the ultimate aphrodisiac, as Kissinger would demonstrate.

In early December, it was announced that Kissinger would become Nixon's national security adviser. The establishment quickly fell into line behind him, expressing confidence that was summed up by James "Scotty" Reston, the eminent Washington columnist for the *New York Times*, who professed relief that it would be Kissinger in that basement office at the White House.

"A reassuring sign," Reston wrote.[1] Kissinger checked all of Reston's boxes: "doctorate degree at Harvard . . . has the respect of most of the foreign policy experts who have served the last three presidents . . . an intelligent, articulate, and remarkably industrious scholar."

But now Kissinger needed help getting up to speed quickly. His most trusted advisers were at RAND, which functioned as the Pentagon's alter ego. Kissinger wanted RAND to prepare an options paper that he could use to prepare for his first National Security Council briefing in January. It was a coup for RAND, because the think tank had never had such direct access to the White House.[2] But RAND's involvement would need to be kept quiet; Kissinger just wanted advice and talking points. And even though Ellsberg, by this time, had made his views on the futility of the war known, Kissinger nonetheless wanted his star pupil—steeped in the encyclopedic Vietnam study that McNamara had asked for—to lead the assignment. Absolute discretion was required.

Ellsberg reassured him. He could keep a secret.[3]

Ellsberg quickly returned to the Pentagon for a debrief with his Harvard chums: Morton Halperin was now the Johnson administration's deputy assistant secretary in charge of international security, and Les Gelb was handling the day-to-day oversight of the three dozen analysts who were compiling the Vietnam history.[4]

After spending a week in and around the Pentagon, Ellsberg returned to Santa Monica and prepared a twenty-seven-page report for Kissinger. He wrote how the most important thing for Kissinger to know was that there was now a distinct split, even within the Pentagon, about the American involvement in Vietnam. This internal skepticism was new, and, to Ellsberg's mind, it validated the various strategies that his options paper laid out. All were variants on American withdrawal, with such scenarios titled "Communist Fadeaway" and "Negotiated Victory." The direction of Ellsberg's thinking was clear.

Ellsberg spent Christmas Eve in Malibu with his two children, then drove them back to his ex-wife's house the next morning and got on a plane to New York. He carried with him the report for Kissinger.[5]

On Christmas Day, 1968, Ellsberg and Kissinger were together again, this time at the Pierre Hotel on Fifth Avenue in New York City. It was the headquarters of President-elect Richard Nixon's transition team. Kissinger, now forty-five years old, was working out of a room at the posh hotel. Nixon's other aides and advisers were scattered up and down the halls.

When Ellsberg got to Kissinger's office, he was surprised to see Tom Schelling, his Harvard economics professor. Schelling was Ellsberg's mentor, the official adviser on Ellsberg's PhD thesis, and the dominant influence on Ellsberg's work concerning game theory in decision-making. Schelling would later be awarded the Nobel Prize in Economics for his pioneering work on game-theory analysis.

It would be Schelling, not Kissinger, who would pick apart Ellsberg's twenty-seven-pager.

Schelling's critique was twofold. His first objection was that Ellsberg hadn't included a "win strategy." By that, Schelling meant "a strategy that you think would win, even if you wouldn't recommend it because you think it would cost too much or would be too dangerous, or for some other reason. You'd say, 'Here's what you'd have to do for victory,' even if you don't think he should do it."

Ellsberg acknowledged that he hadn't included a "win strategy"—and the reason, he said, was that the war was unwinnable. "You could kill all the people with nuclear weapons. I wouldn't call that winning."

Schelling and Kissinger didn't press the point. Ellsberg interpreted the silence as skepticism. Schelling moved on to his second critique, which Ellsberg found more telling: "You haven't said anything in here about threats. You don't have a threat tactic."[6]

Ellsberg instantly recognized he'd left out the one scenario that he, of all people, should have included. It was embarrassing. A decade earlier, Ellsberg had made his reputation with the lecture titled "The Theory and Practice of Blackmail," and he'd reprised it for Kissinger, his admiring professor. Ellsberg had been all in on the theory that sometimes the upper hand in a negotiation could be attained through irrational threats—and, occasionally, even making good on them. It even had a name: the Madman Theory.[7]

If Ellsberg needed confirmation of where Kissinger soon would be taking the National Security Council, he got it when Kissinger finally spoke. "How can you conduct diplomacy without a threat of escalation?" Kissinger asked. "Without that, there is no basis for negotiations."[8]

Threats were what Kissinger really wanted, and that would turn out to be the immediate plan. Two months after taking office, Nixon widened the Vietnam War through a massive bombing campaign aimed at North Vietnamese supply lines and bases in neighboring Cambodia. The bombing went on for years and killed anywhere from 150,000 to five hundred thousand civilians.[9,10]

Suddenly a theory was folded in on itself and became reality. Bombing Cambodia was Nixon's attempt to force the North Vietnamese into serious negotiations to end the war—and his plan, to intimidate North Vietnam by showing that Nixon was a dangerous leader capable of anything, was based on the theory that Kissinger had long espoused, but which now would be tested in real time.

Nixon was all in, even down to the nickname. "I call it the Madman Theory,"[11] he told his chief of staff, H. R. Haldeman. "I want the North Vietnamese to believe I've reached the point where I might do anything to stop the war. We'll just slip the word to them that, 'for God's sake, you know Nixon is obsessed about communism. We can't restrain him when he's angry—and he has his hand on the nuclear button' and Ho Chi Minh himself will be in Paris in two days begging for peace."[12]

But the plan was Kissinger's, and that begged the question: Who was the real madman?

Haldeman kept a diary. When the bombing began on March 17, 1969, he described the first day of Operation Breakfast, so named because the final go-ahead came at an early-morning Pentagon meeting:

> Historic day. K[issinger]'s Operation Breakfast finally came off at 2:00 pm our time. K really excited, as is P[resident].[13]

The news was even better the following day:

> Kissinger's "Operation Breakfast" a great success. He came beaming in with report, very productive. A lot more secondaries than had been expected. Confirmed early intelligence. Probably no reaction for a few days—if ever.[14]

Haldeman's prediction proved wrong. The bombing drew Cambodia into the Vietnam conflict and expanded the war on the ground to neighboring countries. When Nixon finally revealed the extent of the operation more than a year later, in late April 1970[15]—including, for the first time, sending American ground troops into ostensibly neutral Cambodia—it led to riots on college campuses and the killing, by National Guardsmen, of four student protesters on May 4 at Kent State University in Ohio.[16] Each spring for years to come, Mayday protests broke out anew on campuses and elsewhere.

Morton Halperin, the Pentagon whiz kid who'd had overall responsibility for McNamara's Vietnam study, now was working for Kissinger at the White House. Early in 1969, Halperin knew everything about the secret bombing of Cambodia. He saw it as confirmation that the madman plan was afoot.

But when Halperin wanted to alert his friend Ellsberg to what was going on, all Halperin had to do was flag a story that ran on Friday, May 9, 1969, in the *New York Times*.[17] The headline: RAIDS IN CAMBODIA BY U.S. UNPROTESTED.

Reporter William Beecher had the whole story. Halperin confided to Ellsberg that he hadn't been the leaker; Halperin thought the leak came from somewhere in the Pentagon. Whatever the source, Beecher had scored a great scoop for the *Times*—and yet, the story went nowhere for almost a year. The Pentagon denied it the same day, and no other journalist followed up.[18]

The leak had to have come from the tight circle of people who knew about the secret bombing. It enraged Kissinger, whose paranoia ran as deep as Nixon's. Kissinger suspected that even his closest aide, Halperin, could be the mole.

Kissinger asked J. Edgar Hoover to put wiretaps on Beecher's phone, as well as Halperin's and those of fifteen others who, Kissinger thought, might be responsible for the leak. The wiretaps were secret and went on for years.[19]

Within days, Hoover was delivering reports from the wiretaps directly to Nixon at the White House. One year later, the wiretap reports were still coming in. The FBI director couched his reports in a bureaucratic code that he knew Nixon would understand. The ongoing stream of information, Hoover explained, was "obtained from extremely sensitive sources":

> May 11, 1970
> Dear Mr. President:
>
> Previous communications furnished information obtained from extremely sensitive sources concerning contacts made by members of the White House staff and other Government officials. The same sources have furnished the following additional information.
>
> Morton H. Halperin, a former member of the White House staff who is now employed by the Brookings Institution, during a conversation with an individual employed by the Massachusetts Institute of Technology, mentioned that he had resigned as a consultant to the White House. This was apparently in opposition to the present United States action in Vietnam and Cambodia. He said he was not going to make a press release concerning his resignation but was going to "quietly tell people" so that if anyone wanted to write about it, they could. He also told this individual that he could feel free to mention the fact he was resigning to anyone in the press. Halperin said he was becoming a "revolutionary or at least a radical." He defined radicalism as "telling the truth in simple language." He also stated that the result of the Cambodian invasion would be the killing of a large number of Cambodian civilians who will be "labeled Viet Cong."[20]

Whether Hoover or anyone else knew it at the time, the wiretap on Halperin's home telephone had most likely also picked up Ellsberg, who by 1970 had left RAND and was working as a senior researcher at MIT.

Hoover continued his report to Nixon by describing another phone conversation the FBI had overheard, this time involving the Democratic ambassador and Vietnam troubleshooter Averell Harriman, whose criticism of the Cambodia operation was also bedeviling the president:

> Averell Harriman contacted Ambassador Bill Sullivan of the State Department. Harriman asked what the situation in Cambodia looked like. Sullivan stated that he thought the communists would fall back to the northeast sections of Cambodia which they will use as main bases. Harriman then inquired whether or not Sullivan was one of the 250 individuals of [the] State Department who signed a protest of United States action. Sullivan said he was not. Harriman then asked whether Ambassador Bunker was going to resign. Sullivan said he wanted to but that the President would not let him. Harriman also commented that the President has "lost the country." Sullivan said that his main effort is to try to get a cease fire. Harriman commented that the trouble is Kissinger will not negotiate.
>
> Harriman said that the State Department employees who signed the protest plan to meet at his house May 17, 1970 and invited Sullivan to join them. Sullivan agreed to attend.[21]

Hoover knew how to push Nixon's buttons. The president had an innate distrust of Harriman, whose Georgetown mansion provided a harborage for all manner of Vietnam doves, diplomats, and out-of-favor Democrats. Harriman's N Street mansion, because of what the FBI learned through the wiretap, now would be under FBI surveillance.

In private, Nixon mocked what he perceived to be Harriman's undue deference to the North Vietnamese:

> We never have any trouble getting messages from North Vietnam. Harriman's idea that they are tender flowers who send signals that we can't read is not the case at all. They are tough cookies, and when they have a theme to get across, they get it across.[22]

Privately, Kissinger, too, disparaged Harriman, who, along with Cy Vance, had led the Paris peace negotiations for LBJ:

> If only the guys who got us into this would give us the chance to get out of it. I wasn't second-guessing Vance and Harriman, when I told them privately we couldn't win the war. I said, How could I help? All we needed was for the criticism to hold off for another couple of months.[23]

Harriman had his own ax to grind. As the Cambodian incursion went on, Harriman muttered:

> Nixon had the chance to do something in Paris [with peace negotiations], and he blew it. . . . Vietnam is crazy. It is preposterous for us to think that we can win that war; and, secondly, that we can create a democracy in South Vietnam is insane. We can't even create a democracy in Mississippi.[24]

Arthur Krock, the legendary Washington bureau chief and columnist for the *Times*, understood the egos involved. He wrote this memorandum to Neil Sheehan[25]:

> I suppose that you were taught at Harvard that Longfellow was "camp," though he was the first poet to bring the old culture of Europe into American literature. Anyhow, in Evangeline there is a line which explains—to me—Harriman's dislike of Nixon to the point where he

> revises history to put Nixon in the wrong: "Envy, the vice of Republics."[26]
>
> Harriman has aspired to be president ever since he became the protégé of Harry Hopkins and rode on Harry's back, as Harry did on FDR's, to power. That Nixon made it and Harriman couldn't, though Mr. Truman supported Harriman for the nomination against Stevenson at the Democratic National Convention of 1956, has plagued Harriman like a thorn deep in a man's heel. Harriman also is jealous of [Nelson] Rockefeller because Rockefeller not only won the governorship of New York against him, but was several times re-elected whereas Harriman was given only one term by the voters.
>
> Such matters as these are the driving force of many men in public life, not to speak of newspaper men who aspire to executive jobs which go to their colleagues: the head of the *Times*' Washington bureau [Max Frankel] and executive editor of the *Times* [Abe Rosenthal] for examples.
>
> End of lesson.

A year after the Cambodian bombing began, the campaign was still "secret." By now it was April 1970, and Ellsberg's friend Lloyd Shearer, the gossip columnist, had a lunch date with Kissinger at Nixon's Western White House. Shearer invited Ellsberg to come along to San Clemente.[27]

Kissinger, it turned out, had an agenda for that luncheon. He wanted to dish about his Hollywood life, and he didn't want Ellsberg in on the discussion. Instead, Ellsberg took lunch with Al Haig, Kissinger's new military aide. (Haig's predecessor, Halperin, had publicly resigned in protest over the Cambodian bombing.)[28]

Before sending Ellsberg away, Kissinger offered an ingratiating compliment in front of Shearer and Haig[29]:

> You know, I have learned more from Dan Ellsberg than from any other person—about bargaining.

Kissinger was referring to the lectures, about Hitler's blackmail of Austria and Czechoslovakia, that Ellsberg had given to Kissinger's Harvard seminar eleven years earlier. The Madman Theory.

"You have a very good memory," Ellsberg replied.

"They were very good lectures," Kissinger answered.

Ellsberg later recalled: "On the drive back to Santa Monica, Lloyd told me about his conversation with Kissinger. He had asked him one question that I'd suggested: Could he imagine any circumstances under which he would leave his position and oppose the president's policy? Kissinger's first answer was *No, none at all.* But when Lloyd pressed him, he said: "Well, I suppose, if there were plans for gas chambers. . . ."[30]

Neil Sheehan had been itching to get sprung from his *New York Times* beat at the Pentagon. The former Vietnam War correspondent wanted more exciting assignments. Just as Nixon entered the White House, he was given the title of "special investigative reporter."[31] Sheehan would still work the Pentagon beat. But, with Abe Rosenthal's blessing and support, he would get time to do some deeper reporting.

Nixon's still-secret Cambodian operation brought an opportunity. The *Times* Washington bureau was putting together a reporting team for an investigation into how and why Nixon made the decision to bomb the neutral country. Hedrick Smith, thirty-six, who'd worked for the *Times* in Vietnam when Sheehan was there for UPI, now was in the newspaper's Washington bureau. Smith would be writing the story. Sheehan and a few others would be contributing reporting, with bureau chief Max Frankel directly overseeing everything. Among those involved, the Cambodia investigation became known, simply, as "the project." It was expected to take months to complete. And it was to be kept a secret from others at the newspaper.

Sheehan, typically a loner on stories, jumped at the chance to join the team, because he was interested in going after Kissinger. Coincidentally, editors at the paper's Sunday magazine had asked him to write a feature profile on Kissinger. Sheehan thought the assignment could give him the perfect pretext to dig deeply into Kissinger's involvement in the Cambodian operation, without letting on what he and the *Times* were really up to. It would not be the first time Sheehan would be complicit in such a ploy within his own newspaper.

Sheehan wrote to Frankel:

> I have taken an assignment from the Sunday magazine to do a profile of Kissinger. I took the assignment because my spare time after this weekend will not be used up on my book. It goes into galleys on Monday.

Sheehan had just completed his first book, *The Arnheiter Affair*. Publication of the book would result in years of libel litigation, and would become an ongoing distraction for him:

> I have a proposition for whatever it is worth if you decide to go ahead with the project discussed at lunch the other day. I would do the magazine profile on Kissinger on office time, with the understanding I would not be paid for it when it was published. The profile would give me a convenient cover to conduct what interviews you'd want me to do for the special project, because I will inevitably have to ask people I see what Kissinger's role in the Cambodian affair was. I don't think there'd be any conflict in substance between the magaziner and the project, because only a small portion of the profile will deal with Kissinger's role in the

> Cambodian crisis. There would be some conflict, of course, but it would be fairly minimal. But I would have a pretext to steer each conversation to Cambodia while I was getting what I will need for the profile and once brought up, I could swing off on the subject of Cambodia with the sources to milk them of whatever I could get. What do you think?
>
> If you do decide this proposition is sound, I suggest we not tell the magazine people about the arrangement. They are rather talkative up there and word of what we're up to down here would leak.[32]

Right away, Sheehan set up a meeting with Kissinger, whom he met with, off the record, on April 16, 1970.

Kissinger spoke cautiously about the Cambodia bombing, confirming details that the *Times* already had revealed the year before, which had resulted in Kissinger's ordering wiretaps (at that moment, still secret) on his closest aides and others. The newspaper's earlier reporting hadn't gotten traction after the Pentagon's denials. But now, face-to-face with Kissinger, Sheehan did get Kissinger to confirm a key point, which was that Kissinger "felt sure" the bombing would encourage Hanoi's "willingness to negotiate." Kissinger was, in essence, affirming his view that Nixon's so-called Madman Theory—a theory Kissinger also had long taught and espoused, albeit with a more palatable name—eventually would pay off.

Sheehan typed up his notes and sent an insightful memo to Hedrick Smith, the lead reporter on the story, documenting what Kissinger said during the meeting:

> 1. We do not want another client state in S.E. Asia, it's the last thing we want. So we don't want to get deeply involved with Lon Nol govt. [Lon Nol, the Cambodian defense minister, led a coup the previous month, overthrowing Cambodia's leader, Prince Norodom Sihanouk.]

2. On the other hand, it's a shame that this country is in such a state that we can't get any help to a little country of 7 million begging for help.
3. It would be militarily advantageous to do something about the sanctuaries. [Nixon and Kissinger believed North Vietnam was harboring troops and weapons in Cambodia.] Militarily, events in Cambodia are a short-term plus but a long-term unknown. The Commies have already lost the use of Sihanoukville.[33] They have suffered a setback and must believe (he said several times) that we arranged for Sihanouk's overthrow. (He never actually said we didn't.)
4. The military "temptation" of striking at the sanctuaries is offset by the effect such action would have in discouraging Hanoi from a willingness to negotiate. He said he felt sure—though he lacked evidence—that Hanoi must at this stage be seriously considering the desirability of negotiating. Perhaps also they would find it easier to negotiate in the larger context of Indochina than just about South Vietnam, but either way, we want to encourage any such interest.
5. When I said that he seemed to be balancing tangible temptations of a short-run against an "unknown" factor of diplomatic advantage, he demurred at that formulation but in effect assented to it.

   5a. In a music [*sic*], sad and speculative sort of way, he commented at this stage that if Cambodia and Laos were to fall in Communist hands, then the U.S. effort in South Vietnam would come to appear illogical. When I showed signs of interpreting this in military terms, he went on to indicate that he meant the intellectual rationale for our sacrifices in South Vietnam made no sense if we simply shrugged off Cambodia and the rest of Indochina—something like "if the communists are in Cambodia and in Laos and in North Vietnam, then what is the purpose of our effort in [the] South?"

6. In a peroration of some length he gave it as his definitely "personal" view—presented more as a hunch—that before this year is out, Hanoi will agree to engage us in serious negotiations. He offered no evidence or claim of secret information. He placed it in the context of his having literally guessed right on Hanoi's thinking before, once besting Cy Vance [Averell Harriman's deputy in LBJ's efforts to get peace talks going in Paris] on a matter of timing. Thus, it came over more as a hunch than anything else. (I have the impression, shared by Mac Bundy [national security adviser to JFK and LBJ, by this time president of the Ford Foundation] and some others that Kissinger rather freely tailors the emphasis of what he says to his audience, so that with presumed doves he always stresses the diplomatic track more than he might in his own calculations.)

Sheehan's instinct was correct. Kissinger was already privately strategizing with Nixon about moving U.S. forces across the border into Cambodia. Nixon made the decision on April 25, 1970, and announced it in an April 30 speech to the nation, carried live on the three broadcast television networks ninety minutes after U.S. soldiers crossed the border. "It is not our power but our will and character that is being tested tonight," Nixon told the nation. "The time has come for action."[34]

Haldeman extensively documented the internal debate in his diary at the time. The ad man had probably never heard the term "threat tactic," but he recognized it nonetheless in Kissinger. The national security adviser, Haldeman wrote, had doubts about the audacity of invading a neutral country, but in the end, gave his full support to the plan:

> Kissinger takes whole deal as test of President's authority, and I think would go ahead even if plan is wrong, just to prove President can't be challenged.[35]

Demonstrations and riots immediately broke out on college campuses across the country. Nixon had promised an end to the war, but his actions in Cambodia signaled the opposite.

Two weeks later, May 15, the *Times* reporters were still working on the special project, which now had a name: "Why Cambodia?" The investigation was ongoing. Sheehan put together a memo for Max Frankel with a list of fifty potential sources he planned to interview, and got busy setting up meetings with as many as would talk to him.[36] The list—filled with elected senators and representatives, congressional staff, Pentagon officials, and "White House legislative liaison who would have had to do explaining to various congressmen"—showed the depth of Sheehan's sources. Sheehan had developed relationships with officials a level or two down from the very top, and they frequently were in a position to know everything, and to speak more freely off the record. When he knew someone personally, Sheehan made sure to let Frankel know that only he, Sheehan, should talk to them. There were some noteworthy examples.

One was Vice President Spiro Agnew's military aide, Colonel John M. Dunn.[37] Agnew was a Vietnam hawk with little nuance. But Sheehan felt Dunn could be trusted: *Very smart man, good politician. I know him and I should be the one to see him. If he knows anything, he would not open up to a stranger.* Dunn agreed to talk to Sheehan, and they set up a meeting for a Thursday evening later in June.[38]

Another second-echelon name on Sheehan's list—put there because of proximity to power and possible willingness to talk—was Kissinger's former special assistant (and, two decades later, Bill Clinton's national security adviser), Anthony Lake. Kissinger, unbeknownst to anyone other than Nixon and J. Edgar

Hoover, already had Lake's home phone wiretapped after the leak about the Cambodia bombing the year before. Sheehan made this comment to Frankel about Lake: *Another personal friend. Might have something to say.* This put Lake off-limits to other *Times* reporters.

Sheehan almost certainly would have worked his close friend Tony Lake as a source. One week after Sheehan put Lake's name on the interview list, Lake resigned from Kissinger's White House staff, letting it be known that his opposition to the Cambodia bombing was the reason.[39] Lake's friendship would be important to Sheehan for another reason: Lake would reconnect Sheehan to Daniel Ellsberg a few months later.

The opportunity came during a dinner at Lake's Washington home. Sheehan and Ellsberg were invited. The two hadn't been in touch with each other since Ellsberg leaked documents to Sheehan about LBJ's troop buildup plans in March 1968. Now they were talking again.

At the dinner at Lake's house, Sheehan unburdened himself. He felt misused and misunderstood by his *Times* editors. Sheehan wanted to do some serious on-the-ground reporting about the war in Vietnam, and was angling for permission from Frankel and others to return as a war correspondent for three months. But his editors were dragging their feet: *I have tried to get the question settled one way or the other for some time now without success. It looks like the question will still be hanging fire for weeks to come.*

Sheehan confided to Ellsberg that the *Times* "is done with Vietnam."[40] Ellsberg figured then there was no use considering Sheehan for any future leaks:

> [Sheehan] says, "They won't let me cover Vietnam. They've got me covering other domestic stuff. They're just not interested." And so I had the feeling from that, well, no use giving them top-secret stuff.[41]

Another name on Sheehan's interview list was one of LBJ's Wise Men, the retired four-star general Maxwell Taylor. Taylor had been one of the few in Johnson's inner circle who favored doubling down on U.S. involvement in Vietnam. *The hawk of hawks,* Sheehan called him. *Perhaps was consulted.*

Omitted from the list was a source Sheehan turned to for off-the-record confirmation that the Cambodian invasion was Nixon's call, and not the result of puppeteering by Kissinger. That source was Bryce Harlow.

Harlow was one of Nixon's confidants, a shrewd lobbyist who had swung through Washington's revolving door more than once. Harlow had served as Eisenhower's congressional liaison—essentially, the White House's chief lobbyist—during Ike's second term. Nixon, then vice president, grew to know and trust Harlow. Harlow had been Procter & Gamble's chief lobbyist in Washington during the JFK and LBJ years. Although he wasn't inside the White House, the affable Oklahoman retained easy access, particularly with LBJ. When Nixon returned to the White House in 1969, he called Harlow back to run congressional relations.

On June 19, Sheehan sent a long memo to the "Why Cambodia?" team, cryptically titled "Interview with H." The person Sheehan referred to as an "informant" almost certainly was Harlow, Nixon's trusted confidant, who had been at Nixon's side as he made the decision to send troops across the border.[42,43] Sheehan began the memo by quoting "H":

> Said if the story came out in the end as saying this was anything other than "Richard Nixon's personal decision, then the story will be wrong." Said "Richard Nixon made this decision himself, after he [had] gotten all the advice and all the information he wanted." Smiled and commented with some amusement on all the swimming and backpedaling that's now going on in Washington about [Secretary of Defense Melvin R.] Laird having reservations and [Secretary of State William P.] Rogers opposing the decision. Said Rogers may have been opposed "but he and the president talked about this *in extenso*." Noted "in the

> stories of these battles for the mind of the president you always hear more about it from the participants than you do from the president." Said he'd now seen three presidents in operation. All of them were men with very strong ideas on various subjects, and Nixon was no exception. On the big ones they made up their own minds."[44]

Inadvertently or not, "H" also gave full credence to Nixon's Madman Theory:

> Informant said the meaning of the action, far's Nixon was concerned, was credibility and a warning in general. Said Nixon had asked about and looked towards the effect of the Cambodian action "in the Middle East, in Europe, everywhere." I said, You mean he had to prove he wasn't a pantywaist, and he said, "Yeah."

An afterthought on Sheehan's interview list was Martha Mitchell, the wife of John Mitchell, Nixon's attorney general and former law partner, campaign manager, and closest confidant. John and Martha were polar opposites in the company town of Washington, DC.

It would have been next to impossible for the *Times* to get anything out of Attorney General John Mitchell. John Osborne, a Mississippi-born, Washington-based journalist for the *New Republic*, whose Old South mannerisms and slow drawl seemed discordant with everything else in political Washington, penned a weekly column he called "The Nixon Watch." Osborne wrote up his notes after interviewing Mitchell at the Nixon-Agnew campaign headquarters[45] during the 1968 campaign:

> Mitchell is a calm, possessed man. Pipe smoker. Talked for 30 minutes but said very little revealing of himself. Obviously used to such interviews; another reporter waiting to see him when I left.

Mitchell's wife, Martha, was a different story. She was as garrulous as Mitchell was taciturn: A "*bon vivant* on the Washington social scene" from Pine Bluff, Arkansas, "with a penchant for drinking whisky and calling journalists late at night."[46] When she made the cover of *Time* magazine in 1970, the reason was clear:

> About a year ago, as the wife of the U.S. Attorney General, she told a TV reporter that the November peace demonstration in Washington reminded her husband of a Russian revolution. . . . This month the Gallup poll announced that fully 76 percent of the American population realizes who Martha Mitchell is, establishing her as a personality who is already better known than many politicians or entertainers, and is fast approaching the celebrity of Jacqueline Onassis (91 percent), who has been at it considerably longer and with some notable advantages.
>
> Martha's trademark is her mouth, literally and metaphorically.[47]

Martha Mitchell would turn out to be a martyr to her husband's complicity in Nixon's later scandals—a whistleblower and truth teller of the highest order, facing gaslighting and discreditation for her efforts to reveal the truth. But in 1970 she was still a caricature, an afterthought in Sheehan's memo to Max Frankel about sourcing the Cambodia story:

> Someone ought to try to get to Martha Mitchell. That wacky woman may just have heard something from her husband.

Sheehan's hunch would turn out to be prescient. During the Watergate scandal, still to come, she was a truth teller about her husband's misdeeds.

Neil Sheehan's wife, Susan, thirty-two years old, was a staff writer for the *New Yorker*, having joined the magazine in 1961, just a few years out of Wellesley and after a brief stint at *Esquire*. The two were a journalistic power couple, introduced to each other by *Esquire's* star writer, Gay Talese[48]; both later would win Pulitzers for deeply reported books. But their writing styles were vastly different. Susan's pieces for the *New Yorker* often were highly observed, whimsical, offbeat "Talk of the Town" pieces rather than in-depth profiles. Only her later work would delve deeply into intricate portraits of troubled lives. Neil, meanwhile, wrote in the fact-heavy, rat-a-tat-tat telegraphic style of a wire service reporter—a style honed, of necessity, with UPI in Vietnam.

There was another thing that distinguished the two of them. Despite his wire-service background, Neil could be an agonizingly slow writer—an angst-filled perfectionist who labored over stories and sometimes tossed the entire typescript in the trash can and started over. His issues with deadlines caused him problems in the *Times* newsroom.[49]

Susan, on the other hand, worked quickly—so much so that she had slack time, despite a steady output for the *New Yorker*, to take on ambitious long-form assignments for the *New York Times* Sunday magazine, and also to assist Neil in researching his own stories. Frankel, running the bureau in Washington, had problems with Susan, convinced that both she and Neil were prideful and self-important. Frankel felt Susan's "exaggerated estimation of [Neil's] talents" was at least partly responsible for his own sour relationship with Neil.[50]

Still, the *Times Magazine* editors in New York gave her regular work. Her writing was dishy and sprightly, in a magazine better known for its gravitas. Her *Times Magazine* stories were conversational in tone, but unsparing in substance, exposing the foibles of her subjects.

Susan's profile of Jackie Onassis came out in the *Times Magazine* on May 31, 1970. It was based on interviews with "friends" of Jackie, because—of course—JFK's widow, now Ari Onassis's wife, didn't talk to reporters. Susan's piece was cleverly titled "The Happy Jackie, The Sad Jackie, The Bad Jackie, The Good Jackie." The wordplay reflected Susan's description of the various emotional masks that Jackie wore, none of them revealing her true self:

> The main difficulty with this supposed transformation of Jackie from fairy princess to gold-digging, superconsuming, jet-setting hedonist (according to a recent series of newspapers articles, she and her second husband spent between $15 million and $20 million during the first year of their marriage) is that, upon examination, it seems to have more to do with the making and debunking of a legend than with the subject of the legend. What is interesting about Jackie is that she hasn't evolved from "good" to "bad" but that she has always been a very diverse personality, a mixture of the provocative, the willful, the fey, the bitchy and the sensitive, along with a good many other paradoxical qualities as well. . . .
>
> Jackie, who speaks in a feathery little-girl voice, paints naive little-girl paintings, and throws little-girl tantrums, takes pleasure in such little-girl activities as going to amusement parks, wearing costumes (some new Greek acquaintances were surprised to see her in native dress on Corfu on New Year's Day) and donning disguises. . . .
>
> For now, my only answer to a tiresome question I have been asked a lot lately —"Why are you writing a piece about Jackie?"—is, "Why are you reading this?"[51]

The following Saturday, June 6, Susan dashed off a note to Neil, who was away. *My days as a Jackie-authority are, I hope, over.*[52] Susan was heading off that evening on another *Times Magazine* assignment, this time for a story about Senator Edmund Muskie, of Maine, the man who then seemed the most likely

Democratic presidential nominee. Her story, some months later, would have the same zing as the one about Jackie, right down to the title: "Pro: He's a Nice Guy. Con: Nice Guys Don't Necessarily Make Good Presidents."[53]

> Pro: He's a Horatio Alger hero. Con: Horatio Alger heroes are from Dullsville. . . . Senator Muskie's admirers . . . claim it is Muskie's good character that came across to the public during his quest for the Vice Presidency in 1968 and turned him from an obscure Senator into the Cinderella of the campaign.
>
> Senator Muskie's nonadmirers, who include a segment of the Noisy Minority—the intellectual elite, the Eastern Liberal Media Establishment, the left wing of the Democratic party—make short shrift of Muskie's '68 success. They believe it was a success based on comparison: Muskie looked so good because the other candidates were so bad. "In the kingdom of the blind, the one eyed man is king," a Harvard professor put it. (In the kingdom of the Harvard professor, exaggeration always puts the point across.)

Clever stuff. Needless to say, Muskie didn't get the nomination.

Susan's reporting trip to Harvard would yield something beyond that precious turn of phrase above. She expected to be in New England at least two weeks on the Muskie story, and she might have some time to spare on a side project Neil was contemplating. Neil's work on the "Why Cambodia?" story, still underway, had got him thinking—about starting another book.

Sheehan was seriously considering Kissinger as the subject.

The "Why Cambodia?" team published its five-thousand-word exposé on June 30, 1970: "Cambodian Decision: Why President Acted."[54] The story was datelined from Washington, and Rick Smith got the byline—with an unusual "written in collaboration with Max Frankel" postscript that also credited nine others from the bureau, including Sheehan, for their reporting. Sheehan's reporting with Kissinger barely registered. Harlow wasn't mentioned, but his off-the-record comments to Sheehan a few weeks earlier were crucial to cementing the conclusion that the invasion was Nixon's personal decision. The reporting team had put in a workmanlike effort, resulting in the sort of "first draft of history" that the *Times* specialized in, but the story was anticlimactic, without any bombshells. Two months had gone by, and most of the world was inured to the Cambodian invasion.

Sheehan continued thinking about a possible future Kissinger project.

Sheehan talked to some friends in publishing to gauge interest. Richard McAdoo, the editor in chief at Houghton Mifflin in Boston, encouraged him. Sheehan scrawled McAdoo's comments, along with some observations of his own, into his reporter's notebook:

> [Kissinger] is interesting as a focal point for a book on how power is exercised in the White House. How Kissinger has taken away power from the cabinet officers. Irony—for a president who was supposed to return to a more traditional form, [Nixon] has gone [instead] for greater centralization of power than ever before. [Kissinger] operates independently of the power centers. Inscrutable behind the glasses, a cold clammy handshake. Likes to show the guise of a swinger. Another aspect of [his] personality he seems to want to fill in.[55]

One of McAdoo's well-regarded senior editors was Dorothy de Santillana, who had acquired many notable books, but was also the editor who rejected Julia Child's French-cooking masterpiece.[56] Santillana apparently had been Kissinger's dinner companion at some point—likely chatting up the prolific Kissinger about a future book. Sheehan put it down in his notebook:

> Dorothy de Santillana found him a very dull dinner partner—behind inscrutable bottle-bottom [glasses], always calculating the quid and the quo of power.
>
> If Kissinger stays on for two more years, a book on this subject will be durable. How power is exercised in the White House in this administration.

Sheehan made a reminder: *Get details on the meetings between [Kissinger] and his friends from Harvard.*

Susan would get to work on that.

Meanwhile, Neil continued his research—taking notes on Kissinger's TV interviews[57] (*a plump little man, self-satisfied; looks for loyalty and trust, then intelligence*) and digging into Kissinger's doctoral dissertation about Metternich (*contempt Dr. K shows for naïve, honest men by praising this contempt in Metternich*).[58]

You could see where this was going.

Neil didn't have much use for Kissinger's dissertation. But when Susan was at Harvard that summer, she stopped by the International Seminar offices, Kissinger's old turf, and pulled off the shelf Kissinger's 1957 book, *Nuclear Weapons and Foreign Policy*—the book about limited nuclear warfare that had caused such a stir when it came out.

In careful cursive that was a counterpoint to Neil's squiggles, she wrote her husband a note:

> I picked up a copy of Henry's book on nuclear war and foreign policy, and inside the front flap was a poem some student had written about K's advocacy of limited nuclear war:
>
> *Don't you cry now, honey chile,*
> *Don't you cry no more.*
> *It's just a nuclear weapon in a little ole limited war.*
> *It's just a limited warhead on a little ole limited shell*
> *And all it will do is blow us all to little ole limited hell.*[59]

CHAPTER 5

Red

AMERICA WASN'T JUST AT WAR in Vietnam. There was another struggle taking place at home—and it was dividing the country every bit as much as the ongoing events in Indochina.

Violent crime and civil unrest were on the rise. The threat was real, and the country was feeling it. During the decade of the 1960s, in the capital city of Washington, DC, the number of murders more than tripled, and robberies increased an astonishing twelvefold.[1] The murder rate in New York City doubled.[2] The situation was equally dire on the West Coast. Murders in California more than doubled, and robberies in the state nearly tripled.[3]

The Gallup polling organization had been measuring the public's fear of walking alone at night within a mile of home, and each year the percentage of people calling themselves afraid ticked higher and higher, always setting a new record. By the end of the decade, Gallup's results showed that almost half the country was too scared to walk alone after dark.[4] The assassinations of John F. Kennedy, his brother, Robert, and Martin Luther King Jr. gave further credence to the fears.

Into what seemed a lawless void walked two men who promised to fix things: Richard Nixon and Ronald Reagan.

A Black Communist activist soon became their foil.

Fifty years before Black Lives Matter became a rallying cry for a movement seeking to end systemic racism and police brutality in the United States, twenty-five-year-old Angela Davis was the face of a noisy, angry revolution to expose racial injustice within the American prison system and broader societal structures. Davis's backstory was formative and impressive. She was a fearless and articulate advocate for her people, possessing unquestioned passion and dedication. Tall, slender, and regal, with a trademark full-on Afro,[5] she exuded Black pride.

All this was undeniable.

Yet, within a year, she would be facing the death penalty.

Running for president in 1968, Nixon and his campaign managers tapped into the public's craving for order. A half century before other candidates ran against "the swamp" of Washington, Nixon set the tone by tapping into the nation's fear. He declared the nation's capital to be America's crime capital, and promised to make the city a showcase for public safety.

Nixon discerned, correctly, that much of the increase in violent crime was due to drugs. Whether that was the president's sole motivation for declaring the consequential War on Drugs[6] is arguable. Regardless, Nixon was the first in a long line of politicians to politicize the issue.

Accepting the 1968 Republican nomination for president at the convention in Miami, Nixon spoke to what he called "the great majority of Americans, the forgotten Americans, the non-shouters, the non-demonstrators." The first civil right in America, Nixon said, was the right to be free from the violence of civil unrest.

Roger Ailes would later gain notoriety as the television genius behind Fox News, but in 1968, Ailes was the new kid on the campaign, orchestrating Nixon's television appearances, and in the process writing the script for the modern presidential campaign. A resultant book describing Nixon's transformation by Ailes, *The Selling of the President*, would turn Ailes and the book's author, a young *TV Guide* writer named Joe McGinniss, into media stars. Nixon had failed to master the new medium in 1960, but Ailes and his handlers turned things around eight years later.

From the *Harper's* review of Rick Perlstein's 2008 epic book, *Nixonland*[7]:

> Nixon, edgy, sweaty and never photogenic, was a more difficult but more rewarding charge. Ailes carefully staged climate-controlled televised panel shows packed with rank-and-file Republicans to give the impression that Nixon was one of the people, not some out-of-touch, meddling social engineer. Nixon's ad team also produced brilliantly effective campaign spots, with ominous music and shots of angry protesters and rubble-strewn streets, which captured Americans' anxieties about civil disorder.[8]

In those live televised town meetings, Nixon took questions from a handpicked crowd of supporters and answered them conversationally. The idea was to "destroy the image of Nixon as a loser by showing him as a fighter, someone who could survive tough questions on the public stage."[9]

On October 1, 1968,[10] the campaign filmed Nixon at what it called a Southern Town Hall in Atlanta. A Black man named "Mr. Hutchins" asked a question about crime, and Nixon was prepared with the answer he'd rehearsed:

> MR. HUTCHINS: Mr. Nixon, does "law and order" now take on a new meaning since Black Americans are making a demand for equality, while for years the Ku Klux, white citizen councils and other organized bigoted groups have slaughtered, murdered, maimed and burned the churches and edifices of the Black people all over this nation and especially in the South?

Tough question, right? Mr. Hutchins and the rest of the audience were handpicked for the event. This exchange allowed

Nixon to use one of his stock lines, to resounding applause. A true made-for-TV moment:

> NIXON: Mr. Hutchins, you've put your finger on a very troublesome question for every American—white American, Black American. And let me be quite direct in the answer: I don't go along with people that say that "law and order" is a code word for racism. I don't go along with that because my studies of this situation indicate that Black Americans have as just as great a stake in a law-and-order society as white Americans.[11]

But the real motivations behind the war on crime—and, by implication, its disproportionate burden on young Black men—were never that simple. Twenty years after Nixon resigned, his disgraced chief domestic policy adviser, John Ehrlichman, would bluntly suggest—after his stretch in federal prison—a different catalyst[12]:

> We knew we couldn't make it illegal to be either against the war or Black, but by getting the public to associate the hippies with marijuana and Blacks with heroin, and then criminalizing both heavily, we could disrupt those communities. We could arrest their leaders, raid their homes, break up their meetings, and vilify them night after night on the evening news. Did we know we were lying about the drugs? Of course we did.[13]

Ronald Reagan also saw the political expedient in bluntly taking on quality-of-life issues facing the state. He ran for governor in 1966 on a no-nonsense platform of getting tough on crime and civil disobedience. Crime was an overriding issue in the campaign; the state was experiencing a frightening increase in violent offenses. But alongside that was another phenomenon that unsettled life in 1960s California: riots in the Los Angeles ghetto of Watts, and student unrest in the state university system, notably at the flagship University of California campus in Berkeley.

The Watts riots,[14] which took place the summer before Reagan began his gubernatorial campaign, were on a scale never seen up to that time in Los Angeles. They were sparked by a routine LAPD drunk-driving stop at 116th Street and Avalon Boulevard, which quickly spiraled out of control. A crowd of fifty gathered on a sultry night. Words were exchanged with the police attempting to arrest the driver. A police baton drew blood. Rumors circulated as the crowd grew larger. When more police arrived to disperse the crowd, people broke into smaller groups and roamed the streets. White motorists in the area were pulled out of cars and beaten. Store windows were smashed.

The violence escalated the following day and night. Rioters looted machetes and rifles from pawnshops. Firefighters attempting to douse blazes throughout the neighborhood were forced to take cover; rioters had begun shooting at them. As more fires broke out in South LA on the second night, a firefighter was killed by a collapsing wall; an LA County sheriff's deputy died after he was shot by friendly fire during a clash with rioters; a Long Beach police officer also died as unrest broke out in several neighboring cities.

Across six days and nights, the *Los Angeles Times* catalogued the toll:

> As the death toll rose, 13,900 guardsmen poured into Watts, along with nearly 2,000 LAPD officers and sheriff's deputies. Contingents of armed officers escorted firefighters so they could start to contain the blazes that had burned throughout Watts the entire day.
>
> The chaos that enveloped South L.A. left 34 people dead and 1,032 injured.
>
> The vast majority of those who were killed or hurt were civilians. Of those who died in the riots, 23 were killed by LAPD officers or National Guardsmen.

The Watts riots left 600 buildings damaged by fires or looting; 200 were completely destroyed. Almost 3,500 people were arrested. The violence in Watts eclipsed the death and destruction of all seven race riots that had struck various East Coast cities the year before.

Media-savvy LAPD chief William Parker had built his department into a PR juggernaut. He coined the term "thin blue line" to describe his crisp, militaristic officers, who were glorified in the long-running TV series *Dragnet*. Parker dismissed any notion that his officers bore any responsibility for the violence. Like the generals in Vietnam, Parker felt the real problem was that the police hadn't been forceful enough; the LAPD, he said, was handling Black residents with "kid gloves."[15] Members of the Black community, however, traced the unrest to years of discrimination and overpolicing.[16]

With the press on his side, Parker dismissed the rioters with the kind of statements that others would be excoriated for in later years. After riots broke out again in 1992, the *Los Angeles Times* singled out its own reporting and reconsidered the free pass the newspaper had given to Parker, who'd used all manner of stereotypes and pejoratives during his tenure as chief to describe Blacks and Latinos:

> . . . but the media were not terribly interested, and the chief remained a media darling. When he died in 1966, the *Los Angeles Times* said in an editorial: "Los Angeles is in deep mourning for William H. Parker—the man who devoted his life to making this the best-policed city in the nation."
>
> Neither before nor after Parker's death was there any examination of why "the best-policed city in the nation" had one of the highest crime rates of any major city in the country.[17]

The following year, during Reagan's first campaign for governor, rioting again broke out, this time in San Francisco. The

Hunters Point neighborhood where it started was an impoverished and largely Black ghetto in the city's southeast corner. Drugs and violence were rampant in the area, and most people lived in squalid public-housing projects. The spark for the riot came after a police officer shot and killed one of three teenagers who were joyriding in a stolen car.

Five days of rioting saw 146 people arrested, two police officers hurt, and forty-two civilians injured, including ten with gunshot wounds. Governor Edmund "Pat" Brown, who was running for a third term against the Republican newcomer, Reagan, sent in two thousand National Guard troops with tanks. That was in addition to officers already in the area from the California Highway Patrol and San Francisco Police Department.[18]

Reagan was a political novice, but the actor certainly could deliver a line. Up against Reagan, Governor Brown's campaign was already floundering.

Reagan had outflanked Brown on the crime issue from the very first day of his campaign, when he made a coded racial appeal advocating for more muscular law enforcement and depicting the streets of the state's cities as having become "jungle paths after dark."[19]

Six months after Watts, on the day he announced his candidacy, Reagan showed Californians what the rest of the country would see once he made it to the White House. This was Reagan on January 4, 1966:

> California also leads in some things that, unfortunately, give us no sense of pride. The only thing that's gone up more than spending is crime. Our city streets are jungle paths after dark, with more crimes of violence than New York, Pennsylvania, and Massachusetts combined. Narcotics arrests among youngsters under age 18 are up 40 percent over last year. Now, these aren't delinquents; these are our children, inquisitive as puppies and filled with the spirit of adventure. They're no match for that character leaning against the lamp-

> post down the block from the school. They need more help than just our love and lectures. And they can have such help if we'll untie the hands of our local law enforcement officers.

It was yet another "Vietnam general" moment, this one for a future president. Reagan's simple message was that the solution to crime was more strength, more firepower, unleashing the cops to do what they were trained for.

Reagan had another button to push in his get-tough campaign. There were student protests at flagship Cal Berkeley, beginning in the fall of 1964, over the university's restrictions on political activities on campus.[20] Berkeley's policy, enforced by the campus police, prohibited advocacy of political causes or candidates, outside political speakers, recruitment of members, and fundraising by student organizations. When a student[21] was arrested on campus after violating the ban—he was collecting donations for a civil rights group—matters quickly escalated. Soon as many as ten thousand[22] students surrounded the police car. The Free Speech Movement's leader, Mario Savio, jumped atop it. He and others made speeches into the night.[23]

The large-scale rallies and protests demanding free-speech rights on campus continued for the full academic year. Joan Baez showed up to sing "We Shall Overcome."[24] When Savio called for a campus-wide strike, and students occupied the main administration building on December 2, police arrested over eight hundred students.[25] It was the largest mass arrest in California history,[26] and by far, the largest police invasion of an American college campus.[27] As the news of the occupation and arrests spread, volunteer lawyers began showing up at the Santa Rita Jail, where the students were charged and booked.

National television audiences accustomed to seeing civil rights demonstrations on their evening news now watched as privileged, mostly white students battled police.[28]

Reagan had been handed another issue. "That mess in Berkeley."[29]

Campaigning in Los Angeles, Reagan depicted Berkeley's protests as "not just lewd, but mentally sick."[30] He described a dance that had occurred at the university "against a backdrop of sexual misconduct" backlit by "films of naked torsos of men and women." Hallucinogenic drugs and marijuana filled the air so much "you could hardly breathe."

Beset by Communist influence, Berkeley, and by extension the California university system, needed to be saved by traditional morality and religion. "Reagan tied the 'rioting' and 'anarchy' of Berkeley students to academic freedom run amok and communist professors indoctrinating the next generation," author Livia Gershon[31] observed[32]:

> For Reagan's gubernatorial campaign, campus radicalism was a goldmine. Rhetorically, he tied the "rioting" and "anarchy" of Berkeley students to academic freedom run amok and communist professors indoctrinating the next generation. He promised that, if elected, he would institute a code of conduct for faculty and appoint former CIA chief John McCone to investigate why "the campus has become a rallying point for communism and a center of sexual misconduct."[33]

Reagan trounced Brown in the gubernatorial election. And he kept his word about going after the Communists.

Angela Davis would be collateral damage.

Angela Davis's story began in Birmingham, Alabama, in the segregated Jim Crow south, at a time when the Ku Klux Klan terrorized Blacks with impunity. Those who dared to move across the color line—leafy Center Street, which separated the white and Black neighborhoods—risked dynamite bombings by the Klan. There were forty-plus unsolved bombings between the late 1940s and the mid-1960s. Center Street became known as "Dynamite Hill." The city had a nickname: "Bombingham."

Alabama had a proud history of electing racist governors. In 1968, ex-governor and avowed segregationist George Wallace[34] ran for president and carried five Deep South states, spoiling the election for Democrat Hubert Humphrey and sending Nixon to the White House.[35]

Born in 1944, Angela was the oldest of four children. Her father owned a gas station; her mother was a schoolteacher. When Davis was four years old, the family moved from their Black neighborhood to a white neighborhood across town. The following spring, a neighbor's house was firebombed. It wasn't the first time.

In Angela Davis's own words:

> The first organization I can remember being involved in was an interracial discussion group that took place at the church I attended. *(Davis was eleven.)* I didn't think of myself as an organizer, but I knew there was something very different about doing that work, because the church got burned as a result of our meetings.[36]

Davis was bright, and curious, and eager to get out of Birmingham. She'd already fallen in love with New York when she visited as a six-year-old with her mother. She got the opportunity to return as a high school junior, winning an American Friends Service Committee[37] scholarship to New York's progressive Elisabeth Irwin High School. The school was a cooperative run by teachers, many of whom had been kicked out of the public school system because of their politics during the Communist-baiting McCarthy era.[38]

This was the era of the Red Scare; Joe McCarthy was part of the past, but he was still in the rearview mirror. Davis lived with a white family in Greenwich Village—and joined the school's Communist youth group[39]:

> As far back as I can remember, I've had some relationship to the Communist Party.[40]

By now, Davis was proving herself to be a brilliant young academic, with an extraordinary intellectual life ahead of her. She received a scholarship to Brandeis University, and studied in Paris, France, and in Germany (under Marxist theorist Theodor Adorno).[41]

In 1963, while she was abroad, Davis learned of the bombing of the Sixteenth Street Baptist Church in Birmingham in which four girls, friends of the Davis family, were killed. Big changes were happening back home. Blacks were rising up; the civil rights movement was erupting.

Davis returned to the United States in 1967 to study for her doctorate in philosophy under Marxist scholar Herbert Marcuse at the University of California at San Diego. In Europe, she'd become interested in mass movements opposing racism, classism, and colonialism. San Diego—where, at age twenty-three, she had her first brush with the police, during a sit-in[42]—proved to be less inviting:

> When I first attempted to get involved in Black movements in San Diego, people thought I was an agent. It took me a while to figure out why no one was responding. They said, "Well, she just came from Europe and she did this and she did that, so she must be an agent."[43]

Davis sought ways to get more deeply involved in the struggle. Soon she was the tip of the spear in organizations such as the Black Panthers and the Student Nonviolent Coordinating Committee, known as SNCC. Both organizations were calling for radical change in the United States, and were feared by mainstream America. But Davis soon tired of what she saw as sexism in the Black organizations, and also didn't feel a kinship with the rapidly growing feminist movement. "There wasn't a place for me there. I felt no connection with what the white women's liberationists were doing. And this was the case with the overwhelming majority of Black women. The feminist movement, even though it was sparked in part by contributions made by Black women, did not attract Black women. This was true for other women of color as well."[44]

Davis had worked it all out. She saw a connection between institutionalized racism, the oppression of Blacks, and "the exploitation inflicted upon the working class as a whole." There was a budding movement of Black Communists who bridged that ideological divide. She felt most at home with the Communist ideology.[45]

Davis paid her dues—fifty cents[46]—to the Che-Lumumba Club. She was officially a card-carrying Communist.

By the spring of 1969, the twenty-five-year-old Davis—with a PhD soon to be in hand from the University of California, San Diego—had an offer to teach at Swarthmore.[47] But Davis chose to remain in Southern California. A teaching job—acting assistant professor of philosophy, at a salary of $9,684 a year[48]—awaited at the University of California, Los Angeles.

With the UCLA offer wrapped up, Davis traveled to Cuba that summer as part of a delegation of Communists who had been invited to spend a month in the "first free territory of America."[49]

The appointment of a Black Communist would only add to turmoil already swirling on the UCLA campus.

Two-and-a-half months earlier, two UCLA students had been shot to death in a campus lunchroom during a Friday afternoon meeting that was open only to Black students. About 150 Black students, out of 450 on the 28,000-student campus, attended.[50] The ostensible purpose of the meeting was to settle on a candidate to lead the university's Black Studies program. But what the shootings pointed to was a violent leadership struggle among rival campus organizations: the Black Panthers, the Black Student Union, and a group that called itself US. All three were competing for recruits, and some of their leaders brought guns.

The two students who were killed, John Huggins and Alprentice "Bunchy" Carter, were Black Panthers.

As the *Daily Bruin* later reconstructed the events, the shootout was started by two US members.[51] The meeting had just adjourned. Harold "Tuwala" Jones entered the room and Huggins confronted him about the harassment of a fellow Panther. As a fight broke out between the two, Carter tried to intervene. Then Claude "Chuchessa" Hubert, a member of the rival US organization, came in and shot Huggins in the back. Huggins, who was armed, fired a couple of shots back as he fell, wounded.

Carter attempted to find cover behind a chair, but was also shot by Hubert. "Chuchessa shot through the chair and killed him instantly," recalled J. Daniel Johnson, a student who was present in the room.

In seconds, it was all over and two men were dead.

That evening, the LAPD raided Huggins's home and arrested seventeen Panthers, confiscating a homemade bomb, a rifle, several shotguns, ten handguns, and hundreds of rounds of ammunition.[52]

With Black Panther leaders Huey Newton already in prison and Eldridge Cleaver on the run, it fell to a Panther "captain," David Hilliard, to explain things to reporters at a press conference the next day:

> Nobody lives forever. The ultimate point is how you die. The brothers died courageous, revolutionary deaths. The people who murdered them are criminals, and the masses share this view.[53]

The *LA Times* led its story about the news conference with Hilliard's pledge that the Panthers would "bear arms against 'any aggressor—policemen, whites, or Blacks.'" At Carter's Los Angeles funeral, Panther co-founder Bobby Seale delivered the eulogy to righteous shouts of "amen" and "right on." Author James Baldwin and Eldridge Cleaver's wife, Kathleen, were among the mourners. More than a hundred cars followed the hearse to Woodlawn Cemetery.[54]

Thirty-eight years later, a special committee of the U.S. Senate revealed that Hoover's FBI had a hand in stoking tensions between the rival groups. FBI informants infiltrated both the Panthers and US; the Bureau forged hate mail to each group in the name of the other. The FBI's actions were highly organized and intended to provoke violence. The Bureau had a covert action program known as COINTELPRO (derived from the starting letters of Counter Intelligence Program), formed to disrupt and "neutralize" organizations that the Bureau characterized as "Black Nationalist Hate Groups." According to the Senate report:

> The Black Panther Party (BPP) was not among the original "Black Nationalist" targets. In September 1968, however, FBI Director J. Edgar Hoover described the Panthers as:
>
> > "the greatest threat to the internal security of the country. Schooled in the Marxist-Leninist ideology and the teaching of Chinese Communist leader Mao Tse-tung, its members have perpetrated numerous assaults on police officers and have engaged in violent confrontations with police throughout the country. Leaders and representatives of the Black Panther Party travel extensively all over the United States preaching their gospel of hate and violence not only to ghetto residents, but to students in colleges, universities and high schools as well."
>
> By July 1969, the Black Panthers had become the primary focus of the program, and was ultimately the target of 233 of the total authorized "Black Nationalist" COINTELPRO actions.[55,56]

By early 1969, Nixon's new attorney general, John Mitchell, had approved Hoover's request for wiretaps on Black Panther phone lines in New York and Los Angeles.[57] Racial tensions were high on both coasts, UCLA was in turmoil, and the FBI was in on it.

The appointment of Angela Davis to the UCLA Philosophy Department faculty made the front page of the student newspaper, the *Daily Bruin*, on April 7. The lead story that day was about ferment and dissension within the department. Donald Kalish, the department head, was under pressure from students to revise the curriculum. After a daylong meeting, he still professed not to know what the students were upset about, or exactly what they wanted: *While it isn't too clear what the problems are, it is obvious that there are some real grievances. That everyone in the department must work together to discover what they are is a basic premise of all this*. Kalish pledged changes. Davis's coming in would be one of them. The *Daily Bruin* sandwiched in this squib about her:

> The department has invited a black PhD candidate and student of Herbert Marcuse at UC San Diego, Angela Davis, to a post as acting professor. The usual duration of acting professor appointments is two years.[58]

The *Daily Bruin* incorrectly listed her title as "professor." In fact, Davis would be coming in as an acting assistant professor. But the student paper was correct about something else: Davis's academic mentor was the controversial Marxist professor Herbert Marcuse.

Marcuse was a magnet for controversy and had been having problems of his own with the university system. At seventy, he was past the university's mandatory retirement age of sixty-seven, and thus required an annual waiver to keep teaching. Conservative lawmakers, along with the American Legion, wanted him gone. Marcuse was resisting: "I have not pursued any militant activity for a long time. The Russians consider me an agent of Wall Street. There must be something good about me if I'm equally condemned by both sides."[59]

Meanwhile, Davis's activism on behalf of SNCC and the Communist Party had already aroused suspicion within the FBI. Under J. Edgar Hoover, the Bureau had begun maintaining files on "individuals who have demonstrated by their actions and speeches that they have a propensity for fomenting racial disorder."[60]

By 1968, at age twenty-four, Davis was under FBI surveillance:

> **NATIONAL SECURITY INFORMATION**
> **Unauthorized Disclosure Subject to Criminal Sanctions**
>
> ANGELA YVONNE DAVIS, also known as "Tamu," resides at 1107-1/2 West 87th Street, Los Angeles, California. DAVIS is presently unemployed. Background data is being set out. On 6/21/68, DAVIS was elected as a staff member of the Los Angeles Chapter of SNCC. DAVIS dropped out of SNCC and joined the Communist Party. DAVIS is a member of the Che Lumumba Club, Moranda Smith Section, SCDCP (Southern California District Communist Party). DAVIS' activities in connection with the SCDCP are set out. Description data set forth.
>
> DETAILS:
>
> Investigation in this matter was predicated upon receipt of information from LA T-3 that ANGELA YVONNE DAVIS was a member of the Communist Party in 1969.[61]

The FBI relied on paid informants—including on the UCLA campus[62]—to report on groups it considered "subversive." Davis fell into the dragnet. The FBI's detailed surveillance reports noted Davis's comings and goings at various 1968 and 1969 meetings of the all-Black Che-Lumumba Communist collective, as well as the views she expressed.[63]

Hoover had informants and wiretaps all over. T-3 wasn't the only source passing along information about Davis. Another was T-14, who tipped off the FBI when Davis bought a shotgun.

MISCELLANEOUS
LA T-14 (7/24/68)

On 7/24/68, source was shown a photograph of ANGELA YVONNE DAVIS taken 10/5/67. Source stated that the woman in the photograph strongly resembles the woman who, on 9/11/67 with a male companion, purchased a shotgun at Sportstown, 2673 La Cienega, Los Angeles. Source added that if the woman in the photo is about 5'7", 135 pounds, and has pierced ears, she is almost certainly the woman who assisted in purchasing the shotgun.[64]

The FBI's informant T-3 also reported that Davis was living in South Central LA with a man called Deacon Alexander, "a Negro youth organizer for the Southern California District Communist Party"[65]:

> Source stated that Davis is not employed at the present time but that she is traveling periodically between Los Angeles and San Diego.

Another source, T-2, reported Davis as a suspected burglary suspect:

> Source advised that on March 13, 1968, ANGELA DAVIS was interviewed by the Los Angeles Police Department as a burglary suspect but was released without arrest.

On April 15, a week after the *Daily Bruin* story revealing Davis's connection to Marcuse and Davis's plans to teach at UCLA, the FBI began keeping closer tabs on her. Davis's FBI dossier quickly filled up. The Bureau almost certainly also passed along information to the California Board of Regents, the governing body of the state university system.

The Bureau had a mole planted among the Communists, a UCLA undergraduate anthropology student named William

Tulio Divale. It turned out he had been feeding information to the FBI about "subversives" for all four years he was on campus.

Divale had been paid almost $15,000 (about $131,000 in today's dollars) for his four years as an informant for J. Edgar Hoover's FBI—and the Communist hunters in the new Nixon Administration, including the attorney general, John Mitchell, now saw a way to cash in on that investment.

"Red baiting," as it was colloquially known at the time, was Nixon's early political hallmark.[66] When Nixon finally got to the White House in 1969, his administration almost immediately resuscitated the 1950s McCarthy-era Subversive Activities Control Board and set it back on a path to hunt down Communists. The Board scheduled a hearing for June 17 and 18, 1969, to take place in downtown Los Angeles at the new federal building, with the stated purpose of blacklisting two Communist students—both members of Students for a Democratic Society (SDS)—from getting federal jobs or federal student aid.

And there would be a star witness for the prosecution: The aforementioned William Tulio Divale, who, having completed his four-year FBI undercover assignment at UCLA, was being brought forward to reveal the Communists hiding in plain sight.

This was, in effect, a show trial on Nixon's and Reagan's home turf, complete with two hapless SDS "defendants," who were represented by the Communist Party's chief counsel.[67] Three hundred demonstrators massed outside the hearing, some carrying signs reading STOP FASCISM and DEFEND FREEDOM OF IDEAS. More than a hundred more supporters of the two SDS defendants jammed the hearing room. One hundred fifty police officers were called in to keep order.[68]

After the hearing revealed Divale as the FBI's campus operative, Divale wrote an open letter to the *Daily Bruin* in response, seeking to explain and defend himself. The campus newspaper published it two weeks after the Subversive Activities Control Board hearing, on July 1.

As Divale saw it, he brought clear-eyed academic objectivity to his work for the FBI: "My approach was as an anthropologist studying a group." He allowed as how he had come to know the names of "hundreds" of Communist Party members throughout the country—but denied any animus toward them. "If I was a witch hunter, I would be dropping names all over."

Instead, he had singled out Davis. He called her "well qualified for the post," and "also a member of the Communist Party. . . . Unfortunately, this person will probably be subject to attack now."[69]

If there was any doubt earlier about the controversy soon to erupt around Davis, the FBI informant's open letter put an end to it. The California Board of Regents now faced what had long been an imponderable on campuses everywhere, and remains so to this day: balancing free speech and academic freedom with the political realities of the moment.

California's new governor, Ronald Reagan, was a reflection of the new brand of righteous conservatism taking hold. And, as governor, he automatically had a seat on the Board of Regents. Davis's appointment would quickly become a divisive political issue. The Regents Board had no easy way of avoiding that, largely because of their own contradictory actions.

The Regents Board had a policy, adopted in 1940 and reaffirmed in 1949, against hiring Communists. Even UCLA's faculty senate had voted to ban Communist Party members, in 1950.[70]

But in the aftermath of the Free Speech Movement at Berkeley, the Board of Regents also had just adopted a policy assuring faculty and employees of the state university system that "no political test shall ever be considered in the appointment and promotion of any faculty member or employee."[71]

The two policies were irreconcilable.

The Regents Board was already saddled with their own prior actions. They couldn't claim ignorance: Even if the FBI informant Divale had kept quiet, the impending arrival of the young Communist firebrand had already been front-page news in the *Daily Bruin*. Davis's affiliation had been widely known on campus almost from the moment she was hired by the Philosophy Department.

Seeking a way out, the Regents Board instructed UCLA's chancellor[72] to confirm whether Davis was, indeed, a Communist. Davis replied with a straight-up yes, although she claimed a First Amendment right and questioned the chancellor's authority to even ask the question, or "to deprive me of employment on such grounds"[73]:

> I am now a member of the Communist Party. While I think this membership requires no justification here, I want you to know that as a Black woman I feel an urgent need to find radical solutions to the problems of racial and national minorities in white capitalist United States.[74]

As far as a majority of the Board of Regents was concerned, that made it an open-and-shut case. Supported in their action by Reagan, they fired Davis as classes got underway for the fall term. Reagan was unapologetic.[75] Davis went to court.

The controversy over academic freedom and free expression was about to blow wide open at UCLA. Life-altering aftershocks would follow, and there would be blood.[76]

Davis would soon feel the obloquy of Ronald Reagan.

CHAPTER 6

Revolutionary

COMMUNIST.

Governor Ronald Reagan had a new issue.

The story of an admitted Communist in UCLA's midst burst onto the front page of the *Los Angeles Times* as classes began in the fall.

The unfolding Angela Davis story—a brilliant twenty-five-year-old Black Communist on campus, stirring up trouble—stoked white fears that sold papers. The story was too good to drop.

The right-leaning *LA Times*, controlled by four generations of the dynastic Chandler family,[1] churned out profits as it dictated what to think and what was news in Southern California. The newspaper's weekday circulation was over 1 million, with hundreds of thousands more copies on Sundays.[2] The *LA Times* carried more advertising than any other newspaper in the country. The Chandlers and their paper were, truly, the stuff of legend. In a widely quoted *Atlantic Monthly* cover story in 1979, David Halberstam wrote[3]:

> No single family dominates any major region of this country as the Chandlers have dominated California. It would take in the East a combination of the Rockefellers and the *[New York Times']* Sulzbergers to match their influence. The Chandlers did not so much foster the growth of Southern California as, more simply, invent it.

Halberstam still turned a phrase with the cold detachment of the young Vietnam War correspondent he earlier had been. The Chandlers, he observed drily, "stood at the center of California life, making and breaking political careers, directing the economic progress of Los Angeles—and profiting, always profiting."[4]

The *LA Times*—with its recurring headlines about the ADMITTED RED, sometimes conveniently shortened to RED if space was tight—kept the story in the news for weeks. The paper's conservative editorial page also weighed in. In the news columns, as well as on the editorial page, the Chandlers left no doubt about where the ruling dynasty of Los Angeles stood.

The first story in the *LA Times* appeared on September 19, the day the Board of Regents met to vote on Davis's firing. Under the headline PROFESSOR ADMITTED COMMUNIST: EXPLOSIVE ACADEMIC FREEDOM CASE CONFRONTS UC REGENTS, the lengthy article quoted UCLA's chancellor (Davis's dismissal "will make the loyalty oath fight look like a Sunday School picnic") and her Marxist mentor ("Marcuse called her one of the five top graduate students he ever had"). The story left little doubt about how Davis would be treated in its news pages:

> The dangers of the Angela Davis case are magnified by the fact that she is a militant Black who has strong support from Black students and faculty members at UCLA. . . . UCLA officials expressed concern that the case might lead to a coalition of Black students and white radical students, an alliance that has not formed on the Westwood campus in the past. . . .
>
> Who is Angela Davis? On first meeting, she is an attractive, tall, bronze-skinned woman of 25 with a natural hairdo. She is direct, soft-spoken, and self-possessed.[5]

Reagan didn't express any remorse. He told a news conference that "membership in the Communist Party is a bar to teaching at the University of California." Further, Reagan said, the American Communist Party wasn't a political party but, rather, a "subversive organization."

Reagan had been president of the Screen Actors Guild during the McCarthy era, and had opposed Hollywood's blacklisting of communists (note with a lower-case *c*) during the 1950s. But Davis's case was different, he said. "Communism with a small 'c' is different from active membership in the American Communist Party."[6]

Cornered by reporters as he was leaving the Regents Board meeting after Davis's firing, Reagan was unapologetic, adding simply, "Well, she knew the matter was on today's agenda."[7]

Lest anyone doubt where the Chandlers and the ruling elite of Los Angeles stood on the matter, the *LA Times* weighed in with an editorial titled, "The Case of Angela Davis":

> What smells unmistakably like a carefully contrived plot aimed at provoking new tensions between the university and the public is now unfolding at UCLA in the case of Angela Davis, the admitted Communist Party member and philosophy teacher.
>
> How successful this shrewd but transparent effort at confrontation politics will be depends to a great extent on the political sophistication and calm good sense of the UCLA community, the University of California regents, and the general public.
>
> If reason and perception on the part of all these concerned groups prevail, then the revolutionaries who are stage-managing the Davis case will be defeated. But if emotions are permitted to become dominant and dictate responses, then the purposes of the communists and their allies will be served.[8]

By then, Davis's lawyer, John T. McTernan, had already filed a constitutional challenge to her firing.[9] McTernan specialized in defending Communists. He quickly scored a victory for

Davis when, within a month, a California judge declared the Board of Regents' policy against employing Communists to be unconstitutional.[10]

Even before that, Davis scored a big public-relations win when the regents backed down and reinstated her to teach a non-credit course, "Recurring Philosophical Themes in Black Literature."[11] In a sign not only of support for Davis, but of more turmoil to come, a crowd of more than two thousand students came to her first lecture and gave her a standing ovation.[12]

Davis used her first lecture to poke the regents in the eye. "The first condition of freedom is an open act of resistance—violent resistance," she told the students. In an off-campus speech later, she doubled down on the theme: "When people start saying that we are subversive, we should say, 'Hell, yes, we are subversive. Hell, yes, and we are going to continue to be subversive until we have subverted this whole damn system of oppression." Addressing a group of students in San Diego, she said, "As I see it, capitalism does not contain the solution to our problems. We have to talk about radical solutions."[13]

Davis had begun amassing a mini-arsenal of guns. There was the shotgun the FBI already knew about. Added to that was a Browning .380 semiautomatic pistol[14] she purchased at a Los Angeles pawnshop. Then, on the same day that the *Daily Bruin* first wrote about her, she bought a rifle—a Plainfield carbine, also semiautomatic.[15]

The California Board of Regents was still intent on firing Davis.

Meanwhile, in New York City, the Black Panthers were enmeshed in allegations of more violence to come. The NYPD rounded up twenty-one Panthers who were accused by the Manhattan district attorney of conspiring to kill police officers and dynamite Macy's and other city department stores.[16]

By January 1970, the jailed defendants, by now known as the Panther 21, had an unlikely group of supporters. Leonard Bernstein, the New York Philharmonic laureate conductor, and his friends were trying to raise bail money. Charlotte Curtis, a society reporter from the *New York Times*, was at the Bernsteins' cocktail party where the hat was passed. The guests were household names from the arts. The next morning, there was a story that name-checked everyone. The headline was innocuous. But the writing—uncharacteristically cheeky for the staid *Times*—was deadly, and it made clear the dichotomy between Davis's real-world experience and that of the coastal elites.

> BLACK PANTHER PHILOSOPHY IS DEBATED AT THE BERNSTEINS
>
> The conductor laureate of the New York Philharmonic did most of the questioning. Donald Cox, the Panther field marshal and a member of the party's central committee, did most of the answering, and there were even moments when both men were not talking at the same time.

Curtis's story replayed the back and forth between Bernstein and Cox in painful detail. She pointed out how Bernstein had shushed other guests who wanted to ask questions. The Panther field marshal, after all, spoke of wanting "peace." But Cox didn't disavow violence, and Curtis quoted Bernstein as agreeing:

> "But if they," he (Cox) said, meaning representatives of what the Panthers call the oppressive establishment, "attack us in our homes, and we have been attacked in our homes and murdered in our beds, we have the right to defend ourselves."
>
> "I agree 100 percent," Mr. Bernstein said.

The story went on like that.

The Bernsteins were livid. Felicia Bernstein, Leonard's wife, told the *Times* just that, in a letter that she personally delivered to the newspaper.[17]

It got worse. The next day, the *Times* ran a scolding editorial that characterized the Panthers as a "so-called party, with its confusion of Mao-Marxist ideology and Fascist para-militarism":

> FALSE NOTE ON BLACK PANTHERS
>
> Emergence of the Black Panthers as the romanticized darlings of the politico-cultural jet set is an affront to the majority of black Americans. . . . [T]he group therapy plus fund-raising soirée at the home of Leonard Bernstein, as reported in this newspaper yesterday, represents the sort of elegant slumming that degrades patrons and patronized alike. It might be dismissed as guilt-relieving fun spiked with social consciousness, except for its impact on those blacks and whites seriously working for complete equality and social justice. It mocked the memory of Martin Luther King Jr., whose birthday was solemnly observed throughout the nation yesterday.
>
> Black Panthers on a Park Avenue pedestal create one more distortion of the Negro image. Responsible black leadership is not likely to cheer as the Beautiful People create a new myth that Black Panther Is Beautiful.

The Bernsteins never got over it. As their daughter Jamie put it after their deaths:

> With the "New York 21" episode, the FBI nearly succeeded in discrediting Leonard Bernstein. For a time, my father's stature as a musician was overshadowed by his awful new role as object of trendy ridicule, embarrassing to his acquaintances and infuriating to his fellow Jews. Sadly, we weren't the only ones to suffer. The FBI had deliberately pitted Jews and African Americans against each other, fanning flames of animosity and mistrust that burn to this day.[18]

The author Tom Wolfe was at the Bernsteins' that evening, and he got an earful of anger from them about the intrepid *New York Times* society reporter who'd spoiled the party. "It wasn't anything she wrote that infuriated them," Wolfe recalled. "It was that she put down exactly what they said. That's always what seems cruelest of all, to hold up a mirror to people that way."[19]

Wolfe had his own go at the Bernsteins a few months later in a legendary *New York* magazine piece that went on and on and sank the shiv in deeper. "Radical Chic: That Party at Lenny's"[20] was a pioneering work in what came to be known as New Journalism. Just a taste here:

> Shootouts, revolutions, pictures in *Life* magazine of policemen grabbing Black Panthers like they were Viet Cong—somehow it all runs together in the head with the whole thing of how *beautiful* they are. . . . And here they are, right in front of you, trucking on into the Bernsteins' Chinese yellow duplex, amid the sconces, silver bowls full of white and lavender anemones, and uniformed servants serving drinks and Roquefort cheese morsels rolled in crushed nuts. But it's all right. They're *white* servants, not Claude and Maude, but white South Americans. Lenny and Felicia are geniuses. After a while, it all comes down to servants.

The Panthers were deadly serious in their fight and used violence to make their point. But in articles like these they became caricatures—straw men easily knocked down in the debate. The leading magazines and newspapers of the day were signaling to the ruling class that it was all right to push back against, even taunt, those who fought for Black equality.

Similarly, when major newspapers covered the controversy swirling around Davis, it wasn't to come to her defense, but, rather, to lament the turmoil her dismissal from UCLA would cause.

Outwardly, Angela Davis seemed to absorb the blows. But she was radicalized—and soon would be charged with murder.

George Jackson, just twenty-eight years old, had already been in California prisons for a decade when his family learned about Davis's activism and reached out to her. Davis initially didn't respond.

Jackson's first crime as an adult—a gas-station robbery of $70 at gunpoint—led to a guilty plea and an indeterminate prison term, one year to life.

But Jackson wasn't a compliant or obedient prisoner. He spent most of the subsequent years in solitary confinement at San Quentin, resisting prison authority and studying Marxism. He wrote passionately and eloquently about the injustices of America's prisons. In frequent letters to the outside, Jackson compared his imprisonment to slavery.

And, in ways that he could, he fought back and found solace in his resistance. Guards were "uniformed pigs. . . . Cretins with guns."[21]

By January 1969, Jackson had been transferred to Soledad Prison, a three-hour drive south. "Soledad" is a Spanish word meaning "loneliness," and that was a fitting appellation for the restive Jackson, who'd spent most of his adult life locked down, alone. The prison sat along picturesque Highway 101, near some of the most beautiful places in California: Carmel, Monterey, Pebble Beach, Big Sur. But the hothouse atmosphere inside Soledad was just one step from hell—2,570 inmates and 275 guards, two cellblocks, too much violence. Stabbings, riots, attempted escapes. Authorities counted six violent deaths at Soledad during the first half of 1970, including three Black inmates who were killed by a tower guard during a brawl in the prison's exercise yard. A grand jury exonerated the guard who fired the shots.

Three days later, a twenty-six-year-old novice guard was beaten, dragged up three flights of concrete steps, and tossed headfirst to his death. It was a revenge killing, and the killers left no doubt: "One down, two to go." Shortly after, two other guards who'd been seized by inmates were rescued by fellow guards, who used tear gas.[22]

Three inmates charged with the murder became known as the Soledad Brothers. George Jackson was one of them, and became their self-styled leader. If convicted, he faced the gas chamber at San Quentin.

Davis, meanwhile, had been amping up her rhetoric, in speeches at UCLA and on campuses elsewhere, while trying to fend off the regents who remained intent on firing her. She had already become, in the words of a *Reader's Digest* article of the time, a "martyr"[23]:

> The radical scene thrives on martyrs, and slender, attractive Angela Yvonne Davis . . . is ideally cast for the role. "No Black person in recent years has aroused more public interest—outrage, bewilderment and sympathy—than has this self-proclaimed communist," says the Christian Science Monitor. At once a lofty intellectual and a vituperative rabble-rouser, Miss Davis has been posed in the press as something of an enigma. But she has been far from enigmatic in explaining herself: "I am a Black communist revolutionary," she says, "in a revolutionary movement designed to overthrow all the conditions that stand in the way of our freedom."

The ongoing controversy swirling around Davis only emboldened her.

She also reconsidered her reticence to join in George Jackson's defense. A Soledad Brothers Defense Committee had been set up, with offices across the state: San Francisco, Santa Cruz, San Diego, San Jose, and Stockton.[24] The group needed defense funds, and Jackson's family saw Davis's involvement as key to fundraising. Davis got to know Jackson's mother, Georgia, and his seventeen-year-old brother, Jonathan. When she needed a bodyguard (there were always threats), the younger Jackson was at her side.

Davis gave Jonathan her .380 Browning pistol. *It has a 13-round clip,* Jonathan wrote to George. *I keep one in the barrel, 14 shots. Save me a cell on murderers' row there, I could have 14 murder charges any day now.*[25]

When the Soledad Brothers had a court hearing on May 8, in nearby Salinas, Davis was there. She saw George Jackson—manacled, in chains—for the first time:

> I had not really expected the scene that confronted me when I walked into that courtroom and sat down and saw, coming into the courtroom, three Black men who were chained and shackled. I had never seen Black men before with chains, all over their bodies. It was certainly reminiscent of slavery.[26]

Davis said the sight of Jackson in chains affected her strongly, but even that would turn out to be a dramatic understatement. Davis professed herself to be immediately, impossibly, in love with Jackson. She began writing poignant, profoundly personal letters to the prisoner she now considered not just a soulmate, but her husband.[27] Davis was ready to commit.

> June 2
> Dear George,
> ... Believe me it happened so abruptly, so spontaneously. I was not seeking a love when I walked into a Salinas courtroom on Friday, May 8, 1970.... My love—your love—reinforces my fighting instincts; it tells me to go to war.[28]

Davis, who called George "a beautiful Black warrior,"[29] was fighting her own war on multiple fronts. There were "lectures to brainwashed students," as she put it in another letter to Jackson.[30] On another front, the California Board of Regents was still battling to kick her off campus—and they were using her firebrand rhetoric as the new justification. Amid all that, Davis now was walking picket lines and holding news conferences as the head of the Soledad Brothers Defense Committee.

On June 6, there was another murder of a UCLA Black activist. The twenty-two-year-old president of the Black Student Union was found on an abandoned farm in the driver's seat of a car. Melvin X, as he was known, had been killed gangland execution–style on a Saturday night, on his way to a party; two gunshot wounds to the head—one from the front, the other from the rear. The murderer or murderers were in the car with him.[31]

Davis felt the world closing in. She wrote to George:

> Pigs? Minutemen? Not one clue. What is certain, however: this was undoubtedly a political assassination. I think back to one of your first letters: your reflections on preparedness. Absolutely correct. Precautions must be taken—for it is also certain that this will not be the last attempt.[32]

The Monday following Melvin X's murder, the UC Regents Board met in secret in San Francisco and reached their decision about Davis. She would be fired—again. But instead of basing the dismissal on Davis's Communist affiliation, they decided to base their action on her off-campus speechmaking at rallies and other events. Lawyer William French Smith, the Board of Regents' vice chairman, and a close friend of Governor Reagan's, led the meeting. As they met, four UC Berkeley faculty members picketed outside.[33]

The Board of Regents was scheduled to meet again, in Los Angeles, on June 19. The final vote on Davis would be taken then, and they would face the press after.

Davis got a jump on the Regents Board, calling a news conference one day prior to their meeting. She wasn't about to capitulate to them, and planned to announce what George Jackson already knew: Davis would be the public face of the Soledad Brothers Defense Committee. Her revolution had begun.

"Three unarmed Black men are shot to death. This is called justifiable homicide," Davis told reporters. "One white guard is found dead. This is called murder." Davis was joined at the news conference by the mothers of the three Soledad Brothers. An impressive retinue of politicians, authors, poets, and entertainers added their names to the committee, including Marlon Brando, Jane Fonda, Allen Ginsberg, Lawrence Ferlinghetti, Pete Seeger, Jessica Mitford, Julian Bond, Noam Chomsky, and Tom Hayden. Lawyers for the inmates had been lined up. The committee wanted an end to a court-imposed gag order on the defendants, and the removal of shackles on the prisoners during their court appearances.[34]

The next afternoon, Davis was leading a picket line for the Soledad Brothers at the state office building in downtown Los Angeles when she heard that the Regents Board had voted, 15 to 6, to fire her.

"What has happened to me," she said when told of the vote, "is only a tiny, minute example of what is happening to [the Soledad Brothers]. I suppose I just lost my job because of my political beliefs. The Soledad Brothers lose their lives."[35]

Davis was asked if she planned to challenge or appeal the decision.

"I challenge everything the oppressor does. . . . I appeal what is happening to me by struggling for people like Bobby Seale and others who are in prisons on trumped-up criminal charges."

Governor Reagan took the microphone after the meeting and defended the firing as based on "unprofessional conduct" and "speeches on those campuses where there was already trouble and dissension"—not on her membership in the Communist Party.[36] But that was a tenuous distinction, because Davis had, after all, been speaking *like a Communist.* The Regents Board called out, in particular, Davis's comments about academic freedom. She'd referred to that as "an empty concept and a real farce if divorced from freedom of political action, or if exploited to maintain such views as the genetic inferiority of Black people." Davis had stated publicly that "education is inherently political and political values should be made explicit in the classroom." She had called the university an "outmoded feudal institution" and described the regents as "'unscrupulous demagogues intent upon representing and maintaining the prevailing oppression." And finally, Davis had stated in speeches that "mass demonstrations" were "necessary to secure the objectives" she supported.[37] She certainly wasn't inciting a riot, but it was enough for the board. They were done with her.

Davis drove north the next day to San Jose with Georgia and seventeen-year-old Jonathan. Davis would be leading a statewide gathering of the Soledad Brothers Defense Committee. She wrote to George:

> San Jose
> June 22, 1970
> Dear George,
> Since that day I described to you, my life, all my life-efforts, have gone in one direction: free George Jackson and the Soledad Brothers. Man, I have gotten into a lot of trouble—but I don't give a damn. I love you, I love my people—that's all that matters. Liberation by any means necessary: these means are determined by the nature and intensity of the enemy's response. . . .
> Hasta La Victoria!
> *Angela*

In that letter, Davis also told George: *There are beautiful plans ahead.*

What did she mean?

Davis and Jonathan Jackson were in the process of acquiring an arsenal of weapons and ammunition.

The best description of what followed came from a book published thirty years ago, *The Road to Hell*, written by journalist Paul Liberatore. He described how three weeks before that "beautiful plans" letter, Jonathan and Angela took George's mother, Georgia, to the Western Surplus Store in Los Angeles, where they bought one hundred rounds of .30-caliber ammunition in her name.

On June 15, Davis accompanied a "Stephen Mitchell" to Western Surplus, giving him money to buy a Jetfire 9mm pistol. The gun buyer's name matched the first and middle names of a civil rights lawyer who was on the approved list to visit George Jackson in prison: Stephen Mitchell Bingham. Davis later exchanged it for an M-1 carbine, two hundred rounds of .30-caliber bullets, and two banana clips.

Davis was a regular at Western Surplus, making an impression on the clerks with her big Afro and smoking a jaunty Tiparillo cigar. The previous April, she'd bought a Plainfield carbine with a collapsible stock, two thirty-round banana clips, and one hundred rounds of ammunition for the rifle. Later, more bullets: fifty rounds of .38-caliber bullets and another one hundred .30-caliber rounds.

On July 14, Angela, Jonathan, and George's father, Lester, traveled north to Berkeley, and appeared the next day in San Francisco Superior Court. Davis was there for a hearing on her petition to get visiting privileges with George—ostensibly as an investigator for his legal team. The judge denied it.

In the days following their return to Los Angeles after the hearing, Jonathan and Angela spent a great deal of time together. Soon law enforcement would be following that trail.

The pair crossed briefly into Mexico, returning the same night. On August 1, LAPD officers picked up Jonathan while he was driving Angela's car. She came to the police station and told officers he had her permission to drive it. The following day, Jonathan returned to San Francisco. Angela flew up a day later.

They both tried to visit George, who by now had been transferred from Soledad back to San Quentin. The guards turned them away; visiting hours were over. The two went back the next day. Jonathan got in and talked to his brother; Angela waved to George from the waiting room. When Jonathan and Angela left the prison, they went to a San Francisco pawnshop and bought a 12-gauge shotgun and a box of shells.

The next morning, Thursday, August 6, Jonathan rented a yellow Ford van from Hertz and paid cash for it. He drove it across the Golden Gate Bridge to the Marin County Courthouse in San Rafael. Jonathan walked into the courtroom, where another San Quentin inmate, James McClain, was on trial for assaulting San Quentin guard. The charge was possession of a knife and stabbing a guard. McClain, acting as his own lawyer, was a prison friend of George's. McClain was calling other San Quentin inmates as character witnesses in his case; waiting to testify, they were kept in adjacent holding cells. San Quentin guards were nearby. It was a hot summer day, but Jonathan wore a heavy, long coat.

Jonathan didn't stay long in the courtroom. He was worried about the van. He went back to the courthouse parking lot. The van had a dead battery. Angela, also on the scene, got behind the wheel while a gas-station attendant from across the street gave her a push to get it started. The attendant remembered Angela; she was smoking a cigar.

Later that Thursday, Angela and Jonathan again drove back to San Quentin. Jonathan was able to get in to see his brother. The two huddled across the visiting room table. Jonathan and Angela left San Quentin and drove to the courthouse in San Rafael, but when Jonathan tried to get back into the courtroom, the bailiff told him court had adjourned early that day.

Jonathan planned to return the next morning, Friday, August 7.

Friday, August 7, 1970, 10:45 a.m.

Judge Harold Haley, three months shy of sixty-six years old, was presiding in court, on the bench in his black robe. McClain had fellow Black Panther prisoner Ruchell Magee on the stand, the fourth witness in the third day of testimony.[38] Other prisoners were waiting to testify,[39] sequestered in a holding cell adjacent to the courtroom.

Jonathan Jackson walked into the courtroom and sat down in back. He was wearing a heavy, long coat again, despite the summer weather. A bailiff took notice and moved toward Jackson. At that point, Jonathan pulled out the Browning .380 pistol that Angela had given him, leapt to his feet, and shouted: "All right, gentlemen. Just hold it right there."

Jonathan took over the courtroom. The inmates appeared to be ready for what was coming.

He threw his gun to McClain, then pulled the M-1 with the twenty-round banana clip from his coat and also took out the 12-gauge shotgun, now sawed off, from his satchel. Those guns were Angela's. More guns came out and were passed around. McClain, with his gun to Judge Haley's head, forced deputies to remove the shackles on himself and the other prisoners. He sent Magee into the corridor to free another prisoner, William Arthur Christmas, who was waiting outside to be called in to testify.

Jackson and the three San Quentin prisoners—McClain, Magee, and Christmas—started taking hostages in what would become the worst episode of courtroom violence in American history. Courtroom security protocols would forever change as a result of this August day.

Judge Haley was the first to be taken. Jackson had brought a roll of tape, which McClain began looping around Haley's neck in order to fasten the sawed-off shotgun under the judge's chin. The convicts took four other hostages: three suburban housewives, who were serving on the jury, and the assistant district attorney prosecuting the case, thirty-two-year-old Gary Thomas. McClain kept his finger on the shotgun's trigger. A fall or jostle surely would set it off.

Jackson's plan was to trade the hostages for the Soledad Brothers. One of the prisoners told the judge to get the sheriff on the phone, to guarantee safe passage for the whole group. But word had spread quickly about the violence that was unfolding, and sheriff's deputies and San Quentin guards were already on the scene. The San Quentin guards had been trained never to allow prisoners to take hostages, under any circumstances. This was headed to a shoot-out.

Ken Combs was the official court transcriptionist that day, responsible for taking down every word of testimony as it was given. The moment Jackson leapt to his feet, Combs had taken down his words—*All right, gentlemen. Just hold it right there*—and attributed them to "Voice from the Audience." Those would be the last words he'd transcribe that day—and, Combs feared, perhaps the last ever.

The convicts had used piano wire to tie together Combs, Judge Haley, and the other three hostages. Combs stood face-to-face with the judge. As Combs later recalled:

> Three or four jurors were now strung together with me by one long piece of wire. The assistant district attorney was brought to his feet. Then Magee took my arm, held a handgun to my head and uttered his words, "Let's get one of them now, so they know we mean business."
>
> Everyone was talking at the same time—chaos, chaos, chaos, voices overlapping and shouting, giving instructions. Someone shouted, "Where's the van?" while someone else was saying, "Is it clear out in front so we can get out of here?"
>
> Then someone said, "Let's go." Others kept shouting instructions and giving orders. It was obvious no one was in charge. All the while, Judge Haley and I were looking at each other feeling absolutely helpless.
>
> That moment was when I made my decision: I'd rather get shot here on a carpet than go outside and be shot on the asphalt. It was time to try to get away. I put my hands together, and the wires practically fell off. I moved both hands in front of me, but the wire was still tangled and hung up on the right sleeve button of my suit.
>
> I remember watching Judge Haley's eyes move downward and fix on my hands as I struggled to remove the last piece of wire. Even though he knew what I was doing, he said absolutely nothing but gave me a

> very slight nod to show his recognition. He had a calmness about him that I still cannot adequately describe.
>
> Using the least amount of movement I could muster, I slowly returned to the face-down position on the floor to await my death, because I knew someone must have seen me.
>
> Then the front door of the courtroom swung open as the group moved out into the hallway of the Marin County Civic Center—without me.[40]

One of the hostages asked where they were being taken. McClain, sliding behind the wheel of the yellow Ford van, told them they were headed to the airport to catch a plane.[41] McClain wanted the judge to be up front with him. "I want Judge Haley here where they can see him," McClain ordered. But somehow the judge remained in the rear.

McClain couldn't manage the stick shift, so Jackson got into the driver's seat and the van took off.

The group didn't make it out of the parking lot. Two Marin County police cars blocked the parking lot exit.[42] Jackson lurched the van to a stop.[43] He had a .357 Magnum revolver in his right hand, taken from one of the deputies. Jackson pointed the gun out the window and fired a shot at the deputies and guards, who had flocked to the scene. Two shots were fired in response by the officers. When Jackson pulled his hand back into the van, still holding the gun, his wrist was bleeding. A split second later, the shotgun taped to the judge's chin blew his head off.

Gary Thomas, the prosecutor who was a hostage, looked at Haley:

> When I last saw his face, he was alive. An instant later, I saw the right side of his face slowly pulling away from his skull.

Thomas turned toward Jackson, who still had the gun in his hand. There were five shots left in that .357. Instinct took over:

> I turned to my right, took the gun in Jonathan Jackson's hand. I took it out of his hand and shot in his direction, one, maybe two times. McClain (who was in the front, passenger side of the van, opposite Jackson) was moving toward the left. I shot him in the back. I turned and fired a shot in the area of Christmas (who was in the rear of the van) and then I shot Magee (also in the rear, next to the judge) in the chest; shot Magee once. He was moving. I tried to shoot again. The gun clicked. He stopped moving and I yelled out [to the lawmen outside], "Stop firing. Please stop firing."
>
> About the same time I felt a sharp pain in my back, my legs gave out and I crumpled down.

In the fusillade from the officers that followed, Thomas had been shot through the spine. He would survive, but was paralyzed for life from the waist down. Haley, Jackson, McClain, and Christmas were dead inside the van; Magee was seriously wounded. All had been hit by .357 Magnum rounds fired from inside the van.[44] In addition to Thomas, another hostage was wounded.[45]

When the police searched Jonathan Jacksons body, they found a little over $2 in cash and a slip of paper with the telephone number of a pay phone near the American Airlines ticket counter at San Francisco International Airport.

Within three hours of the shoot-out, Angela Davis was at the Pacific Southwest Airlines ticket counter at SFO, no luggage, hurrying onto a PSA shuttle bound for Los Angeles.

Jonathan Jackson was given a full Black Panther funeral in Oakland.

Angela Davis dropped from sight. Soon she would be deep underground.

Almost instantly Davis became an internationally recognized cause célèbre. Her portrait became a fixture on buttons, T-shirts, and other memorabilia worn by the Woodstock generation. "Free Angela Davis!" would be their rallying cry—in the summer of '71.

PART II

SUMMER

CHAPTER 7

Mayday

THE FIRST ANNIVERSARY OF NIXON'S Cambodia incursion[1] loomed—and, with it, the threat of mass protests by a disparate group of activists: veterans, college students, domestic terrorists known as Weathermen, and newly emboldened gay rights groups.

"Mayday" was no longer a plea for help; now, it was a rallying cry for resistance. The May 1970 campus killings of student protesters by National Guardsmen at Kent State[2] in Ohio and by police at Jackson State[3] in Mississippi were memories as fresh as yesterday. Plans were being made for the biggest act of civil disobedience in the nation's history—an attempt to shut down the government in Washington.

The president was determined to fight back.

Nixon had campaigned on ending U.S. involvement in Vietnam, but by the summer of '71, that wasn't happening fast enough. The Vietnam conflict was being played out in every living room on nightly television newscasts, and it was ugly and grotesque.

A month before Mayday, Lieutenant William Calley was convicted in a military trial of committing twenty-two premeditated murders during a massacre by U.S. forces in the Vietnamese hamlet of My Lai. As many as 504 civilians had been killed that day when Calley took his platoon into the undefended village, and Calley was responsible for killing many more than twenty-two.

It was Calley who gave the order to start killing the civilians, an action he later defended as adherence to clear orders.[4] Calley testified that his military superior, his captain, informed Calley's platoon that they were to "kill every living thing—men, women, children, and animals—and under no circumstances were they to leave any Vietnamese behind them as they passed through the villages en route to their final objective."[5]

Courtroom testimony later revealed how one of Calley's enlisted men, Private First Class Paul D. Meadlo, rounded up and guarded a group of between thirty to forty old men, women, and children:

> Calley approached Meadlo and told him, "You know what to do," and left. Calley returned shortly and asked Meadlo why the people were not yet dead. Meadlo replied he did not know that Calley had meant that they should be killed. Calley declared that he wanted them dead. He and Meadlo then opened fire on the group, until all but a few children fell. Calley then personally shot those children, expending four or five magazines from his M-16 rifle in the incident.
>
> Calley and Meadlo moved from this point to an irrigation ditch on the east side of My Lai 4. There, they encountered another group of civilians being held by several soldiers. Meadlo estimated that this group contained from 75 to 100 persons. Calley stated, "We got another job to do, Meadlo," and he ordered the group into the ditch.[6]

The operation was meant to ferret out enemy guerrillas, but there were not any. Instead, the soldiers herded innocent civilians into ditches and shot them. Women were raped. Livestock were destroyed. Huts were set ablaze. Calley threw a baby into the ditch and shot it. The violence didn't end until a helicopter landed and the pilot intervened.

The helicopter crew held off Calley and his men at gunpoint so they could evacuate survivors. "Shoot them if they shoot me," the pilot told his gunner.[7]

When his Army superiors learned of the massacre, Calley was quietly sent back to the States to await discipline at Fort Benning, Georgia. Senior officers engaged in a cover-up.[8] Eventually word of the crimes leaked to Seymour Hersh, a young freelance journalist who would later become a famed *New York Times* colleague of Neil Sheehan's. Hersh investigated and broke the story. Now the world knew.[9]

Calley's defense wasn't just that he was following orders—although, to be sure, that was part of it. His justification for the killings was that he was trained to do what he did—and that he was being singled out and scapegoated by the government for the entire immoral war in Vietnam.

Astonishingly, given the opposition to the war, a majority of Americans agreed and thought Calley was unjustly accused.

"This boy is a product of the system," argued Calley's chief counsel, George Latimer. "He was taken out of his own home, given automatic weapons, taught to kill. They ordered him to kill. And then the same government tries him for killing, and selects the judge, the court, the prosecutor."[10]

Calley was convicted and sentenced by the military court to life with hard labor at the military prison at Fort Leavenworth, Kansas.[11] The same day that the Calley verdict came down, a jury in Los Angeles recommended death in the gas chamber for cult leader Charles Manson and three of his followers. Nixon had already disdainfully pronounced them "guilty"[12] during their trial the year before for the murders of actress Sharon Tate and six others. But Nixon had a different view of Calley, and how the lieutenant's plight might give Nixon a boost.

The White House quietly commissioned a poll and learned what a Gallup poll already had revealed: Nearly 80 percent of the public disapproved of the guilty verdict against Calley. Before the week ended, Nixon intervened, ordering that Calley remain at Fort Benning until the president himself could review the findings. Calley never left house arrest at Fort Benning. He was paroled three-and-a-half years later.

Draftees were still being sent to war. A restless public wanted action. There was a bill pending in Congress to put a firm year-end deadline in place for the withdrawal of the 284,000[13] American soldiers still in Vietnam, and a vote was set for later that summer. Nixon's Republican Party was in the minority in both chambers; privately, he feared a humiliating defeat.

The Weathermen struck first. The group was an offshoot of Students for a Democratic Society, an antiwar group that by 1969 had splintered into different factions. The Weathermen, also known as the Weather Underground, were the most radical and violent of those offshoots.[14] "Our intention is to disrupt the empire . . . to incapacitate it, to put pressure on the cracks," claimed the group's 1974 manifesto, *Prairie Fire*.[15]

The Weathermen were domestic terrorists—embracing crime-as-protest with a torrid manifesto, a cache of dynamite, and a specialty in bomb building.[16] By 1975, the group had claimed credit for twenty-four other bombings, including at the Pentagon, the California attorney general's office, and a New York City police station. Later, the group turned to robbery and murder in a Brink's armored-truck robbery that left two policemen and a Brink's guard dead.[17] They took their name from a Bob Dylan song of the time, 1965's "Subterranean Homesick Blues": *You don't need a weatherman to know which way the wind blows.* In other words, some things were just so damn obvious, you didn't need to be an expert to know them.

Nixon's war in Vietnam was one such thing.

Early on a Monday morning, March 1, 1971, the Weathermen set off a bomb at the U.S. Capitol.[18] No one was injured because the Weathermen typically provided a warning before they struck. A caller told the Capitol switchboard, around 1:00 a.m., that a bomb was about to go off—"in retaliation for the Laos decision." (The month before, American and South Vietnamese forces had invaded Laos to cut off North Vietnamese supply routes.)[19] The bomb went off at 1:32 a.m. The damage was considerable—about $2.3 million in today's dollars.

Opponents of the war used the bombing to call attention to their cause. Senator George McGovern (D-SD), already a declared candidate for the Democratic presidential nomination and the co-author of the Senate bill to pull out all American forces from Vietnam, called the bombing a barbaric act. But he couldn't resist a dig at the man who would be his opponent in the coming presidential election:

> The massive bombardment we are continuing year after year against the peoples of Indochina has its counterpart in the mounting destruction of human values in our own land. It is not possible to teach an entire generation to bomb and destroy others in an undeclared, unjustified, unending war abroad and not pay a terrible price in the derangement of our own society.[20]

People found different ways to protest. Jane Fonda and Donald Sutherland rebelled against the war with biting satire. The two had just finished shooting Alan J. Pakula's neo-noir psychological thriller, *Klute,* in New York—a film that would become one of the big hits of the summer of '71. After the picture wrapped, but before its June release, they hit the road to entertain troops with a show that was decidedly *not* your typical USO fare.

The duo called their antiwar show *FTA*, which stood for "Fuck the Army"—or, if you were J. Edgar Hoover and averse to the F-bomb, "Free the Army." To the GIs, the title didn't matter; the recruits just seemed to love it as much as the Nixon administration hated it. FBI agents and informants reported on every show; thousands of pages of files were amassed.

Fonda and Sutherland put on their show at venues and coffeehouses all over the country, always just outside the gates of a military base because their antiwar comedy certainly wasn't sanctioned by the authorities. They were aided by such talented and like-minded compatriots as Black comedian Dick Gregory (telling the GIs to vote in a bloc to raise the draft age to seventy-five years old "and send all them older cats to Vietnam with John Wayne leadin' them"), writer/cartoonist Jules Feiffer (who contributed scripts when the group wasn't doing improv), and actor Garry Goodrow.

Their skits were precursors of what would be seen a few years later on *Saturday Night Live*, like one about Dick and Pat Nixon, as played by Goodrow and Fonda at a venue outside Fort Bragg, North Carolina, that March.[21] The set-up: Protesters are trying to storm the White House:

> FONDA: Mr. President, there is a massive demonstration going on outside. . . .
> GOODROW: What are they asking for today?
> FONDA: Free Angela Davis and all political prisoners. Out of Vietnam now. And draft all federal employees.

In the skit, Goodrow-as-Nixon has an easy answer: He'll call in the Army. But Fonda-as-Pat says that won't work—because it's the Army that's trying to take over the White House.

Nixon and J. Edgar Hoover didn't see the humor. FBI agents shadowed Fonda at her shows and campus lectures and sent back reports to headquarters about her. She was, in the agents' telling, an "anarchist." In an era long before social media and the Internet, her speeches would have gone unarchived, but for the fact that the FBI recorded and transcribed everything she said.

In a speech at Southern Colorado State College,[22] Fonda told students about another antiwar group, Vietnam Veterans Against the War, that was making waves. The new group had just held a three-day meeting—dubbed the Winter Soldier Investigation—in Detroit. Fonda called it "a war crimes investigation," and said one hundred thirty veterans ("Black, white, Chicano, Asian, Indian") gave first-person testimony about "war crimes they had committed in Southeast Asia":

> The purpose of it was to show the American people that the My Lai massacre is not an isolated incident.

> That it happens—perhaps on a lesser scale—but that it happens daily in Southeast Asia. And, more important, that these atrocities are the result not of aberrant individual behavior, but of the policies that are formulated in Washington by our leaders, by the CIA, by the Joint Chiefs of Staff, and by the Pentagon.

Fonda told the students what she'd heard in Detroit—testimony from "fifteen or twenty men from the 101st Airborne, representing the entire time span of the 101st Airborne":

> [They spoke openly] about how they were trained at Ft. Holabird, Md. in prisoner-of-war interrogation tactics, where it is implied that there are ways to get information from prisoners: attaching field radios to the genitals. You then crank the field radios and they send electric current through the body of the prisoner of war. The degree of current depends on how fast you crank the field radio.
>
> One by one, the men talked about the massive indiscriminate killing of civilians in the presence of officers—a standard operating procedure. The massive rapes, the skinning alive, the cutting off heads and hands and ears and fingers, the wearing them around their necks and their waists, the rapes of Vietnamese women with their children in their arms, the putting them on posts, on bamboo posts, in the villages for all to see.

Fonda was being brutally serious; no improv comedy that day. The Winter Soldier Investigation did, indeed, happen as she described it, at a Howard Johnson's Motor Lodge in Detroit. The meeting got its name from a reference to Thomas Paine's writings, where he criticized "summer soldiers," who deserted during difficult times, contrasting them with "winter soldiers," who stayed strong through hardship; essentially, the name was chosen to signify the Vietnam veterans who were coming forward to testify about their experiences despite potential backlash, much like the "winter soldiers" in Paine's analogy.

In her speech, Fonda omitted the fact that she was the event's sponsor and one of its principal fundraisers, along with conspiracy theorist Mark Lane. The *New York Times* Detroit bureau sent Neil Sheehan a press release about the forthcoming event and invited him to cover it. Weeks earlier, Sheehan had caused a furor with a scathing review of Lane's book about Vietnam atrocities, *Conversations with Americans.*[23] Sheehan's review accused Lane of fabricating interviews—the worst journalistic crime. Lane ended up getting dropped from the Winter Soldier program, and Sheehan avoided covering it.

Fonda wanted the gathering held in Detroit in order to reach the "working class." As Fonda stated, the gathering received scant notice at the time. But, in her exhaustive recounting of events that day, there was a relative newcomer to the cause that she failed to mention.[24] He was a charismatic twenty-seven-year-old on the make. His name: John Kerry.[25]

Amid the ragtag antiwar groups and long-haired protesters who comprised the movement, John Forbes Kerry stood out. He was a young Navy veteran with a striking appearance, lean and angular; a New England Brahmin educated at St. Paul's School and Yale; a Swift Boat commander in Vietnam with a Silver Star, a Bronze Star, and three Purple Hearts. He was also something of a walking, talking contradiction. Kerry looked and acted the part of the well-bred Yalie, with patrician manners and stock patriotic phrases. He favored tailored suits, Gucci loafers, and monogrammed "JFK" sweaters (yes, his initials, too) that other vets kidded him about. But he harbored, and openly expressed, an everyman's opposition to the war and the politicians behind it.

Testifying in Congress against the war, and speaking on campuses for a fee, in today's money, of $10,000 per appearance, plus expenses, he seemed straight out of central casting—a highly credible opponent of Nixon's policies that the average American had to pay attention to. And Kerry knew it. He was already being talked about as a possible senatorial candidate from Massachusetts,[26] except there was a problem—he was too young to run.

Kerry considered running for Congress, instead, in his home state of Massachusetts; unlike for the Senate, the minimum age to serve in the House was twenty-five. But Kerry thought better of it and instead traveled in 1970 to Paris with his new wife to meet with the Viet Cong and Communist representatives to the peace talks that weren't going anywhere. A "fact-finding mission," Kerry called it.

When Kerry got back, the Vietnam Veterans Against the War (VVAW) were about to start a three-day, eighty-six-mile Labor Day march along George Washington's "winter soldier" route, from Morristown, New Jersey, to Valley Forge, Pennsylvania. Three hundred veterans planned to march, carrying toy M-16 rifles and performing "search and destroy" skits in towns along the way to demonstrate the shameful things they said they'd been asked to do in Vietnam. The authorities expected violence.

Kerry was asked to join the group—but, fearing the clashes with onlookers that the vets would come close to, he arranged to show up only for the speeches in Valley Forge, skipping the march. Kerry would be the warm-up speaker, ahead of Fonda and Donald Sutherland. But it was Kerry's speech, not Fonda's, that turned out to be the high point. The FBI, of course, transcribed everything.

"We are here," Kerry told the crowd, "because we, above all others, have earned the right to criticize the war in Southeast Asia. We are here to say that it is not patriotism to ask Americans to die for a mistake, and that it is not patriotic to allow a president to talk about not being the first president to lose a war—and using us as pawns in that game."

Kerry that day seemed to believe, and be genuinely affected by, the atrocities the vets described, and he expressed support for Ho Chi Minh, calling him "the George Washington of Vietnam"—comments that would receive scrutiny years later when he was a U.S. senator and, later, secretary of state.

After Kerry's stirring speech, one of the VVAW's founders exclaimed, "Whoa! He looks like Lincoln, and he sounds like a Kennedy. Get him on the road!" From then on, Kerry was the new national spokesman for the VVAW. He hit the road again, making speeches on campuses across the country to raise funds for an epic protest that the VVAW was planning for the weeks before Mayday.

The event was called Operation Dewey Canyon III, named after Nixon's secret invasions and bombings of Laos—"limited incursions," in the jargon of the day. The military had code-named their operations Dewey Canyon I and II. With Dewey Canyon III, Kerry's group had its own plan for a "limited incursion of Congress." A thousand vets would be bused into Washington from all over the country, working the halls of Congress in jungle fatigues for a full week in mid-April, buttonholing lawmakers and staff and making their case for an end to the war.

Washington became ground zero for protest. Other antiwar groups built their plans around the VVAW's operation. Almost the entire month of April would be devoted to demonstrations against the war, culminating in a Mayday effort to shut down the federal government through civil disobedience.

A Women's March on the Pentagon was planned for the second Saturday in April. The following weekend, the VVAW demonstrators would start arriving; they planned to set up an "encampment" as close to the Capitol as possible and would hold demonstrations there and at the Supreme Court. There would be a candlelight service at Arlington Cemetery.[27] The vets also planned guerrilla theater, reenacting atrocities as they had on the Winter Soldier march a few months before, and then gathering at the Capitol, where they intended to strip off their medals and decorations and deposit them in a body bag of the type used to evacuate dead soldiers. Kerry would testify before the Senate Foreign Relations Committee; the panel was chaired by the antiwar senator J. William Fulbright (D-AR), and the friendly forum would give Kerry and the vets a powerful megaphone for their message.

Riding on the shoulders of the VVAW was the People's Coalition for Peace and Justice, which planned an enormous rally on the Ellipse and a march to the Capitol for the day after the vets ended theirs, on Saturday, April 24. The Southern Christian Leadership Conference (arriving via a Poor People's Mule Train, a dramatic protest caravan of mule-drawn wagons), the National Peace Action Coalition, and the National Welfare Rights Organization also put their support behind that event, as did McGovern, who was the co-sponsor of the bipartisan amendment that would set a year-end deadline for ending the war. It would turn out to be the largest antiwar march Washington had ever seen, with at least two hundred thousand participants (the official estimate) and as many as five hundred thousand (according to the organizers).

The groups leading the April 24 rally scheduled more demonstrations the following week outside the Justice Department, the Pentagon, the CIA, and the Department of Health, Education and Welfare.

Gay rights groups planned their own Gay Mayday, two years after Stonewall. Organizers designed their own logo featuring an upraised fist above male and female gender symbols, circled by the words "Gay Mayday Tribe. An Army of Lovers Cannot Lose." There was a Gay Peace Treaty with this Preamble:

> We, gay women, males, transvestites, and transexuals, in America who have been systematically and deliberately oppressed and exploited in this country's history through sexism, male chauvinism and supremacy, racism and capitalism, feel that the war waged against the Southeast Asian people by the government of the United States is an extension of our oppression.
>
> War, American style, is a man's game, where to prove his masculinity he must maim or kill women, children, the very old, the very young, and his own brothers. War is an extension of our own oppression

> because it reinforces the masculine image of males and forces them into playing roles where the end result is the death of millions of people.
>
> We as gays are a part of the struggle of the Vietnamese, Laotian, and Cambodian people and feel solidarity with them. In this spirit we sign this treaty of peace, love, and struggle.[28]

The capstone of this month of events would come as SDS and Chicago Seven antiwar radicals, led by Rennie Davis, planned a "celebration of peace" with sit-ins and massive civil disobedience by tens of thousands, all intent on disrupting business as usual.[29] The Mayday motto: "If the government won't stop the war, then the people will stop the government."

Inside the White House, Nixon's chief, H. R. Haldeman, took note, and expressed his concern. He reached out to five people in Nixon's innermost circle, including speechwriter Bill Safire:

> There is a great deal of anti-President/Administration activity being generated on the college campuses. The effort is calculated to begin the campaign to defeat the President in 1972.
>
> How do you feel this stirring up of campus attitude against the President and the Administration can be countered? Should anything be done at this time? What should our strategy be for the next few months?

Safire cautioned against making "any overt moves to 'cool' campuses this spring."[30] But the young speechwriter had an idea for Haldeman that he thought could be "the most poignant and human-interest-laden moment of this Administration."[31]

Safire wanted to get Nixon to retell the story of the president's predawn visit, the year before, to meet with protesters at the Lincoln Memorial. It had been a spur-of-the-moment thing, just Nixon and a few aides and Secret Service agents, in the wake of the Cambodian invasion and the campus rioting that followed.

Nixon, after an evening news conference where questions about the invasion predominated, slept fitfully, if at all. He arose at 4:00 a.m., roused his valet, Manolo Sanchez, and off they went. Nixon's small group had encountered a handful of college students, and Nixon talked to them. Then, astonishingly, Nixon wanted to go to the Capitol and sit in his former seat in the House chamber. This, too, happened—his valet giving a "speech" from the rostrum as Nixon listened approvingly and clapped (joined by the cleaning crew). Then Nixon topped off the bizarre early-morning cavalcade with a stop at the Mayflower Hotel, blocks from the White House, for a breakfast of corned beef hash and eggs.

Haldeman gave Safire the green light. He agreed it would be good to get Nixon to talk about his motivations for the meeting with the student protesters. Nixon played along. The president saw the dialogue with the students at the Lincoln Memorial as an attempt "to lift them a bit out of the miserable intellectual wasteland in which they now wander." He spoke his recollections onto five Dictabelts that Safire got transcribed. "To get the conversation going," Nixon said:

> I asked them how old they were, what they were studying, the usual questions. Two or three of them volunteered that they had not been able to hear the press conference because they had been driving all night in order to get here. I said I was sorry they had missed it because I had tried to explain that my goals in Vietnam were the same as theirs—to stop the killing and end the war. They did not respond, so I took it from there by saying I realized that most of them would not agree with my position, but I hoped that they would not allow their disagreement on this issue to lead them to fail to give us a hearing on some other issues where we might agree. And I particularly hoped that their hatred of the war, which I could well understand, would not turn into a bitter hatred of our whole system, our country and everything that it stood for. . . .

> One spoke up and said, "I hope you realize that we are willing to die for what we believe in." I said I certainly realized that. I asked if he realized that many of us, when we were his age, were also willing to die for what we believed in—and were willing to do so today. The point is that we are trying to build a world in which nobody will have to die for what he believes in.[32]

Nixon's "memoir," as Safire called the transcribed Dictabelts, was lengthy but not particularly revelatory, despite what Safire promised. Haldeman wasn't impressed. He told Safire to show the transcript (but not allow quotes) to friendly *Newsweek* columnist Stewart Alsop, and also to conservative author Victor Lasky, who was working on a book about Nixon. It turned out that Alsop wasn't interested "since the ability to quote was essential," Safire reported back. "Lasky will use the info in his book, but that will not have the impact this deserves."

Safire pleaded with Haldeman to do more with the transcript, and offered up names of some other reporters who might bite on the story. Telling the rest of the story would be "a big plus" for Nixon, Safire promised. "As of now, all that is remembered of that night is one coed's sarcastic reference to 'he talked to us about football.'"

The ad man in Haldeman saw no upside, and he shut down the plan with a note scrawled at the bottom of Safire's memo:

> This should be left as is. No further exposure beyond Alsop and Lasky. If no results, we can reopen it in a year or so.

Haldeman seemed pretty sure there would be Maydays to come.

Meanwhile, Kerry was busy on a public-relations blitz. He visited the DC office of NBC's *Meet the Press*, the top Sunday-morning interview show, and pitched VVAW's plans for the coming demonstrations. Lawrence E. Spivak, the taciturn moderator of the show, and Betty Cole Dukert, his producer, agreed they "were much impressed with his intelligence and manner and his articulateness." His Yale background was a plus, they thought. But they were still on the fence about inviting Kerry on the show, in those days broadcast live from the NBC Studios on Nebraska Avenue, in leafy Northwest Washington. They asked Kerry who else he could bring along to demonstrate the breadth and diversity of the movement. Kerry suggested one of VVAW's co-founders, Al Hubbard, a Black former Air Force captain and pilot who'd been wounded in combat while serving in Vietnam.

According to Spivak's notes at the time: *We thought a combination of Kerry and Hubbard could show the scope of the leadership, as Hubbard was a founder, served as chairman at one time, was Black and had been in the Air Force. Kerry is white and a Navy man.*

Spivak and Dukert traveled to New York, where they met again with Kerry and spoke with Hubbard for the first time. Per Spivak's notes: *Found Hubbard intelligent and articulate, though not as much so as Kerry. Decided the two could make an interesting show.*

Kerry and Hubbard were booked for April 18. The show would broadcast live at 1:00 p.m. Neil Sheehan, the *New York Times* investigative reporter who was deeply experienced at the Pentagon, was brought on as one of the questioners. Sheehan was hunkered down on a top secret project for the *Times*, but he couldn't turn down the *Meet the Press* gig. He was paid a fee of $125.[33]

By now, Kerry's barnstorming on the lecture circuit had raised nearly $100,000—surely enough to bring a thousand camouflage-wearing vets to Washington for the big week of Dewey Canyon III. But he was outraged to learn just a week before the big event that $94,000 had been spent for an advertisement that would appear in the Sunday *New York Times*. Only a last-minute $50,000 infusion from a few big Democratic donors—funneled through the Senate offices of Democrat George McGovern and Republican Mark Hatfield (OR)—saved the day. The two senators were pushing their eponymous McGovern-Hatfield Amendment to cut off funding for the war by year's end. The FBI, tracking everything, wondered how Kerry had managed to get his hands on so much cash so quickly. "Subversive elements" were credited.[34]

The *Meet the Press* show came off without a hitch. Sheehan got in a few questions, including one at the very end that Kerry memorably teed off on:

> SHEEHAN: You said the war in your opinion did not justify the loss of one more American life. But in fact 53,000 Americans have died in Vietnam, and we are told repeatedly by men inside the government and some out that one of the basic reasons for continuing the war and trying to leave something solid behind in Vietnam is to justify those 53,000 deaths. It seems to me that what you and Mr. Hubbard are proposing is that the country withdraw from Vietnam regardless of the consequences to Vietnam itself. Doesn't this make meaningless the sacrifice of those 53,000 lives? What do you have to say about that?
>
> KERRY: To answer your question as to the dead, we will have marching with us mothers of prisoners of war, mothers of soldiers who have been killed, wives of husbands who have been killed. We will have Marines coming down here, men with no legs, with Navy Crosses, Silver Stars, Purple Hearts, 100 percent disabled, who are coming here to say to the people of this country: "We have lost our sons; we have lost our husbands; I lost my legs. But the important thing is not that that happened. Let's not keep killing people to justify my loss. Let's not glorify the dead. Let's try and glorify the living. Let's do something for the living." And they would say, therefore, don't let it happen to any more people when it doesn't have to. Don't let it happen to someone else.[35]

What seemed to worry the FBI most was Kerry's impending televised testimony before the Senate Foreign Relations Committee. A warning was passed directly to FBI Director J. Edgar Hoover that public sentiment could shift: "It is probable that considerable publicity would work in their favor and definitely against FBI."

As Kerry delivered his Senate testimony, the Pentagon was double-checking its records to see if they matched the public statements of Kerry and Hubbard. In a big black eye for the VVAW, to say nothing of Spivak and *Meet the Press*, it turned out that Hubbard was an impostor: He was an enlisted man; was a flight engineer, not a pilot; hadn't served in Vietnam; hadn't been wounded in combat. Hubbard confessed: "In this country, it has been very important that one have an image. That is compounded if one is Black and attempting to do something. I don't justify the lie. I'm trying to explain it."

Among the twenty thousand pages[36] of FBI files on the VVAW was this summary of the week in question:

> Kerry was glib, cool, and displayed just what the moderate elements wanted to reflect. It appears that Al Hubbard revealed his own ambitions of becoming the VVAW national leader by lying about his former military rank. He claimed to be a captain, but in reality he was a sergeant.

NBC got out in front of the story first thing the next morning on its *Today* show, and then again on the *Nightly News*. But the incident soon was eclipsed by the dramatic theater later that Friday when the vets, throughout an emotional three hours, one by one, threw back their Vietnam medals and ribbons onto the Capitol steps. Some spoke angrily as they did so; others, tearfully. They wore old uniforms and combat fatigues. The spectacle led the evening news.

Kerry soon moved on. He faced growing opposition from enlisted veterans who had borne the brunt of the fighting in Vietnam and who now wanted control. He planned to make a second trip to Paris that summer to continue his freelance negotiations to bring home American prisoners of war. But first, there were bills to pay. He scheduled a fundraiser at Averell Harriman's Upper East Side mansion on Eighty-First Street, just off Fifth Avenue. Three Democratic members of Congress were expected, along with a hundred guests.

As the vets left Washington, a new, unruly contingent took their place. Mayday had finally arrived.

Rennie Davis had a simple plan, at least on paper.

Once all the vets and other demonstrators had cleared out and returned home, he would bring thousands of activists back into the city to camp out and disrupt business as usual. The May Day Tribe, as it became known, comprised hard-core activists, as well as pranksters who called themselves Yippies—the name a comic riff on "hippies." Their plan was to disrupt the Monday-morning rush hour using hit-and-run tactics to block commuter routes and the bridges across the Potomac with old cars, trash cans, and their own bodies.[37]

Davis was no stranger to civil disobedience—or political theater. He had been a leader, along with Tom Hayden, of Students for a Democratic Society. He'd marched on the Pentagon, immortalized in Norman Mailer's 1968 book, *The Armies of the Night*. And he was still facing a five-year jail term as one of the Chicago Seven defendants for his 1968 Democratic Convention role as rioter-in-chief (and a bloodied victim of police violence) in Grant Park. He was part rabble-rouser, part salesman—"smart, charismatic, and a blur of energy and engagement," in the words of one writer.[38] As he planned the grand finale of the months' worth of demonstrations in DC, Davis straddled the line carefully.

The tens of thousands of protesters who hung around after the VVAW left town, along with others who showed up to join

Davis's group afterward, were told to expect a wild time—bridges and intersections blocked, fires set—basically, a full-on riot. There was even a convenient map handout that showed the twenty-one locations where the action would take place. Everything was planned out.[39] The leaders coached people to plan to be arrested if and when they blocked traffic, but then to post $10 bail and return to the streets. Police activity and arrests were key to getting media attention, and that was the name of the game above all else.

The government, on the other hand, heard a different sales pitch from Davis: Mayday would be a peaceful demonstration, with a two-week campout by the protesters in West Potomac Park. The park was situated at the end of the National Mall, near the Washington Monument, and alongside the famed cherry trees, just past peak blooming.

Surprisingly—because there had been a lot of back-and-forth about it, and multiple trips to various courts—the government finally granted the campout permit. Thus, by Saturday night, May 1, nearly forty thousand people were sleeping, many in tents or other makeshift arrangements, in West Potomac Park. The weekend was unfolding smoothly, everything proceeding as planned for the Monday-morning disruptions to come.

But it was a trap. Davis and his ragtag band of protesters had been snookered.

The Nixon administration had no intention of allowing the demonstrators to run roughshod over the streets in an attempt to shut down the government.

Nixon confided to Haldeman[40]:

> The party's over, and it's time to draw the line.

Nixon's Justice Department, led by Attorney General John Mitchell, coordinated the government's plan. Determined to keep the city open, the president refused to give federal employees the day off (traffic was snarled all over). Most of the 5,100 members of the DC police force were placed on full alert. In addition, the government brought into the city paratroopers from the 82nd Airborne Division[41] and soldiers from the 2nd Marine Division,[42] as well as four thousand Army reservists and fourteen hundred National Guardsmen—an astonishing deployment of the military against civilians in peacetime. An additional four thousand reservists were stationed nearby. Four hundred U.S. Park Police were also on alert. Almost all the firepower was under Nixon's direct control, and the one group that wasn't—the DC police—was cooperating.

So, once all the protesters had doused their (illegal) campfires and returned to their tents and sleeping bags for the night, the police went in. "Move out!" the police said. "Your permit has been revoked."

Indeed, the permit had been pulled—at 6:00 a.m. on Sunday, the day before the Mayday disturbance was to begin.

The police swept in, using tear gas, clubs, and whatever force was necessary to clear out the protesters.[43]

The goal of the sudden sweep was to break up the May 3 action, even before it could get underway. The government calculated—wrongly, it would turn out—that the thousands of demonstrators would leave the city after the raid. But those who had stayed this long were in it to finish. They regrouped in clusters elsewhere, and they still had their maps. The disruptions were still on. Protesters were out in full force by 7:00 a.m. that Monday.

Civil liberties be damned, Nixon intended to teach the protesters a lesson. In three days of mass arrests all over the streets of Washington, police rounded up more than thirteen thousand people, including many innocent bystanders. When the first cases came up for trial, the ACLU represented the defendants and got the charges dropped. The government didn't pursue the remainder. It was such a blatant violation of basic constitutional rights that the victorious ACLU came out the following year with a ninety-one-page report, intending that it stand as the definitive document of those tumultuous days, and as a warning for the future[44]:

> This report is being issued more than a year after Mayday. But even though a full year has passed since the events described took place, it is still too early to assess their full significance. It is possible that Mayday will become just a curious historical footnote. It is equally possible that it will set the pattern for government action from now on. Which course our country chooses for the future will depend in some part on how well we understand what happened a year ago.[45]

In the aftermath of the police sweeps, there was a huge problem: The DC jail was already at capacity, and there was nowhere those arrested could be held. A makeshift outdoor jail was quickly set up by authorities, who erected an eight-foot-high chain-link fence around a Washington Redskins football practice field at RFK Stadium. No food, water, or sanitary facilities were made available; sympathetic citizens brought supplies and passed them through and over the fence.

In its exhaustive after-the-fact report, the ACLU described what happened next:

> Nobody will ever know how many had planned to participate in the illegal traffic blocking. For it became clear immediately that the government's elaborate plans for handling Mayday did not include any attempt to limit arrests only to those blocking traffic. Instead, the government elected to clear the key intersections by sweeping the streets clean by mass arrests, without stopping to ascertain whether the individuals swept into the police net were participants, passersby, spectators, etc. Special targets for mass arrest were the young and the long-haired, no matter where they were or what they were doing. Among the various threads running through the May 3 affidavits collected by the ACLU, the most common is that in certain areas, a great many people who had absolutely

> nothing to do with the demonstration were arrested simply as a means of keeping the sidewalks clear.[46]

The three days that followed constituted pandemonium, with the police abandoning any semblance of probable cause or due process and simply throwing out a dragnet. Some officers removed their badges so their misconduct couldn't be documented. Again, from the ACLU fact finders:

> During this three-day period, normal police procedures were abandoned. Most of the 13,000 people arrested—including lawbreakers caught while attempting to impede traffic, possible potential lawbreakers, war protestors engaged in entirely legal demonstrations, and uninvolved passersby and spectators—were illegally detained, illegally charged, and deprived of their constitutional rights to due process, fair trial and assistance of counsel. The court system, unable to cope with this grand scale emergency caused by the police, was thrown into chaos. The scale of arrests—and of official illegality—was unprecedented in Washington. Indeed it has few equals in the 20th Century history of our country. All in all, Mayday was a profound blow to civil liberties, and one in which the federal and local governments share responsibility.[47]

It fell to William Rehnquist, the future chief justice of the United States Supreme Court, to defend the government's action, which he did with gusto. At the time, Rehnquist headed up the Justice Department's Office of Legal Counsel. Essentially, Rehnquist served as the attorney general's in-house lawyer. As the Mayday arrests began, he was asked to find—or, a better description, concoct—a legal basis for the mass arrests and preventive detention taking place. Rehnquist came up with a theory that had no basis in the Constitution, but rather evoked the "double secret probation"* of *National Lampoon's Animal House*: The government had declared "qualified martial law"—without actually declaring it.

The protesters, according to Rehnquist, had "Communist-oriented or related backgrounds." Suspending ordinary civil rights, Rehnquist asserted, was justified because there was a civil emergency. "The doctrine which there obtains is customarily referred to as 'qualified martial law.' In that situation, the authority of the nation, state or city . . . to protect itself and its citizens against actual violence or a real threat of violence is held to outweigh the normal right of any individual" to insist on normal constitutional rights when arrested.

But there was no such doctrine. Rehnquist just made it up.

In its post-Mayday report, the ACLU said:

> This is an extraordinary statement from one of the chief law officers in the country. There is no doctrine of "qualified" martial law. . . . By invoking the doctrine of "qualified" martial law, the government was attempting to eat its cake and have it, too: to avoid a formal proclamation with its legal requirements, but to impose the conditions of martial law in fact. This doubletalk was a forerunner of the tortuous line the government was to pursue in court to justify its actions.[48]

The Nixon Administration's actions were an egregious violation of constitutional rights, and the government eventually paid millions of dollars in damages. But Nixon and Attorney General Mitchell were pleased. The ends justified the means. Mitchell

---

*"Double secret probation" is a fictional disciplinary status first used in the 1978 comedy film *Animal House*. In the movie, Dean Vernon Wormer places the Delta Tau Chi fraternity on double secret probation—a made-up term meant to sound like a severe administrative punishment, but with no real definition or precedent. In popular culture, it's since come to mean a comically exaggerated or unofficial warning—when someone is said to be in trouble or under scrutiny, but the punishment itself is vague, arbitrary, or lacks any real authority.

called the decisive action a model for the future. One week to the day after Mayday, Nixon and Mitchell welcomed Washington's police chief, Jerry Wilson, and the city's mayor, Walter E. Washington, to the Oval Office to personally thank them for handling everything with "firmness and restraint."

Nixon's speechwriter Bill Safire was one of those who got caught up in the rioting. Safire certainly knew that Nixon was capable of egging on protesters and inciting violence. He had been with Nixon at a speech in San Jose, California, a few days before the 1970 midterm elections. Thousands of antiwar demonstrators gathered outside were boisterous and profane. Instead of avoiding them when his speech ended (there was a police barricade and plenty of protection), Nixon purposely threw red meat, standing atop the hood of his limousine and thrusting out his arms to make the double-*V* for which he was known. "This is what they hate to see," Nixon said. A hail of rocks, eggs, and rotten tomatoes came flying back at him—but Nixon had the law-and-order moment he wanted, right before a critical election.[49]

Still, Safire sided with Nixon on the mass arrests of Mayday. When the ACLU, which had sued the city for the false Mayday arrests, won a $12 million jury verdict[50] for twelve hundred of those arrested, Safire—by then a columnist and conservative curmudgeon in residence at the *New York Times*—used his new bully pulpit to defend his former boss and excoriate the protesters.

Safire's point was that his bosses at the time had prevented anarchy—"the real threat of mob rule had been averted with a minimal application of force." The rioters, Safire argued, "were not gentle souls carrying candles, but largely the toughs and crazies who marred the peace movement." In Safire's telling, "justice has miscarried." The "terrorizers" weren't entitled to anything for having simply been rounded up as "guests of the city in a football stadium overnight."[51]

This set off a debate.

Anthony Lewis, a liberal columnist for the *Times* who'd previously been the newspaper's Pulitzer-winning Supreme Court reporter, dashed off a letter to Bill Safire the day his column ran:

> For once I do disagree, and enough to write. Your characterization of the 1971 protest is silly. Those so-called "terrorizers" included some stuffy Boston lawyers and a number of my pastoral neighbors on Martha's Vineyard. Maybe it looked like terror from inside the White House. But then, as we know, Mr. Nixon was determined to find that whether it existed or not.[52]

The dig at Safire's White House days was too much to ignore. Bill Safire shot back a reply:

> I know you feel strongly about the Nixon White House's response to protest and I'm glad you wrote. When you think of "terrorizers," you think of your pastoral neighbors, who undoubtedly were there. But I wasn't looking at it from inside a bunker-style White House that night. I was in Georgetown. I saw people being chased by young hoodlums. I saw—with my own eyes—garbage cans being dumped in the streets by what we used to call "Fascist bully boys." Ordinary people were scared. It wasn't a concoction of some law-and-order nuts. The May Day Tribe, which ran that "rally," and the one in Dupont Circle that I also saw, was a group of people who took delight in what they were doing.
>
> In some situations, we have to respond not by what we read or want to read, but by what we live through. God knows, the Nixon men overreacted to protest groups on many occasions, but on that particular one—as in San Jose in 1970—the terror came from the mob and not from the police. And I didn't want people to rewrite history; the hoods I saw were not the friends of yours who might also have been there.

> I only wish you had been with me that night; your reaction might have been like that of Pat Buchanan's in 1968, when he saw the Chicago cops charge out to crack skulls—sometimes you don't want to be on your own side.

Lewis wasn't willing to let it go:

> My objection is to sweeping everyone who was there in 1971 under the classification "terrorizers." I think that is a mistake as a matter of journalism or law. Our whole constitutional premise is that guilt is individual. The fact that hoodlums dumped garbage cans in Georgetown cannot justify John Mitchell's ordering thousands of peaceful people outside the Capitol arrested without any probable cause for thinking that they had committed a crime.

Attorney General Mitchell and his outspoken, mercurial wife, Martha— "that wacky woman," in Neil Sheehan's telling—lived in Washington at the fashionable Watergate complex. The Potomac River bridges nearby were targeted by the demonstrators.[53] Martha watched events unfold, and wrote in her diary:

> When I thought of all those people out there being dictated to by the [Supreme] Court—people who wanted to have their say and couldn't be heard, it made me just that much more angry a couple of weeks later when I looked out my apartment window at the Mayday demonstrations. The streets were being blocked by nasty looking dirty kids, building barricades, harassing passing cars, and generally being horrible. My [10-year-old] daughter and I were afraid to leave the apartment.[54]

Martha wrote how enraged she was that the demonstrators only wanted to tear things down. She thought about all the "good, unheard people" who only wanted to help the country. That reminded her of her own son, Jay, who at that moment was on the front lines, somewhere in Vietnam.

Daniel Ellsberg, meanwhile, had a different Mayday story to tell. He had been back and forth to Washington, talking to various members of Congress about the Vietnam study he'd worked on, and how it should be made public. "Nothing looked very promising." A few days before the big event, he'd given an antiwar speech at Brandeis University—extemporaneous, nothing prepared ahead of time. The lecture hall was packed; students sat in the aisles and on stairways. So Ellsberg decided to use a cinematic analogy to make his point about Vietnam: He'd just seen the movie *Little Big Man*, in which Dustin Hoffman played an old man reminiscing about his life among the Lakota Sioux. There was a line, a saying of the Lakota just before they go into battle: "Come on, brothers. This is a good day to die."

"Well," Ellsberg told the students, "the truth is, it's never really a good day to die. But I think that May first is a good day to get arrested in Washington."

The crowd went wild. Ellsberg was ecstatic. He went home and told his wife, Patricia,[55] "Well, it seems that I'm going to Washington."[56]

Ellsberg pulled together eight of his activist friends for the trip down to DC, including Noam Chomsky and Howard Zinn. Both were outspoken foes of the war and, to anyone on campus or in academia back then, household names. Ellsberg's crew—he called them his "affinity group"—arrived that Sunday night and were "directed to someone's house, where we found scores of people already trying to sleep on every available surface." All the beds were taken; the group settled into a basement rec room and slept for only a few hours.[57]

By about 4:30 a.m. the next day, everyone was up and getting ready to go amid the orangey light from a single lamp in the basement room. Ellsberg and his cohorts, Chomsky and Zinn, observed all the righteous kids in their teens and early twenties filling water bottles, putting food in small backpacks, and writing on their hands the names of lawyers to call when they got arrested. Everybody was focused.

Ellsberg, at this point, was forty years old—two decades senior to most of those he was bunking with. (Chomsky and Zinn were even older, at forty-two and forty-eight, respectively.) But being among the students had an almost mystical effect on him. It brought him back to his days as a Marine, and to his time in Vietnam that he still relished in spite of everything. Ellsberg felt like a much younger man. It reminded him of the dim lights in the hold of a troopship—the troops, apprehensive but excited, adjusting their gear in the narrow aisles between four-high bunks, getting ready to go over the side.[58]

Chomsky recalled Ellsberg leading the trio as if he were still a Marine commander.[59] Chomsky just wanted to be done with the protest, but Ellsberg really relished it. "He was more at ease with the kids on May Day than I was."

Ellsberg and the others chose Fourteenth Street for their first "mobile tactics." The broad thoroughfare was the principal roadway to the Pentagon, "so this seemed like a logical place to stop traffic." The group sat down, shoulder to shoulder; two policemen soon converged on them. One wearing full gear and a mask, the other with his mask atop his helmet. Amid the advancing officers, the affinity group made a hasty decision to scramble up and run away. What happened next was something Ellsberg likened to a "beautifully choreographed" Keystone Kops slapstick: As two police officers converged from opposite directions—one ready with Mace, the other with an upraised truncheon—Ellsberg and his cohorts quickly ran away. So, instead of firing his Mace at Ellsberg & Co., the first officer sprayed it directly into his brother officer's face. The second officer staggered, dropped his club, and clutched his face in his hands. The first officer dropped everything to tend to his comrade, who'd been injured by friendly fire. Ellsberg called it a big win. He and his group set off to look for another place to do the same thing again.

The group's hit-and-run plan was paying off. They would stop traffic, and if an officer approached, they'd simply saunter onto the sidewalk and then find a place to do the same thing again. But then one policeman started following them intently, even as they moved up a sidewalk. Ellsberg took note: middle-aged man, ordinary uniform, no helmet or mask, noncommittal expression. And a can of Mace. The officer was, Ellsberg figured, intent on nailing someone with that Mace. Just as Ellsberg looked over his shoulder, "he calmly held up a can of Mace and shot it at me. He hit me directly in the eyes, as I presume was his intention."

Ellsberg had been tear-gassed in Marine training, but Mace was altogether different. He was disoriented, couldn't see anything, had to be held upright. When finally he could talk, Ellsberg blurted out, "'God, that's good Mace!', as if I were a connoisseur. What I meant was that this was a product that really worked as advertised." Ellsberg took such pride in their shenanigans as part of the May Day Tribe that, when he got back to Cambridge, he showed around a photo to the student editors of the *Harvard Crimson* of himself with Chomsky and Zinn taken during the protest.[60]

The affinity group never did get arrested. One of them called the muckraking journalist I. F. Stone from a pay phone around lunchtime and arranged for him to join them at a Chinese restaurant. Then Ellsberg went to National Airport, got the shuttle to New York, and stopped off at his and Patricia's Sutton Place apartment to rinse out the tear gas before going to McGeorge Bundy's first of three lectures about Vietnam at the Council on Foreign Relations. Bundy, by now, was president of the Ford Foundation, but was hopeful of getting back to Washington if the Democrats defeated Nixon the following November. Ellsberg saw many of his former bosses from the Pentagon, the State Department, and the embassy in Saigon. "The whole Vietnam establishment. . . . It looked to me like the defense dock at Nuremberg."[61]

Ellsberg went up to Bundy afterward and confronted him. Ellsberg still held out hope that the McNamara Report, which he'd worked on, would become public and, thus, destroy the credibility of Bundy and others who continued to advance what Ellsberg considered to be lies about the narrative on U.S. involvement in Vietnam.

"I said, 'Mac, you shouldn't be saying this. The truth about what you're saying is going to be coming out.'" Bundy didn't back down. "He was saying that Congress hadn't been lied to, and there was no intention to deceive anyone."[62]

Ellsberg later told Sheehan about Bundy's speech. "Sixty minutes of lies," Ellsberg called it. Ellsberg knew, from working on the McNamara Study, what the truth was. "Men like Bundy," he told Sheehan, believed "a right-wing dictatorship is better than a left-wing dictatorship, because left-wing dictatorships are forever."

Sheehan found Ellsberg's tales about Mayday of greater consequence. He scrawled a note to himself: *Bizarre life DE leading.*[63]

But it would soon become apparent that Ellsberg wasn't the only one leading a double life. Sheehan had disappeared. He was working on the story of a lifetime.

CHAPTER 8

Choice

ANOTHER ISSUE WAS ROILING THE country in the summer of '71.

Amid the chaos and mayhem of the first day of the Mayday demonstrations, a landmark development in one of the most important cases ever to reach the Supreme Court was almost completely overlooked. The justices announced on May 3 that they would take up the controversial case of *Roe* v. *Wade*.

The states were already grappling with the issue, and the result was a slowly evolving patchwork of statutes that gave women varying rights depending on where they lived.

By the summer of '71, six states and the District of Columbia permitted abortions under various circumstances. Hawaii, New York, Alaska, Washington, and California had reproductive rights laws with the fewest restrictions. Colorado had decriminalized abortion in cases of rape, incest, or when pregnancy would threaten the life or physical or mental health of the woman. A District of Columbia law allowed abortion to protect the life or health of the woman.

The DC law became the first testing ground for Supreme Court action, and it did not bode well for those advocating for a woman's right to choose. Although a federal district court judge, Gerhard A. Gesell, had ruled in *U.S.* v. *Vuitch* that the DC law's abortion restrictions were unconstitutionally vague, the justices had overruled him, 5 to 4, without reaching the question of constitutionality.[1] The Supreme Court, in essence, left the DC law intact, allowing abortions under some circumstances, but severely restricting the procedure. States with similar reproductive rights restrictions could take some comfort that they were following the Constitution.

But because the Supreme Court in *Vuitch* had sidestepped the question of whether all antiabortion laws violated women's constitutional right of privacy, the reproductive rights question was by no means settled.

Pro-choice groups, who argued that reproductive rights restrictions were unconstitutional, still had an argument to make. They took support from a 1965 Supreme Court case, *Griswold* v. *Connecticut*, which legalized contraception. A plurality of four justices in *Griswold* based their ruling on what they called a "zone of privacy" created by "penumbras" emanating from the Bill of Rights[2] and the Fourteenth Amendment.[3] Privacy wasn't explicitly mentioned in the Constitution, but the majority opinion, written by liberal William O. Douglas, said it was implied. (Douglas, married four times, argued that the right to marital privacy was "older than the Bill of Rights.") Although not all of the justices agreed with Douglas's reasoning, a solid majority of seven did agree on the outcome, which overturned Connecticut's ban on contraception. Only two justices had dissented. That was a promising portent for reproductive rights advocates who looked ahead to extending this new constitutional right of privacy. The *Griswold* decision certainly opened the door to a more expansive interpretation.

Nixon, meanwhile, was eager to close the door on such a broad reinterpretation of the Constitution—thereby stopping any further High Court moves to expand reproductive rights.

Nixon had campaigned in 1968 on a pledge to appoint judicial conservatives, and he was about to make good on the promise. A huge political miscalculation by Lyndon Johnson would allow Nixon to name a new chief justice as soon as Day One of his presidency. To get a second pick, Nixon would resort to dirty tricks, and it wouldn't be the last time.

The new president intended to quickly push two liberals off the Supreme Court.

When Richard Nixon took office on January 20, 1969, it was already clear that he would have one important vacancy to fill on the Court. The prior June, at the end of the Court's term, Chief Justice Earl Warren had gone to the White House to tell President Lyndon Johnson of his intention to retire. His departure date was open; Warren agreed to stay on until a successor was in place.

Warren was seventy-seven years old, and in a letter to Johnson, he said his departure was "solely because of age." It was time "to give way to someone who will have more years ahead of him to cope with the problems which will come before the Court." But Nixon's former White House counsel John W. Dean, in his book *The Rehnquist Choice*, saw a different motive in the timing of Warren's resignation.[4] The politically savvy Warren (he'd been governor of California) believed that Nixon would win the coming election, and Nixon had made it clear that he would appoint judges who would reverse the precedents of the Warren Court. Warren wanted to give Johnson a chance to reshuffle the lineup at the Court, before it was too late.

Warren's timing was off. The Vietnam War raged on and demonstrations against it were escalating. Johnson was already a lame duck, having announced on March 31 that he would not run for reelection. The beleaguered president had little political clout left, but he nonetheless decided to move forward with a controversial choice to succeed Warren. Johnson nominated his friend and confidant, Associate Justice Abe Fortas, whom he'd named to the Court in 1965, to be the next chief. Fortas was a reliable vote for Warren and would carry on in his stead. To replace Fortas, Johnson nominated another crony, Homer Thornberry, a Texan who had taken over Johnson's seat in the House of Representatives before being nominated to the U.S. Court of Appeals.

Naming Thornberry was intended to mollify Southern Democrats who were skeptical about Fortas. Johnson was under the same political pressure as Richard Nixon later would be to rebalance the Court whose decisions had tilted decidedly leftward under Warren, and he particularly felt the heat from the South. Johnson cynically tried to palm off Fortas as a Southerner. Calling the press into the Oval Office to announce Fortas's nomination, Johnson referred to his man as "Justice Abe Fortas, of the state of Tennessee," but the ploy was transparent and Johnson should have known better. Fortas had, indeed, been born in Memphis, but he lived in an ornate mansion in Georgetown and his roots as an insider's insider were beneath Johnson's feet. It was a craven political move by Johnson, and it backfired.

The Republicans smelled blood as the November elections neared, and there was no way that they were going to give Johnson either of those appointments without a fight. Senators used Fortas's confirmation hearings that fall as a forum to attack the Warren Court's decisions, like *Gideon* and *Miranda*, claiming they aided criminals and damaged the state. There were also claims that Fortas's closeness to Johnson violated the principle of separation of powers. Fortas became the first sitting justice to testify at his own confirmation hearing for chief justice. But Fortas didn't help himself, reinforcing with his own testimony his reputation as an inscrutable opportunist, LBJ's alter ego, and his all-around fixer. Even one of Fortas's own clerks later said, "It wouldn't surprise me if he was robbing banks on the side or writing novels under another name."

Fortas's nomination was doomed when it was revealed that Paul Porter, one of his old law partners, had raised $30,000 on Fortas's behalf from Fortas's friends and former clients, and that half of the money (40 percent of a justice's salary at the time) had been paid to Fortas for teaching a summer course at the American University Law School. When the Fortas nomination finally came to the floor, Republicans and Southern Democrats launched a historic filibuster—the first ever against a Supreme Court nominee. A cloture motion to stop the filibuster failed. Unlike today, the Senate's parliamentary rule required a two-thirds majority to put an end to debate, or sixty-seven votes if all senators were present. It was an almost impossible hurdle to get over.

Johnson had overestimated his Senate support and didn't have enough clout left to help his old friend. Nixon stayed above the fray, but sent word through back channels that he supported the alliance against Fortas. His reputation in tatters and his confirmation prospects hopeless, Fortas asked Johnson to withdraw the nomination on October 1, 1968. Earl Warren would open the Court's new term a week later.

As soon as Nixon won the 1968 election, he began shrewdly calculating how and when he could pick off some of the members of the Court's liberal bloc. Hugo Black was eighty-two years old. Douglas was seventy. Replacing Warren, the chief, was already a given, so Nixon could actually take his time with that; Nixon arranged for Warren to remain until the end of the Court's full term, in June 1969. Having bought himself some time on the chief justiceship, Nixon set about creating one more vacancy. He intended to drive the weakened Fortas from the Court entirely.

White House counsel John Ehrlichman orchestrated the plan against Fortas, with the help of the Justice Department. Justice officials had learned about a $20,000 retainer that Fortas, while a sitting justice, had accepted from the family foundation of Louis Wolfson, who was under investigation by the Securities and Exchange Commission (SEC). (Fortas kept the money for eleven months, but returned it after Wolfson was indicted on federal stock fraud charges.)

The information was passed to a Nixon-friendly *Life* magazine reporter named William Lambert. Lambert was a tough investigator and a Pulitzer Prize winner, but he also was a reliable, trusted conduit when the White House wanted to get a story out without leaving fingerprints. *Life* had Lambert's exposé about Fortas ready for its edition that would hit newsstands on Sunday afternoon, May 4, 1969. Whether true or not, the revelation would be incendiary, far worse for Fortas than the prior year's revelation about the law school payments.

Ehrlichman already had an advance proof of the *Life* story, and he saw an opening for the White House to use the new revelations as leverage to quickly force Fortas off the bench—under the threat of a grand jury investigation. But this was a delicate matter, because there was no precedent for the Justice Department going after a sitting Supreme Court justice. Only Congress had the power to remove a sitting justice, through impeachment. The White House needed protective cover for its threatened investigation.

On May 1, three days before publication by *Life*, Attorney General Mitchell's trusted Justice Department counsel, William Rehnquist, sent Mitchell a memorandum providing a precedent for the Department of Justice to investigate the Fortas-Wolfson relationship. Mitchell had instructed Rehnquist "to assume the most damaging set of inferences about the case were true" and to "determine what action the Justice Department could take." In essence, Mitchell had instructed Rehnquist to ignore the facts. This Rehnquist did, providing the scenario that became the Nixon game plan to drive Fortas from the bench.

Rehnquist connected the dots inferentially, as instructed; he later would be rewarded when Nixon appointed him to the Supreme Court (and later still would become the chief justice). Rehnquist began by assuming that the *worst* inference to be drawn was that Fortas, while sitting on the Court, had intervened in the government's prosecution of Wolfson. (In fact, Fortas had not.) In essence, the worst-case scenario was that Fortas had taken bribes. Rehnquist next searched the federal criminal code and found an obscure statute that made it a crime under certain circumstances for an officer of the judicial branch to be paid for services on behalf of a third party. Having found this possibly relevant federal statute, Rehnquist had to determine whether the Justice Department could prosecute Fortas while he was a sitting justice. In pursuit of that, Rehnquist, who had little time for legal precedent generally, unearthed a 1790 law, along with an attorney general's opinion from 1796, which he thought supported prosecution. By this tortured logic, Rehnquist sent Mitchell the requested memorandum advising that if the department had the evidence, it could prosecute Fortas, even though he was a sitting member of the Supreme Court.

Rehnquist's memo gave Mitchell what he needed to move the game forward. The *Life* story was front-page news, and Mitchell boasted at a White House staff meeting that there would be more revelations. The *Washington Post* was already calling for Fortas's resignation. Then Mitchell made his move.

Mitchell went to the Supreme Court for a secret meeting with Earl Warren. The attorney general asked the chief justice for his help in getting Fortas to resign, and he hinted that the Justice Department would go forward with its criminal investigation—the Rehnquist memo vouchsafed that—if Fortas demurred.

To ratchet up the pressure even more, Mitchell had his department reopen an old investigation that focused on Fortas's wife, Carolyn Agger, a highly paid tax law specialist, and Fortas's former law partner, Porter. A grand jury was convened, even though a previous investigation found nothing improper.

Within a week, Fortas submitted his resignation. Nixon now had two Supreme Court vacancies to fill, less than four months into his first term. There was a toast among the higher-ups in Mitchell's office at the Justice Department. Nixon called in to congratulate them.

Exactly a week later, Nixon announced that Warren Burger would be replacing Earl Warren as chief justice. When Mitchell and his deputy, Richard Kleindienst, snuck in a meeting with Burger during the fracas over Fortas, both were struck by what a perfect fit Burger was. With his wavy white hair, resonant baritone, courtly demeanor, and conservative views, he was right out of central casting. To make the surprise announcement, Nixon smuggled Burger and his wife into the White House through an underground tunnel in the adjacent Treasury Department building. Two weeks later, Burger was confirmed in the Senate by a vote of 74 to 3.[5] Now Nixon could turn to filling Fortas's seat.

Nixon's first choice for the vacant Fortas seat was Clement Haynsworth, a federal judge from Greenville, South Carolina. Rehnquist, quarterbacking the vetting process, did not take long to give the green light. He reviewed twelve years of the judge's decisions and affirmed, in a memorandum for Mitchell, that Haynsworth was indeed a "strict constructionist" who "will not be favorably inclined toward claims of either criminal defendants or civil rights plaintiffs." In other words, Rehnquist liked Haynsworth because he was tough on criminals and was a segregationist. That was what he assumed Nixon wanted. FBI Director J. Edgar Hoover also gave Haynsworth two thumbs-up as a law-and-order conservative.

Haynsworth was a wealthy man, a Southerner, and had a segregationist past—all strikes against him by the lights of the Northern Democrats who held sway on the Senate Judiciary Committee. Opposition quickly mounted. Haynsworth protested that the 1950s were a different time, "when none of us was thinking or writing as we are today." But Democrats, with memories of the Fortas filibuster still fresh, exacted some street justice against the new president and defeated Haynsworth's nomination, 55 to 45. It was the first time since 1930 that the Senate had voted down outright a Supreme Court nominee, and only the second time in the twentieth century. Adding to the sting, all three of the top Republican leaders in the Senate voted against confirmation.

Nixon's next choice, early the following year, was a Florida judge, G. Harrold Carswell, who seemed superficially to have the right credentials, but who, in fact, turned into a far greater embarrassment for the White House than Haynsworth.

At age fifty, Carswell had already climbed high, serving five years as a federal prosecutor in Florida before moving to the federal court, where he'd been for eleven years. Nixon had elevated him to the federal appeals court a mere seven months earlier. Rehnquist vetted Carswell's decisions and affirmed him to be a strict constructionist. Moreover, Carswell passed another important litmus test: He'd already been confirmed *three times* by the Senate; already investigated *three times* by the FBI. Surely any skeletons in the closet had come out by now. Mitchell called the choice too good to be true. And it was. Carswell was carrying all sorts of embarrassing baggage, not least his prior statement that "I yield to no man as a fellow candidate, as a fellow citizen, in the firm, vigorous belief in the principles of white supremacy, and I shall always be so governed." Carswell's nomination went down in flames on the Senate floor by the same vote, 55 to 45.

"A colossal mistake," White House counsel John Dean later said of the nomination. "A complete screwup by Nixon's advisers," Rehnquist among them.

By now, the Court had been sitting with only eight justices for almost a year, and important cases loomed. Nixon had to get that Fortas vacancy filled, so he took what he could from the two defeats and moved on. He reminded his Southern base about how hard he had worked to put one of their own on the Court, and then declared that he was putting his strategy on ice. Nixon had concluded that the Senate as "presently constituted" would not confirm a nominee to the Supreme Court "from the South who believes as I do in the strict construction of the Constitution":

> [Haynsworth and Carswell] have endured with admirable dignity vicious assaults on their intelligence, their honesty and their character. As long as the Senate is constituted the way it is today, I will not nominate another Southerner and let him be subjected to the kind of malicious character assassination accorded both Judges Haynsworth and Carswell. I understand the bitter feeling of millions of Americans who live in the South about the act of regional discrimination that took place in the Senate yesterday. They have my assurance that the day will come when men like Judges Carswell and Haynsworth can and will sit on the High Court.[6]

Burger quietly passed another name on to Nixon and the president wasted no time in acting on it. This time his nominee was Burger's boyhood friend from Minnesota (and the best man at Burger's wedding), Harry Blackmun, a sixty-one-year-old federal appeals court judge. Burger and Blackmun were jocularly called the Minnesota Twins, and the fact that he would vote like Burger was taken for granted. Nixon was sailing into a safe harbor to the North, and he wasn't going to waste any time getting there. Blackmun was a Northerner and the Senate had tired of the jousting. The senators confirmed him by a vote of 94 to 0 on

May 12. By the time Blackmun took the oath, the Court had been shorthanded for 391 days. Not since the Civil War had there been such a long stretch without a full Court.

Abortion cases were quickly making their way to the Supreme Court. Burger and Blackmun were Nixon's best shot at making sure there would be at least five conservative justices to hold the line.

Nixon decided to leave no doubt where he stood on the reproductive rights issue. In April 1971, he used his executive power to make it more difficult for women to get abortions on military bases, reversing a more permissive policy. Nixon issued a statement from the Western White House in San Clemente:

> Historically, laws regulating abortion in the United States have been the province of states, not the federal government. That remains the situation today, as one state after another takes up this question, debates it and decides it. That is where the decisions should be made.
>
> Partly, for that reason, I have directed that the policy on abortions at American military bases in the United States be made to correspond with the laws of the states where those bases are located. If the laws in a particular state restrict abortions, the rules at the military base hospitals are to correspond to that law.
>
> The effect of this directive is to reverse service regulations issued last summer, which had liberalized the rules on abortions at military hospitals. The new ruling supersedes this—and has been put into effect by the Secretary of Defense.
>
> But while this matter is being debated in state capitals, and weighed by various courts, the country has a right to know my personal views.
>
> From personal and religious beliefs I consider abortion an unacceptable form of population control. Further, unrestricted abortion policies, or abortion on demand, I cannot square with my personal belief in the

> sanctity of human life—including the life of the yet unborn. For, surely, the unborn have rights also, recognized in law, recognized even in principles expounded by the United Nations.
>
> Ours is a nation with a Judeo-Christian heritage. It is also a nation with serious social problems—problems of malnutrition, of broken homes, of poverty and of delinquency. But none of these problems justifies such a solution.
>
> A good and generous people will not opt, in my view, for this kind of alternative to its social dilemmas. Rather, it will open its hearts and homes to the unwanted children of its own, as it has done for the unwanted millions of other lands.[7]

By April 21, the day the Court decided *Vuitch*, seven other abortion appeals already were stacked up in front of the justices, awaiting action.[8] The justices had to decide whether to leave reproductive rights to the states, as Nixon wanted, or to confront the issue head-on.

A New York University law student, Roy Lucas, was the first person to advance the theory of how *Griswold* could be expanded into a constitutional protection for a woman's right to choose. He did so first in a research paper for a class on litigation, then turned it into a full-blown argument in the June 1968 issue of the *North Carolina Law Review*, the university's student-run law journal.[9]

Pro-choice activists took note. Lucas soon showed them the way by filing the first abortion rights lawsuit in New York, in September 1969. He then began seeding other lawsuits around the country through a nonprofit group that he founded. Lucas, twenty-eight years old at the time, called his new operation the James Madison Constitutional Law Institute, named after the chief author of the Bill of Rights. He situated his new institute in Greenwich Village, near the NYU campus, and provided accommodations for other pro-choice activists.

The NYPD Intelligence Unit, aka the Red Squad, already had infiltrated the Black Panthers and hundreds of other groups it deemed "subversive." Lucas and his institute were immediately added to the Red Squad's undercover operations.[10]

Meanwhile, in Texas, Sarah Ragle Weddington had already faced the choice that thousands of other women had to make. The daughter of a Methodist[11] minister, she was working full-time to pay for law school at the University of Texas—she was one of forty women out of sixteen hundred students[12]—when she became pregnant by her future husband. On a morning in 1967, the two drove to Eagle Pass, Texas, where they crossed the border into Mexico and paid $400[13] to a doctor in Piedras Negras for an abortion. The procedure was successful and she was back in class the following Monday morning. Weddington felt fortunate, and didn't discuss it at the time. But the effect on her was profound. Once out of law school, she threw herself into activism for women's rights.[14]

By early 1970, Weddington was working as an assistant city attorney in Fort Worth. Already interested in entering politics and enjoying the stage, she teamed up in her off-hours with another lawyer, Linda Coffee, and a group of activist UT grad students who were responding to the constant need of young women looking to terminate unwanted pregnancies without risking their lives.[15] Weddington and Coffee needed the right plaintiff to challenge Texas's strict antiabortion law. Texas law at the time only permitted abortions to save the life of the mother.[16]

The two sought out another young activist lawyer in Dallas, Henry McCluskey. McCluskey was twenty-seven years old and openly gay, a recent graduate of Baylor Law School. He was a childhood friend of Coffee's. McCluskey worked out of a Dallas strip mall representing an assortment of clients, mostly adoptions and criminal work, including defending sodomy cases.

The Dallas vice squad was tough on gay men, concealing themselves in ventilating ducts and attics of gay meeting places and then jumping out to make arrests. McCluskey had recently taken the case of a Dallas man, Alvin Leon Buchanan, who'd received a five-year prison sentence for sodomy. Coffee was also gay, but quietly so; she was working behind the scenes on the case, helping McCluskey, but not asking for credit. "I wasn't about to touch that publicly," she said. "I would not have enough nerve to even be the counsel of record."[17]

McCluskey was making headway in getting Buchanan's sentence overturned on the basis of the privacy protections of *Griswold.*[18] One of the defendants in McCluskey's lawsuit was District Attorney Henry Wade—yes, *that* Wade, as in *Roe* v. *Wade.* Wade certainly had seen his fair share of controversial and high-stakes cases. He was also known for his prosecution of Jack Ruby for the murder of JFK assassin Lee Harvey Oswald.[19]

The tight group of young activist attorneys was still figuring out whether and how the Court's decision in *Griswold* could help their cause. The whole privacy thing was still very fluid and new, but Weddington and Coffee thought McCluskey could help: Could he suggest an ideal client to challenge the Texas antiabortion law?

"It had to be a pregnant woman wanting to get an abortion," Coffee later explained. "She couldn't have the funds to travel to California or New York for a legal abortion. And we had to have someone who could take the publicity. We weren't able to guarantee her anonymity." Also, she couldn't be so far along that her delivery would moot the case before it was filed.[20]

The answer was yes; McCluskey knew a woman, Norma McCorvey, who was five months pregnant and had come to him for help.[21] She fit the bill as their ideal plaintiff. (A tragic sidenote: McCluskey was murdered three years later by an ex-boyfriend, who drugged him, shot him twice in the back, and dumped him in a lake.[22])

Weddington and Coffee met with McCorvey in a Dallas pizza shop. She was in her early twenties—petite, outgoing, talkative. Her nickname was "Pixie." McCorvey had dropped out of high school in the tenth grade and was working as a waitress. She had already had two babies, both given up for adoption. Pregnant with a third, she wanted an abortion.[23]

On March 3, 1970, Weddington and Coffee filed a federal lawsuit on McCorvey's behalf against Dallas County District Attorney Henry Wade, challenging the constitutionality of Texas's abortion laws. McCorvey was six months pregnant by then, and she never would get that abortion. They used the pseudonym "Jane Roe" to protect McCorvey's identity. A couple of months later, the case was amended into a class action, ensuring that it would not be mooted by Jane Roe's giving birth. *Roe* v. *Wade* was now in federal court.

The constitutional issue was what gave *Roe* v. *Wade* its significance. The case argued for the protections of *Griswold*, and took head-on the Court's sidestepping of the issue in *Vuitch*. Also, because *Roe* was a challenge to a state law's constitutionality, it allowed Weddington and Coffee to put the matter directly in front of a three-judge panel of federal district court judges for a speedy decision appealable directly to the Supreme Court.

Coffee had clerked for a federal judge named Sarah Hughes, the first female federal judge in Texas. Hughes had come to national attention as the judge who swore in LBJ after the Kennedy assassination. She was also a fierce advocate for women's rights—things like equal pay and the right to serve on juries.[24] And here, Weddington and Coffee got a lucky break: Sarah Hughes was one of the three federal judges assigned to hear *Roe* v. *Wade*.

It took only three months for the judges to declare the Texas law unconstitutional. But they also ruled against an injunction, which meant that Henry Wade, the district attorney, could keep enforcing the law. This allowed both sides to make an appeal directly to the Supreme Court: Roe, because there was no injunction; Wade, because the statute was voided. If the justices wanted to tackle the reproductive rights issue, *Roe* v. *Wade* was a good case for that.

The same day, May 3, 1971, that the Supreme Court announced it would hear *Roe* v. *Wade*, the justices in a 6-to-3 ruling also upheld the death penalty in state courts. There were 648 prisoners on death row, including the Manson family members who were awaiting the gas chamber at San Quentin. Angela Davis, now charged with murder and awaiting trial, faced the same penalty if convicted.

On Mother's Day, May 9, Weddington wrote her parents with the good news about *Roe*: *The Supreme Court has granted a hearing in our case, so that will probably be in the fall. I'll definitely go to the hearing in Washington, but Roy Lucas of New York will probably argue it.*[25]

The exact date of the oral argument hadn't yet been set, but Roy Lucas, who had been the first to see the pro-abortion prospects in *Griswold*, and who was already advancing the cause through his James Madison Institute, seemed the logical choice, and he certainly wanted to do it. It seemed like Weddington and Coffee were going to defer to Lucas and let him take the argument. The two women had split the presentation when the case was argued in front of the three-judge panel, which included Judge Sarah Hughes; Weddington focused on *Griswold* and its broad privacy protections, while Coffee took the narrow but equally important points of jurisdiction and standing.[26] Coffee had already decided to take a pass on the oral argument before the High Court; she would sit at the counsel table, but was content to stay in the background.

Weddington went off to New York City for three weeks at the end of May to start preparing the case, and Lucas put her up in a guest room at the Institute's Greenwich Village townhouse. Weddington returned to Austin in mid-June; she and her new husband, Ron, had just moved from Dallas and set up their own law office. There were two phone lines, one for Weddington & Weddington, the other a listing for the James Madison Institute. Weddington wrote to her parents on June 12:

> I've had interviews with the chairman of the OB-GYN Dept. at Southwestern in Dallas, at the Medical School in San Antonio, and at the Medical School in Galveston. I am writing up those interviews for affidavits to

> use in connection with the suit. I'm also gathering information from the Texas Medical Association and regional Planned Parenthood office. Getting lots of calls from everywhere about the case—including one from the National ZPG [Zero Population Growth] office. Got my first contribution from an Austin woman (although she sent the check to New York and I don't know yet how much it was). She took me to San Antonio Wednesday for lunch at the Argyle Club with two of her friends (one of the friends owned one of the horses that ran in the Kentucky Derby). She is about 50—and is really nice—but leads a glamorous-type life. They are always flying off to somewhere; have a private plane; and she has "her own foundation" of some sort. Anyway it's been fun and I'm getting to meet or have contact with some very interesting and some very well-known people.[27]

Weddington got her admission to the Supreme Court Bar on September 15—that was a prior requirement if she planned to argue the case—although the oral argument date wouldn't be set until the following month. Weddington was enjoying the limelight; she traveled to Washington on September 25 to make speeches the following day alongside reproductive rights activist and constitutional lawyer Cyril Means and feminist Betty Friedan.

Weddington wrote her parents again in November, this time with surprising news about the argument. A date for the oral argument in *Roe* v. *Wade* had been set—but there had been a squabble with Lucas over who would do the talking:

> As you'll see, the case is set for argument Dec 13th. I had assumed Roy [Lucas] would do the argument but my clients sent him a telegram last night saying they wanted me to do it. Hate to get into a big fight over it. Don't know what will work out. Get very scared and nervous just thinking of being before that Court.

Lucas, not yet thirty, was deeply disappointed that he'd been aced out.[28]

By the standards of the staid Supreme Court Bar, all three of them—Lucas, Coffee, and Weddington—were misfits and outright anomalies. Still, as Joshua Prager, who interviewed Coffee in 2017 for *Vanity Fair*, later put it, "optics mattered."

Coffee, twenty-eight, would be sitting with Weddington at the counsel table, but wouldn't say anything. "Despite her brilliance," Prager wrote, "Coffee could come across as bedraggled." Weddington, on the other hand, had more of a command presence; she was, quite proudly, anything but a submissive female. "I was able to work well with men perhaps because I had learned leadership in traditional ways, beginning in the Canyon Junior High Band; I was the drum *major*, not the majorette."[29]

"She was younger than I was," Coffee added. "She was blonde, blue-eyed."

Douglas, author of the Court's majority opinion in *Griswold*, had long wanted to face the issue of reproductive rights head-on. But he also knew that Nixon's new chief justice, Burger, saw *Roe* and a companion abortion case from Georgia, *Doe* v. *Bolton* (scheduled to be argued on the same day, immediately following *Roe*), not as an opportunity to legalize abortion, but instead as a way to get rid of bothersome constitutional challenges to state laws. Douglas was discouraged. In his view, Burger wanted to use *Roe* and *Doe* for the sole purpose of further limiting the intervention of the federal courts in state court proceedings—a jurisdictional issue—not to make a grand statement about reproductive rights. It was safe to assume that Burger also had a sure vote from his best man, Blackmun, in his back pocket. (Blackmun's diaries from 1971, although cryptic, show that he wasn't thinking about *Roe* or *Doe* at all.) The private back-and-forth between the justices and their clerks about the two cases early in the term made it pretty clear that there was not much hope for overturning state restrictions.[30]

Weddington was all of twenty-six years old.[31] She would be the youngest person ever to argue a case before the Supreme

Court.[32] And, unaware of the interplay between the justices over the jurisdictional question, she was ready for a different argument: a woman's constitutional right to privacy.[33]

Weddington went squarely at that point, and it did not take long for Burger and a few of the other justices to interrupt her. That was the norm for any argument. Weddington kept her footing, and quickly got to her key point, still unaware that the justices were thinking differently about her case. Weddington pointed out to them that even though she and Coffee had won *Roe* in the federal court below, Wade was still enforcing the statute, forcing Texas women to go out of state if they wanted an abortion. She sounded self-assured as she laid things out for the justices:

> Since the time of the lower court ruling, the district attorney in Texas has said that he considers the Federal court decision there not to be binding. And he is—we do have a letter from him, the first thing in our appendix to the brief—stating that he will continue to prosecute.
>
> So the doctors in Texas, even with the federal decision and even after the Vuitch decision, do not feel free to perform abortions. And, instead, 728 women in the first nine months after the decision went to New York for an abortion.
>
> Texas women are coming here. It's so often the poor and the disadvantaged in Texas who are not able to escape the effect of the law[34]. . . . In Texas, the woman is the victim.[35]

Weddington had nailed her argument—and the opposing counsel, who went next, flubbed his. Jay Floyd, the thirty-seven-year-old Texas assistant attorney general tasked with defending the state's abortion restrictions, opened with an aside about Weddington and Coffee, who were seated at the adjacent table.

"It's an old joke," Floyd began, "but when a man argues against two beautiful ladies like this, they are going to have the last word."[36] All nine justices just stared back at him, dumb-

Daniel Ellsberg in Vietnam, c. 1966.

Neil Sheehan covering the Vietnam War for UPI, c. 1962. He joined the *New York Times* in 1964 and continued reporting from the region.

Ellsberg takes aim in a rice paddy, c. 1966. Years before turning against the war, he was seduced by Vietnam's exoticism and rawness.

Ellsberg speaks at a news conference, New York, 1972.

Nixon and Kissinger on the White House grounds, August 10, 1971.
Nixon initially wasn't worried about the Pentagon Papers, but Kissinger urged action: "The press has no freedom to publish highly classified materials." Nixon advised Kissinger: "Skip the parties; get some rest. I wouldn't try to fight the battle with the press guys."

Two weeks before Mayday, 27-year-old John Kerry led antiwar demonstrations in Washington.

Vietnam veterans protesting the war gathered at the Capitol. Kerry told them, "We are here because we, above all others, have earned the right to criticize the war in Southeast Asia."

Marines land at the Washington Monument, May 3, 1971. At least 10,000 active-duty Marines and Army paratroopers were staged in and around Washington in response to the Mayday protests.

Over three days in the streets of Washington, police rounded up more than 13,000 people, including many innocent bystanders—the largest mass arrest in U.S. history. With nowhere to put all the prisoners, a practice field adjacent to the city's RFK Stadium became a makeshift jail.

Sarah Weddington, 25, attorney for Jane Roe, moderates Citizens' Hearings on Abortion, Austin, Texas, January 1971.

Angela Davis, 26, leads a picket line for the Soledad Brothers at the state office building in downtown Los Angeles, June 20, 1970, the same day the UCLA regents vote 15 to 6 to fire her. "I just lost my job because of my political beliefs. The Soledad Brothers lose their lives."

August 7, 1970: With weapons purchased by Davis, 17-year-old Jonathan Jackson, brother of Soledad Brother George Jackson, storms the Marin County Courthouse, taking Judge Harold Haley hostage and demanding release of the Soledad Brothers. The ensuing gun battle kills four, including Jackson and Haley, and leaves others gravely wounded.

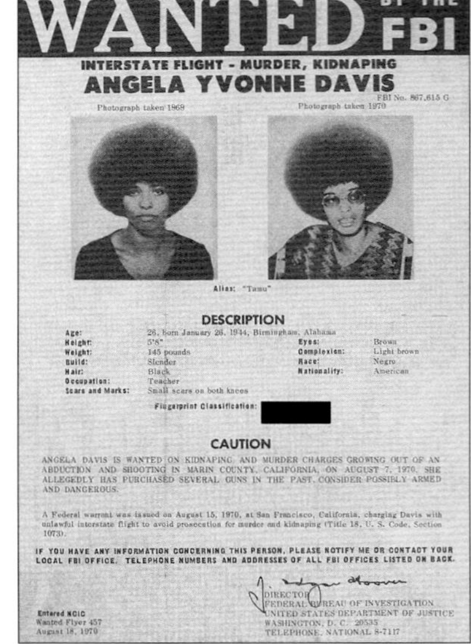

WANTED BY THE FBI

INTERSTATE FLIGHT - MURDER, KIDNAPING

ANGELA YVONNE DAVIS

FBI No. 867,615 G

Photograph taken 1969

Photograph taken 1970

Alias: "Tamu"

DESCRIPTION

Age:	26, born January 26, 1944, Birmingham, Alabama		
Height:	5'8"	Eyes:	Brown
Weight:	145 pounds	Complexion:	Light brown
Build:	Slender	Race:	Negro
Hair:	Black	Nationality:	American
Occupation:	Teacher		
Scars and Marks:	Small scars on both knees		

Fingerprint Classification:

CAUTION

ANGELA DAVIS IS WANTED ON KIDNAPING AND MURDER CHARGES GROWING OUT OF AN ABDUCTION AND SHOOTING IN MARIN COUNTY, CALIFORNIA, ON AUGUST 7, 1970. SHE ALLEGEDLY HAS PURCHASED SEVERAL GUNS IN THE PAST. CONSIDER POSSIBLY ARMED AND DANGEROUS.

A Federal warrant was issued on August 15, 1970, at San Francisco, California, charging Davis with unlawful interstate flight to avoid prosecution for murder and kidnaping (Title 18, U. S. Code, Section 1073).

IF YOU HAVE ANY INFORMATION CONCERNING THIS PERSON, PLEASE NOTIFY ME OR CONTACT YOUR LOCAL FBI OFFICE. TELEPHONE NUMBERS AND ADDRESSES OF ALL FBI OFFICES LISTED ON BACK.

J. Edgar Hoover
DIRECTOR
FEDERAL BUREAU OF INVESTIGATION
UNITED STATES DEPARTMENT OF JUSTICE
WASHINGTON, D. C. 20535
TELEPHONE, NATIONAL 8-7117

Entered NCIC
Wanted Flyer 457
August 18, 1970

Angela Davis is added to the FBI's Ten Most Wanted list, August 18, 1970.

Top cops:
Nixon thanks
Attorney General
John Mitchell
and FBI Director
J. Edgar Hoover
after Mayday,
May 26, 1971.
(Also pictured is aide
John Ehrlichman.)
Mitchell called
the Mayday arrests
a model for the future.

Two pals:
Henry Kissinger
and Frank Sinatra.
Kissinger was a regular
in the Hollywood
gossip columns.
Sinatra became his buddy.

Attica aftermath: Police carrying out wounded on stretcher, September 13, 1971.

founded. After the stony silence, Floyd struggled to regain momentum throughout the argument.[37] His comment would go down as the worst courtroom joke in legal history.[38]

It would take two more years, and another argument before the Supreme Court by Weddington, before the justices would be ready to decide the issue.

CHAPTER 9

Deceit

INSIDE THE *NEW YORK TIMES*, multiple major dramas were unfolding, and they went way beyond routine newsroom politics.

Neil Sheehan, as usual, was at the center of things.

He was seriously late with an important article about Henry Kissinger for the newspaper's Sunday magazine. Sheehan had blown off deadline after deadline, and his editors were growing impatient.

In truth, Sheehan had no intention of turning in the article about Kissinger. When he first took on the assignment, it was as a pretext for interviewing Kissinger for the Washington bureau's special investigation of Nixon's invasion of Cambodia, without revealing the paper's intentions ahead of time. Washington bureau chief Max Frankel was complicit in that; he and Sheehan agreed that even their own colleagues at the magazine couldn't be trusted to keep a secret, and shouldn't be told what Sheehan was really up to. Both Frankel and Sheehan had deceived their Times teammates, but the magazine was still expecting an article. So where was it? As usual, Sheehan was late. Very late.

Editors hate reporters who are late with copy. Sheehan, already four months late with the Kissinger story, which he had no intention of delivering, was being pestered, initially rather politely, by editor Nona Brown, who worked out of the Washington bureau and brought her Vassar politesse to such things[1]:

9/28/70
Neil:

A reminder that both Susan and you have pieces due shortly—Susan on October 1st (we devoutly hope) and you within the next week. Will we see copy?

nb

Sheehan ignored the deadline for as long as he could, but he was falling further behind—and the magazine's editors were running out of patience. A message came down from New York via telex from Lewis Bergman, the magazine's chief editor:

GOOD MORNING, TUESDAY, OCTOBER 13TH, 1970
SHEEHAN
WASHINGTON
NEIL—WHERE'S THAT MAGAZINER?
IF YOU WAIT UNTIL 1972 KISSINGER MAY NO LONGER BE IMPORTANT. AND EVEN THE PYRAMIDS WERE BUILT TO A DEADLINE. CAN'T WE HAVE COPY WITHIN A WEEK?
REGARDS
BERGMAN

No answer from Sheehan.

Again, from Bergman:

CAN WE DEFINITELY COUNT ON KISSINGER MAGAZINER BY DECEMBER 7?
REGARDS
BERGMAN

Now at least six months past his deadline, Sheehan typed out a reply to buy himself more time:

> Pro Bergman Sunday magazine
>
> Lewis I am shooting for the end of December as I mentioned earlier to Shapiro and I cannot deliver by Dec. 7.
>
> Regards Sheehan[2]

Sheehan was bedeviled by phone calls and memos from the Sunday magazine's editors, who didn't know that he was working on something much bigger. Sheehan continued to ignore their entreaties.

Soon there was a pink phone-message slip on Sheehan's desk from the aforementioned Harvey Shapiro, a roguish charmer playing the good cop. Shapiro was the magazine's resident poet and would later become editor of the *Book Review*. It's unclear whether Sheehan returned the call, but Shapiro's nudge didn't get action. Still, Sheehan put the message slip to good effect. He used every available space on the back of it to scribble a note to himself—about Kissinger.

Garry Wills had just come out with an important book, *Nixon Agonistes*,[3] and Sheehan's scrawled note reminded himself to check out what the book said about the man whom Sheehan had every intention of writing about someday, just not for the *Times Magazine*. Sheehan's "note to self" indicated the low regard he had for Kissinger—or, perhaps to put it more aptly, for Kissinger's opportunism:

> Have to go into his background. The people who came to [Kissinger's] summer seminar were important people who gave him a network. He's exercising a tremendous amount of power. It was all very calculated. He signed himself on to William Yandell Elliott (Kissinger's doctoral adviser at Harvard).[4] He asked people to give parties there. He must always have wanted to be the "in" guy.[5]

Sheehan was about to get wrapped up in a reporting project that would shock the world when finally revealed, months later. In the meantime, the existence of the *Times Magazine* assignment continued to provide a convenient cover for another of Sheehan's distractions.

Sheehan had become increasingly strident in his opposition to continued U.S. involvement in Vietnam, and was looking for a way to channel his frustration.

Sheehan's first opportunity came when editors at the newspaper's venerable *Book Review* asked him to review Mark Lane's book *Conversations with Americans*.[6] The review was slated for the last issue of the year, December 27, 1970.

Lane, a forty-three-year-old New York attorney, was a conspiracy theorist and a publicity hound with major name recognition. He'd been comedian/activist Dick Gregory's vice presidential running mate on the Freedom and Peace ticket in 1968. Before that, Lane waged an all-out assault on the findings of the Warren Commission investigation into the assassination of JFK, turning his skepticism about the guilt of assassin Lee Harvey Oswald into a number one best seller, *Rush to Judgment*. That book tapped the public's nerve; it spent twenty-nine weeks on the *Times* best-seller list.

Now Lane was back with a new effort, this one just as timely—and controversial—as his previous effort. *Conversations with Americans* comprised thirty-two first-person accounts by soldiers who committed atrocities in Vietnam, as tape-recorded by Lane. The book's timing coincided with the Army's trial and conviction of Lieutenant William Calley for the My Lai massacre. The stories were horrific, describing war crimes of savagery, sadism, torture, terrorism, and murder.

The *Times* had already favorably reviewed the book in its news pages, but the Sunday *Book Review* always represented the last word. Sheehan was asked to do a "reportorial" review, befitting his experience.[7] He came to Lane's book expecting it to be what he later called a "fine thing"—after all, Sheehan knew what he had seen as a war correspondent in Vietnam; and after the Calley case, he certainly didn't need persuading that atrocities had been proved.

But when Sheehan undertook his own investigation of the soldiers' stories, he found gaping holes in some of their accounts. At least four of the men, Sheehan said, had lied about their military service, and Lane hadn't bothered to verify their accounts. Sheehan's review was scathing—an intentional takedown that came off as an all-out attempt to destroy Lane's credibility.

The review also exposed a darkness within Sheehan; it seethed with a kind of generalized rage and frustration. Sheehan, by that point, had made clear his personal animus for the ongoing war, and his frustration in covering the Pentagon. He had been brooding about—and was increasingly motivated to write about—what he saw as American war crimes in Vietnam:

> This book is so irresponsible that it may help to provoke a responsible inquiry into the question of war crimes and atrocities in Vietnam. Conversations with Americans is a lesson in what happens when a society shuns the examination of a pressing, emotional issue and leaves the answers to a Mark Lane.
>
> Mr. Lane is a New York lawyer who charged admission six years ago to his lectures in an East Side theater about a conspiracy behind the assassination of President Kennedy (a conspiracy Mr. Lane did not prove in his book attacking the Warren Commission report). He now purports to have assembled a collection of interviews with American soldiers and Marines who witnessed or participated in atrocities in Vietnam.[8]

The review went further downhill from there. Lane's publisher, Simon & Schuster, had taken out an ad in the *Times Book Review* the previous month, calling Lane's book "one of the most shocking, eye-opening books ever encountered in the annals of wartime reporting." That allowed Sheehan to take aim at Simon

& Schuster. Unlike Lane, Sheehan had relevant, on-the-ground experience as a war correspondent in Vietnam, and he did not disguise his disdain for what he considered Lane's disregard for basic fact-checking, and the publisher's complicity.

"Mr. Lane did not bother to cross-check any of the stories his interviewers told him with Army or Marine Corps records," Sheehan pointed out. "I asked him why in a telephone conversation."

"'Because I believe the most unreliable source regarding the verification of atrocities is the Defense Department,' he said.

"'But what about simple and obvious facts . . . which might throw light on the credibility of his witnesses?' I asked.

"'It's not relevant,' he said."

Sheehan accused Lane of engaging in "a new McCarthyism, this time from the left. . . . Those on the left who cherish their integrity might do well to take a careful look at Mark Lane's methods."

Although Sheehan had issues with the specifics of Lane's accounts, and with Lane's fact-finding, Sheehan couldn't argue about the brutality of the war and the obvious civilian casualties. Certainly, crimes had been committed. And that brought him back to the point he'd made at the outset:

> It has always been my understanding that it is the task of the Army and the Marines to kill the enemies of the country when they are ordered to do so. The rub is whom they should kill, when they should do the killing, and how they should do it. This is what has torn the nation apart over the Vietnam war.
>
> The country desperately needs a sane and honest inquiry into the question of war crimes and atrocities in Vietnam by a body of knowledgeable and responsible men not beholden to the current military establishment. Who these men are and how that inquiry ought to be conducted are questions I do not have the space to discuss here, but the need for the inquiry is self-evident. Too large a segment of the citizenry believes that

> war crimes and atrocities have taken place for the question to be ignored.

Sheehan was making a personal statement with the Lane review: He intended to confront the war-crimes demon head-on. To do so, Sheehan's forum would once again be the Sunday *Book Review*. And this time he would be writing under the direction of the *Review's* brash new editor, John Leonard.

Although Leonard's predecessor had assigned the *Conversations with Americans* review to Sheehan, it was set into type on Leonard's watch—and Leonard liked what happened next: Sheehan's rant got attention, and Leonard wanted more of that. Leonard thus now had motive and opportunity for showcasing Sheehan's opinionated style of journalism in the *Review's* pages—and Sheehan was up for it. Leonard asked Sheehan to get busy on an even more ambitious project for the *Book Review*: a panoramic appraisal of books about war crimes, notably referencing America's involvement in Vietnam. A rageful, far-reaching commentary on war crimes would be Sheehan's next plum assignment.

In 1971, the *Times Book Review* was trade publishing's category killer—it was, literally and figuratively, the house organ for the thriving New York–centric industry, lush with display advertising and a huge moneymaker for the *Times*. In taking the *Review's* helm, thirty-one-year-old Leonard wanted to make a bold statement about new directions: not just about the rapidly changing industry, which was getting more conglomerated and best-seller driven, but also about literary criticism and, ultimately, the *Review* itself.[9]

Leonard was, to his *Times* colleagues, an "ardent leftist all his life,"[10] but he had gotten his start as a twenty-year-old Harvard dropout in 1959[11] with William F. Buckley's *National Review*—"state media" for conservatives—before jumping to the *Times* eight years later. Leonard thus felt a certain license to play both sides against the middle. He wanted the *Review* to take chances, be edgier, and shake things up.

Inviting Sheehan to return to the subject that obsessed him—war crimes, particularly those alleged in Vietnam—guaranteed controversy and attention. So much the better. If that's what Leonard wanted, he was assured that the *Review* would get it with Sheehan—just as before.

When Sheehan's review of *Conversations with Americans* hit, kudos came in from all over. *Newsweek* spun it into a splashy story that featured a photo of the thirty-four-year-old Sheehan sitting at his typewriter, looking formidable, a long-stemmed pipe tightly clenched in his teeth. *Newsweek's* reporter on the piece, hard-boiled Liz Peer,[12] sent Sheehan a note: *Not even President Nixon got nearly three full columns in Newsweek this week.*[13]

The Canadian Broadcasting Corporation scheduled a debate between Sheehan and Lane. Abe Rosenthal's watchful ally, Allan Siegal, the paper's assistant foreign editor in New York, and a newsroom arbiter who called balls and strikes on good stories and bad, signaled approval in a telex to the Washington bureau, via Frankel's deputy, Bob Phelps:

> 1/4/71
>
> WASHINGTON
> PHELPS FOR NEIL SHEEHAN
> OUR OPINION OF NEWSWEEK'S PRESS SECTION JUST SOARED. OUR OPINION OF NEIL SHEEHAN HAS BEEN UP THERE ALL ALONG.
> BEST REGARDS
> SIEGAL[14]

Before any of those missives arrived, there was a note from the top editor himself, Abe Rosenthal, who still favored Sheehan and did his best to look out for the mercurial reporter in times of potential controversy. The newsroom always got the *Book Review* a week ahead, which meant Rosenthal could front-run everybody. He sent an "attaboy" to Sheehan, who was now back on what Sheehan considered the dreary Pentagon beat. Sheehan sent back a gracious reply a few days before Christmas:

> Dec. 22, 1970
> Dear Abe,
> Your note on the review of Mark Lane's book arrived at the end of a grey day filled with interviews on weapons procurement, a subject only slightly more stimulating than the weather. Notes like that wipe away rain and Pentagon gibberish. It was a very nice Christmas present. Susan sends her best.
> Many thanks,
> *Neil*[15]

Sheehan soon went to work on the war crimes piece. The result would be a tour de force for Sheehan and the *Book Review*, three months later. But the path along the way would be rocky. For one thing, Sheehan still owed the Sunday magazine that piece about Kissinger, and he was taking constant fire from the Sunday editors, who had no idea that Sheehan wasn't just late with the story, but rather wasn't even working on it.

Another stress factor for Sheehan was the opposition from inside the *Times* to the moralistic stand that Sheehan intended to make. Tension built as his intentions about the war crimes review became clear. Sheehan was, after all, still a beat reporter at the Pentagon, not an opinion columnist. There was no telling how the powers that be at the Defense Department would react.

As his essay "Should We Have War Crime Trials?"[16] neared publication, Sheehan worried that opposition from inside the *Times* would force him to water it down. Because the *Book Review* worked on a longer lead time than the rest of the paper, Sheehan already had a galley of his essay in hand on Tuesday evening, March 2, when he received an unexpected phone call.

Daniel Ellsberg needed a place to sleep for the night.

Sheehan was so frustrated by pushback at the *Times*, as he tried to expose wartime criminality in Vietnam, that he welcomed the opportunity to talk to someone who understood his fury. Motive met opportunity.

Ellsberg had come to Washington that evening to have dinner with friends. He was planning to stay with his and Sheehan's mutual friend, John Paul Vann, the buccaneering former Army colonel turned senior civilian adviser in Vietnam. Vann was the go-to guy when someone wanted to know what was really happening on the ground in Vietnam, and he was admired by both men. But, on this particular evening, Ellsberg wasn't able to connect with Vann. So Ellsberg phoned Sheehan. Did Sheehan have an extra bed? Ellsberg figured Sheehan would say yes.

The story of events that then began to unfold has been told and retold many times. Despite that, some facts are still open to debate and interpretation, not least because of the secrecy that Sheehan and, later, the *Times* stood firm about. Sheehan and Ellsberg and most of the other principals are gone. During his lifetime, Sheehan steadfastly refused to discuss these events, although he recorded a posthumous oral history that the *Times* later quoted selectively and has never published in full. That left Ellsberg, in his late years, to explain matters as he saw them—a still-incomplete version of events because Ellsberg never fully knew everything that Sheehan had been up to.

But some things are clear, a half century later: Both Sheehan and Ellsberg were using each other in service of their own self-interested, if noble and well-intentioned, aims—and neither was being fully truthful with the other, on that Tuesday night or thereafter. The two men, each at the top of their own peculiar game, circled each other and traded information like two spies from rival nations, boastful yet always wary. It is a testament to their circumspection that some of the finest reporting about these events involving Ellsberg and Sheehan in the run-up to, and during, the summer of '71 didn't come out for another half-century. Journalist James Risen, a former *Times* reporter, filled in some of the remaining blanks after the death of both men. Risen's story, published in October 2023 in The Intercept, was titled "The Secret History," and informs much of the account that follows.[17]

When Sheehan welcomed Ellsberg that evening, Sheehan had already been tipped off by sources that Ellsberg had the entire forty-seven-volume, seven-thousand-page McNamara Report on the history of U.S. involvement in Vietnam—and Sheehan very much wanted it all. Ellsberg had spirited the forty-seven volumes out of RAND, page by page, later using his Santa Monica circle of colleagues, close acquaintances, and ex-girlfriends to laboriously remove the *Top Secret* markings and xerox multiple sets. Ellsberg's theft and copying of the document was an open secret among those who knew him well. And Sheehan wanted everything.

The *Top Secret* document was still being referred to, by those who were aware of it, as the McNamara Report, or the Vietnam Study—euphemisms for the 2.5-million-word document that described the self-serving deceit and outright lies underpinning America's involvement in Southeast Asia over the prior two decades. Later, Sheehan and his editors would kick around some other names and settle upon one that finally resonated: the Pentagon Papers.[18]

That evening in early March, Sheehan already knew what Ellsberg was up to. Sheehan was among a select few who were aware that Ellsberg had been quietly trying for months to get someone high up in Washington to go public with the Pentagon Papers. Ellsberg believed—incorrectly, it would turn out—that the war would quickly end if he could get someone of prominence to go public with what the Pentagon Papers revealed about how multiple administrations had lied to the public about American involvement in Southeast Asia.

But even the most dovish politicians wouldn't risk prosecution, or the wrath of the Nixon administration, by revealing the top secret report. Ellsberg had been rebuffed by, among others, Senator George McGovern, already announced as a Democratic challenger in Nixon's coming reelection campaign, and Representative Pete McCloskey, a California Republican and ex-Marine who planned a quixotic battle in primaries as an antiwar candidate against Nixon.

Frustrated by the timidity of politicians, Ellsberg next tried to dribble the story out by leaking a tantalizing thousand pages of the Papers to three left-wingers at the Institute for Policy Studies in Washington, who were writing a history of American involvement in Vietnam. His deal with Marcus Raskin (the father of Representative Jamie Raskin), Richard Barnet, and Ralph Stavins, of IPS, was that the trio could use the Papers for their book "as long as they did so only on background, meaning they wouldn't acknowledge publicly that they possessed the classified history or quote from it directly," Risen explained over fifty years later in The Intercept.[19]

The IPS activists hadn't kept the secret. Sheehan knew all about it because, in February 1971,[20] Raskin and the other two didn't just tell him about it, they went ahead and gave a copy of everything they had to Sheehan. Then, as now, Washington was a leaky place. Thus, when Ellsberg showed up that night at Sheehan's house in Washington, Sheehan *already had a partial set* of the Papers. And, unbeknownst to Ellsberg that evening, it was Ellsberg *himself* who had indirectly been Sheehan's source through the circuitous path.

The IPS authors had duplicated their thousand pages of the Papers for Sheehan in exchange for Sheehan's promise to coordinate favorable publicity and a review in the *Times* once their book came out. Sheehan made those promises without the knowledge of the *New York Times*.

"[T]here is no evidence that Sheehan ever actually talked to any of his editors about it," Risen wrote after interviewing Max Frankel, one of the last remaining *Times* editors who was involved. "Sheehan never told me he got some of the documents from Raskin and IPS," Frankel told Risen. "I never heard of any deal that Sheehan had made with IPS and Raskin. They would have to have been very naïve to believe that Sheehan could make that deal."[21] James Greenfield, the *New York Times* foreign editor, was also in the dark.[22]

Sheehan "simply lied to them as a reporter," Ellsberg said of the supposed deal, which Raskin told Ellsberg about thirty years after the fact. That was "totally in line with my dealings with Sheehan," Ellsberg added. Ellsberg wanted Raskin to tell him why he'd kept the secret for so long. Raskin told him he was too embarrassed by the deceit, and the double crossing, to even talk about it.[23]

Regardless, it's clear in retrospect that by early March, even before his war crimes essay came out, Sheehan already had the first of what ultimately would be *three* sets of the Pentagon Papers eventually obtained by him. Higher-ups at the *Times* soon would know Sheehan had something afoot, but even his bosses wouldn't know that Sheehan was in the process of secretly amassing *multiple* sets of the Papers, each with its own set of conditions attached (and which Sheehan was implicitly agreeing to, whether he had the authority or not). Ellsberg wouldn't find out about all this until decades later.[24]

Sheehan set up a cot for Ellsberg in the basement, but there was no sleeping that night; the two stayed up talking. Sheehan showed Ellsberg his war crimes essay, and Ellsberg was impressed. He'd been dubious about the newspaper's stance on Vietnam since hearing Sheehan's complaints the year before at Tony Lake's house. But that night, Ellsberg came away convinced he had found a reporter he could once again confide in. Risen, who interviewed Ellsberg a few months before Ellsberg died in 2023, picked up the story from there, describing the March 2 meeting when Sheehan showed Ellsberg his draft of the war crimes essay[25]:

> "He said, 'I'm having a lot of trouble with the editors on this,'" Ellsberg recalled. "I read it in his D.C. basement. Very good! This is very good stuff. So I thought, 'OK, he's the guy.'"

That March night, Ellsberg began to tell Sheehan about the Pentagon Papers. He explained how the IPS guys, Barnet and Raskin, had suggested he seek out Sheehan. Ellsberg also told Sheehan that he'd given IPS a big chunk of the secret documents. Sheehan replied that he figured IPS had some of the material—

but, according to Ellsberg's later recollection, Sheehan never mentioned that he, too, already had the same one thousand pages.

As they stayed up all night talking, Ellsberg invited Sheehan to come to Cambridge, Massachusetts, where Ellsberg was then living, to read the Papers in their entirety.

Sheehan now had confirmation (from Ellsberg himself) that Ellsberg was the IPS's source. He also now knew that Ellsberg had the full set of the Papers.

Sheehan's reportorial gut told him that the story wouldn't hold for much longer. He needed to go full speed ahead.

The next morning, March 3, Sheehan approached the deputy Washington bureau chief, Bob Phelps, with his next big story idea. This would be the first that anyone at the *Times* heard of the Pentagon Papers. Sheehan told Phelps he had a "source" who would make the Pentagon Papers available if the *New York Times* "would handle it properly." There would be some "conditions," including the newspaper agreeing to use it all or in very large chunks. He asked Phelps what he would advise.[26]

Phelps thought the idea was worth pursuing, but wanted a second opinion. He suggested Sheehan talk to Tom Wicker. Wicker had previously been the Washington bureau chief. Now Wicker was a left-leaning political columnist and, like Sheehan, a source of pride or irritation at the paper, depending on whom he'd recently antagonized.

Wicker, too, liked the idea, but he told Sheehan they'd need a policy call from New York as to what the paper might or might not be willing to agree to in advance of seeing the Papers. Importantly, Wicker advised Sheehan not to take the idea to New York by himself. Use James Reston as your go-between, Wicker suggested. Just leave it to Reston and see what he comes back with.

James "Scotty" Reston, sixty-one years old, was a mentor to younger journalists and an éminence grise at the *Times*—a two-time Pulitzer Prize winner who'd been a war reporter, foreign correspondent, and Washington bureau chief, all for the *Times*, before moving up to the executive ranks as a vice president in Washington.

Reston agreed to get the reading from New York. A few days later, Sheehan met with Frankel to brief him about what was going on. On his way to the elevator after the meeting, Sheehan bumped into Reston. "You have clearance, young man," Reston told him.

Sheehan was about to disappear—back to Cambridge, to fetch the whole megillah that he thought he had been promised by Ellsberg. It would turn out that the two weren't on the same page.

The annual Gridiron Club white-tie gala at the Statler Hilton[27] was an inexplicable rite of spring, a weird but revered throwback to another century. It was here that, once a year, the cream of Washington's journalism colony made nice with the politicians they criticized the other 364 days, each poking fun at the other with skits and spoofs and finely crafted gags from the president. Everything off the record. The club was limited to sixty members, but their prestigious annual affair drew ten times that number.[28]

Max Frankel and James Goodale of the *Times* were suited up for the annual Gridiron Dinner on March 13. Walking in, they and others were confronted by thirty-five picketers, mostly young women, who were protesting the Gridiron Club's policy of excluding women from membership.[29] The women had sent letters to 125 of the expected guests, urging that they boycott the event, but only four had done so. Two of the boycotters, Senators George McGovern and Edmund Muskie, were Democrats vying to replace Nixon. The other two were Senator Mike Mansfield, the majority leader, and Walter Washington, DC's mayor.

Ted Kennedy, Chief Justice Warren Burger, and Henry Kissinger were among the Gridiron's guests. The vice president, Spiro Agnew, would have the speechmaking honors this night. The year before, Nixon and Agnew had both been on stage—Nixon at the piano playing ballads; Agnew constantly interrupting with a raucous version of "Dixie" that got louder and louder with the audience's laughter.[30] Nixon, while having some fun on stage, was showing who he really was, and what his Southern

Strategy was all about. This year, Nixon had decided to stay away. He was at the Florida White House in Key Biscayne.

Humor, with more than an edge of truth, was the Gridiron's specialty. Agnew's stock in trade was that of an attack dog on the media, but lampooning was the order of the evening, so he asked his pal, comedian Bob Hope, to feed him some good lines. Hope gave Agnew some zingers, carefully typed out in ALL CAPS on index cards, which Hope figured would get laughs from the all-white, all-male audience[31]:

> LADIES AND GENTLEMEN, AND MEMBERS OF THE EASTERN LIBERAL ESTABLISHMENT.......
>
> CONTRARY TO POPULAR BELIEF, I HAVE NOTHING AGAINST (CBS ANCHOR) WALTER CRONKITE. I'M SURE IT WAS JUST A SLIP OF THE TONGUE WHEN HE REPORTED SEEING ME COME OUT OF A MOTEL WITH ANGELA DAVIS.
>
> I AM GRATEFUL FOR THIS VERY INTERESTING EVENING. IN FACT, I SHALL THANK YOU ALL PERSONALLY. THE CIA HAS ALREADY HANDED ME THE ADDRESS AND FINGERPRINTS OF EVERYONE INVOLVED.
>
> LET'S FORGET THIS HOGWASH ABOUT J. EDGAR HOOVER OR ANYONE ELSE BECOMING "ALL POWERFUL" IN WASHINGTON. NO ONE HAS "GOT ANYTHING" ON ANY MEMBER OF THIS ADMINISTRATION, I CAN ASSURE YOU! THE PRESIDENT WOULD BE HERE TO TELL YOU HIMSELF, BUT HE COULDN'T MAKE IT—HE'S BABYSITTING HENRY KISSINGER'S PEKINGESE.

During the festivities, Frankel took aside Goodale, the newspaper's general counsel, to give him the first heads-up about what Sheehan might be up to. Frankel told Goodale to read the law on classified documents, because the newspaper might have a story involving a lot of them.[32]

Kissinger reported back to Nixon the following morning, Sunday, March 14. *The President called this morning on just a few general odds and ends,* Haldeman wrote in his diary. *He had a report from Henry on the Gridiron last night, where apparently the Vice President saved the evening for the Administration.*

Sheehan, meanwhile, went off to meet Ellsberg in Cambridge. The Monday after the Gridiron, Sheehan rented a Plymouth[33] at the Hartford airport and drove to Harvard Square,[34] checking in to the Treadway Inn under the cleverly assumed name of "Samuel Johnson"—the noted man of letters from two centuries before. The Treadway was a fleabag and a weekend crash pad for students, which Sheehan would have known quite well. As a twenty-year-old Harvard senior, he'd been arrested (and later released) by Cambridge police on a drunk charge.[35]

When Sheehan signed the hotel registry, he gave his corporate affiliation as "Control Data Corporation" and a fake Wall Street address, 25 Broadway, New York City. Sheehan's room was $28 a night—including $10 extra per night for a bed board to stiffen the mattress; Sheehan needed that because of his bad back.[36] Sheehan always paid cash.

But he also got careless, leaving tracks that the FBI later would follow. Sheehan used his White House press pass as check-cashing identification at Western Union offices around town.[37]

Sheehan stayed in Cambridge for two days, then dropped off the Plymouth at Boston's Logan Airport and hopped on a shuttle back to Washington.

He told Susan that Ellsberg had everything at his Cambridge apartment—all seven thousand pages of the Pentagon Papers.

"Xerox it," Sheehan remembered Susan saying.[38]

Sheehan hadn't told Ellsberg about that cache of Papers he had gotten from IPS—and never would. Meanwhile, the IPS trio had connections that even the FBI couldn't figure out. Around the time Ellsberg gave the IPS trio the thousand pages, likely the prior September, the far-left group had suddenly begun getting an infusion of huge donations from an unknown source or sources—totaling $704,000 in four big monthly deposits, equivalent to more than $5,522,000 today. The FBI began monitoring IPS's bank account. J. Edgar Hoover asked the head of the Criminal Division at the Justice Department to find out who was fronting all that money: "The coincidence of the deposit of one quarter million dollars during September 1970, together with the alleged acquisition of the McNamara Study by IPS, should be resolved."[39]

It's likely that Ellsberg, on Sheehan's initial brief trip to Cambridge, showed Sheehan the whole tantalizing set of Pentagon Papers, but didn't let him copy anything. What is clear, however, is that after returning to Washington on Friday night, Sheehan went straight to the *Times* bureau the following morning, Saturday, March 20, to make some copies on the office Xerox machine. The bureau was typically quiet on weekends, so Sheehan would have been able to work efficiently without having to answer questions about his recent whereabouts.[40]

Later that same day, early on Saturday afternoon, Sheehan returned to Boston and checked back into the Treadway Inn, once again as Samuel Johnson and using the same fake company name and address.[41] Sheehan was back in room 215 by 4:30 p.m.[42] This return trip carried some urgency for Sheehan. Daniel and Patricia Ellsberg told him they would be leaving for a vacation in Trinidad and Tobago, and they planned to be gone for a week.[43] Ellsberg said Sheehan could review—but not copy—the Papers while they were away. He gave Sheehan a key to their Cambridge apartment and told him: You have free rein, look through everything, but don't make copies.

Sheehan quickly made a duplicate of the key.

Sheehan agreed to Ellsberg's terms. But he fully intended to violate the deal he'd just made.[44] Sheehan planned to start copying the Papers—every last page—as soon as the Ellsbergs left their apartment. The question was, how? The logistics of copying seven thousand pages of top secret documents were formidable.

As Ellsberg had done when he began pilfering the Papers from RAND in 1969,[45] Sheehan now sought help from people he trusted most. He phoned Susan and told her to come up and bring suitcases, large envelopes, and all the cash in the house.[46] Susan flew up and checked in under an assumed name at a different hotel—the Continental, also in Cambridge. Then she linked up with Neil at the Treadway. Unless they were alone in Neil's room, the two acted as if they didn't know each other.

It was going to be expensive, and time consuming, to copy all seven thousand pages. And Neil needed to work quickly. He had already been phoning copy shops near Harvard. Some were open 24/7—that was good. But they wanted big bucks, banks were closed on the weekend, and Neil was way short of cash.

Sheehan phoned a friend.

Dun Gifford, thirty-two years old, had been a few years behind Sheehan at Harvard. He was a well-connected Bostonian who'd earlier knocked around Washington in various jobs for JFK's younger brothers, including as a campaign aide to Robert Kennedy (and a witness to RFK's 1968 assassination) and a legislative assistant to Ted Kennedy.

Gifford had quit Washington the year before, returning to his hometown to begin a career in commercial real estate. He was just starting out with a Boston developer, Cabot, Cabot & Forbes, when Sheehan called him for help. Gifford would help his friend, but he soon regretted his involvement. As an aide to Ted Kennedy, Gifford had a top secret security clearance. Gifford worried, with good reason, that if the FBI later found out he'd been involved, Nixon would try to pin involvement in the Pentagon Papers leak to Ted Kennedy. Gifford later went back and read the security oath he'd taken, and it confirmed that he'd broken that oath by assisting Sheehan. Indeed, just as Gifford feared, the FBI later harassed Gifford in an attempt to tie Kennedy to the leak. Gifford hired Herbert J. Miller, a Washington, DC, criminal lawyer who had strong ties to the Kennedy brothers and who'd represented Ted Kennedy two years earlier following the drowning of Mary Jo Kopechne, off Chappaquiddick.

Sheehan documented Gifford's misgivings in a note to himself that he later jotted down:

> Dun wasn't ashamed of what he did, but he went back and read his security oath that he had to sign when he went into government. It was an indefinite security oath, [and it's clear that] somebody would say you broke your oath to the U.S. government. He thinks what he did was patriotic, but the crazies wouldn't see it that way.[47]
>
> Dun said the Nixon Administration harassed the hell out of him after the Pentagon papers to try to tie Ted Kennedy into the publication and hurt him politically. It was part of the paranoid business [White House Plumber Egil] Krogh and his crowd went through in thinking that publication of the PPs was part of a great big conspiracy by Clark Clifford and Warnke and others in the Democratic party establishment, including Ted Kennedy, and they [meaning Nixon] would have them all indicted (not Kennedy, but Clifford, etc.) and destroy the Democratic party in the process. The Nixon prosecutors called Dun before the Boston grand jury and he spent hours in testimony. They would ask him questions about whether he knew me and when I had been in Cambridge. And he would say that he knew me but then waffle about what he knew of what I was doing in Cambridge. The FBI was also after him for months, but he kept his mouth shut to them.
>
> He would tell them Yes, he knew me. But he didn't know what I had done in Cambridge, etc. Dun was afraid he was going to be hauled before the grand jury and cited for contempt. He ran up thousands of dollars in bills with Miller, the Washington lawyer.[48]

Gifford's wife, a socialite who went by the nickname "Pebble," recalled the frantic call that came in early on Sunday morning:

> We were in bed and the phone rang and it was Neil who called and said, "Dun, I need help. I've got the Papers. Is there any way you could help me Xerox these Papers?"
>
> Dun of course said right away, Yes. Dun worked for Cabot, Cabot & Forbes. Lots of Xerox machines. Big ones. And they went up to the umpteenth floor. Dun at this point said, "Oh, my God, What am I doing here?" He started Xeroxing and there was just thousands of sheets of paper. Every one of them said Top Secret stamped on it. And so Dun said, "What are we doing here?" But he was glad to help Neil.[49] And it took quite a bit of time.[50]

Gifford had agreed to let Sheehan into the Cabot real estate offices, quiet on the weekend, so Sheehan could use the copying machine there.[51] But, given Gifford's misgivings, they didn't finish the job. Sheehan returned to the Treadway. It was time for Plan B.

Neil phoned the New England bureau chief, Bill Kovach. Kovach had been with the *Times* three years and had just moved up to Boston from the national desk in New York. He was thirty-nine years old, originally from Tennessee, and had made a reputation covering renegades in the antiwar movement. The two had never met. As Kovach later told the story[52]:

> I get a call. Neil Sheehan. I knew him because he and Abe [Rosenthal] were pals. We knew each other, but we hadn't met. And he said, "I don't want to talk on the phone. I'm down here at the Treadway Inn. Come down and see me. Ask for Mr. Johnson."[53] So I drove down and went, and asked for Johnson. And I go up to the room, door opens [he indicates, just by a crack] and Neil pulls me in. There's this woman sitting there

on the desk, and there's papers all over the place. The whole bed's covered and the whole room was full of documents. And it was Susan, his wife. He introduced me to Susan.

He said, "Look Bill, I can't tell you what this is. These are things, these are important papers. I can't tell you what they are. But I need your help."

So, this was late.[54] "I've gotta get them back in the office at MIT before classes start on Monday. And I've gotta get 'em copied." He said, "I've got to find a place—can't be in Cambridge because of the FBI is all over town—I've gotta find some place."

I said, "I know the perfect place. A place in Bedford just opened up last week, I saw it as I was driving into town." And so, I said, "I can arrange to get whatever it is copied."

He said, "Also, I don't have any money." And I said, "Jesus, Neil, my bureau account is flat, it's toward the end of the month." I said, "I gotta call New York and get some money."

He said, "You can't tell anybody in New York. There's only three people that know about this. And nobody except Abe in New York knows it."[55]

And so I went by the place and said, A friend of mine has a book manuscript that he was finishing up and he had to get it copied this weekend because it had to be at the publisher first thing Monday morning. And would he be willing to rent us that machine over the whole weekend, because he was not going to be open anyway.

He said he'd do it for fifteen hundred dollars. So I wrote him a check for fifteen hundred dollars. And they went out and copied the stuff.

The copy shop in Bedford, Massachusetts, was called Victor Publishers.[56] But the $1,500 check that Kovach wrote didn't ensure victory. The machines in the copy shop crashed under the strain.[57] The whole job still wasn't done. The Sheehans called around and found another shop in Boston's financial district, Liberty Square Press, that was open and promised a quick turnaround.

But when the guy running that shop noticed that the documents were classified, he became nervous. Susan, who had taken over the copying chores at that point, called Neil at the Ellsbergs' apartment. "Get down here!"

Sheehan rushed back and reassured the manager that everything was on the up-and-up. The material, Sheehan told him, was from some Harvard professors who were doing a study, and they'd already gotten the documents declassified in bulk. The manager seemed to understand.[58] Early Tuesday morning, March 23, Susan and Neil hopped in a cab and stopped off at each of the copy shops that helped them, in order to pick up straggler copies. "Rapid conversationalist," the cabbie later recalled Sheehan to the FBI. "Wore a hat."[59] The Sheehans now had a complete set of the stolen Pentagon Papers and were ready to lug everything back to DC in the suitcases that Susan brought with her.[60]

That night, back in DC, Sheehan phoned Frankel: "I got it all."[61]

The following Sunday, March 28, Sheehan's war crimes essay hit the stands.

"Book Review" certainly would be a misnomer to describe the resultant work that appeared in the newspaper's Sunday *Book Review* supplement on March 28, 1971.

Sheehan's essay, retaining the provocative title "Should We Have War Crime Trials?,"[62] started out on a type-dense cover page of the *Book Review* and continued for seven more pages on the inside. Cascading down the middle of the front cover was a drawing by a twenty-eight-year-old Dutch political cartoonist, just arrived in America, named Fons van Woerkom[63]: Vietnamese peasants were leaping, one after another, onto an increasingly crowded powder keg of TNT, which was resting on the shoulders of a beleaguered American soldier, who was intolerably weighted down. If you traced the image down the page and looked at it more closely, the soldier took on the form of an eagle, yet the raptor's head also bore more than a passing resemblance to LBJ. And if you tried hard enough, you could maybe see Richard Nixon in there, too. The eagle/soldier/politician's talons were gripping a skull-and-crossbones dynamite plunger, the growing weight of it all tipping at any moment to the inevitable: blowing everything and everyone to smithereens.

Sheehan's eight-thousand-word essay began with an editor's note:

> The *Book Review* received the accompanying bibliography from Mr. Mark Sacharoff, assistant professor of English at Temple University, and sent the books to Neil Sheehan for review.

There were thirty-three books in all, and the list ran the gamut: academic treatises, congressional hearings, journalistic investigations (Seymour Hersh, first to reveal the My Lai massacre, had two books), even Lane's maligned *Conversations with Americans*. The alphabetical list ran down the center of each page until it stopped with *Why Are We Still in Vietnam?*

Sheehan began his essay with a question: "Do you have to be Hitlerian to be a war criminal? Or can you qualify as a well-intentioned President of the United States?" After meandering around in that daisy field for a while, he got back to the answer:

> If you credit as factual only a fraction of the information assembled here about what happened in Vietnam, and if you apply the laws of war to American conduct there, then the leaders of the United States for the past six years at least, including the incumbent President, Richard Milhous Nixon, may well be guilty of war crimes.

The new *Book Review* editor, John Leonard, had scored a direct hit with Sheehan's bombshell review. More than any other review or essay, it would define Leonard for the rest of his life. When Leonard died in 2008, his *Times* obituary called the war crimes issue "one of the signal events of his tenure." That certainly was true. The obit also called it "a widely praised issue." That, as the paper's fact-checkers might say today, would require more context.

Within the *Times* newsroom, controversy was stirring even before Sheehan's essay came out. Leonard and his editors at the *Book Review* wanted the daily paper to hype Sheehan's piece ahead of its publication, in order to draw maximum attention to it. The newsroom resisted, with some editors arguing that Sheehan—ostensibly, still the paper's beat reporter at the Pentagon—had gone way beyond journalistic objectivity with his blunt accusations of war crimes.[64] The balkanized structure of the *Times* placed the *Book Review* under Daniel Schwarz, the autonomous Sunday editor, who reported not to Rosenthal, but directly to the publisher, Arthur Ochs "Punch" Sulzberger. Schwarz also had to give the OK to Sheehan's piece, which he ultimately did.

Rosenthal found himself torn between siding with his editors over the ethical issue and supporting his favored reporter. Sheehan's essay wasn't the only source of conflict Rosenthal grappled with. Tom Wicker, the former Washington bureau chief who now was a political columnist and fierce critic of Nixon's, also frequently rankled Rosenthal. What really got to Rosenthal were Wicker's extracurricular efforts.

Around the same time that Sheehan's war crimes essay came out, Wicker gave a speech at Columbia University criticizing the mainstream press, including his *Times* colleagues, for laziness in reporting. The speech became a Wicker-bylined feature, "The Greening of the Press,"[65] in the next issue of the *Columbia Journalism Review*. Wicker bluntly criticized what he called the media's lack of enterprise reporting and its overreliance on "the official statement, the official explanation, the background explanation from the official source."[66]

Rosenthal had tried to stay out of the debate over Sheehan's essay, but he felt no such compunction about Wicker. Rosenthal wrote in his private journal:

> I am weary to death of confrontations, but I think that this is something so important to the paper that over the long run I will not be able to turn away from it. . . . People like Wicker have taken to making strong political statements and speeches on their own before militant groups. He may think he is speaking as a person, but there he is listed on the masthead as an associate editor, and I think it is expecting too much to disassociate one from the other.

Still putting his thoughts into the journal, Rosenthal unloaded next on John Leonard, the newly promoted *Book Review* editor responsible for Sheehan's war crimes essay:

> The latest turn is that John Leonard has made it clear he is going to make the book review into a political-social journal. This was my great complaint about Leonard as a book reviewer. He was brilliant stylistically. But over and over again he used the book merely as a pretext to launch into a political discussion in which he was primarily interested. The important thing became Leonard's views rather than the book itself. When he came up for consideration as Book Review editor, I told Punch and [Daniel] Schwarz [Sunday editor] that I was afraid he would do this to the Book Review section. He has done that specifically and in an article in the current issue of Newsweek, he states so. I've discussed this this morning with Sydney [Gruson,[67] Sulzberger's assistant and alter ego], and I think he understands it but he keeps advising me to keep cool and not to get involved in confrontations. I find it difficult to do either.[68]

In the moment, Rosenthal took Gruson's advice, since staking out a position either way was bound to alienate someone.

As if on cue, days after Sheehan's piece came out, Rosenthal received an effusive letter praising Sheehan, and the new attitude at the *Book Review*, from his friend David Schoenbrun. The two had a common bond as foreign correspondents, and Schoenbrun was journalistic royalty; he'd worked for CBS alongside Edward R. Murrow during World War II, and following the war ran CBS's Paris bureau. Schoenbrun had just returned from a lecture tour, and he reported back to Rosenthal about the buzz that Sheehan's essay had created:

> The highlight of my trip was the discussion, in L.A. and Chicago, of Neil Sheehan's magnificent essay-review of war crimes books. . . . We need more work to find the right balance between essay and review, but the substance of Neil's piece was so strong that form and structure become unimportant.
>
> It was brilliant reporting and analysis and the highest form of patriotism. . . .
>
> Best personal
> regards,
> *David*[69]

Rosenthal couldn't bring himself to agree—or disagree. Third rail. He wasn't going to touch it.

> April 5, 1971
> Dear David:
>
> That was a very sweet letter but I am passing it on to Dan Schwarz and John Leonard, who are responsible for the Book Review and the Sheehan Piece.

Within the Pentagon, there was a scramble to compile a point-by-point rebuttal to Sheehan's assertion that the war was, in itself, an atrocity punishable by law. Army staffers went so far as to put together a document that justified the conduct of the war and exonerated the commanding general, William Westmoreland, of complicity in war crimes. But when they presented it to the Army's chief information officer at the Pentagon, General Winant Sidle, he counseled silence. Sidle was wary. The document the historians had prepared was open to interpretation, and might prove the opposite.[70]

Meanwhile, intentionally or not, with his war crimes essay, Sheehan telegraphed where he was already headed next—the sprawling Pentagon Papers project that ultimately would consume the *Times* and become the newspaper's singular defining event:

> This bibliography represents the beginning of what promises to be a long and painful inquest into what we are doing in Southeast Asia. The more perspective we gain on our behavior, the uglier our conduct appears. At first it had seemed unfortunate and sad; we were caught in the quicksand of Indochina. Then our conduct had appeared stupid and brutal, the quagmire was of our own making, the Vietnamese were the victims and we were the executioners. Now we're finding out that we may have taken life, not merely as cruel and stubborn warriors, but as criminals. We are conditioned as a nation to believe that only our enemies commit war crimes. Certainly the enemy in Indochina has perpetrated crimes. The enemy's war crimes, however, will not wash us clean if we too are war criminals.

Rosenthal had begun keeping a private journal earlier that year not just as a way, he said, to become more self-aware, but also as a means of channeling his own prideful anger about criticisms of the *Times*, which he felt acutely. The very first entry, on January 29, was noteworthy in that it showed Rosenthal's prescience.

It was also astonishing, because it demonstrated an introspection that few in the newsroom ever saw[71]:

Journal—Friday, January 29, 1971[72]

Manny Freedman (assistant managing editor of the *Times*)[73] died the day before yesterday, and in a couple of hours I will be going to the funeral. Is that one of the reasons I have decided to write a journal? Thomas Wolfe wrote that no young man ever really believes that he will die. I'm at an age now that I have no doubts whatsoever that I will die. Like most editors, I am seized with the reality of death, and of course because of my family, it has never been too far from my mind.

Something very much on my mind, and perhaps more the reason that I am writing the journal than Manny's death: the incessant attacks on the *Times* from the left and the liberal community. Somehow, the attacks from the right do not bother me—they never liked the paper or what it was trying to do. But the past few years the antagonism of the far left—which also never bothered me very much—has spread rightward into the center.

I think I tend to exaggerate the importance of the attacks on the *Times* because I am so deeply involved, and of course I see an attack on the *Times* as an attack on me. But I think there are some significant things operating. . . . The radical left has become a deep and powerful establishment of its own. If there were a real revolution in this country, the *Times* would not be the first to go. Perhaps the second. The first would be the present bourgeois leaders of the left. It might almost be worth having, just to see the look of astonishment on the faces of those people who have done most to destroy a free society as they are being led off to the American equivalent of Lubyanka (the Russian KGB headquarters in Moscow).

> But what bothers me most, I suppose, is the fact that the liberal leaders of society are so joyfully cooperating in their own destruction. I think they try to chop away at the *Times* because it represents something sane and decent in their own lives, a mirror of what they once were. They mistrust and detest themselves, and so they try to smash the mirror. It has happened before in other societies and it can indeed happen here.

When he wrote that first journal entry, Rosenthal was about to leave for a reporting trip to Vietnam. His inner fear was that he might be running away from one bloody war, standing up for the honest values of the *Times*, and into another over Vietnam. At the time of that writing, he did not know that Sheehan soon would be pulling him into both.

A big day was coming up for Daniel Ellsberg—his fortieth birthday, on April 7. There would be a big bash for him in Cambridge. Ellsberg had a wide circle of friends, many of whom he'd told about his role in compiling the still very hush-hush Pentagon Papers; a favored few learned that he'd surreptitiously made copies, and were allowed to read some of the more incriminating portions. Discreetly or not, spreading the word about the Papers among like minds was Ellsberg's modus operandi as he tried to figure out a way to push out the Papers without getting arrested.

But people talked. And *especially* at Ellsberg's festive fortieth birthday party, they talked. Because during all the idle cocktail chatter, there were some pretty interesting stories to drop. In the course of the evening, one celebrant bragged to another that she knew about a top secret operation in Vietnam called Operation 34A. That was a highly classified American program of clandestine raids against North Vietnam, during the early days of the Johnson administration.

The Pentagon Papers would reveal Operation 34A as a key element in Lyndon Johnson's escalation of the war. But on the night of Ellsberg's party, Operation 34A was still very secret. Nevertheless, at least two guests at Ellsberg's party were familiar with it. One was Dun Gifford, Sheehan's accomplice in copying the Papers a few weeks earlier. Gifford had learned of the still-secret operation while working in the Senate for Ted Kennedy. The other was someone to whom Ellsberg had blabbed about it, and she was going on and on. Gifford got tired of listening, and told her, in so many words, to shut up.

Gifford immediately regretted the interaction, but it was too late. Sheehan described getting an earful about it afterward from Gifford[74]:

> At Ellsberg's birthday party Gifford was talking to a girl who knew Ellsberg, and she was talking about Operation 34A and what the documents in the PPs said about it. Dun had read some of the information on the Operation for Ted Kennedy. She started questioning Dun. DE had let her read some of the documents. The way Ellsberg was going to use these papers was to dribble them out to his friends bit by bit and let them write newspaper & magazine articles—that sort of thing.
>
> Dun got tired of the questions she was asking him & said in exasperated fashion: "It's a waste of time bec[ause] the *Times* is going to publish the whole goddamn thing in a couple of months." She told DE what [Dun] had said afterwards. DE called Dun in a fury & came over to see him. He wanted to know how Dun knew the *NYT* was going to publish the Papers & what Dun's involvement with me had been.
>
> Dun put him off by saying, "Oh hell, everyone in Washington is talking about this thing. They know the *Times* is working those Papers." But he flubbed DE off on the specifics of what I had done with him (they had Xeroxed the Papers together) & did not tell DE that I

> had used the Xerox machine at Cabot, Cabot & Forbes
> to copy the part on Tonkin Gulf & Operation 34A.*

Dun Gifford wasn't the only person who was deceiving Ellsberg.

Sheehan now had multiple problems with him as well. For one thing, Ellsberg was still waiting to hear, via Sheehan, whether the *Times* would agree to his conditions for publishing the papers. Knowing Ellsberg's propensity for indiscretion, Sheehan certainly didn't want to tell him the truth, which was that Sheehan had stolen the Papers from him the previous month and now was working furiously with a growing team (to get the Papers into print). Ellsberg was a gadfly who couldn't keep his mouth shut. Word would be out in no time; the scoop would be ruined.

There was also the question of the journalistic ethics of what Sheehan had done in deceiving Ellsberg about his copying the Papers.

Sheehan had assured Bob Phelps and Max Frankel, his bosses at the *Times* Washington bureau, of his confidence that he would, at some point, get explicit approval from Ellsberg to publish. When Sheehan first brought the Papers to the *Times*, he estimated those odds (of Ellsberg's eventually assenting to publication) at 90 percent. A few weeks later, after Frankel had gone to New York and sold the top editors about going all in on the project (using a memo Sheehan prepared, and some examples from the Papers), Sheehan seemed to walk that back. That wasn't something Frankel, his neck on the line with Rosenthal, wanted to hear,

*When Ellsberg later realized he'd been lied to by Gifford, he angrily confronted Sheehan about it. Sheehan recounted Ellsberg's reaction in private notes he kept: "[Ellsberg] confronted me after talking to Gifford. . . . DE nevertheless had the impression that Dun had somehow gotten a copy of the papers, prob[ably] through me. After *NYT* published & then was enjoined, DE sent him a copy of the papers to distrib[ute] to another paper. 'Hugh Sidey & Cronkite & the [Boston] *Globe* were all over me,' Dun said. They apparently were told by DE that Dun had a copy. Ellsberg thinks that Gifford had a copy all along. He is still fussing with Dun and thinking that Dun somehow betrayed him. He badmouthed Dun to [Harrison] Salisbury [the esteemed *Times* journalist]. 'He (DE) believes that I (Dun) dissembled to him about it—and so I did.'"

and he made that clear to Sheehan. Frankel had "told New York it was [a] 90 percent chance Neil can talk his source into it. Let's not go back to New York now and tell them it's 89 percent."[75]

Two more sets of the Papers were xeroxed in New York, and the "originals" were returned to Sheehan. More copies would be made as the project expanded. All the copying was done on publisher Punch Sulzberger's Xerox machine on the fourteenth floor of the *Times* building, at 229 West Forty-Third Street, by his two trusted secretaries and a news clerk from the Foreign Desk.[76] "You've got the journalistic hydrogen bomb," foreign editor James Greenfield told Sheehan, with Rosenthal present, on April 19.[77] Assistant managing editor Seymour Topping, Rosenthal's trusted second-in-command, called a meeting for the following week.[78] The project was underway.

CONFIDENTIAL
MEMORANDUM for: Mr. Rosenthal
From SEYMOUR TOPPING
April 16, 1971

The Washington project has now reached a point where decisions must be made, and, on the recommendation of Mr. Mooney,* we are scheduling a meeting in Mr. Reston's office for 11:00 A.M., Wednesday, April 21. We are using Mr. Reston's office as a security measure.

Tentatively, we are planning to have the following people present at the meeting:

Mr. Rosenthal
Mr. Topping
Mr. Greenfield
Mr. Mooney
Mr. Gold
Mr. Roberts

---

*Richard E. Mooney, deputy foreign editor.

Mr. Frankel
Mr. Sheehan

On April 21, the top editors gathered in Scotty Reston's office, away from the newsroom's view, to plan out what was to come.

It is fascinating today to be able to see into this meeting from multiple perspectives, through memos and journal entries that have only recently come to light.

Sheehan's pro bono attorney, Mitch Rogovin, of the Washington law firm of Arnold & Porter, prepared a lengthy memorandum at the time, marked *Privileged and Confidential*, which laid out the entire timeline of the Papers' saga from Sheehan's perspective. Fifty-two years later, Rogovin's revelatory memo came to light.

Sheehan had pulled in Rogovin as his personal lawyer—completely independent from the *Times*—because of the obvious personal jeopardy Sheehan might be in after stealing and publishing top secret materials. Rogovin prepared the fact memorandum to aid in Sheehan's defense, should that be necessary.

In 2023, it was reporter James Risen who, in The Intercept, unearthed Rogovin's memo. He wrote, "The long-buried memo contains Sheehan's contemporaneous and confidential account of his relationship with Ellsberg, as well as Sheehan's version of events inside the *Times* as it prepared to publish the Pentagon Papers. It offers an unprecedented, real-time depiction of Sheehan's actions—including his phone call to Frankel ["I got it all"] and his admission to his editors that he had lied to his source."[79]

Beginning on page 7 of the thirteen-page memo, Rogovin described the Wednesday, April 21, meeting when the top editorial brass convened their Go/No Go meeting and closely questioned Sheehan about his actions. Rosenthal also recounted the aftermath of the meeting, and what was to come, in his journal. Both contemporaneous accounts are presented here.

First, Rogovin's:

> On April 20th Neil met with Frankel and arranged for the two of them, along with Phelps and [Gerald] Gold

[assistant foreign editor], to travel to New York for the Wednesday meeting. Frankel asked Neil to prepare another memo on how the stories would be written.

[On] Wednesday Neil, Gold, Frankel and Phelps first met in Seymour Topping's office. From there they went to James Reston's office and were joined by Turner Catledge, Sydney Gruson, Abe Rosenthal, James Greenfield, James Goodale, [and] Peter Millones.

Neil was given the floor and briefed the group for over an hour on what he had and how it was organized. In response to a question by Goodale, Neil said that the documents were not stolen, but copied. The meeting ran from 10:30 a.m. to about 1:00 p.m.

Neil told the group that he had Xeroxed the materials without permission and the source was unaware that he had done so. He explained how the papers had been obtained, including his wife's involvement. He also told them of the involvement of the Institute for Policy Studies. No one asked and Neil did not tell who his source was. There were, however, questions regarding the authenticity of the papers and the stability of the source. The group was told that the source had seen a number of Senators in an effort to have them publicly reveal the content of the papers but to date had been unsuccessful. Neil also told the group that he did not have the volumes on secret diplomacy. He explained that the Senate Foreign Relations Committee had the volumes in its safe and that his source was not going to let him see them because they could contain channels still in use. As to the materials he had, Neil said "The stuff is all publishable; there might be a few names of U. S. agents we'd want to leave out to protect them. That's all."

The morning meeting had settled the question of publishing. In the afternoon another meeting was held to consider the mechanics. Reston, Greenfield, Topping, Rosenthal, Frankel, Gold and Millones were present in Rosenthal's office. Their discussions centered upon how to run the stories; the use of 10- to 12-page inserts and the need for security. As to security, the concern was twofold: (1) the government might try to seize it: and (2) the competition. It was decided that the number of Times people to be involved should be limited. Goodale told Neil he wanted a lawyer (presumably outside of his office) to look at the papers. Neil expressed concern about the lawyers seeing the material. A hypothetical case was suggested as an alternative to showing actual documents.

Neil was asked who he would need to help. The people selected were picked for competence and loyalty by Topping, Rosenthal and Gold. (One reporter was rejected because his wife was a "peacenik," he wasn't considered discreet and she might talk.) The group then turned to the question of where the team would work. Washington was determined as inappropriate. Tarrytown and Charlottesville were considered before the Hilton Hotel was finally decided upon. Millones obtained a suite in the name of the *Times* before the day was over. (The rooms were actually in Gold's name.) The bills went to Millones and then directly to the Chief Accountant, McCabe. Typewriters, filing cabinets, a safe and other supplies were obtained by Millones.

On April 22nd Gold and Neil, having returned to D.C., packed and returned to New York where they checked into the Hilton and began work. They had with them two working copies of the materials. The third set, which had been at 229 West 43rd Street, was moved to Greenfield's apartment at Rosenthal's direction as Goodale wanted it out of the *Times* building.

During the next month work began, additional people joined the Hilton group and the pressure to meet deadlines started to build.

On Friday, April 23, Abe Rosenthal made the first entry in his journal about what had been going on all week:

Journal—April 23, 1971

This paper is now involved in one of the biggest, most voluminous and probably one of the saddest and most damaging stories it has ever confronted journalistically. And yet I believe that we all agree at this point that we must publish.

I will have to be elliptical as I dictate this, because even though the confidentiality of my secretaries is beyond question, nobody can guarantee the security of the files, and the lives of men are involved.

We have total access to a vast collection of documentation relating to the decision and conduct of the war. I am dictating this now simply because I want to record some of the thinking and discussion that went into our decision to go ahead and put ourselves in a position to publish—to prepare the stories and the documentation. At this point there is still a 10 percent chance that for reasons as between the reporter and his sources that we might not be able to publish. We will face that when we come to it.

As far as I know, there is no question of the military security of the United States involved. If such information does crop up as we proceed, we will delete it. We are all agreed on that.

The documents are of the highest degree of government security classification. But the security was imposed not to protect the military security of the United States but to protect the political decisions and the political reputations and the political thinking of the men in high government places involved. I do not really feel that we have a moral dilemma here. I believe that the public's right to know what took place is of a far higher order of priority than the protection of the reputation of the statesmen and politicians involved.

Furthermore, we know that this documentation is known to a very small group of former top officials of the United States, including President Johnson and McNamara and Clifford and Bundy. We also know that government officials, once they leave office, use documents and studies of this sort to write their own version of history. The difference is that they include only what makes them look good or buttresses their point of view.

We have a task force working in a New York hotel on this massive story. It consists of Neil Sheehan, who got the story and is at its center, Jerry Gold and Al Siegal as editors trying to block it out and put it into shape, [and] young Fox Butterfield as a researcher and a secretary. It's under the personal supervision of James Greenfield, our foreign editor, and Topping and I will move in directly as the story begins to take shape.[80]

Over the next two months, Sheehan deceived Ellsberg into believing that the *Times* was indecisive about how to handle the Papers. Sheehan told Ellsberg he'd gotten sidetracked on other things—that bothersome Kissinger deadline. Neither was true.

Meanwhile, like almost everyone else at the newspaper, Sheehan's editors at the *Times Magazine* were oblivious to what was going on. Bergman just wanted Sheehan's Kissinger story, now about twelve months overdue. His request was dripping with sarcasm, imagining a scenario in which, just as Sheehan was at long last finishing the piece, Kissinger had lost the power struggle with his longtime rival, Secretary of State William Rogers, mooting Sheehan's story:

> Memorandum for: Neil Sheehan—Washington Bureau
> From: Lewis Bergman
> April 28, 1971
>
> Scenario Number 41. June 15, 1971. Nixon in Peking announced nonaggression pact with the People's Republic of China. In Washington, Neil Sheehan called away from his typewriter, which has page 7 of his manuscript on Kissinger in it, to listen to Secretary Rogers' announcement that Kissinger has been made charge d'affaires in Liechtenstein.
>
> Come on, Neil, before it's too late. Can you give us an honest and firm deadline for delivery of the Kissinger?
>
> Sincerely,
> Lewis Bergman
> Editor
> *The New York Times Magazine*[81]

CHAPTER 10

Shadows

Averell Harriman had been LBJ's man at the Paris peace talks in 1968, sent over after LBJ announced he wouldn't run for reelection. Following Nixon's inauguration, Harriman returned to his Georgetown mansion; his second wife, Marie, died the next year.

In the summer of '71, Harriman, comfortably rich from his forebears' Gilded Age interests in railroads and banking, yet chafing at his outsider's status—since the Democrats no longer had the White House—operated a kind of shadow diplomatic operation from his Georgetown living room. His diplomatic experience had spanned Europe, Russia, and Southeast Asia, and he seemed genuinely to want to help Nixon and Kissinger on each of those fronts—and certainly to extricate America from its involvement in Vietnam. After-meeting notes by Harriman show he was mostly frustrated in his efforts, though he kept up his connections and occasionally sent off letters to Nixon and Kissinger suggesting options for diplomatic breakthroughs: in Europe, for the reunification of East and West Germany; in Vietnam, for a way to achieve a principled end to the war.

J. Edgar Hoover's agents kept an eye on the N Street mansion's assorted comings and goings of visiting exiles, expats, and potentates. Hoover himself occasionally passed along to Nixon intelligence about Harriman's efforts, gathered from an expanding web of FBI wiretaps.

That summer, Harriman's visitors included: the West German chancellor, Willy Brandt; South Vietnamese politician

Dang Duc Khoi; JFK's former press secretary, Pierre Salinger; various U.S. senators and congressmen; longtime Soviet Communist Party adviser Georgy Arbatov; Soviet Ambassador to the United States, Anatoly Dobrynin; LBJ's Vietnam hawk McGeorge Bundy, now the Ford Foundation president; South Vietnamese Ambassador to the United States, Bui Diem; and South Vietnamese senators Don van Sung and Tran von Don, the latter whom Harriman had known since the Diem coup; and French diplomats secretly acting as intermediaries in the Paris peace talks. The foreign envoys passing through town invariably hoped that Harriman could be a back channel to Nixon and Kissinger. Harriman kept in touch with Kissinger.

Indeed, Kissinger cannily used Harriman when it served his purpose—sometimes just to give the impression of listening to or seeking Harriman's advice when, in fact, he wanted nothing more than to stifle it.

One of Kissinger's aides bumped into Kissinger and Harriman at the White House mess, which was Kissinger's favored place for a working lunch. When Harriman left, the aide asked Kissinger what they talked about. "I urged the governor (Harriman had served a term as New York's governor, and preferred that title to any other) not to denounce our actions in Vietnam. I told him that if he held off, I would urge the president to appoint him as the U.S. government's Vietnam peace negotiator again, when the time came."

The aide knew there was no chance of that ever happening. He gave the Kissinger tactic a nickname. When Kissinger promised something that could never, ever happen, that was "a Harriman."

Saturday, May 22, 1971

This was the weekend that the LBJ Library would be dedicated on the campus of the University of Texas at Austin. Johnson was ailing; he'd suffered a heart attack the year before, and his friends worried about him. Harriman didn't want to miss seeing the ex-president who had trusted him with the Paris peace talks. Lyndon's wife, Lady Bird, promised a barbeque at the ranch of movie mogul Arthur Krim,[1] and apologized for the unprepossessing accommodations during the busy weekend—the best she could do for Harriman was a room in a dorm near the campus.

> Austin is long on hospitality but short on good hotel space and so we are suggesting that some of our special friends with adventurous spirits be housed together in Hardin House, a new girls' apartment-dormitory near the University of Texas campus. You may find a left-over poster or two, but frankly I think you'll have fun in your "personal campus weekend."

Abe Fortas and Hubert Humphrey, and their wives, would be roughing it with Harriman.

You'll find friends all around you, Lady Bird added in a handwritten postscript, *and it will be just like a house party.* Nixon and his wife, Pat, would be there.

Antiwar protests were planned. The Austin police made arrests and did their utmost to keep the violence out of view. LBJ sent a warm letter to Nixon on June 1: *In the fullness of time perhaps you can throw [*sic*] me around the Richard M. Nixon Library at its opening.*

Johnson would not live that long. In less than two years, he would be dead at age sixty-four.

When Harriman learned that his old friend and China hand, Chester Ronning, had scored an invitation to the People's Republic of China, Harriman pestered him for help. Western visitors had to be officially invited, and the United States was off-limits because it still recognized Taiwan as the official government. But the country was showing signs of opening to the West, and Harriman was keen to get there. Ronning, born in China of missionary parents and fluent in Chinese, was widely regarded as Canada's leading expert on China. Working closely with Harriman, he'd been a go-between with North Vietnam during the early Paris peace talks. Harriman sent a cable to Ronning in Peking, via the Canadian Embassy in Washington. The cable used the spelling of Premier Zhou Enlai's name that was accepted at the time:

> HAVE BEEN ATTEMPTING SINCE 1959 TO GET PERMISSION TO VISIT CHINA. HAVE RECENTLY APPLIED AGAIN. WOULD BE GRATEFUL IF YOU COULD SAY KIND WORD TO PREMIER CHOU EN-LAI AS I AM MOST ANXIOUS TO COME AS SOON AS POSSIBLE. WOULD BE ACCOMPANIED BY TWO PERSONAL COLLEAGUES. WARMEST REGARDS.[2]

One of the "personal colleagues" likely would have been his renewed love interest, Pamela Digby Churchill Hayward. The two had been wartime lovers, when Pamela was the teenage bride of Randolph Churchill, and Harriman was a dashing wartime diplomat bedding Pamela in London while Randolph was fighting the war.[3] When her second husband, Hollywood mogul Leland Hayward, died the previous March, Pamela wasted no time reconnecting—although, initially, she made a play for Frank Sinatra. Sinatra was a longtime friend of Leland and Pamela's; and after Leland's passing, Sinatra (divorced from Pamela's friend Mia Farrow) invited Pamela to his Palm Springs home for "a rest." They hung out, played backgammon. The gossip columns took note. Pamela ordered a giant marble backgammon table custom made in Portugal, and had it shipped to Sinatra in Los Angeles as a gift.[4] But the romance fizzled. By May, Pamela had returned to the apartment that she and Leland kept at 575 Park Avenue, on New York's Upper East Side. And, by September, she would marry Harriman.

Harriman wanted his new bride to meet LBJ. They visited Johnson at his ranch before the Christmas holidays the following year. Harriman wrote an encouraging letter to Johnson after the visit, commending him about being: *fit and vigorous as ever [and] taking an interest in everything that's going on. Never having been to Texas before, Pam was, of course, fascinated and much impressed with everything. After all, there is only one Texas!*

But privately, Harriman expressed deep concern about the state of Johnson's health. The former president was on oxygen for his angina.

Johnson also confided something to Harriman during the visit. The former president was a conspiracy theorist when it came to the assassination that elevated him to the presidency. It was a stunning admission. Johnson flat out told Harriman that he did not believe the conclusion of the Warren Commission that Kennedy assassin Lee Harvey Oswald acted alone.

Harriman wrote up Johnson's confession immediately after the visit: *LBJ said he was convinced Oswald was tied in with Castro to get even over the Bay of Pigs. Oswald had been in Cuba not too long before the assassination.*[5]

Harriman made a note to himself to check the date of Oswald's supposed visit, but there is no evidence that he later did that. If Harriman had checked, he would have found that Oswald obtained a visa, a month before the assassination, to immigrate to Cuba. But Oswald apparently never traveled there.

It was the last (and perhaps only) time the two spoke about the assassination. Johnson died six weeks later.

When Ronning returned from China in June, he delivered unwelcome news. Mao and Zhou Enlai were intrigued by the idea of meeting Harriman and his entourage, but they weren't going to invite Harriman or any other official delegation from the United States just yet. In Harriman's retelling of his conversation[6] with Ronning, it's clear, in retrospect, just how little Beijing has budged from the position it expressed over a half century ago. Harriman memorialized his conversation with Ronning:

> The major issue between the United States and Peking (as Beijing was called at the time) is Taiwan. It would not be sufficient for us to take our troops out. We would have to stand aside and let relations between Peking and Taipei be settled entirely by the Chinese themselves. I said "What about our treaty against forceful takeover? We, of course, would agree to any arrangements made voluntarily for reunification or continued independence." He said we would have to trust them. We would have to renounce our treaty and break all diplomatic relations with Taipei just as the Canadians had done. I asked if we were to end all trade and pointed to Japan. He said we could trade without representation, as the Canadians were doing.
>
> I didn't pursue the subject further, as I want him to continue to help me get invited to Peking. He made it plain what we would have to do or, as he said, there would be no agreement between us.[7]

A delegation of French diplomats visited Harriman at N Street a week later[8] with back-channel messages from Hanoi (the United States needed to stop the bombing and get serious about the Paris negotiations) and Beijing (nothing positive would happen unless the United States stopped blocking China's entry into the United Nations). The French diplomats conveyed the Chinese side's position on the UN; if the United States stopped using its veto on China, "China would regard this as a very positive step and our relations would improve even without mutual recognition." As to the latter, Harriman was skeptical. "It would be unthinkable," Harriman told the French, "for the United States to abandon its defense commitments to Taiwan."

Still, Harriman persevered, and he wasn't alone in seeking favor with the Chinese. As Ronning had signaled to Harriman the week before, in their phone call, the Chinese were "concentrating on newspapermen"—shrewdly using the American news media to send their own signals. The first two invitations had already gone to the *Times*: in April to the newspaper's China specialist, Tillman Durdin, and the next to Rosenthal's deputy, Seymour Topping, who would sit down on May 20 with Zhou for two-and-a-half hours in the Great Hall of the People.

But there was hope for a Nixon visit. The U.S. ping-pong team had been invited to the Mainland, and when they arrived on April 14, Zhou told them, "You have opened a new page in the relations of the Chinese and American people." Nixon sent a signal back to China the same day by easing some controls on shipping, currency, and travel with China. Two days later, Nixon told a group of newspaper editors that he wanted to visit China. "As a matter of fact, I hope sometime I do."[9]

Two weeks later, Nixon received encouraging news.

On April 27, Premier Zhou Enlai, responding to a December 1970 message from the president that had been delivered to Beijing through the Pakistani government, sent a message to Nixon via the Pakistani ambassador. It was a signal that China would be willing to receive publicly a high-level representative from the United States, such as Kissinger or Rogers, or even Nixon himself.[10]

This message immediately triggered a phone call between Nixon, who was at his home in California, and Kissinger over who should go. Nixon wanted complete secrecy. During the call, Nixon was, as he put it, "thinking out loud" about sending a statesman with gravitas—someone with sufficiently prestigious name recognition to the Chinese. Other criteria Nixon mentioned: The emissary would have to be a reliable order-taker, sticking closely to the White House instructions on how to handle this first important step. And, finally, Nixon's ideal candidate was someone whose absence wouldn't be a matter of speculation among the curious Washington press corps.

Nixon knew that Governor Nelson Rockefeller, of New York, his challenger for the 1968 Republican nomination, was a Kissinger ally; in fact, Kissinger had been Rockefeller's chief foreign policy adviser during the campaign. So Nixon floated Rockefeller's name to get a reaction. Interestingly, Kissinger cagily batted it down; he couldn't have two masters. As the twenty-minute conversation went on, the conversation steered toward Kissinger, who might have been Nixon's first choice all along. The call took place on Tuesday, April 27, at 8:16 p.m.[11]:

> NIXON: Let me just throw a real wild one out. How about Nelson [Rockefeller]?
>
> KISSINGER: No.
>
> NIXON: Can't do it, huh?
>
> KISSINGER: Well, he wouldn't be disciplined enough.
>
> NIXON: He's outside of government, you see.
>
> KISSINGER: I might be able to hold him in check.
>
> NIXON: And the idea being that he's not there to love the Chinese, but for the purpose of getting something done for us. I mean, the war and all. See? It's intriguing. I mean, if we're going to go close, then you have the [Secretary of State] Rogers problem. On Nelson, just thinking it out loud, you have a man who's, you know, I mean, that the Chinese would consider him important. And he would be. Of course, [chuckles] we know Nelson's sort of a wild hare when he gets running around, and he'd get some silly staff with him.* That's the problem that I see with him.
>
> KISSINGER: Well, I'd think for one operation I could keep him under control.
>
> NIXON: Let's just put it in the back of your head and keep it.
>
> KISSINGER: Nelson has possibilities.
>
> NIXON: He's a possibility, yeah. That, of course, [chuckles] that would drive [the Department of] State up

---

*Whether intentional or not, this was a backhanded dig at Kissinger, a longtime Rockefeller protégé.

the wall, but they couldn't really complain a hell of a lot about that.

KISSINGER: Well, Mr. President, you made it possible.

NIXON: We have played a game, and we've gotten a little break here. We were hoping we'd get one, and I think we have one now.

KISSINGER: [Speaking about Rockefeller] He'd do what I tell him on this. For one operation, you know. For a long period, he'd be hard to keep under control. But for one operation he'd follow his script.

The conversation meandered. Kissinger contrasted the Chinese with the Russians:

KISSINGER: The difference between them and the Russians is that if you drop some loose change and try to pick it up, the Russians step on your fingers and fight you for it; the Chinese don't do that. And I've reviewed all the communications with them. And all of it has been on a high level. I mean, if here you look at the summit exchange, they haven't horsed around like the Russians. And compared to what the game was, the Russians squeezing us on every bloody move [President Nixon agrees] has been just stupid.

I've never said this before. I've never given it more than one in three. I think if we get this thing working, we'll end Vietnam this year. [Pause. President Nixon exhales.] The mere fact of these contacts is one of—

NIXON: Haig was pretty pleased, was he?

KISSINGER: Oh, yes. If anyone had predicted that two months ago, we would have thought it inconceivable.

NIXON: Yeah, yeah. That's what I mean. What is really intriguing about this is that after Laos, when these bastards were all saying, "Well, this broke it off with the Chinese and their—"

KISSINGER: Cambodia, they were saying the same thing.

NIXON: Yeah. But here comes Laos, though. Let's look at that one, where, after Laos, when the people over 2-to-1 think it failed and all of that, you know, they've had all the polls show that, and so forth, and we know that. And yet, here comes a Chinese move, the ping-pong team, and now something that is so much more significant.[12]

Nixon eventually decided Kissinger was the man to send over first. In effect, this settled the jockeying between Kissinger and Secretary of State Rogers. The two men were bitter rivals, each vying for primacy when it came to setting American foreign policy and speaking for the administration. Although both denied the rivalry, Kissinger had once bluntly confided to Safire, "If Rogers doesn't knuckle under, I go. You and Haldeman don't think I'm serious about this, but I mean it."[13] Nixon's decision made clear that Kissinger was the winner.

Planning for the mission began in complete secrecy. Even Rogers did not know about it, and he wouldn't be told until Kissinger returned from China.[14] ("I won't give Rogers anything," Kissinger promised at the time.[15]) Later, when Nixon got blindsided by the Pentagon Papers, he would be glad he'd chosen Kissinger for the assignment. No leaks.

Friday, May 7, 1971, 2:50 p.m.

Kissinger needed a trusted go-between to ferry messages and signals back and forth to the Chinese, via the Pakistanis. He ordered the U.S. ambassador, a crusty former FBI agent named Joseph Farland, to fly to the West Coast from Islamabad. No reason for the trip was given.

Kissinger was, in essence, off the grid for the meeting; he was hiding out with his security detail at the Palm Springs home of a wealthy Republican businessman, Theodore Cummings. Kissinger used a secret cable back channel, rather than the official

State Department system, to send the message to Farland. To further disguise Farland's tracks, and his own whereabouts, Kissinger arranged for a private jet to take the ambassador to Palm Springs. Farland, always the curious FBI agent, noted that the ashtrays on the jet had a familiar name on them: *Frank Sinatra*.

Kissinger met Farland on the patio, drink in hand, wearing short sleeves. In a three-hour meeting, the two cooked up an elaborate scheme to smuggle Kissinger into China via Pakistan. The plan was for Kissinger to announce a mission to various countries—a fact-finding tour through Asia (including Vietnam, Thailand, India, Pakistan), concluding in Paris, France—and then to become "sick" after he arrived in Pakistan. The cover story would be that Kissinger was ill and resting for a few days. Kissinger would arrive in a larger aircraft, which would remain parked on the tarmac while Kissinger was ferried to a smaller, pre-positioned plane at a military base nearby, with a Pakistani navigator. (On the day of the flight, the Boeing actually had two Chinese pilots and a Chinese navigator in the cockpit. "That scared a couple of the small group nearly to death, including the Secret Service men who were with us," Farland said.) The smaller aircraft would take Kissinger over the Himalayas to China, while the larger one parked on the tarmac was "proof" that Kissinger was still in Pakistan.

Tuesday, June 1, 1971

At 8:30 p.m., Nixon held a half-hour prime-time news conference in the East Room.[16] He favored these evening events: It meant a bigger audience, and they suited the style of this politician who limited those he dealt one-on-one with, and who favored the staged over the impromptu. Questions reflected the issues of the day.

There was a drug problem among soldiers returning from Vietnam. Fifteen percent of U.S. soldiers in Vietnam were addicted to heroin. It was cheap and plentiful there. Nixon blamed the Saigon government for letting this happen. He announced more drug-addiction help for the vets.

Marijuana was illegal in the United States, but it was as widely available at home as heroin was in Vietnam. A questioner asked about legalizing it, and Nixon was ready: There's no moral or social justification. That would only encourage more youths "to start down that long, dismal road that leads to hard drugs and eventually self-destruction."

Russia and China were familiar tropes for Nixon. He knocked Russia and cautioned its leaders against a "new arms race." And China was knocking on the UN's door. It was tricky, threading the needle between China and Russia. Nixon said he was open to considering membership for the Communist regime there. What he didn't say was that Kissinger had been making secret entreaties to Zhou Enlai, leader of the Chinese Communist Party.

A surprise was coming.

The China trip was still top secret; not even Secretary of State Rogers knew about it. Farland and Kissinger had earlier discussed whether the Chinese should meet him halfway, in Pakistan. But Farland counseled that was too risky. The Chinese and the Pakistanis would have eyes and ears on Kissinger and his small entourage every minute, but being wiretapped by the Chinese represented the lesser of two evils. As Kissinger summarized it days later in a *Top Secret/Sensitive/Eyes Only* memo for Nixon, Farland said "it would be better to be taped by the Chinese than the Pakistanis."

Farland picked up the story from the point he arrived in Palm Springs[17]:

> I got to the house and saw some big men standing around. They looked like Secret Service people. I saw Henry was out on the patio with a drink in his hand. He was in a sport shirt and was relaxed. I was anything but relaxed. I said, "Henry, I've come halfway around this damn earth and I don't know why." He said, "I want you to put me into China."

> I said, "I don't think that's very funny, Henry."
>
> He said, "It's not funny. You know it. Haig knows it. Nixon knows it. I know it."
>
> I said, "I didn't ask for this job." He said, "You are going to do it."
>
> I said something about "Don't be so damned dictatorial. I'm not up to that yet." We talked for a while. I calmed down a bit. It was still exasperating in no uncertain terms. I said, "Look, Henry, you fly west of K2, the Russians are going to pick you up on their radar. There is no question about this. If you fly east of the K2, the Indians have got you pegged. How are you going to get into China?" He said, "That is for you to figure out."

Kissinger's secret mission to China would have to wait until July, after the dust from the Pentagon Papers had settled. But the trickery had worked. Zhou's first words to the small entourage that arrived with Kissinger mocked the elaborate backstory Kissinger had fabricated: *There is special news this afternoon: You are lost!*

And then came an offer of hospitality; cigarettes, politely declined.

Zhou: *No one wants one? I have found a party that doesn't smoke!*

Kissinger and his aides stayed in a Chinese government guesthouse. The talks went on for two more days, long discussions about normalizing relations and trade, and the sticking point: Taiwan.

When Kissinger returned on July 13 to San Clemente from China via Paris, the last scheduled stop on his itinerary, the reporters traveling with the president were way off base with their prying questions to Press Secretary Ron Ziegler about what Kissinger had been up to.

"We hear secondhand that he is having dinner with Jill St. John," one reporter asked.

Ziegler: "I would prefer to let Henry speak on his own in relation to his activities in Paris this evening." (Laughter)

"Is Jill St. John in Paris?"

Ziegler: "I would not know her schedule."

On Thursday, July 15, at 7:30 p.m. West Coast time, Nixon, shuttled by Marine One to the NBC Studios in Burbank, announced Kissinger's breakthrough to China. In the vernacular of the day, Nixon was tanned, rested and ready,[18] and decided to walk out to the camera rather than having the shot open with him behind a lectern. The president told the nation that he would visit China soon. "There can be no stable and enduring peace without the participation of the People's Republic of China." Later, Nixon exulted that no one saw this coming.

Haldeman, once and always an advertising exec, thought Nixon still had some selling to do back in Washington. He wrote in his diary:

> We're going to appear to be letting our friends down, and they will object. Also, the liberals, on the other side, will make the Tricky Dick claim, and will complain that there was no consultation with Congress.

Oh . . . and Treasury Secretary John Connally called Haldeman at the studio and threatened to resign. Nixon couldn't afford to lose Connally; he would be playing the central role in a drama to come: the imposition of wage and price controls to fight inflation.

Haldeman related that story to his diary as well:

> He had been told that we had hired a new Treasurer of the U.S. and that this had been done without consulting him.* We had hired this Mexican woman. And this got Connally extremely upset. And he said that he, as a result of this, and other things, was going to check

*That was true. In nominating Romana Acosta Bañuelos, Nixon was hoping to make inroads among Latino voters in his reelection campaign after a poor showing with them in his 1968 election. See https://www.nytimes.com/2018/02/05/obituaries/romana-acosta-banuelos-us-treasurer-under-nixon-dies-at-92.html

> out—in other words, resign. . . . He said that he just wasn't going to tolerate this kind of thing; that obviously it's forecasting what's to come; that these things build up; and he can see it coming and went into the point that he was not a peon and was not going to function as a slave to the White House staff; and that he knows when he's got a problem, when [Secretary of State Bill] Rogers is out here knifing him with the President, referring to him as a "gunboat diplomat," et cetera. . . . Once again, I get to do the dirty work.

When Kissinger got back to Washington, he was greeted by Pete Peterson, another of the president's advisers, in this case for international economic affairs. Peterson, forty-five years old, had been chairman and CEO of Bell & Howell, and was being groomed for commerce secretary. Kissinger had him figured out. "We were both considered to be promising young men. Some commentators predicted a grim bureaucratic struggle." Instead, they became unlikely friends, a kind of two-man White House comedy act for a bemused Washington press corps.[19]

"It's marvelous to have something to congratulate you for other than your presumed sexual experiences," Peterson chided.

Kissinger was always quick to return a quip, using diplomatic lingo. He put on a Groucho Marx leer: "Ah, but I'm a believer in the linkage theory."[20]

CHAPTER 11

Secrets

SHEEHAN KEPT TRYING TO WEAR down Ellsberg, trying to get Ellsberg to "give" him permission to copy and publish the full seven-thousand-page set of the Papers—and not telling Ellsberg that this was, in fact, going to happen regardless. To apply added pressure, Sheehan reminded Ellsberg that there was a de facto deadline for a decision, since the IPS trio of Raskin, Barnet, and Stavins already had a thousand pages of the Papers, and they had a book coming out.

In fact, as the world now knows because the story has been told over and over in some excellent works that you'll find in this book's bibliography, Sheehan and a growing group of editors and reporters were working feverishly toward a blockbuster series of stories featuring the documents that Sheehan had taken from Ellsberg.

As the date for publication neared, Sheehan still hadn't told Ellsberg the truth about how he had taken the Papers from Ellsberg's apartment and then copied them, and that the *Times* soon would begin publishing its blockbuster series. This preyed on Sheehan; he had pledged to his editors to resolve the situation with Ellsberg before the series began. Pressure was building, as Rogovin recounted in his 1971 legal memo:

> In the meantime, Neil was still unable to get permission from the source and more and more people outside of the *Times* became aware of the project. In addition, Congressman McCloskey now had portions of the

> papers. To compound the pressure, Neil was told at a dinner meeting at Greenfield's home that Louis Loeb thought that "publication was illegal." During the period, Neil sent one of the secretaries, Muriel Stokes, to Washington to deliver some materials to Susan who, in turn, gave them to IPS. On May 26th Neil finished his first piece and delivered it to Rosenthal's wife.

The significance of the return of the thousand pages to IPS soon would be clear. Sheehan was about to claim to legitimately have a full set of the Papers, no strings attached. He could give back the IPS subset and, in effect, rescind any promise previously made.

Sheehan had been coming up with various excuses to keep Ellsberg warm to the idea of collaborating with the *Times*, and to ensure that Ellsberg didn't leak them to another newspaper. Now, two-and-a-half weeks before the *Times* intended to drop the first part of the series, Sheehan wanted to put himself on the right side of what he'd promised his editors, and also extricate himself from a journalistic dilemma. Sheehan decided to seek what he referred to as "a moral release—in my mind."[1]

Sheehan did not tell Ellsberg his real intentions—or his real motive.

Thursday, May 27, 1971

Ellsberg's wife, Patricia, was the daughter of a famous toy mogul named Louis Marx. She had a trust fund, and a posh Sutton Place apartment in Manhattan. On Thursday, May 27, Sheehan left what he called his submarine-like[2] quarters at the Hilton and visited the couple's elegant Sutton Place apartment.

When Sheehan left the apartment, he did so with a set of the Pentagon Papers—his *third*, although as far as Ellsberg knew, it was Sheehan's first time possessing the Papers.

Ellsberg had finally relented and given Sheehan permission to possess a complete set of the Papers.

But did Ellsberg know what was coming next? Had Ellsberg given "official permission" to publish? According to Sheehan's later notes, the answer was no. Even though Ellsberg had handed over a set of the Papers, he still had no idea what Sheehan and the *Times* were up to, and thus couldn't possibly have given explicit approval for the *Times* to proceed with publishing.

In the moment, Sheehan chose to ignore that moral dilemma, and he steadfastly refused to talk about it during his lifetime. As far as Sheehan was concerned, on that day, May 27, he finally had his "moral release," and there was no further need to equivocate. "A moral release in my mind" was the term Sheehan used.

Rogovin's memo to the files was unequivocal as to what he called Sheehan's "official permission." As Rogovin saw it, Sheehan had given the *Times* the ethical and legal cover the paper required. Rogovin related it this way:

> On May 27th Neil's source gave him "official permission" to possess the papers. Neil moved them to the Hilton that night. An inventory of these materials revealed some important pieces were missing—probably given to Congressman McCloskey.

Tuesday, June 1, 1971

With Sheehan's affirmation of receiving "official permission" from Ellsberg, now it fell to Abe Rosenthal to seek final permission to begin publishing the Pentagon Papers series. Approval was needed from publisher A. O. "Punch" Sulzberger:

> CONFIDENTIAL
> Mr. Sulzberger
> Mr. Reston
> June 1, 1971
> As you will see, the whole series follows some rather decided philosophical and journalistic ground rules.

> What we are presenting is the Pentagon version of the war and its origins. What our reporters have contributed is the essential task of selecting the essence of 7,000 single-spaced pages of Pentagon analysis and documentation and presented it in a sequential and logical manner.
>
> This is not the *New York Times* history, I emphasize, but the *New York Times*'s report on the Pentagon's history—and this is what makes it far different and far more significant, in my opinion, than previously published material.
>
> *A. M. R.*[3]

As far as is known, Sheehan never publicly revealed the moral and ethical dilemma that he had resolved, in his mind, by somehow persuading Ellsberg that the time was finally right for the *Times* to possess the full set of the Pentagon Papers. But Sheehan was an inveterate note scribbler, and he later penned a detailed account that confirmed what happened. The notes show how Sheehan eventually told the truth, *to himself*, about what he had done.

Sheehan had been asked point-blank about the May 27 episode by Harrison Salisbury, the venerable *Times* foreign correspondent who was, some years later, working on a weighty memoir/history of the newspaper titled *Without Fear or Favor*. Salisbury was doing his own original reporting for a chapter about the Pentagon Papers—and, of course, he had been talking to Ellsberg. The subtitle of Salisbury's book was *An Uncompromising Look at the* New York Times, which really was all you needed to know about Salisbury's intentions as a reporter. He was trying to get to the bottom of what happened that day between Ellsberg and Sheehan.

On sheets from a steno pad, Sheehan scrawled a note to himself about what he'd revealed to Salisbury, then stuck it away.

Salisbury had already interviewed Ellsberg. Ellsberg's memory turned out to be somewhat off as to the exact date; Ellsberg recollected that Sheehan's Sutton Place visit took place earlier, in April.

Sheehan, under questioning by Salisbury, once again proved wily. For one thing, Sheehan was willing to let Salisbury go with the approximate timing of the "moral release" deduced from other interviews, even though—as Sheehan's notes show—Sheehan knew the exact date all along. Sheehan held back the precise date in case he someday wanted to use it himself. But there was something else. Salisbury questioned the authenticity of Ellsberg's "moral release."

Sheehan knew Salisbury's reporting was solid—but to Salisbury he admitted nothing, because *Harrison is not quite clear in his doubt, however. He doesn't seem clear enough to write that, although he would be correct if he did.*

Here is what Sheehan's handwritten confessional recounted:

> Oct. 11, 1976
> DE-PPs 1971-72 & Epilogue
> Telecon—Harrison Salisbury.
>
> Harrison called me to straighten out when DE let me take a copy of PPs out of the NYC apt.
>
> At the beg[inning] of the conversation Harrison remarked that DE was a complicated character "but then you're (Sheehan) not so simple either" which may be more indication of what he is going to say about me.
>
> Dan E. told him: "Neil came to see me at my NY apt, prob[ably] in early April. He said he was working on something else" but he wanted me to let him take away a copy so that he could work on it. I let him have one.
>
> "I'd always before said he couldn't take one out, unless the decision had been made to publish." Dan was specifically referring to a decision by the *NYT* to publish, but he also made clear to Harrison that he had always considered turning over a copy to me as permis-

sion from him to publish & that's what he was consciously giving me.

Gerry Gold [assistant foreign editor and Sheehan's earliest compatriot at the Hilton] believed it was in the third week in May, so Harrison doubted DE's timing.

Harrison to me: Since I already had a copy of the PP's why was I seeking a second copy? I said to him: "I was seeking a moral release in my mind."

Harrison: "That is now the way he (DE) understands it. He now believes he gave me the moral release" at that time. Harrison went on to say that DE now believes he consciously gave me permission to publish in releasing a set to me at that time.

Harrison remarked that DE has "a way of neatly tidying thing up in his mind" after the fact, which is why Harrison doubted the chronology DE gave of April. Harrison also doubts whether DE actually was conscious that he was going to give me a moral release, that is permission to publish, when he turned over a set of the PP's to me from the NY apartment. Harrison is not quite clear in his doubt, however. He doesn't seem clear enough to write that, although he would be correct if he did.

What Harrison is writing on the PP's in his history of the *NYT*: The PP's are an opening of a whole new era in the role of journalism in which the *Times* and other newspapers turned from being a mirror of American society & the institution in it to becoming a moving force in American society. I am one character in that story. I am a character in it because I am the instigator, but I am only one character in Harrison's story. There are others who he thinks equally important, partic[ularly] Abe. Harrison says that I am a hero but only one of his heroes.

Harrison believes that I had a moral imperative to go ahead, copy the PP's & get them published by the

NYT despite lack of permission from DE. He said others feel the same way he does.

Harrison asked if DE ever was going to write about the PP's. I said no. . . . [Years later, Ellsberg did write a book about his role with the Papers.]

I told Harrison that DE let me take the set of papers out of the NYC apt. during the second half of May. Harrison said Gerry Gold remembers the third week of May. I told Harrison I would have no quarrel with that & he could write it. But actually that is wrong, since the precise date is May 27, which I did not give Harrison bec[ause] I want to use it myself, & so I will write Harrison tonight & tell him to date the act as occurring sometime during the second half of May.

Harrison said he does not believe his history of the *NYT* will conflict w/ my work in the sense of exposing material I want to use. He thinks it will be complementary bec[ause] he will not go into the details I will have to go into.[4]

Memorandum from: Sunday Department
6/2/71
Neil:

This is just to let you know that the Kissinger profile has definitely been reassigned.

nb[5]

Rogovin's memo showed that Sheehan's declaration of "official approval" cleared the last hurdle:

By June 6th Neil finished his second piece. The possibility that McCloskey leaked the papers he had to the *Los Angeles Times* had, by this time, placed still further pressure on the group. Phelps reported back on the second of his two visits with McCloskey—that the Congressman heard the *Times* was "working on something" and that he would not turn over what he had to another paper.

Around that time Greenfield came over to report the publisher's decision regarding publication. At 6:00 p.m., June 12th the presses began rolling.

Saturday, June 12, 1971

Tricia woke up to a note from her father placed under her door, wishing her well. *Today is the day you begin a long and exciting journey,* he wrote. *You have made the right choice.*

But Nixon was worried. And, at least for a day, not about affairs of state.

Would it rain?

Skies threatened. Pat and Julie told him not to worry, they could bring the event inside; that was always the contingency plan. But Nixon was having none of that. Tricia wanted her wedding to take place outside. She would be the first presidential daughter ever to be married in the Rose Garden.

Ed Cox, a Harvard Law student from a prominent New York family, was Tricia's childhood sweetheart. Tricia would be trading the White House (she lived there with her parents, seldom leaving its safe confines) for life in Cambridge as a third-year law student's wife.

The press was gathered, staff was bustling, a huge cake was ready, and 398 guests were corralled in a big room just off the Rose Garden, waiting to take seats outside.

A drizzle began.

Upstairs in the family quarters, Nixon took a few steps out onto a balcony and looked up at the clouds, as if he could do something about them; as if he could disperse a gathering storm by sheer force of will.

Probably, at some level, he knew that would be futile—certainly as futile as trying to will away the forty thousand Mayday antiwar demonstrators who'd descended on Washington the month before. On this day, only a handful of Quakers gathered outside the Northwest Gate, across from Lafayette Park, praying and singing as they held a peace vigil. An elderly man walked over and told them, "Only divine intervention will stop the war."

The group waiting to take their seats was an interesting mashup, more Nixon's list than anyone else's[6]: Florida businessman and Nixon's close friend Bebe Rebozo was there, of course. Mamie Eisenhower. J. Edgar Hoover, sans Clyde Tolson. The reverends Billy Graham and Norman Vincent Peale. Most of Nixon's cabinet. Agnew and his wife, Judy, with two of their children. And there were a few Hollywood names that Nixon felt at home with: Red Skelton, Art Linkletter, and Freeman Gosden, creator of the original *Amos 'n' Andy* radio show. (Gosden, who was white, voiced Amos and fifteen other Black characters on the show.)

Cox's family had been Republican royalty in New York for generations, but Ed's guest list reached across the aisle. During the summer of 1968, fresh out of Princeton and headed to Harvard Law, Cox had been one of the original seven Nader's Raiders* in Washington. So he added the original Raiders to the invitation list. Ralph Nader wore a suit, and his trademark combat boots.

Military officers who served as social aides in the White House were holding everybody in the South Hall in case the rain worsened and the ceremony moved indoors. But a weather report indicated that the drizzle would taper off in less than an hour.

Nixon, still fidgety, wanted to use the break to walk down to the press tent. He told Haldeman to come along. "Let's see what the setup is."

Haldeman, as chief of staff, was seldom far from the president's side, and he knew what to expect. His boss saw the press

---

*A group of idealistic young lawyers, students, and activists who, starting in the late 1960s, worked under consumer advocate Ralph Nader to investigate federal agencies and corporate abuses. They exposed regulatory failures, published influential reports, and helped spark the modern consumer protection movement.

through a lens distorted by decades of mistrust and antagonism that crossed into outright loathing. The feeling was, for the most part, mutual. Even on a day like this one, Nixon couldn't put it behind him. There were hundreds of credentialed media covering the event, but the *Washington Post*'s reporters were banned. Nixon was feuding with the newspaper.

"They're screwing us. We know it. And we'll handle it," Nixon brooded to Haldeman about the press as they began walking. "Everything is loaded against us. Don't butter them up."

Ziegler fell in behind the two, and pool reporters joined. The group walked out the Southwest Gate and down to the South Lawn, where the press tent was. Reporters were still trying to figure out where the couple would honeymoon, and the gaggle peppered Nixon with questions. But Tricia, twenty-five, and Ed, twenty-four, wanted their destination to be a secret, and Nixon played along. "Wherever they're going, I won't be there." Although speculation had centered on the Caribbean, Haldeman figured that UPI's Helen Thomas had guessed—correctly—that the newlyweds would be going off alone to Camp David.

Barbara Walters was anchoring NBC's live coverage, along with Edwin Newman, a host as grumpy as she was ebullient. Half the country was tuned in to the wedding on various TV networks. Wind whipped, and the storm still threatened, but Walters remained peppy, upbeat. "Whenever there's a wedding like this, there are those who say, 'Oh, perhaps too much attention is being paid to it, and too much money being paid for it.' But why are we so interested? Well, it's historic. And it's a chance perhaps to see a little of the backstage gossip, to view the closest we have to tradition and royalty. To see the powerful in their off-guarded moments."

Once the rain ended, Nixon wanted to get things moving. The White House crew rushed to get the folding chairs outside; Nixon told them not to bother pulling the protective plastic off the carpet. "Stand up straight," Pat whispered to her husband as he prepared to walk Tricia down the aisle. Within eighteen minutes, the guests were back in the Blue Room for the reception.

Army and Marine bands provided the music, heavy on strings, harps, and flutes. Two Marine accordionists performed on military buses that shuttled guests from their hotels to and from the White House. The *Washington Post* estimated the wedding's cost—like the music, most of it billed to taxpayers—at $19,000 ($143,000 today).

An unsmiling Nader eyed the receiving line of Republicans, greeting and being greeted, and crossed his arms. No gladhanding the enemy. *Republicans everywhere,* he thought, *stereotypical in gesture, behavior, and appearance.* Finally reaching Nixon, Nader gave in, extending his hand and introducing himself.

"Ah, yes," the president replied. "Raider's Nader. We were just discussing you last evening because we had a defective toaster." Nader, always fast on his feet, had a wisecrack on the tip of his tongue—he would call the president "Nixon's Richard." But Nader quickly thought better of it. He just smiled and moved on.

Haldeman wrote about the event in his diary: *[Nixon] just wanted to get the chairs up, and the guests seated, and the thing underway. As it turned out, it worked out beautifully, and the whole thing was a sensational success.*

Nixon took turns on the dance floor, not only with Tricia, but also with Pat, Julie, Ike's widow, Mamie, and Lynda Robb, LBJ's daughter who'd also been a White House bride. The president had never danced in public, and never would again. "My parents were Quakers. They didn't believe in this sort of thing. Never again."

Lynda Robb, LBJ's daughter, replied that her father, "a backsliding Baptist," famously never missed a dance step.

Later that evening, NBC had a prime-time wedding special scheduled. Haldeman wrote in his diary:

> Julie wanted to watch the thing on TV. And the President said, "If you do, I'm going to have to leave." But we persuaded him to look at it on TV, on the NBC special which came on right at that time. He saw himself

> going down that aisle and made the comment that, "Well, at least I'm standing pretty straight." Obviously, the ladies in the family had been nagging him about standing up straight, and he was pleased to see himself looking pretty good. The TV was great, and he realized it. So it was a good thing that he did watch it, and I think that bucked him up, too. All in all, the whole thing was a sensational day.[7]

Nixon finally could catch a breath. He had, in effect, just finished watching his own home movie, in real time, on national television. And he liked what he saw. Any looming problems seemed far away.

Publication of the first installment of the Pentagon Papers in the Sunday *New York Times* of June 13, 1971, blindsided Ellsberg. As the presses began rolling in New York on Saturday night, Ellsberg and his wife, Patricia, were at the movies in Cambridge with Howard and Roz Zinn, seeing the Redford-Newman movie *Butch Cassidy and the Sundance Kid*, at the University Theater on Harvard Square. Howard was Dan's Mayday buddy. Ellsberg had seen the picture twice already; it was a favorite.

The first Ellsberg heard about the *Times* publishing the Pentagon Papers was when he received a phone call from Anthony Austin, an editor on the *Times Magazine*, whom Ellsberg had been helping on a book about Vietnam. Austin hadn't been part of the Pentagon Papers team; he was shocked. His book was "ruined."[8]

> Austin's book *The President's War*, publishing in a few weeks, was focused on LBJ's subterfuge about the Gulf of Tonkin. His reporting so impressed Ellsberg that Ellsberg let him use the relevant volume of the Papers that described the Tonkin Gulf incidents. Austin had a Pulitzer winner for sure, Ellsberg thought. But now,

> Austin was almost in tears. His book was ruined. The presses were rolling at the *Times*.[9]

So clueless was Ellsberg about the project that, still intent on getting someone in Congress to make the Papers public, he had plans to fly to DC on Monday to meet with another dovish senator, Mike Gravel (D-AK). The *Times* now forced Ellsberg underground. The FBI would soon be on to him.

Ellsberg tried to get in touch with Sheehan later that Saturday night to find out what was going on. Sheehan was at the Hilton, already on deadline for another Pentagon Papers installment. He ignored Ellsberg's messages until he knew it would be too late in the press run to intervene. He asked an editor to let him know when ten thousand copies had been printed.[10]

Ellsberg wouldn't be the only person who was blindsided.

Saturday, June 12, 1971, 11:00 p.m.

Ben Bagdikian was the assistant managing editor for national news at the *Washington Post*. Bagdikian had been invited to dinner that evening at the Watergate apartment of a friend. He excused himself at eleven o'clock to make his nightly call to the *Post*'s news desk, checking late news as well as the competition. "What do we have?" Bagdikian asked. The guy on the desk replied, "The *Times* is publishing secret papers on the history of the war in Vietnam."[11]

> Well, there are three papers that every politician in Washington reads. They read the *New York Times*, the *Washington Post*, and the *Wall Street Journal*. These were important papers and what we published would make a difference. [*Post* editor Ben] Bradlee hated to be beaten. So when my deputy said, "They're running these stories about the Pentagon Papers," I called Brad-

> lee right away and said, "Ben, we have to run that." And he said, "Yes, we've got to run it."
>
> We knew something was up. We knew it was a big story somewhere. And Bradlee was itchy. He's saying, "Call everybody you know. It apparently has something to do with RAND." That's as much as we knew. It had something to do with RAND. Bradlee thought it was probably an attack on Cuba. "Find out. Find out." So I called Harry Rowen [president of RAND].[12] I said, "Harry, apparently there's a big story that's going to run in the *Times* tomorrow, something about Cuba. Has RAND published anything that would be a big story?" He said, "Nothing I know of." I called other people I knew. They had no idea what it was going to be.

"So that was the beginning," Bagdikian recalled. "I immediately knew I had to do something."

The *Post*'s Sunday edition, sans any mention of the Papers, was already rolling off the presses in downtown DC. Bagdikian would be hustling to the *Post*'s newsroom first thing the next morning.

Sunday, June 13, 1971, 8:10 a.m.[13]

Nixon was up early Sunday morning and had breakfast with Rebozo, who'd stayed over in one of the White House guest rooms. Afterward, the two of them walked the short distance to the Old Executive Office Building next door. Nixon kept a hideaway office there, for when the bustle of the West Wing got to be too much. Nixon and Rebozo had lunch brought in.

Then Nixon made some calls. Vietnam was on his mind, but first he wanted to revisit the evening before. He wanted to hear Pat and Julie tell him again how good it was.

Nixon hadn't yet looked at the Sunday morning newspapers. What he didn't know about—yet—was the bombshell running in the *New York Times*, above the fold, opposite the big photo of him escorting Tricia into the Rose Garden.

The title of the series and the main headline were, as Rosenthal decreed, "as bland as possible"[14]—a conscious act of restraint so as not to overdramatize what the *Times* had done. Sheehan had the first byline:

> VIETNAM ARCHIVE: PENTAGON STUDY TRACES
> THREE DECADES OF GROWING U.S. INVOLVEMENT[15]
>
> A massive study of how the United States went to war in Indochina, conducted by the Pentagon three years ago, demonstrates that four administrations progressively developed a sense of commitment to a non-Communist Vietnam, a readiness to fight the North to protect the South, and an ultimate frustration with this effort—to a much greater extent than their public statements acknowledged at the time.
>
> The 3,000-page analysis, to which 4,000 pages of official documents are appended, was commissioned by Secretary of Defense Robert S. McNamara and covers the American involvement in Southeast Asia from World War II to mid-1968—the start of the peace talks in Paris after President Lyndon B. Johnson had set a limit on further military commitments and revealed his intention to retire. Most of the study and many of the appended documents have been obtained by the *New York Times* and will be described and presented in a series of articles beginning today.

Hedrick Smith had the second front-page story, this one giving context to the undertaking by describing the year-long effort by Ellsberg and others to compile the Papers:

> VAST REVIEW OF WAR TOOK A YEAR
>
> In June, 1967, at a time of great personal disenchantment with the Indochina war and rising frustration

> among his colleagues at the Pentagon, Secretary of Defense Robert S. McNamara commissioned a major study of how and why the United States had become so deeply involved in Vietnam. . . . It was compiled by a team of 30 to 40 government officials, civilian and military, many of whom had helped to develop or carry out the policies that they were asked to evaluate and some of whom were simultaneously active in the debates that changed the course of those policies.
>
> While Mr. McNamara turned over his job to Clark M. Clifford, while the war reached a military peak in the 1968 Lunar New Year offensive, while President Johnson cut back the bombing of North Vietnam and announced his plan to retire, and while the peace talks began in Paris, the study group burrowed through Government files.

Both stories jumped to multiple pages inside. The *Times* also included extensive verbatim excerpts from the Papers on three more pages inside.

Interestingly, the *Times* wasn't yet calling these the Pentagon Papers. It wasn't until Wednesday, June 16, that Abe Rosenthal figured it was time to dump the innocuous "Vietnam Archive" title of the series and go with something snappier. He wrote a memo to Jimmy Greenfield, the foreign editor whom he'd placed in overall charge of the project.

> To: Mr. Greenfield
>
> I would like to change the type of the rubric. It was a very good one but adopted, as you know, because we wanted to get as bland a one as possible. Well, it's all fat to the fire anyway and I think we ought to get something more interesting. Nobody calls them the Vietnam Archives. They call them the McNamara papers or the Pentagon papers or the Vietnam papers or the Pentagon study or something. We should have a rubric

> with which our series would be identified. How about Vietnam Papers?
>
> *A.M.R.*[16]

Bagdikian met with Ben Bradlee at the *Post* on Sunday:

> When I saw Bradlee, I said, "We've got to report what the *Times* is saying." He hated to do that. I said, "I know, but this is big national news. We've got to say the *New York Times* reported today that they had papers that said thus and so." He hated it. He hated [to acknowledge that they were out front], but he realized that we had an obligation to our audience. We had to say that. So we ran our lead story. "The *New York Times* today published information from top-secret documents about the Vietnam War."[17]

The *Post*'s journalists were playing catch-up, grabbing each first edition of the rival *Times* to quickly summarize what Sheehan and others had spent months on, and report on reactions from the principals. It went on this way for days. (Typical *Post* headlines: HUMPHREY SAYS HE, LBJ DIDN'T LIE and TOP SECRECY AT TIMES: FEW KNEW OF PROJECT.)

At eighteen minutes past noon on Sunday, Nixon asked the White House operator to get Kissinger on the line. But Kissinger was en route to Los Angeles; the operator couldn't complete the call.

Nixon still didn't know what was on the front page of the *Times*.

Kissinger was chummy with Frank Sinatra, and right after Tricia's wedding, he'd hustled out to the West Coast to schmooze with his Hollywood connections. Kissinger was one of Sinatra's special guests at what was being billed as the singer's Sunday evening "retirement performance," an end to Sinatra's thirty-six-year career in show business. (Sinatra's retirement lasted about as long as his marriage to third wife Mia Farrow. He was back to performing within two years.)

Unable to reach Kissinger, Nixon next phoned Kissinger's deputy, Alexander Haig.[18]

"Hi, Al. What about the casualties last week? You got the figure yet?"

"No, sir," Haig replied. "But I think it's going to be quite low."

The casualties they were talking about were Americans killed and wounded in the Vietnam War.

Nixon had been elected to end the war. But he had made a calculation that weighed heavily on him now. To ensure reelection in 1972, Nixon would keep the war going. Kissinger had bluntly told him to do so: "We can't have it knocked over—to put it brutally—before the election."[19] That made up Nixon's mind.

To keep Saigon from falling before Election Day, 1972, Nixon would keep soldiers fighting and dying in Vietnam throughout his first term. He periodically announced partial troop withdrawals, reducing the number of American soldiers in Vietnam from over five hundred thousand when he took office in January 1969 to about 245,000 as of June 13, 1971. Men were still dying, but it was enough to convince most voters he was ending the war, and it was sufficient to guarantee that Saigon wouldn't fall until after Nixon had secured his second term.

Vietnam was Nixon's war now, but it was the military that endured the public's contempt and obloquy. No one wanted to be the last to die in a war that America didn't want to fight. Of the 58,000 American soldiers killed during the conflict, more than 20,000 lost their lives during Nixon's first term.

For Nixon, the death toll was a political calculus, more important than any polling number. Under LBJ, several hundred soldiers were killed each week. Nixon had gotten the weekly number down to a few dozen.

The body count of American servicemen was the political barometer that now obsessed Nixon as he reached out—first, unsuccessfully, to Kissinger, and then to Haig. This was real business. In the rearview mirror were the big events of the day before, all the dancing and fun.

The president urgently pressed Haig again. How many dead soldiers? How many?

Haig: "It should be as [low as] last week, or better."

Nixon: "Yeah, should be less than twenty, I would think. Yeah. When will you know?"

Haig replied that he'd have the answer in a day. "We don't get it officially 'til Monday afternoon."

Nixon: "Right. Well, Monday afternoon officially? Well, let's wait 'til then. Fine. OK."

Then, a prophetic question.

Nixon: "Nothing else of interest in the world today?"

Haig: "Yes, sir, very significant. This goddamn *New York Times* exposé of the most highly classified documents of the war."

Nixon: "Oh, that. I see. I didn't read the story."

This was the first Nixon heard about it. The foreign-policy-obsessed, Vietnam-obsessed president hadn't read the Sunday headlines.

As David Dunlap, a former *Times* reporter and the newspaper's historian, later explained[20]:

> What the *Times* had in its possession were 7,000 pages of documents that were a top-secret, classified history of American involvement in Vietnam, in Indochina, going back to the Truman administration, every page of which had been stamped "Top Secret," "Sensitive," "Classified."
>
> Part of the mission of the *Times* was to present the history of the Vietnam War as it had been recorded under the orders of then-Secretary of Defense Robert McNamara, who wanted to find out, How did we get into this mess?
>
> The people who compiled the report had access to all kinds of cables, memos and notes, which betrayed—when you read them closely—that one administration

> after the next had engaged in exactly the kind of double-dealing that critics of the war had always maintained was going on. But here was the Pentagon saying it, in its own voice.
>
> Because of that, it was critical, as far as the *Times* saw it, to reproduce the documents themselves. Not simply interpret them or rely on them for narrative articles, but to actually expose the public to the words of the decision makers. And that meant that we were trading in classified information on a scale that perhaps had never been undertaken before.

Nixon hadn't yet grasped the magnitude of what the *Times* had done. But Haig saw it clearly. He was an Army one-star still on active duty, detailed from the Pentagon to be Kissinger's right hand. Haig was a West Point graduate and Vietnam veteran, who'd served earlier as the military aide to Defense Secretary Robert McNamara. And, as Haig well knew, it was McNamara who ordered up the Pentagon Papers.

"Sir, [that] whole study that was done for McNamara and then carried on after McNamara left by [Clark] Clifford and the peaceniks over there. This is a devastating security breach of the greatest magnitude of anything I've ever seen."

Nixon was still back on his heels, trying to make sense of it all. To him, it sounded like another leak. Nixon hated leakers as much as he loathed the press. Still, his initial reaction was casual, unalarmed.[21] "Well," he replied, "what's being done about it, then? Did we know this was coming out?"

"No, we did not, sir."

Nixon had an interesting take on things, which was to fire the leakers, not punish the press. Fire the bastards who talked to the press, Nixon suggested. "Start right at the top and fire some people. I mean, whoever—whatever department it came out of, I'd fire the top guy."

When Nixon spoke to Secretary of State William Rogers, his friend and former law partner, after that discussion, he was similarly nonchalant, seeming to take comfort from the fact that the Papers' history stopped in 1968, before Nixon took office. "It's hard on Johnson; it's hard on Kennedy; it's hard on Lodge."[22]

Kissinger would soon call in from the West Coast. Kissinger's call would give Nixon's paranoia a jolt of adrenaline. And within a week, the so-called Plumbers would have a black-bag job to do.[23]

Earlier that Sunday morning, Defense Secretary Melvin Laird was preparing for his appearance on the CBS Sunday interview show *Face the Nation*. The Vietnam War was certain to be the main, perhaps only, topic. Laird arrived at his Pentagon office at 9:15 a.m. and went straight into a meeting with five aides to rehearse his answers for the broadcast. Laird was alarmed about the *Times* story, and he tried unsuccessfully to reach Attorney General John Mitchell at home to get advice about how to handle the expected questions about it.[24] Laird and his people spent almost two hours going over responses to possible questions before leaving for the CBS Washington studio at 2020 M Street NW.[25]

One of Laird's scheduled questioners was a military specialist from the *Times*, John Finney. Laird might have assumed that Finney knew about the newspaper's plan to publish the Papers, although there is no evidence that Finney was read in ahead of time.[26] The other two questioners would be from CBS: George Herman, the program's host, and Bob Schieffer, the network's Pentagon correspondent.[27] Surely, one of those three would push for a comment, right?

As Laird surmised, their questions were all about Vietnam, but the newsmen wanted to know about troop withdrawals, combat operations, the Paris peace negotiations, and getting back POWs. Astonishingly, Laird didn't get a single question about the Pentagon Papers. The story had dropped into the pond without leaving a ripple.

It wouldn't stay that way. At least one Sunday evening newscaster[28] had taken notice and was preparing a story.

Sunday, June 13, 1971, 3:09 p.m.

Kissinger arrived in Los Angeles with his Secret Service detail on Sunday afternoon for the Sinatra affair that evening. Upon his arrival, Kissinger returned Nixon's call. By now, it was 3:09 p.m. in Washington.[29]

Nixon related his earlier call with Kissinger's deputy, Haig. "Haig was very disturbed by that *New York Times* thing. Unconscionable damn thing for them to do." Nixon still didn't sound all that disturbed about the story. He was talking, he said, about how "unconscionable" it was "on the part of the people that leaked it. Fortunately it didn't come out in our administration." Nixon asked Kissinger if he knew who the leaker was. Then the president pivoted, because he still hadn't seen the newspaper.

"Give me your view on [the Papers]. In a word."

KISSINGER: It just shows massive mismanagement of how we got there, and it pins it all on Kennedy and Johnson.

NIXON: Huh, yeah [laughing].

KISSINGER: In public opinion, it actually, if anything, will help us a little bit, because this is a gold mine of showing how the previous administration got us in there.

NIXON: I didn't read the thing. . . .

KISSINGER: And McNamara; so from that point of view it helps us . . . proves that, if it's anybody's war, it's Kennedy's and Johnson's.

NIXON: Yeah.

It was a lengthy call, and before it was over, Kissinger began suggesting that Nixon should take some sort of action. The two settled on bringing in Attorney General John Mitchell.

Kissinger then told the president that he'd flown out to Los Angeles with another of the Nixon friends at Tricia's wedding, radio actor Freeman Gosden, who "worships you."

Nixon asked Kissinger what his friend Gosden thought of "all this stuff."

Kissinger chuckled. "He said [Secretary of State John Foster] Dulles always used to say that he had to operate alone because he couldn't trust his own bureaucracy. I said well, that was good for Dulles but we pay for it now because we are stuck with the bureaucracy."

Nixon replied, "Well, I just wish that we operated without the bureaucracy."

Monday, June 14, 1971

Nixon conferred with Haig and Secretary of State Bill Rogers while he waited for Kissinger to get back from the Sinatra celebration. Kissinger was getting used to the VIP treatment from Sinatra, who gave him ten tickets for the performance[30] and also arranged a jet to whisk Kissinger and his two Secret Service agents quickly out to Los Angeles on Sunday, in time for Sinatra's big evening, and then promptly back to DC early the next morning.[31]

Back in DC by 2:00 p.m.[32] local time on Monday afternoon, Kissinger immediately began fielding phone calls, including an important one from Bill Rogers, who was prepping for a news conference and wanted to confirm whether Kissinger had a set of the Papers. Rogers believed Kissinger did.

Rogers pressed him hard, but Kissinger categorically denied knowing anything and stuck to his story. Rogers believed he was being lied to.

Kissinger was a master of going right up to the edge of what was accepted prevarication between diplomats—"I did not technically lie"—but sometimes he went far beyond that. Problems with truth were a recurrent theme. Secretary of State Rogers seemed to think this might be one of those times, because Rogers had a memo from the project leader that named Kissinger as one of the Papers' recipients[33]:

KISSINGER: I never had it.

ROGERS: The Gelb memo for the record says distribution of the task force study—

KISSINGER: I was a consultant for one limited meeting.

ROGERS: I thought perhaps you might have forgotten it.

KISSINGER: I never had it.

ROGERS: Gelb lists "Kennedy Library, [several other names], Henry Kissinger, and the Archives" as being approved.

KISSINGER: I may have been approved but I never saw it.

ROGERS: Sometimes you get things like that and forget it.

KISSINGER: I knew they were doing a study in McNamara's period, but the only time I had anything to do with it was when McNamara was Secretary of Defense, not Clifford. I talked about the [study] in '67. They may have been authorized to give it to me, but I never got it. In fact, I didn't know it existed.

ROGERS: I know what my line on this will be. I don't know what the hell we can do. You can't wink at a violation of the law.

KISSINGER: It's an outrage. Inimical to the national interest. In Britain no one would publish this.

Rogers had just given Kissinger the first taste of what was to come. Kissinger was getting the idea that even though the Papers stopped with Johnson, he—Kissinger—was personally implicated. In fact, Kissinger soon would be told by Laird that Kissinger's involvement was central to the narrative of the final volume of the Papers (Kissinger was name-checked ninety-nine times), which documented in excruciating detail how Kissinger had acted as one of Johnson's secret emissaries between the various parties to the Paris peace talks that were just getting underway in 1967 and 1968, Harriman taking the lead, after Johnson announced he wouldn't run for reelection.

Kissinger was portrayed as cunning in the Papers' last volume, also known as Volume Six,[34] which the *Times* hadn't gotten around to yet. The volume described how, publicly, LBJ sought to bring North Vietnam to the table in Paris by announcing the United States wouldn't bomb above the 19th parallel, staying well away from Hanoi. But the Papers also showed that the North Vietnamese didn't trust the Americans and considered them "two faced," with some justification.

The final Pentagon Papers volume described how Kissinger sought to keep the bombing of North Vietnam going during the talks,[35] since "a total cessation of the bombing is inconsistent with keeping secret the fact that negotiations are taking place."[36] The peace talks hadn't gone anywhere, but actions like Kissinger's arguably served to negate Johnson's late efforts to broker peace, and helped Nixon win the 1968 election. The optics were not good for Kissinger. When Kissinger phoned Laird first thing on Tuesday morning, Laird cast himself as an innocent bystander in the affair. He urged Kissinger, still pleading ignorance, to look at Volume Six:

> LAIRD: One other thing. On these documents, I understand there's some bitching in the White House that I am defending McNamara. I'm not defending anyone; I'm just saying you can't leak these things. I've refused these documents for two years. Justice last week supported the position that this study can't go to the Congress.
>
> KISSINGER: I didn't know the study existed until . . . I knew McNamara was working on it because I was helping him in 1967. But I didn't know they had ever completed a document pulling it all together. Well, it doesn't matter who knew what.

LAIRD: I am not defending McNamara. I am just saying you can't leak this information all over the world.

KISSINGER: Of course not. There are two problems: One is the intrinsic security problem raised by them, and the second is the integrity of the government. If these things are going to be released to the press at the end of every few years you'll have everyone writing their memos for how they will look in the *New York Times*.

LAIRD: Have you read the section [mentioning Kissinger]? . . .

KISSINGER: No.

LAIRD: You ought to read it. It had to do with you. That's Volume Six.

KISSINGER: Do we have it over here [at the White House]?

LAIRD: You do now.

Kissinger had also received a call the prior evening from Walt Rostow, LBJ's emissary in Texas who was helping Johnson to wrap up his memoirs. Rostow conveyed the former president's distress. Johnson and Rostow were selectively using some of the same classified documents that the *Times* now was publishing, and Johnson was worried not just about getting caught up in the fallout from that, but also whether his book might come across as a revisionist history, given the raw truth of what the Papers showed. Johnson's memoir was already in galleys, ready to go on press. The former president told Rostow to make sure the Nixon White House wouldn't undercut him. To make sure that Kissinger got the point, Rostow assured him that nothing in Johnson's book would embarrass Nixon. "That book will not be damaging to President Nixon."

Kissinger responded in kind. "I don't want it said publicly, but then we will not attack you publicly, either."

Was there anything else Johnson wanted?

"As far as we are concerned," Rostow told Kissinger, "the maximum legal effort to stop [further publication of the Papers by the *Times*] and re-establish discipline would have our support."

Kissinger replied, "We are having the Justice Department study that issue."[37]

As soon as Kissinger hung up with Rostow, Frank Sinatra phoned. By now, it was 7:12 p.m. Sinatra's people had made travel arrangements for Kissinger and his Secret Service agents to get back quickly from the previous evening's shindig in Los Angeles; Sinatra had his own jet. More to the point, Sinatra's oblique mention of an intended trip to the East Coast the following week showed that he had something else going with Kissinger. In fact, it would later be revealed that Sinatra had been assisting with arrangements for Kissinger's intended trip to China. Sinatra loaned his jet for some of the official travel, a subterfuge providing an extra measure of confidentiality.

KISSINGER: Thank you for arranging the return. I have talked to more people today who were moved yesterday. You did a marvelous thing.

SINATRA: We were just talking and think you should come back.

KISSINGER: I won't come back [to Washington] if I stay out there.

SINATRA: Your weather there good?

KISSINGER: Muggy.

SINATRA: Warm and lovely here.

KISSINGER: You need some rest.

SINATRA: The [Bennett] Cerfs[38] [Random House cofounder and publisher] just arrived and are going East on Monday with me. I will call you Monday around 3:00-4:00. And I will call during the week.

KISSINGER: It was really a sensitive and moving occasion.

SINATRA: Thank you.

KISSINGER: You even had my Secret Service guys bawling and I didn't know they had feelings. Many thanks again.[39]

While Kissinger was on the phone with Sinatra, Nixon's domestic policy chief, John Ehrlichman, phoned the president. Their 7:13 p.m. call was brief, just a minute or two. Nixon still seemed intent on going after the leaker, not the *Times*.

"Hell," Nixon told Ehrlichman. "I wouldn't prosecute the *Times*. My view is to prosecute the Goddamn pricks that gave it to 'em."

But Ehrlichman had news for Nixon. He'd just gotten off the phone with Mitchell, and the attorney general told him that "unless he [Mitchell] puts the *Times* on notice, he's probably gonna waive any right of prosecution against the newspaper. And he is calling now to see if you would approve his putting them on notice before their first edition for tomorrow comes out." Mitchell was, in effect, advising immediate action to preserve legal options. Everything flipped. This would be moving fast.

A minute later, Kissinger phoned in. Nixon had suddenly changed course. "I am trying to get all our people to hold the line. Mitchell will have to notify the *Times*." Was Kissinger on board?

Kissinger reassured Nixon. "He [the attorney general] must. Rogers called–this is a direct challenge to the integrity of government."

NIXON: Do you agree?

KISSINGER: Whatever you do, I will back you.

NIXON: Well, the press can publish—

KISSINGER: The press has no freedom to publish highly classified materials.

NIXON: They haven't, have they?

KISSINGER: No, not yet.

NIXON: You intend to take this same view?

KISSINGER: I will take a very tough view.[40]

Nixon cut him off. "Why don't you drop over here for a minute, I've got to call Mitchell now." No longer in the White House basement, Kissinger had a new office near the Oval Office—bright, swank quarters befitting his status. But tonight Nixon was in his hideaway office in the Old Executive Office Building,[41] colloquially known to insiders as the EOB. Kissinger rushed over.

As he awaited Kissinger, Nixon immediately phoned his attorney general.

"What is your advice on the *Times* thing, John? You would like to do it?"

Mitchell replied, "I would believe so, Mr. President, otherwise we will look a little foolish in not following through on our legal obligations."[42]

Nixon asked how Mitchell would handle it.

Mitchell: "Low key. You call them, and then send a telegram to confirm it."

Nixon: "Look, as far as the *Times* is concerned, hell, they're our enemies. I think we just oughta do it. And, anyway, Henry, tell him what you just heard from Rostow."

Kissinger had just walked in. He related his earlier conversation with Rostow, who'd phoned on LBJ's behalf: "It is Johnson's strong view that this is an attack on the whole integrity of government. If whole file cabinets can be stolen and then made available to the press, you can't have orderly government anymore. He said if the president defends the integrity, any action we take he will back publicly."

Mitchell had a surprise for Kissinger. He'd been speaking to Rostow, too. "We've got some information we've developed as to where these copies are, and who [is] likely to have leaked them. And the prime suspect, according to your friend Rostow, is a gentleman by the name of Ellsberg"—Kissinger's one-time protégé—"who is a left-winger that's now with the Rand Corporation, who also have a set of these documents."

NIXON: Yeah.

MITCHELL: So, uh . . .

NIXON: Subpoena them. Christ, get them. . . .

MITCHELL: That agree with you?

NIXON: Yep.

MITCHELL: All right, sir. Will do.

While Mitchell handled things, Nixon sought to unwind. He phoned his best friend, Bebe Rebozo, who now was back in Florida; phoned his wife, Pat, back at the White House; phoned Tricia, now on her honeymoon with Ed Cox. The newlyweds were secretly ensconced from the media's eyes at the presidential retreat, Camp David.

Then Nixon went down to the bowling alley in the EOB basement; he spent an hour there. He was a pretty good bowler. Ten pins.[43]

CHAPTER 12

Pressure

Monday, June 14, 1971, 7:30 p.m.

Ellsberg had already disappeared.

Mitchell told his assistant attorney general in charge of the Internal Security Division, Robert Mardian, to immediately phone the *Times* and tell them to stop the presses. If the newspaper didn't do so voluntarily, the government would take the *Times* to court in the morning. The call from Mardian was the low-key effort that Mitchell had told Nixon would come first. Then a telegram—from Mitchell, also as promised—to confirm the threat[1]:

> I HAVE BEEN ADVISED BY THE SECRETARY OF DEFENSE THAT THE MATERIAL PUBLISHED IN THE NEW YORK TIMES ON JUNE 13, 14, 1971 CAPTIONED KEY TEXTS FROM PENTAGON'S VIETNAM STUDY CONTAINS INFORMATION RELATING TO THE NATIONAL DEFENSE OF THE UNITED STATES AND BEARS A TOP SECRET CLASSIFICATION.
>
> AS SUCH, PUBLICATION OF THIS INFORMATION IS DIRECTLY PROHIBITED BY THE PROVISIONS OF THE ESPIONAGE LAW TITLE 18 UNITED STATES CODE, SECTION 793.
>
> MOREOVER FURTHER PUBLICATION OF INFORMATION OF THIS CHARACTER WILL

> CAUSE IRREPARABLE INJURY TO THE DEFENSE INTERESTS OF THE UNITED STATES.
>
> ACCORDINGLY I RESPECTFULLY REQUEST THAT YOU PUBLISH NO FURTHER INFORMATION OF THIS CHARACTER AND ADVISE ME THAT YOU HAVE MADE ARRANGEMENTS FOR THE RETURN OF THESE DOCUMENTS TO THE DEPARTMENT OF DEFENSE.[2]

The *Times* then issued the following statement:

> We have received the telegram from the Attorney General asking the *Times* to cease further publication of the Pentagon's Vietnam study.
>
> The *Times* must respectfully decline the request of the Attorney General, believing that it is in the interest of the people of this country to be informed of the material contained in this series of articles.
>
> We have also been informed of the Attorney General's intention to seek an injunction against further publication. We believe that it is properly a matter for the courts to decide. The *Times* will oppose any request for an injunction for the same reason that led us to publish the articles in the first place. We will of course abide by the final decision of the court.

Rosenthal told his editors to remake page 1 with a big banner:

> MITCHELL SEEKS TO HALT SERIES
> ON VIETNAM BUT TIMES REFUSES

The presses began rolling at 10:20 p.m. Rosenthal grabbed the very first one, and the second one went to Jimmy Greenfield, the foreign editor who was in charge of the project. Pressmen were congratulating them. Rosenthal called the headline "the most majestic words I've ever seen." He reflected on what it would be like if the headline read, instead: AND TIMES CONCEDES. "Our whole lives, not just mine, but all of our lives would have become meaningless."[3]

But there was a problem. Greenfield walked into Rosenthal's office and said the Associated Press was moving a story on the wire, saying that a spokesman at the Justice Department didn't know anything about a telegram.

Greenfield, Sydney Gruson, and Harding Bancroft, the *Times* executive who had spoken to Mardian, were gathered in Rosenthal's office. Now Greenfield told them his worst fear:

> Oh my God, if it's a fraud, the whole thing is a hoax, the Justice Department never threatened us. It was some guy just calling up, some guy sending a telegram.

They all looked at each other and, as Rosenthal recollected, laughed in a gallows-humor way, and said:

> This is the end. Finished. Jump out the window, all of us. Goodbye. A hoax. The *New York Times* comes out with a big, brave stand and it turns out to be a hoax. We can't stand this. We were almost hysterical at that point.

"Where the hell is the telegram?!" Rosenthal demanded.

Someone fetched the telegram from the wire room.

Sure enough, the telegram said what it said. It looked authentic. But there was a curious sign-off at the end. The *Times* operator had typed back to ask who was sending. The operator on the other end typed back: THIS IS THE FBI MACHINE BUT WE'RE NOT THE FBI, WE'RE THE DEPARTMENT OF JUSTICE, USING THE FBI MACHINE.

The *Times* operator had replied: THANK YOU VERY MUCH.

The sender on the other end answered: YOU'RE WELCOME.

The *Times* operator kept the back-and-forth going, replying with a clever four-word sign-off: BI BI BYE BYE.

The anonymous sender, typing on the other end, humorously cabled back: I AM SPEECHLESS.

In those days before emojis, that was the end of the thread.

Greenfield was dumbfounded. Before joining the *Times*, he'd been a senior official at the State Department. He knew what an official government cable looked like. Greenfield looked at the one in front of them and declared, "It's a hoax. An FBI or Department of Justice operator would not sign off saying, 'I am speechless.'"

Rosenthal told Bancroft to call back Mardian, the DOJ guy to whom he'd allegedly spoken. It was late. Mardian didn't answer his phone. And Bancroft now confessed that the person he thought was Mardian could have been an impostor. He was unsure. Finally someone got through to one of the newspaper's outside lawyers, who confirmed he'd spoken directly to Mitchell and knew the telegram was coming. So, Rosenthal relaxed. It wasn't a hoax:

> But for 45 minutes we thought all our careers were wiped out, including Harding's and Sydney's and mine and Jimmy Greenfield's and everything, because we were out with 50,000 papers saying that the Justice Department ordered the *New York Times* to do this, and we thought it all was a hoax.
>
> By this time it was 1 o'clock in the morning. And our great lawyers were looking for a lawyer. They'd only had three months to figure out that we were going to be hit with an injunction; they had warned us we would be hit with an injunction.

The newspaper's law firm of long standing, Lord Day & Lord, had argued all along against publication. "Since we disregarded their advice, they would refuse to represent us in court." That was fine with Rosenthal. "Frankly, I was delighted. . . . They were wishy-washy and wouldn't have had their heart in it."

The Russians took note of what was happening. The *Times* foreign desk had asked all bureaus to advise how the stories were playing abroad. Bernard Gwertzman, the bureau chief in Moscow, cabled back:

> THE SOVIET INFORMATION MEDIA HAVE WELCOMED THE PUBLICATION BY THE TIMES OF THE SECRET VIETNAM MATERIAL. BOTH IZVESTIA, THE GOVERNMENT PAPER, AND PRAVDA, THE PARTY PAPER, TODAY FEATURED THE NEWS, AND TASS HAS PROVIDED LENGTHY REPORTS ON THE MATERIAL AND THE GOVERNMENT'S EFFORT TO STOP FURTHER PUBLICATION.
>
> THE EXCERPTING IS OF COURSE SELECTIVE TO PUT THE UNITED STATES IN THE WORST POSSIBLE LIGHT. THE OVERALL THEMES OF THE SOVIET REPORTS ARE THAT THE MATERIAL PROVES THAT THE UNITED STATES DELIBERATELY LAUNCHED A WAR IN VIETNAM. IN KEEPING WITH STANDARD COMMUNIST POLICY, THERE IS NO INDICATION IN ANY OF THE SOVIET REPORTS THAT NORTH VIETNAM WAS AT ALL RESPONSIBLE FOR ANY MILITARY ACTIONS IN SOUTH VIETNAM.
>
> TYPICAL WAS TODAY'S TASS REPORT WHICH SAID IN PART: "THE *NEW YORK TIMES* HAS STARTED TO PUBLISH PENTAGON DOCUMENTS DISCLOSING THE SECRET PLANS OF THE PREPARATION OF THE AMERICAN AGGRESSION AGAINST THE VIETNAMESE PEOPLE. THESE DOCUMENTS SHOW THE UTTER HYPOCRISY OF THE AMERICAN AUTHORITIES WHICH, CONCEALING THEIR SECRET PLANS FROM

> THE U.S. PUBLIC, DRAGGED THE AMERICAN PEOPLE INTO THE DIRTY WAR IN SOUTHEAST ASIA."
>
> SPECIFIC ATTENTION WAS FOCUSED ON THE TONKIN GULF INCIDENT, AND TASS SAID FLATLY THAT "DOCUMENTS SHOW THAT THE PROVOCATION WAS COMMITTED BY THE PENTAGON."

Mitch Rogovin, Sheehan's lawyer, phoned him at the New York Hilton. Sheehan was still on deadline, working on stories to come. Rogovin had a warning: Ellsberg was already underground, and the FBI likely would be looking for Sheehan. "Prepare to be indicted or arrested. Make sure you can travel. If a warrant is issued, it will be from in[4] New York. Plan to get home at your earliest convenience."[5]

Sulzberger, the *Times* publisher and a scion of the family that had owned the newspaper for generations, carried around a folded-up statement of support for Sheehan in his suit pocket, in case the FBI came for the reporter.

Tuesday, June 15, 1971

Just as Mitchell had warned, on Tuesday morning the government's lawyers asked the U.S. District Court in Manhattan for an injunction to prevent the *Times* from further publishing the Papers. Judge Murray Gurfein issued the injunction, an unprecedented prior restraint of the press. The *Times* appealed immediately, but in the meantime said it would abide by the injunction.

Bagdikian's reporters at the *Post* were following developments. He received a fortuitous phone call:

> The *Times* was enjoined from the district court in New York from printing anymore, and they appealed. So

> after they were stopped, I came out of one of our afternoon editorial meetings. My deputy, a very cool character, said, "Here's something you ought to look at." And it was a message that came in during the news conference. "Call Mr. Boston at this number." And I noticed that the area code was 617, and that is Boston. And I thought, Someone has told me to call Mr. Boston in Boston—something is funny here.
>
> But the message instructed me to call from a secure phone. So I went across the street to the Statler Hotel, which at that time had a bank of public telephone booths. I called that number and someone answered, and asked, "Are you at a secure phone?" I said, "Yes." "All right. Now, here's a number. Go to another secure phone and call this number." So I call that number and Dan Ellsberg answers.
>
> I knew it had something to do with the Pentagon Papers because the *Times* had already been enjoined. And he said, "You have to come to Boston, pick up some stuff. But you better get a reservation because it's commencement time and you can't get a hotel room easily." I grew up around Boston and knew the area and ended up getting a room in a sort of fleabag motel there.

Wednesday, June 16, 1971

Bagdikian flew up to Boston and checked into the motel as "Mr. Medford," an alias that was only slightly less contrived than Ellsberg's. But when the hotel clerk noticed his real name on the credit card, he had to backpedal. "Oh, I write under the name of Medford."

That worked. The clerk said, "I have a message for you," and gave him an address for a street in Cambridge. Bagdikian took a cab there and told the driver to wait.

A woman opened the door. Bagdikian said, "I've been told that there's something here that I should pick up." The woman asked who sent him. Bagdikian answered: "A friend of mine and a friend of yours."

The woman brought out a big cardboard box—Bagdikian recalled it was three feet long and a foot wide. It was so big and heavy that he couldn't lift it and had to ask the driver to carry it to the cab.

Soon Bagdikian was back at the fleabag motel. Then, in walked Ellsberg:

> He looked very haggard. When I came back, Dan was just coming to this room. He found out what room I was in. And he looked terrible. He had a headache and he said, "Do you have any aspirin?" I got some aspirin at the desk and he took it. And then I showed him the box. He says, "Where's the other box?" I said, "What other box?" He said, "There were two boxes." And I said, "Well, you didn't say that and nobody told me that."

They sent a messenger ("somebody who didn't know what was going on") to go back and fetch the second box:

> So now there were two big boxes. And by this time we had spread papers on the bed. And Dan said, "Now, we've got to separate these out." I said, "Yes, we have to separate these out in terms of stories. Not chronological but the ones that are most important first." He said, "Well, we've got to cut off the code numbers of these cables because these are copies of top secret cables with a code and if you print the code publicly, a hostile nation can take that code number, look at what we printed as a plain language, and figure out the code." He said, "The difference for me is ten years or life imprisonment." So we began cutting.
>
> By this time, also, Patricia Marx [Ellsberg's wife] was there with another man, whom I assumed was a

> lawyer, and he said, "At this point, Pat, I think we'd better leave." So they left.

Bagdikian bought two seats for a flight back to DC—one for himself, the other for the boxes.

Thursday, June 17, 1971, 5:15 p.m.[6]

Nixon, Haldeman, Ehrlichman, and Kissinger were in the Oval Office. Press Secretary Ron Ziegler came in to tell them the House had just rejected a proposal to set a December 31 deadline to end the war. The vote was 256 to 158. Nixon liked it. "I did much better than they expected. That's good."

Once Ziegler left the office, Haldeman brought up the Pentagon Papers. He saw an opportunity to blackmail LBJ. Haldeman's theory went like this: Nixon's people suspected that Johnson had an ulterior motive in ordering a last-minute bombing halt in the war: an "October surprise" on October 31, 1968, just five days before the election.[7] At the time, there was speculation (incorrect, as it turned out) that the bombing halt meant there had been a sudden breakthrough in the Paris peace talks. If it looked like the war might end soon, voters might credit the Democrats, and Vice President Hubert Humphrey (not the party's first choice, having entered the race only after LBJ dropped out) might win after all.

But that hadn't happened. Three years after the fact, Haldeman's theory was that LBJ had attempted a blatant steal of the election, fabricating a rationale for the bombing halt to swing public sentiment toward Nixon's challenger.

Haldeman thought there had to be some documents that would prove he was right—and he believed they would be found at the Brookings Institution, a liberal think tank near the White House. Leslie Gelb and Morton Halperin, the main authors of the RAND study, now were at Brookings. Haldeman figured the documentary proof would be with them, somewhere inside Brookings.

It was plausible that Johnson had tried to rig the results—and it wouldn't have been the first time, or the last, that a shrewd politician tried to engineer an outcome. Regardless, Nixon *won* the election. So, what was the point of trying to blackmail Johnson, three years after the fact? Haldeman thought that Nixon could use the threatened disclosure of LBJ's true motivation in the bombing halt as a way to get Johnson to publicly condemn the Pentagon Papers and support Nixon in his quest to discourage government leakers. It was a gossamer theory. But that's what Haldeman thought.

Kissinger already knew Haldeman's premise was baseless, because he had seen LBJ's top secret instructions to Harriman. Why Haldeman would try to persuade Nixon to vindicate himself over an election that he *won* was anyone's guess. (Of course, it would not be the last time that a president who *won* sought retribution for perceived or actual slights.)

Haldeman offered Nixon a way to get back at Johnson: "You can maybe blackmail Johnson on this stuff."

Nixon didn't get it. "What?"

Haldeman repeated: "You could blackmail Johnson on this stuff, and it might be worth doing."

Nixon: "How? Do we have it? I've asked for it. You said you didn't have it, Henry."

Kissinger was still dissembling about the Papers. "We have nothing here, Mr. President."

Nixon: "Dammit, I asked for that, because I need it."

Kissinger: "Yeah, but Bob [Haldeman] and I have been trying to put the damn thing together for three years."

Haldeman: "We have a basic history of it—constructed on our own—but there is a file on it."

Nixon: "Where?"

Haldeman: "[Tom Charles] Huston swears to God there's a file on it at Brookings."

Kissinger: "I wouldn't be surprised."

White House aide Huston had made a secret proposal to Nixon the year before, to increase the use of break-ins, wiretaps, mail opening, and other actions to fight domestic terrorism, Nixon remembered. Now Nixon wanted the Huston Plan implemented—not against suspected terrorists, but against the Brookings Institution.

Nixon: "Bob, now, you remember Huston's plan? Implement it."

Wait a minute, Kissinger interjected. Couldn't federal authorities just show up at Brookings and demand the secret file, if it existed? Why would Nixon need to order a covert operation? "Couldn't we go over? Brookings has no right to classified documents."

Nope, Nixon said. "I mean, I want it implemented on a thievery basis. Goddamn it, get in and get those files. Blow the safe and get it."[8]

Haldeman thought it was possible that, in the still-unfolding aftermath of the Pentagon Papers, Gelb and Halperin might already have gotten rid of the supposed file. But, he added, Johnson wouldn't have known that, so blackmailing him still could work. "Johnson knows those files are around. He doesn't know for sure that we *don't* have them."

Kissinger expressed a belief that the file—if it even existed—could still be at Brookings, but he came back to the central question in his mind, which was why Nixon would want to risk a black-bag operation when he could, as president, simply demand the return of classified documents: "I wouldn't be surprised if Brookings had the file on the bombing halt. But what good will it do you, the bombing-halt file?"

Nixon shot back: "To blackmail him. Because he used the bombing halt for political purposes." Kissinger wasn't going to win this one.

That settled things. The Huston Plan was a go.

Haldeman: "The bombing-halt file would really kill Johnson."[9]

G. Gordon Liddy swung into action. Liddy, forty years old, was a former FBI special agent, well-practiced in the arts of clandestine entry and intelligence gathering. He had connections to the Cuban exiles that the CIA had trained for the Bay of Pigs invasion in 1961. And he had a bizarre, dark side. New to the White House, Liddy boasted about how to kill someone with a pencil, and once threatened to break off a co-worker's arm and beat him to death with it.[10] To show how tough he was, Liddy summed up his life's philosophy by explaining how he held his hand over a candle flame until his flesh burned: "Suffering. That was the key. Whatever the consequences of what I do, I must accept and endure them—outlast suffering to achieve my goals."

Liddy was assigned to the Nixon White House special investigations unit, alongside former CIA officer E. Howard Hunt. Liddy code-named their operation "Odessa," but the unit was known as "the Plumbers" because they aimed to plug leaks by covert means that included breaking into offices to gather intelligence. Liddy's first assignment under the Huston Plan was to figure out how to do the Brookings break-in. He was a lawyer—J. Edgar Hoover's FBI favored lawyers and accountants as special agents—and he figured the investigation into the Pentagon Papers justified whatever was required. "It involved national security and not politics, and that was the activities of the Odessa Group when we were, for example, trying to determine whether Daniel Ellsberg was a romantic loner of the left or whether he was an agent of the KGB."

Liddy sketched out a plan for the Brookings break-in: The Plumbers would buy a used late-model fire engine. They would paint it with markings from the District of Columbia Fire Department. They would issue uniforms to their CIA-trained Cuban "fire crew." Brookings then would be firebombed at night, "by use of a delay mechanism timed to go off at night, so as not to endanger lives needlessly." The Cuban fire crew would rush to the site, empty documents from the think tank's vaults into a van, and speed away, abandoning the fire truck.

"There would be a lot of who-struck-John in the liberal press," Liddy figured, "but because nothing could be proved the matter would lapse into the unsolved-mystery category."[11]

Thursday, June 17, 1971, 5:30 p.m.

Bagdikian brought back the first box of documents to Bradlee's Georgetown home; the second box went into a closet at Bagdikian's house. *Post* reporters gathered at Bradlee's place that Thursday and began working on stories for Friday morning's paper. In the midst of that, Bradlee wanted advice from legendary Washington lawyer Edward Bennett Williams. Should the *Post* pick up where the *Times* left off? That was a big question, and the *Post*'s lawyers argued against taking the risk. Ellsberg was, after all, expecting serious prison time for his efforts, and Sheehan and the *Times* had been similarly warned. The FBI was moving quickly.

Williams not only was the best criminal attorney anywhere, he also was the controlling owner of the Washington Redskins football club—a sportsman who understood the odds on the playing field, as well as in the courtroom.

The two men later told very different stories about that fateful phone call. Bradlee, in his 1995 memoir, *A Good Life: Newspapering and Other Adventures*, gave an account that had Bradlee tracking down Williams at a courtroom in Chicago and desperately seeking a thumbs-up or thumbs-down from him.

In Bradlee's account, he laid out the complexities of the *Post*'s situation for "maybe 10 uninterrupted minutes." Not only was the paper about to publish top secret documents that the government surely would try to stop, but the newspaper's parent company was ready to go public with a $35 million stock offering[12] that might fall through if the government sued. And—oh, yes—the *Post* owned three valuable television licenses that the Nixon administration might try to cancel. Bradlee described what came next:

> Nothing from Williams for at least 60 seconds. I was dying. And then, finally, "Well, Benjy, you got to go with it. You got no choice. That's your business." I hugged him, long distance, and walked casually downstairs back into the legal debate. When I had the right

opening, I told them what Williams had said. . . . Such was the clout of this man.[13]

Bradlee credited Williams's support with helping to persuade Katharine Graham, the *Post*'s owner, to give the go-ahead later that evening. The *Post*'s presses would roll that night with more of the Pentagon Papers.

But Williams privately told Sheehan a much different story—in essence, that Williams had used a football metaphor to counsel Bradlee *against* rushing headlong that night into publishing the documents that Ellsberg had given the *Post*.

Williams related his version of events to Sheehan five-and-a-half years after the Papers case; Sheehan made a contemporaneous memorandum of their conversation, but never made Williams's account public.[14] Bradlee's memoir came out twenty-four years after the fact. By then, Williams had been dead for seven years, so Bradlee's recollection stood as the only available account of what was said on that call. It added further weight to Bradlee's already cinematic reputation as a swaggering, fearless editor, and to Williams's as the daring Mob consiglieri who gave the green light to Katharine Graham and the *Post*. In fact, about the only thing their two stories agreed on was that Williams was in Chicago when Bradlee tracked him down. Williams said he had counseled Bradlee to hold off; he thought the situation that evening called for caution in the moment, not bold action. But there were only two people who could say definitively what each said on that call, and only Bradlee remained.

Here is Sheehan's account[15]:

PENTAGON PAPERS
Conversation, Bob DuPont's[16] House, Edward Bennett Williams, 3/12/77

Williams said that the decision on whether to publish the PPs at the *Washington Post* was very close. This was because [*Post* chairman Fritz] Beebe, [Secretary of State] Bill Rogers and others in his law firm representing that paper, and others on the business side of the *Post*, were saying that the *Post* should not incur the wrath of the Administration by publishing, that they should leave the *New York Times* with its ass hanging in the wind. This is about five days or so into publication after the *NYT* had been enjoined and the *Post* has finally gotten its own copy of the PPs.

Williams was on his way back from a trial in Chicago, or a court session there. He had left the court when it closed at 4:30 p.m. Chicago time (5:30 p.m. Wash. time so this is very close to publication) and was headed for the airport in a hired car. There happened to be a car phone. Bradlee told him they had the PPs finally, told him of the argument within the *Post*, and he (Bradlee) didn't know what to do and what should they do? Williams answered:

"Bradlee, you and I have known each other for 25 years. You're in the fourth quarter. The score is *New York Times* 21 and *Washington Post* zero. You've got eight minutes to play. You've got to punt." Williams doesn't remember if Bradlee said anything in reply. He thinks Bradlee just hung up and the *Post* went ahead with publication.

Friday, June 18, 1971

The *Post* ran its first installment of the Papers on Friday morning. Other newspapers followed. The Justice Department would end up playing whack-a-mole at various federal courthouses, trying without success to keep the lid on.

Monday, June 21, 1971, 10:13 a.m.

Kissinger took a call from Mardian, who'd been unsuccessful at getting an injunction against the *Post*. The government was appealing. "I think our chances are 20 percent," Mardian confided to Kissinger.

Minutes later on June 21, 10:17 a.m.

Meanwhile, Nixon and Haldeman—by now working out of Nixon's Florida residence in Key Biscayne—had secretly asked for "phone checks" to be run on possible leak suspects for the Pentagon Papers—a warrantless search so questionable, if not outright illegal, that Haldeman's reporting it to his diary was classified as secret for forty-two years.

It was a week after the first installment of the Pentagon Papers in the *New York Times*, and the phone reports came back. Haldeman gave Nixon the bad news; nothing there.[17] Nixon said the next step was to double down on the Huston Plan—break-ins, black-bag jobs, covert wiretaps—for the Plumbers. That would also involve pulling in Charles Colson, another White House hatchet man who specialized in dirty tricks on Nixion's perceived enemies:

> We also discussed the findings of our phone checks on the *New York Times* papers. And, the reports really don't give us any clear cut picture, so the President was weighing a number of options. He called Ehrlichman to get an update; made the point to him that our whole concern from now must be the PR aspects. The morality, and so forth, is moot now because the papers are already out, and we've got to get off the wicket of appearing to cover up for LBJ. He made the point that he wanted to get Huston back in to work with Colson, helping on the Democratic attack. Also, he does not want them to indict the *Times*, just the thief.[18]

Minutes later on June 21, 10:35 a.m.

Nixon phoned Kissinger after he wrapped up with Haldeman in Key Biscayne. Kissinger had stayed back in Washington. Nixon evidently thought his national security adviser needed bucking up. Kissinger had expressed a worry the day before that the Pentagon Papers controversy would put a chill on their plans for the secret China trip.

> NIXON: Is your morale a little better today?
>
> KISSINGER: I don't know why you think it is bad, Mr. President.
>
> NIXON: Well, you're bound to be depressed to have these bastards raise these questions [about Kissinger's involvement in the Pentagon Papers].... You have got to remember that this is a battle. When we smoked everybody out on Laos and that time with the demonstration,[19] it's the same thing. From the standpoint of enemies at home, we have really got them smoked out now. Even Ted [Kennedy] and the whole bunch.... You know, the impact around the country on this is not as big as it seems. You would think from reading the *New York Times* and the *Washington Post* that it's the biggest story in the world. But it doesn't have the emotional impact of the Calley [My Lai massacre] story.
>
> KISSINGER: I think we can still turn it to an advantage [in] a period of weeks.
>
> NIXON: We may well be able to. But whether or not we are able to do that, we know that it is going to go away. You know that because, due to the fact that after you water it all down, what is it? An old story. They have been saying for a long time that Johnson lied and it's an immoral war. They'll try to make a hero out of the guy that did it though—we can't allow that. It's like they tried to make a hero out of [Nixon nemesis Alger] Hiss.
>
> KISSINGER: It's exactly the same phenomenon.[20]

It went on like this, the two men reassuring themselves that all would turn out fine in the end. And if everything wasn't fine—well, then it wasn't yet the end. The government still had court appeals going in what were now multiple Pentagon Papers cases. Kissinger likened it to a poker game.

> KISSINGER: Well, next week some of our cards are going to fall and we will know what we are holding. We can play it the other way then.
>
> NIXON: Well, it's too bad you had to come down with all these problems, but are you all right now?
>
> KISSINGER: Mr. President, I am fine, and we got a lot of very good work done down there (as Nixon remained in Key Biscayne).
>
> NIXON: Henry, for the next couple of weeks, skip the parties; get some rest. I wouldn't try to fight the battle with the press guys. I don't think this is the week to do it.

That was interesting advice, given the numerous First Amendment cases now making their way to the Supreme Court.

Wednesday, June 23, 1971

With court actions pending in Washington and New York—and both cases on a speedy path to the Supreme Court—Nixon and Haldeman began planning how to get back on the offensive.

Nixon called Senate Majority Leader Mike Mansfield to the White House for a working breakfast and made an offer that Mansfield accepted: Nixon would turn over the still-classified Pentagon Papers to Mansfield and his House counterpart, Speaker Carl Albert (D-OK). The two top congressional Democrats then would have the authority to do whatever they wanted to with the documents, including holding hearings (which Nixon thought they would do). This pleased Nixon, who thought he had just walked Mansfield into a trap—because the revelations in the Papers were about the lies and misconduct of Democratic administrations. Haldeman recounted the breakfast meeting in his diary:

> The President worked out a deal whereby we will turn the papers over to Mansfield and Albert, and they can figure out how to handle getting them to the proper Congressional committees, etcetera. This puts the heat completely on them. It fits in with Ehrlichman's strategy on the basis that they will then have to hold hearings, etcetera, to follow up on this, which will be an enormous problem for the Democrats to figure out how to cope with.

Next the president brought up the Democrats' efforts to set a deadline for pulling out all American troops from Vietnam. Kissinger would soon be leaving for London, the first leg of a round-the-world mission that would eventually secretly take him to Beijing. One of Kissinger's stops was to be Paris, where the national security adviser intended to try to get the peace negotiations back on track. Nixon warned Mansfield in no uncertain terms that, if the Paris negotiations failed, he would blame the Senate's meddling, unless Mansfield backed off.

But privately, Nixon was playing a game of chess about the war that had him thinking two moves ahead. His first concerned Kissinger, whose Paris visit, Nixon told him, was do-or-die for the negotiations. Economic problems at home required more focus, and the Paris stop would be the talks' last hurrah, as far as the president was concerned. "This is it," he warned Kissinger that morning.

Nixon's second move looked ahead to the war itself. If the North Vietnamese delegation in Paris remained intransigent, Nixon would blame Mansfield and the Democrats. But Nixon planned to up the ante. If the talks remained stalled, he would "flush the whole deal" and bomb the hell out of the North—"a total bombing of the North to eliminate their capability of attacking, so in order to get out, we escalate to accelerate our withdrawal."

Haldeman's diary entry for that day explained it fully:

> The president, after leading Mansfield on [about turning over the Pentagon Papers to Congress] and finish-

> ing that up, indirectly led him into the question of the Mansfield amendment yesterday calling for a date certain to end the war in nine months, and the president gave him a basic ultimatum regarding the harm that the Senate did, and he rather happily described this to Kissinger and me and Ehrlichman, who was there for it, in his office. He made the point that we are in the middle of negotiations that started May 31, and we'll know within a month whether the Senate action has ruined those negotiations. If so, the President will have to go on to the people and explain that the reason for the collapse was the action of the Senate, and that Mansfield will have to take that blame.
>
> He made the point to us that, if we do get to the point where we have to withdraw because the negotiations failed, he will do it with a total bombing of the North to eliminate their capability of attacking; so in order to get out, we escalate to accelerate our withdrawal. Henry was in and out several times in the morning, as he was getting ready to leave for London for his cover-up to his move on to Paris this weekend for the negotiations. The President made the point to him regarding Paris that, this is it: he's got to get it settled, that from here on everything is based on the domestic political outlook, and he's got to realize that. He makes the point, too, that with the Mansfield resolution, now maybe we have the excuse for flushing the whole deal. That we had to make that decision last year, either to stand up or to flush, and we made the decision to stand up, feeling that we'd never have the chance to decide it again. But now we probably do have that chance, because of the Senate resolution; and if the negotiations fail, that may be exactly what we will do.

Nixon and Haldeman had some other tricks up their sleeves. Now that Nixon had his own man in charge at the IRS, Haldeman reported they wanted to "pull the Clark Clifford file" and cause some tax problems for the former defense secretary, lest Clifford get any ideas about weighing in on the Papers. The White House wasn't going to stop there; Haldeman laid out plans to go after "all the top supporters of the doves—the full list with a full field audit—and see what we can make of it on analysis." Nothing like an IRS audit to get an enemy's attention.

The conversation turned to two others that Nixon considered either an outright enemy (Ted Kennedy) or simply unworthy of support (LBJ). As for the latter, political adviser Charles Colson was advising "don't defend him, but no overt attack."

Regarding Ted Kennedy, Kissinger said he'd observed Kennedy's womanizing a few weeks earlier at a gala benefit[21] for the brand-new John F. Kennedy Center for the Performing Arts, which was slated to officially open in September.[22] Based on what Kissinger reported back to Nixon, Haldeman thought they might be able to set up Kennedy in a "compromising"—read, blackmail—situation. Haldeman didn't recount how Kissinger knew any of this salacious stuff, particularly the floor numbers at the ritzy Carlyle Hotel in New York, where Kennedy supposedly propositioned automaker Henry Ford II's jet-set wife, Cristina. But the proposed setup to blackmail Ted Kennedy had all the makings of another job for Liddy:

> Kissinger reported that Teddy Kennedy is now in the position of practically being a total animal. At the opening of the Kennedy Center, he went to work on Cristina Ford,[23] who he had also propositioned at the Carlyle before he went to Paris for de Gaulle's funeral.[24] She was on the thirtieth floor, he on the seventh. He walked up to her floor, said he wanted to screw her, and she said that they couldn't because of the press, and he said that the press will never touch me. He pulled the same thing on Edgar Bergen's daughter [Candice Bergen],[25] according to Mrs. Bergen. So we need to take advantage of this

> opportunity and get him in a compromising situation if we can.
>
> We had a couple of political sessions today, one with Colson, at which he wanted to be sure that we lay off of LBJ, don't defend him, but no overt attack on him. Instead, attack the JFK, Eastern elite. Also, we should lay off the newspapers and go after the thief, playing up the stolen top secret documents. And, on the Mansfield amendment, for those who voted for it have to take the responsibility now for the failure of negotiations, if they do fail.[26]

The *Pentagon Papers* case, decided 6 to 3 by the Supreme Court on June 30,[27] would become a First Amendment story for the ages. The Court ruled that the government could not prevent the *New York Times* and the *Washington Post* from publishing classified documents about the Vietnam War, affirming the strong protection of the First Amendment against prior restraint. Before long, Ellsberg, with help from friends and employing the hit-and-run tactics that Bagdikian described, would manage to leak the Papers not only to the *Washington Post*, but to many other newspapers. Books and movies would celebrate journalism's epic win.

Meanwhile, Nixon's decision to implement the Huston Plan and blow the Brookings safe "on a thievery basis" set him on a path to disaster.

Thursday, July 1, 1971, 8:45 a.m.

The day after the Supreme Court's ruling in favor of the *Times* and the *Post*, Nixon was raging as he met with Haldeman. As if Liddy and his men weren't already on top of things, the president reiterated that he wanted his chief of staff to find a tough guy to stop what Nixon considered to be rampant leaking to the press. He also revealed his opinion of himself as a shrewd manipulator of the press when it was called for. Nixon pointed to his famous sound bite of the year before, calling Charles Manson "guilty of eight murders" even before the trial took place:

> I want you to find me a man by noon. A recommendation of the man to work directly with me on this whole situation. You know what I mean? I want a son of a bitch. I want somebody just as tough as I am for a change; just as tough as I was, I would say, in the Hiss case, where we won the case in the press. These goddamn lawyers, you know, all whining around. I'll never forget that they were all so worried about the Manson case. I knew exactly what we were doing on Manson.* You got to win some things in the press. These guys don't understand. They have no understanding of politics. They have no understanding of public relations. Do you think the *New York Times* is worried about all the legal niceties? Those sons of bitches are killing us! I want you to shake things up around here. Now, you do it! Shake them up! Get them off their goddamn dead asses. We're up against an enemy!

The White House Plumbers planned more break-ins and bugging. The unit never pulled off that job at Brookings; instead, its first operation targeted Ellsberg through a break-in at the Los Angeles office of Ellsberg's psychiatrist, Dr. Lewis Fielding.[28] The chaos had begun. A year later, Liddy's men would be caught burglarizing the Democratic National Committee's offices at the Watergate.

---

*The previous August, as Charles Manson and his followers were on trial for the murder of actress Sharon Tate and others, Nixon called Manson "guilty, directly or indirectly, of eight murders without reason." After criticism for prejudging the trial, Nixon's press secretary walked back the remark. But Nixon had his law-and-order sound bite.

CHAPTER 13

Distress

INFLATION WAS RAGING, AND THE war in Vietnam dragged on. The electorate was restive. Nixon was vexed by his critics in Congress. He and his vice president, Spiro Agnew, campaigned hard for Republicans in the 1970 midterms—Nixon the (relatively speaking) good-guy statesman, Agnew the attack dog. As was usually the case in a midterm election, the party in the White House would lose some seats in the House of Representatives. But Nixon sought an opportunity in the Senate.

Seeking more influence in the upper chamber, Nixon and Agnew ganged up on one of their own, Senator Charles Goodell, a loudly antiwar Republican whom the state's governor, Nelson Rockefeller, had appointed to fill Robert Kennedy's seat after RFK's assassination.

Agnew went on the attack against Goodell (father of the future NFL commissioner Roger Goodell). Agnew's line was that Goodell was a Republican in name only. The vice president (and Nixon) urged voters to support the candidate who was running on the Conservative Party line, James Buckley—the older brother of conservative firebrand and *National Review* founder William F. Buckley.

To show the Republican faithful how little he and Nixon thought of Goodell, Agnew crudely—but memorably—likened Goodell to someone who'd undergone a sex change. There was a pioneering transgendered actress and activist of the time, and

Agnew made the comparison to Goodell: "He is truly the Christine Jorgensen of the Republican Party."[1]

The strategy was for Nixon and Agnew to brand both Goodell and the Democratic candidate, Representative Richard Ottinger, as dreaded liberals, so that the two would split the Democratic votes, while Republicans united solidly behind Buckley and gave him the plurality win. And it worked. Goodell finished dead last, Ottinger second. Buckley won with just 39 percent of the vote. Buckley's was one of two Senate seats that Nixon's party picked up in the midterms.

As lawmakers returned to Washington in the New Year, Nixon met in the Oval Office at 10 a.m. on Tuesday, January 5, 1971, with Republican governors Rockefeller, Louie Nunn, of Kentucky, and Raymond Shafer, of Pennsylvania. The purpose of the visit was to build support for a new concept of Nixon's, which he called "revenue sharing."

The centerpiece of the president's "new federalism"—another Nixon catchword—was to eliminate hundreds of targeted federal programs that funneled money back to states and localities, replacing the mélange of categorical programs with pooled funding that the cities and states could spend as they wished. That was the idea of revenue sharing; states and localities could spend the money where it was needed most. But there was suspicion among the intended recipients, and in Congress (which ultimately passed Nixon's bill), that revenue sharing was really just a stalking horse for budget cuts, particularly in big cities, where more money was desperately needed.

Naturally, there was institutional resistance to change. Nixon sought to assure the governors that the money would still flow. He wanted their support.

New York City was on the brink of bankruptcy, and Rockefeller was in the Oval Office to plead for $10 billion in new federal funding to stave that off.[2] John Lindsay, the city's telegenic but beleaguered Republican mayor, was seriously considering bailing on his job and running for president—as a Democrat. Lindsay called being mayor of America's most populous city "the second toughest job in America."[3] New York City, Rockefeller feared, was falling down around him—and Lindsay was all good looks and no action. Rockefeller wanted to be rid of him. "He's a fella that we're trying to promote for a good part in a movie."

Rockefeller grew more animated. "It's the cities that are going down the drain," Rockefeller told Nixon.[4] New sources of revenue were desperately needed. "We're going down the drain right now.[5] New York City will not actually go bankrupt, but they will have to cut down on police and close some schools."

Nixon: "That's bankruptcy to me."[6]

Rockefeller agreed. "Social bankruptcy." (Only a federal and state bailout in 1975 saved the city from bankruptcy.)

Rockefeller told Nixon he could support revenue sharing, but he wanted Nixon to push for something even bigger at the same time: a value-added tax, VAT for short. The tax was the equivalent of a national sales tax, and it was the main revenue-raiser in most of the rest of the world—and highly efficient, at that. What made VAT so attractive was its simplicity: It was a tax on consumption, not earnings, and it was collected at each stage of the supply chain. VAT was tried and true in Europe. The progressive income tax, with all its complications and exemptions, was virtually unheard of elsewhere on the scale that it existed in America.

A European-style VAT as a revenue-raiser made sense from a practical standpoint, but the public and their elected representatives didn't understand it. And although Nixon was personally a VAT fan—a lot of accountants and tax lawyers would be looking for new lines of work—he knew the battle would be steep. Nixon didn't want to tangle with the powerful chairman of the tax-writing House Ways and Means Committee, Wilbur Mills (D-AR). When it came to tax legislation, Mills was all powerful. The standing joke in Washington at the time was that Mills's bedside reading was the tax code.

Rockefeller said he had already talked to Mills, and the chairman was receptive to a twofer—VAT and revenue sharing. But the governor also worried Mills might have been fibbing.

"I know how you feel, Nelson, about the value-added tax," Nixon told Rockefeller that January morning. "It is on my mind, but if we put it on [Mills's] plate with welfare reform and revenue sharing, he'll never be able to wheel it out."

Nixon told Rockefeller to smile, because New York was at least going to get revenue sharing.

Rockefeller: "I'm not going to commit myself with a smile. The value-added tax is absolutely essential for the country."

Rockefeller advised Nixon that he would have to "run against the Congress" in 1972. "So you shouldn't just propose what Congress is likely to accept. You should go in with a big proposal."

"Later," Nixon replied. Because, in fact, he was pondering some bold economic moves—and, befitting a president known as a trickster, few would see them coming.

There soon would be a new sheriff in town, a political gunslinger bringing order to the economic beat. His name: John Connally, the larger-than-life former governor of Texas.

Connally was tall and suave—all swagger and cowboy boots—and a natural politician who had switched sides numerous times to get where Nixon now placed him, as his new treasury secretary.

"He looked and behaved like a Texan, but with some of the rough edges smoothed over," wrote a British journalist, Peter Pringle.[7] Pringle had a keen eye for America's wiliest politicians. He would eventually write the big man's obituary[8]:

> They called him a suave Lyndon Johnson, who was his mentor. He was a political opportunist, without compassion. . . . Johnson reportedly once said of Connally's political campaign tactics that he "could leave more dead bodies in the field with less remorse than any politician I ever knew."

Coming from a shrewd politician like Johnson, that was the highest of praise.

Connally had an up-from-the-bootstraps story that propelled him to political stardom: raised on a Texas farm; wartime naval hero; awarded the Bronze Star for valor in the Pacific; University of Texas law degree. He got his start in politics campaigning for LBJ in 1948, when Johnson first ran for the Senate. Then Connally switched sides and jumped to the presidential campaign of Dwight Eisenhower. In 1960, Connally was back with Johnson, serving as LBJ's chief wrangler of delegates at the 1960 Democratic convention.

But Connally's true loyalty was to himself. After JFK won the nomination, and then the presidency, Connally quickly became a trusted Kennedy man. Defense Secretary Robert McNamara insisted upon naming Connally to be secretary of the navy, in spite of JFK's initial reservations about putting in an LBJ loyalist. JFK didn't say yes right away; he asked McNamara to run Connally's name past LBJ and another Texan, House Speaker Sam Rayburn.[9] Both approved.

McNamara trusted Connally and held him in the highest esteem,[10] as he later told Peter Osnos, McNamara's editor at Random House[11]:

> I was right on Connally. Connally was one of the loyalest people in town for Kennedy. . . . [The president] knew he had made a deal with me. He knew he was going to lose a secretary of defense if he didn't go along this way, and he would have.

Connally's time in the navy secretary role was brief, but eventful—he resigned at the end of 1961[12] to run for governor of Texas the following year. After he left the Pentagon, a handwritten letter came in from an ex-Marine, personally addressed to Connally.

The January 30, 1961, letter[13] was from a former Marine whose honorable discharge had been changed to dishonorable after he attempted to defect to the Soviet Union. The sender listed his return address as Minsk, USSR. The sender wanted his discharge changed back to honorable. A reply[14] was sent back under Connally's name, telling the sender that Connally had passed it along to his successor.

The ex-Marine was Lee Harvey Oswald.[15]

Connally was sitting in the front row of passenger seats in Kennedy's limousine when JFK was assassinated on November 22, 1963. Connally was seriously wounded and almost died. Were the shots fired at the limousine that day in Dallas in 1963 meant for him? Oswald had no clear motive for killing Kennedy. Did he, for going after Connally?[16] For once, Connally kept his mouth shut.

Stubborn inflation, driven upward by the Vietnam War deficits, was a dagger pointed directly at the heart of Nixon's coming re-election campaign. To make sure that voters blamed Republicans for the hellacious increases in prices and rents, House and Senate Democrats had pushed through a bill the prior year that put squarely on the president the onus for doing something about inflation.[17] The bill was aptly named the Economic Stabilization Act. Of course, who wasn't in favor of economic stability?

The new legislation made clear that it was solely the prerogative of the president to take action against inflation. The legislation set up a wage-price regulatory agency called the Cost of Living Council, and even gave Nixon authority to temporarily freeze wages, prices, and rents with the stroke of a pen. This was unprecedented. It was a surprising, politically motivated grant of authority giving Nixon a power over wages and prices that had never been used in peacetime. If he didn't deploy the weapon that the Democrats had given him, well, too bad for Nixon.

The president now owned the nation's inflation problem.

Nixon had a new, and compliant, Republican chairman of the Federal Reserve Board, Arthur Burns. Burns had started out as a White House economic adviser, and he was working in lockstep with Nixon on economic matters. Burns favored controls. But the White House party line was that Nixon wasn't going to use the extreme power that Congress had given him.

Nixon kept saying the same thing. On the evening before he met with the governors, Nixon sat down with anchors from the four television networks—ABC, NBC, CBS, and PBS—and was asked straight up about it by CBS's Eric Sevareid:

> SEVAREID: Mr. President, you described what you want to happen with your new economy program in the New Year, but what is going to be in it? You have sounded as though there is going to be nothing about controls of prices or wages, or anything of the sort. Is that what we are to assume from what you have just said?
>
> NIXON: Mr. Sevareid, I do not plan to ask for wage controls or price controls. And I have noted, incidentally, that all of you, the four commentators here, have commented upon controls in one way or another. I know Mr. [Howard K.] Smith [of ABC], for example, has talked about the possibility of wage-price guidelines or a wage-price board, and Dr. Arthur Burns has hinted that possibly that might be something we should turn to.
>
> I have considered all those options. I have decided that none of them at this time would work. And consequently I feel that the best course is to proceed, as I have suggested, with an expansionary budgetary policy, but one that will not exceed full employment revenues, and at the same time with a monetary policy that will be adequate to fuel a growing economy. I believe this will reduce unemployment, and also I believe it will do so at a time that inflation will continue to come down.
>
> If I could come back, Mr. Sevareid, to another point that you raised, I also should point out that we do not plan—despite the speculation that you have heard about—I do not plan to ask for new taxes. I have considered the possibility of the value-

> added tax as a substitution for some of our other taxes, and, looking to the future, we may very well move into that direction.
>
> But this year, I do not think it is realistic to propose a new tax, either new taxes or tax reform, because I am going to give the Congress—and particularly the Ways and Means Committee of the House and the Finance Committee of the Senate—a very full plate in other areas requiring their attention, including, for example, welfare reform that I will submit again; and including also a new health program which will go to those committees; and including also a new, what we will call revenue sharing, going far beyond anything that we have suggested to date.[18]

Nixon's mentioning health care was noteworthy; he was nearly four decades ahead of Congress on the revolutionary idea of providing health care coverage for all Americans. Ted Kennedy ensured that the issue was being seriously debated in Congress, and in 1971 it also was the top agenda item at the American Medical Association's summer convention in Atlantic City.

Kennedy was the author of the most ambitious proposal. His plan would pay almost all the costs of medical services and would cover everyone. It would be operated by the federal government and financed through general tax revenues and a payroll tax on employers and employees that would be earmarked for health care. A half century later, an identical proposal from progressives would be known as "Medicare for all."

National health care, revenue sharing, VAT, federal controls, no new taxes. Nixon was planning a "big play"—that was the phrase he used—that the Democrats wouldn't see coming, but his valued speechwriter, Bill Safire, would. The possibility of wage and price controls continued to loom large. By summer, Nixon would be telling his economic advisers that "if and when we do it, we're gonna leapfrog 'em all."[19]

Safire understood what that meant:

> Liberals found a perverse pleasure in complaining about his pre-emption of some of their positions, as if accomplishment counted only if it had been preceded by long-held views or deep-seated urges. Yet on the big decisions, he was remarkably consistent in the way he made up his mind; the "big play!" as he called it, usually centered around a reversal of field. A handful of common denominators: (1) When circumstances change, a leader has not only the right but the obligation to change his policy to meet them. (2) Half measures are useful on small problems but on major matters accomplish nothing. (3) When the moment comes to jump—leapfrog over the position immediately ahead. (4) Resolve impasses on narrow issues by raising the level of discussions, so that dickering can take place along a broad front. (5) A comprehensive approach excuses internal inconsistencies and permits specific departures from philosophy. (6) Never apologize or look back.[20]

As the first president since the nineteenth century[21] to take office without a majority of his own party in either the House or the Senate, reaching across the aisle was a necessity. Nixon wanted a Democrat to be his chief ass-kicker on the economy. John Connally was the guy to deliver a Texas-sized surprise to Democrats, and the nation.

"Well," Nixon said to the governors who were with him in the Oval Office that day in early January—Rockefeller, Nunn, and Shafer—"now the nut cutting. We are going to reorganize this government come hell or high water. That's why we have Connally—not for Texas politics, but for national politics. He'll be pitching those congressmen hard as hell and sitting on top of the IRS. He'll be able to pitch pretty hard. He'll handle the Democratic governors"—the Republicans had fared poorly in the 1970 gubernatorial elections, losing eleven states—"you'll have to help him with the Republican governors."[22]

Nixon clearly thought John Connally would be able to work miracles, pushing through economic reforms, cutting the deficit, and bringing inflation under control. Connally, a vigorous fifty-three-year-old, with what seemed like a lifetime's worth of achievement already behind him, would take over the Treasury Department the following month—the only Democrat in Nixon's cabinet.

Nixon wrapped up his meeting with the governors. The chief justice was at the White House for Nixon's next appointment, and the president used that to his advantage, cutting the meeting short.

Chief Justice Warren Burger was "the only man I can't keep waiting," he told the governors. "He could put me in jail."[23]

By mid-April, the conservative columnist Stewart Alsop, writing in *Newsweek*, was piling on criticism. Alsop was a graduate of Groton and Yale and lived the gentleman's life in Georgetown, but he had his finger on the pulse of middle America.

In a trenchant (and, more than fifty-five years later, prescient) column titled "The Shafting of Mr. Average," Alsop recited grim Census Bureau statistics about the "average" head of an American household, ending with the "average family's income—$10,577 (about $85,000 today).

The realities that Mr. Average faced included high taxes, high inflation ("the money he has left is worth 19 percent less than it was only five years ago"), lots of bills, and college tuition expenses that he couldn't afford.

"Meanwhile, welfare and other benefits for the poor are ballooning out of sight and forcing up Mr. Average's taxes at a dizzying rate."

Alsop sought to explain why so many Mr. Averages felt fury at the murder conviction of Lieutenant William Calley for the My Lai massacre: "Calley *looks* like Mr. Average, Jr. He is the ideal symbol of the little guy who is getting shafted by the higher-ups, and Mr. Average has a deep and instinctive sympathy for him."

In case you couldn't see where this was headed, Alsop spelled it out: politics was mostly all about money, but the "radical left" just kept "nattering about how wonderful the Berrigan brothers (jailed for plotting to kidnap Henry Kissinger) are." Alsop foresaw a rageful chorus forming on the right, loudly demanding "that the system stop shafting poor Mr. Average. The Calley phenomenon is clear warning that, otherwise, Mr. Average will sooner or later move angrily toward the radical right."[24]

Nixon seemed to be getting the message—or was he?

With inflation continuing unchecked in the United States, European allies began to see rising prices as America's number one export. The European allies were blaming their own inflation and economic problems on America.

For twenty-seven years, America and its allies had relied on the 1944 Bretton Woods Agreement to maintain price and monetary stability between trading nations. The United States was the agreement's linchpin. The Bretton Woods Agreement set fixed rates of exchange between currencies, and allowed central banks to convert their holdings of dollars into gold, at the fixed price of $35 per ounce (about $275 today, and far from gold's price per ounce, at this writing, of over $3,000). But the agreement was breaking down in an increasingly fast-moving global marketplace. European central banks, wary of holding overvalued dollars, began cashing them in for the gold. Meanwhile, currency arbitrageurs were profiting. Corporations, banks, and others who controlled large sums of money exchanged unwanted dollars for West German marks, Swiss francs, Dutch guilders, and other "strong" European currencies. Most of the flow went into marks. The German central bank had to intervene in the foreign-exchange market to prop up the dollar.[25]

The world economic forecast was, well, let's call it cloudy, with a chance of catastrophe. On May 5, the Germans, Dutch, Belgians, and Austrians shut down their currency markets for the rest of the week in order to avoid having to take in more dollars. This was very bad news for the increasingly globalized economy.[26]

Connally offered reassurance to skeptical Democratic lawmakers, although secretly his department had already drawn up a contingency plan for unprecedented economic intervention.

Connally tried to assure lawmakers that the bad news was a blip, "transitory."[27] But June didn't bring any better news. On Friday, June 4, the report from the Labor Department showed *rising* unemployment—to 6.2 percent (the target was 4 percent). Wages were spiking; the steelworkers union had just won a multiyear wage settlement of 31 percent. The next Consumer Price Index report showed a year-on-year increase of 7.2 percent. A recession loomed.

The Fed's Burns told Congress that the "first priority" should be given to "a new government move to try to moderate price and wage increases." He expressed concern over the spread of "inflationary psychology" in this country. A few days later, the AFL-CIO president George Meany backed wage and price controls.

Interest rates kept rising in lockstep with the murder rate. New York City municipal bonds hit a record 7.6 percent, and murders in the city were up 30 percent year-over-year. New York's total of 714 murders in the first six months of 1971 set a record.

Also in the city, there was an influx of new residents arriving to apply for welfare benefits—and the city was pushing back. A new law required a one-year residency for welfare. Welfare applicants found ineligible were being bused back to where they came from. Some applicants decided to stay anyway, even though they didn't qualify for welfare.

Monday, June 21, 1971

Prices in May rose at twice the rate of just a few months earlier. Nixon's secretary of commerce, Maurice Stans, tried to reassure anxious CEOs. He repeated the Nixon party line that inflation was being brought under control.

Inflation had slowed somewhat during the first quarter, but now it was running hot again. Stans had to concede the problem was "stubborn."[28] Nixon knew it was even worse. He called his top economic advisers, with Connally the pack leader, to Camp

David for the first of what would end up being two summer weekends there to brainstorm solutions. Nixon had been distracted by Mayday, then the Pentagon Papers, then the secret planning for Kissinger's trip to China. But by the time Congress recessed for the summer, the president would be hatching a bold plan. It would catch the absent lawmakers flat-footed.

Saturday and Sunday, June 26 to 27, 1971

At Camp David, Nixon's advisers discussed realities both political and economic: stubborn inflation, rising unemployment, looming recession, and the exigencies of a coming reelection campaign. At the conclusion of the weekend, Connally said publicly that Nixon had ruled out using the power the Economic Stabilization Act granted him. The president, Connally said, "has confidence that we're on the right path."

Privately, however, Connally was selling—not telling—a very different line. He wanted bolder action from Nixon, including import restrictions to help domestic industries. Connally hoped Haldeman could break through to the boss.

Haldeman had a long one-on-one with Connally at Camp David that Sunday, and recorded it later that night in his diary:

> Connally feels strongly we shouldn't overlook international trade as a domestic issue, and he'll have a position paper on overall trade policy. He feels we have to have some restrictions on imports, and this will be popular domestically. The President has to be shown doing something about unemployment, fiscal responsibility, inflation, etcetera. He can win labor by showing an interest in protecting their jobs. We don't have to solve the problem, just work towards it, showing visible understanding and articulation. For example, steel: Just the fact of meeting with them [the steelworkers, who were threatening to go on strike][29] is worthwhile.

> One big problem is our own troops. That is, businessmen [who] think that we've given up on inflation, because we're not putting in controls, wage controls. . . . He feels strongly that [Nixon] has to do some unexpected things in an impromptu fashion, to keep people off balance, and pushes hard for this.[30]

Unexpected things. Impromptu fashion. Keep people off balance. Connally knew what played with Nixon. The Democrats were going to be surprised at what Nixon would do with the power they'd given him to impose wage and price controls.

Still brooding about business confidence after the Camp David economic summit, Nixon called a group of bankers, businessmen, and labor leaders to the Cabinet Room two days later and gave them a pep talk. Connally and George Shultz, the head of the Office of Management and Budget (OMB), were there to listen and provide backup. It was interesting to hear Nixon talk about what he thought the world would look like—in fifty years. The president leaned his elbows on the table, put his head in his hands, and spoke with closed eyes for a few moments[31]:

> After World War II, our position was this: We produced 50 percent of the world's steel. The American economic position was so dominant we were concerned about the dollar gap. The Soviet Union was prostrated. Western Europe had had it. Japan was a defeated nation.

Nixon opened his eyes and recalled visiting Latin America as Eisenhower's vice president, in 1958. The leader of Colombia had lectured him: "The problem is like a great poker game. The rest of the world can't play. You must give chips to others around the table, so they can play."

Nixon carried the analogy forward, to the world economic situation of the day. The United States had spread around the poker chips. Now the challenge for America was how to stay in the game:

> The most significant areas of the world in the immediate future are like five fingers of the hand. Other areas like Africa and Latin America are 50 years away. But here are the five fingers.

Nixon held up his hand and ticked them off:

> First, the thumb, the U.S., still the strongest; next, Western Europe, and boy, that Common Market is coming along fast; third, the Soviet Union; fourth, China; fifth, Japan. With that kind of world, the United States of America is entering a very interesting period. Our vision is obscured by our obsession with the war in Vietnam. God knows, that war will be over quite soon. If we had such control over our other problems, it would all be easy.
>
> We will have a live-and-let-live situation with the Soviet Union; we will have a strong ally in Western Europe, but not doing much for its own defense; we will have a competing China, no longer isolated. (*Nixon knew what the others didn't, which was that Kissinger would be there soon.*) And we will have a growing Japan.
>
> Now, the U.S. looks at low labor rates around the world and its immediate reaction is, "Boy, we better put up some quotas." Congressional pressure along these lines is enormous. But the U.S. cannot build a fence around itself and expect to survive as a great nation.[32]

Fifty years later, Nixon's predictions, including about the pressure for tariffs and quotas, would prove to be amazingly prescient.

Every August, the city of Washington virtually shuts down—as mandated by law. Lawmakers leave town. There are no hearings in session. It's been ever thus, but the time-honored tradition of a congressional summer break lasting at least thirty days was enshrined the year before, in the 1970 Legislative Reorganization Act. Members of Congress wanted a more predictable legislative schedule and a designated vacation time. They gave it to themselves. Starting with the Summer of '71, Congress voted itself an official five-week break, extending from Friday, August 6, through the Labor Day weekend.[33]

Monday, August 2, 1971, 10:00 a.m.

By Monday of Congress's recess week, lawmakers were already filtering out of the city. The international currency markets were roiling again. Inflation was moving the wrong way. Shrewdly, Connally showed up in the Oval Office and, one-on-one for an hour with Nixon,[34] began pushing the president to make a surprise move.

Connally's people at Treasury had been working on a contingency plan to head off an international monetary crisis since the May disruptions. Treasury's plan called for closing the gold window, floating the dollar, and imposing a 10 percent import tax. To this, Connally added a freeze on wages and prices. In essence, Connally was forcefully selling Nixon on all the elements of a complete remaking of the administration's economic policy, in one fell swoop.

In addition to the immediate freeze on wages and prices (allowed in the law passed by Congress the previous year), Connally's plan called for reinstitution of the investment tax credit, and various federal expenditure reductions and/or deferrals. He offered numbers to illustrate exactly what the positive impact on the budget would be.

On the international side, the treasury secretary proposed suspending convertibility and floating the dollar, along with a 10 percent import surcharge—in effect, an additional tariff on all imports. This would hit America's trading partners hard, and Canada worst of all. But Connally portrayed the tariff as an attractive part of the domestic program; he estimated tariffs would bring in an additional $4 billion annually into the federal coffers (about $31 billion today).

Everything was linked, Connally argued. Freezing wages and prices would give Nixon the protective cover needed in order to close the gold window and impose the tariffs. And taking action now, while Congress was away, would show bold leadership. It would demonstrate that Nixon was in charge of events rather than responding to them, and show that the president had the courage to take a position before being forced into it.

Under no circumstances was the State Department to be consulted, Connally advised Nixon, because State would take the side of foreign governments. Connally thought two of his colleagues on the four-man economic Quadriad—Fed Chairman Burns and OMB head George Shultz—would be tough sells, but they could be brought around.

Nixon was initially wary, but he seemed to gradually warm up to Connally's proposal, despite still having some reservations about a wage-price freeze and closing the gold window.[35] The president was inclined to favor a November/December time frame, but Connally warned of the increasing danger of leaks if the program was delayed. He urged the president to act quickly.

Wednesday, August 4, 1971, 2:19 p.m.

Connally was a master persuader when left alone with Nixon. The president met again with him in the Oval Office for almost an hour—much of the time just the two of them, until they were joined midway through by Shultz of OMB.[36] Connally was upping the ante. He was urging Nixon to act more quickly on the economy, although he counseled September—when the World Bank and International Monetary Fund would be holding meetings in Washington—would be soon enough.

Nixon told Connally they needed to run against the tide; they needed to turn the tide. Connally was a Texan, after all, so he tried out a stampede analogy in reply: You don't get in front of the cattle during a stampede, you run alongside the thundering herd and gradually turn them. Connally advised Nixon that he needed to think that way. Run *with* the issue, use the opposition's momentum to bring them your way; don't fight it. Connally was saying, in effect, that politicians and the public could be brought back into line—they would understand and go along with "dramatic action." Nixon would turn the herd.

The State Department historian's account of Connally's salesmanship that day gave a blow-by-blow of the Oval Office discussion:

> The two discussed several aspects of the program and the President seemed to be on board. Connally, thumping the desk, advised the President not to defend or explain what was happening, but instead simply to acknowledge there were problems that the administration will solve. He advised the President to create the perception that he was as interested in domestic as foreign affairs, where he already enjoyed high marks, and said that when they returned in September and the President took the strong actions, that perception would change overnight. Connally advised against attempting to change the perception during August, but told the President he would have no choice but to do something before bilateral meetings with the Japanese scheduled for September 9 and before the Bank/Fund meetings in Washington at the end of September.
>
> Midway through that meeting they were joined by Shultz. The three then discussed several unrelated domestic issues before Nixon outlined for Shultz his discussion with Connally on the new program. The President thought the positives outweighed the negatives and that the day after Congress returned in September would be the best time to announce the program, which would give delegates to the Japanese bilateral meetings and the Bank/Fund meetings time to get instructions. Connally was to work it out. Shultz

> stated, somewhat in the form of a question, "You have decided to go with this big program, including the gold window and all that? Our task between now and September 8 is to think it through." The President said he needed to have it by August 23 to have time to reflect on it. He was concerned with leaks and said it was to be just between the three of them; [Pete] Peterson (special assistant for international economic affairs) was not to be told.[37]

Hours later on August 4, 3:50 p.m.

Nixon took the rest of the afternoon off. He and Pat left the White House on Marine One and helicoptered to Andrews Air Force Base, then took off for New York to visit Tricia and Ed Cox. The newlyweds were ensconced in tony digs at the Essex House on Central Park South. Tricia cooked dinner, and then all four took in a Broadway show: *No, No, Nanette.*[38]

"After an evening like this, you go away feeling better," Nixon said. By 12:15 a.m., Dick and Pat were back at the White House, and soon the president was back on the phone with Kissinger, talking to him for almost a half hour, until 12:52 a.m.[39] Nixon was restless. His full cabinet would be meeting later that morning, and the economy was top of mind.

Thursday, August 5, 1971, 9:40 a.m.[40]

Back at the White House on Thursday morning, Nixon was busy talking again by phone—in turn, to Kissinger and Connally and Haldeman. Nixon was coming around to Connally's way of thinking—but he was leaning toward even faster action because of the continuing bad news about the economy.

The wholesale price index, announced that morning, showed another big jump. And stocks were trapped in a grinding bear market; the Dow Jones Industrial Average now had been hovering for years at or below 850.[41] (It would not be until the Reagan years that the Dow finally reached 1,000.[42])

Then came the cabinet meeting.[43] It was scheduled for an hour, but lasted two, because Nixon wanted to talk about the economy and the plans being hatched by the Quadriad, Nixon's four top economic advisers: Connally (as chairman), Burns from the Fed, OMB Director Shultz, and Paul McCracken, the chair of the Council of Economic Advisers.

Nixon viewed the economic problems through a PR lens. "We can't let the opposition dominate the talk on the economy," Nixon told the group—a sign that Connally's salesmanship was working.

Later that day, Alabama's governor, George Wallace, the avowed segregationist, announced he would run for the Democratic presidential nomination. The field of Nixon's challengers was becoming crowded.

It wasn't safe to leave town, because Nixon was making big economic plans that would be every bit the surprise as Kissinger's trip to China.

Thursday, August 12, 1971

From Haldeman's diary:

> Connally called me today to say he was going to come back up—he was in Texas on vacation. He was going to come back up this afternoon as soon as possible, because we had a bad day in the gold market yesterday and another bad day today, and he anticipates a really bad one tomorrow. He says the uneasiness is continuing in many countries and deteriorating daily. He's going to have [Treasury Under Secretary Paul] Volcker send the figures over to me, and all, but he thinks we can move on the whole deal, and at least we can move on the international front, close the gold

> window, and so forth today and maybe wait until Monday on the domestic front. But when we do any one of them, we've got to show all the planning and preparation and do some more. He says there's no panic, but it is getting worse and worse, and we're losing the initiative.
>
> So Connally came on up and met with the President at 5:30 today, after which the president called me while I was out to dinner to say that they had decided to go ahead on the whole move on Monday, and that we were going to pack up the key people—including Arthur Burns and the key Treasury and economic group—go to Camp David tomorrow afternoon, spend the weekend there and get it worked out, and make the announcement on Monday. We'll cover the whole thing when we do it, apparently, so it's going to be quite an earthshaking operation.

Nixon had given the green light to a full ninety-day freeze of wages, prices, and rents, plus a plethora of other things that would be worked out among the participants at Camp David that weekend.

Friday, August 13, 1971, 2:30 p.m.[44]

The big game was on. Nixon and his economic Quadriad—Connally, Burns, Shultz, and McCracken—hopped into Marine One for the half-hour helicopter trip to Camp David, in Maryland's Catoctin Mountains. Pat stayed behind; this was a working weekend. Nixon told the rest of the group—including his favored speechwriter, Bill Safire, who would be writing Nixon's announcement of the freeze and other actions—to take a different Marine helicopter, from the helipad at the Anacostia naval base. That was a few minutes away. Nixon wanted zero leaks, and he thought the staggered departures from separate locations would arouse less suspicion.[45]

Nixon called the group together that evening. The first thing he said was, "Nobody is bound by past positions in this discussion. Circumstances change."[46]

That first evening, the president stayed back at Aspen Lodge, while the rest of the group took their evening meal in the formal dining room at Laurel Lodge, the central hub at Camp David. But Nixon was getting reports by phone about the table talk from Ehrlichman, who periodically left the table to update his boss. After one such call by Ehrlichman, Nixon asked him to call Safire to the phone. It was time for some ego stroking. Nixon said:

> Ehrlichman has been telling me of the contribution you're making. That's good. You know, Arthur is a fine man. A fine man. Tell him I said that.

Safire did exactly that, during a midnight walk with Burns the following night:

> I did so, without telling him the president told me to tell him, and [Burns] was moved. We talked about Connally. "He's an ambitious man, a forceful man. I think he'll help the president." He was sorry, on an institutional basis, that McCracken and the Council [of Economic Advisers] had been eclipsed by [OMB's] Shultz. "The personal chemistry isn't there between Paul [McCracken] and the president, which is unfortunate. I tried so hard not to get in his way when I was a counselor."[47]

Paul Volcker, forty-three years old and Connally's under secretary, was in on the Camp David discussions. It would be Volcker, as Fed chair more than a decade later, who would finally get credit for stopping the inflationary spiral. But on this weekend, he brought his New York banker's sensibility to the meeting. As Safire recounted it in his contemporaneous notes:

> At the Friday dinner, Volcker told Haldeman of the need for secrecy—"Fortunes could be made with this information." Haldeman, mock-serious, leaned forward and said, "How?" Volcker, when the plan was still to make the speech Monday night, told Shultz: "How much is your budget deficit?" Shultz: "$23 billion" (about $188 billion in today's dollars). Volcker: "Give me a billion dollars and a free hand on Monday, and I'll make it for you on the money market."

Needless to say, the group decided that Nixon would announce the freeze on Sunday night, before anyone could front-run the markets.

Saturday, August 14, 1971, 3:15 a.m.

Middle of the night. Alone in Aspen Lodge, Nixon was restless. Couldn't sleep. Nixon started writing the speech that he intended to deliver to the nation on Sunday evening. He filled up three pages of White House stationery, both sides. He then used those notes to dictate onto four Dictaphone tapes his speech draft for Safire to start working on. Finally done with that, at 5:45 a.m., Nixon went for a half-hour swim.

From Safire's diary of that weekend:

> Around 6 a.m., I think, he put on a bathrobe and walked out onto the pool terrace, where he ran into a Navy chief [petty officer] who had been using the sauna. The chief was startled: "Good morning, ma'am—I mean, sir!" He handed the tapes to the chief and told him to take them to Rose Woods (Nixon's secretary). She told me she heard her screen door open and bang shut about 6 a.m. She got up soon after, and started work on them. The president then went back to sleep while I melded together my draft and his.

After that, Nixon finally slept for two hours. He was up again at 8:30 a.m.

The presence of Fed Chairman Burns at Camp David was noteworthy, given the Fed's independence and the obvious political overtones of the economic moves being planned. Burns, sixty-seven, was an old-school economist, and he was wary of all the international monetary actions that Connally was proposing, particularly when it came to the gold standard. The orderliness of the Bretton Woods Agreement was sacrosanct to Burns.

Nixon wanted to make sure he had Burns's support. And Burns, a loyalist who had been slotted into a counselor's role at the White House until the Fed vacancy opened up, fell into line. During a Friday evening meeting between Nixon and the Quadriad, Burns gave Nixon his word on that.

"I argued pretty strenuously against the gold move," Burns confided in his midnight walk with Safire that weekend. "But when it was decided, I told the president he would have my wholehearted support."[48]

Sunday, August 15, 1971, 4:00 p.m.

On Sunday afternoon, before the group disbanded, Burns affirmed the pledge he'd made to Nixon on the first night at Camp David. He meant it to be an inspirational pitch to the whole group:

> A proposal of this scope has not been put forward by an American president since Franklin Roosevelt—and even then, he put out a series of programs, not such a sweeping, overall proposal.
>
> We have the problems of unemployment, rising prices and inflation—which we needed to administer a shock treatment—a balance of trade problem to restore, a balance of payments to restore equilibrium. Not a small step—not small steps at the margin, but

> major action. Productivity, new and faster path of economic growth.
>
> Proliferation of government: The president called a halt to the expansion of bureaucracy and actually is pulling it back. The new economic policy has been evolved over a period of time. This is a program for the first time that's been thought through, thoroughly integrated so that the pieces fit together.
>
> There's been a lot of talk about gold. Very few people understand it. Any questions on this should be referred to the Treasury and the Fed. There's been talk about devaluation. This is a word that's used loosely, especially by laymen. The answer is, the president has stabilized the dollar. Regarding the freeze: it'll be followed by another stage. We have not embarked on a policy of controls. This is not the policy. We're trying to speed the transition from inflation to price stability. We continue to believe in free markets and will return to free markets. There's a lot of foolish talk in the press about differences between Burns and the President. You can quote me as saying I support this program fully.[49]

Later on Sunday afternoon, August 15

It's a twenty-six-minute trip from Camp David to the White House; Nixon arrived back at the executive mansion at 4:50 p.m. He was alone in the residence—except for Haldeman, Safire, and his makeup artist, forty-year-old Ray Voege, on call for Nixon's special request. Voege was the makeup man for Johnny Carson, the king of late night. Nixon was in good hands.[50]

Shortly before 9:00 p.m., Nixon walked into the Oval Office and gave his twenty-two-minute address to the nation. The big headlines were about an end to the gold standard, a ninety-day freeze on wages and prices, a 10 percent tariff on imports, and a 10 percent cut in foreign aid. But there was much more to the plan: a federal pay freeze, a 5 percent cut in the federal workforce, new tax breaks for R & D spending, and a big reduction (about $36 billion in today's dollars) in overall federal spending.[51]

Afterward, Nixon spent hours on the phone, calling around, asking dozens of friends, lawmakers, and his economic officials how he did.[52] Of course, they loved it. And the stock market got a bounce up the next morning. Haldeman made a diary entry that night: *We're in good shape.*

A few weeks later, Nixon addressed a rare joint session of Congress about the economy. He'd be followed to the rostrum by men who were being feted as true heroes: the triumphant Apollo 15 astronauts—just back from the Moon, and a ticker tape parade in New York.[53]

In the moment, there was optimism.

It wouldn't last.

Despite the ebullience of the moment, Nixon's dark side soon would get a jolt of adrenaline—from his White House counsel, John Dean.

Monday, August 16, 1971

Dean had been pulled into the machinations of Huston, Liddy, and the Plumbers. His task was to find ways to make life miserable for Nixon's enemies. Dean did so with lawyerly efficiency, dispatching a memo to Haldeman and Ehrlichman entitled "Dealing with our Political Enemies."

Dean's memo left no doubt about Nixon's intentions:

> August 16, 1971
> CONFIDENTIAL
> MEMORANDUM
> SUBJECT: Dealing with our Political Enemies
>
> This memorandum addresses the matter of how we can maximize the fact of our incumbency in dealing with persons known to be active in their opposition to our Administration. Stated a bit more bluntly—how

> can we use the available federal machinery to screw our political enemies.

Dean marveled at the simplicity of the plan that could be hatched. All the White House would need to unleash the full "federal machinery" on Nixon's enemies would be a "good project coordinator and full support for the project":

> The project coordinator should then determine what sorts of dealings these individuals have with the federal government and how we can best screw them (e.g., grant availability, federal contracts, litigation, prosecution, etc.).[54]

The Plumbers would soon have more work to do.

CHAPTER 14

Revolution

By May 1971, a vicious summer of racial mistrust and unrest had begun.

It was dangerous to be a cop in New York City. Police officers were being murdered at an alarming rate. Two patrolmen were killed in a nighttime ambush on the northern edge of Harlem, cut down by .45-caliber bullets. Police traced the murders to the Black Liberation Army.[1] One night earlier, two cops were wounded by automatic-weapon fire on the Upper West Side—all brazen, targeted attacks.[2]

Five individuals were sentenced to prison for planning to dynamite or firebomb numerous buildings in New York—including a bank and the offices of President Nixon's former law firm. Another person in the plot had been involved in the bombing at the U.S. Capitol two months before.[3]

Court-approved wiretaps used by federal and state law enforcement to target terrorists had doubled in one year.[4]

The Supreme Court was sounding tough about the death penalty, ruling 6 to 3 that juries could be empowered to impose executions, and to do so immediately after deciding someone's guilt. No person had been put to death for a crime in the United States in almost four years, and 648 people were on death row. The High Court's ruling cleared the way for resuming executions.[5]

Thirteen members of the Black Panther Party were on trial in New York City, charged with attempted murder and conspiracy in a plot to kill police officers. Yippie Abbie Hoffman, indicted earlier in the month in Washington for being one of the masterminds of the Mayday demonstrations,[6] was raising money for the Panther defense fund.

Bobby Seale, one of the Panther founders, was on trial in New Haven—also charged with murder.

Angela Davis, captured by the FBI after two months on the run, faced the death penalty in California for her alleged role in the San Rafael courthouse murders the year before.

A group of Native American activists protesting federal Indian policy and asserting their ancestral rights occupied Alcatraz Island—site of the former maximum-security prison, aka the Rock—for eighteen months, just over a mile off the coast of San Francisco. Nixon and his racist third-party challenger in the 1968 presidential election, Alabama Governor George Wallace, further added to the drama. Wallace planned to run again for the Democratic Party's presidential nomination. Nixon would likely be facing a rematch with Wallace in the coming presidential election.[7]

All this happened at the start of a long, violent summer of '71.

Thursday, May 13, 1971, 4:35 p.m.

After an eight-month criminal trial in New York City, the longest and most expensive in the state's history, thirteen members of the Black Panther Party were found not guilty of all 156 attempted-murder and conspiracy charges against them.[8] Huey Newton and Bobby Seale, the Panther founders and supreme leaders, figured prominently in the trial, although they were not defendants.

The Panthers were a reflection of the times, a Black Power group unquestionably advocating—and, authorities said, engaging in—mayhem and murder.

But the big question at the New York City trial of the thirteen Panthers was whether NYPD undercover cops encouraged the specific acts the Panthers were accused of: plotting to dynamite police precincts, bridges, department stores, railway and subway stations, and the New York Botanical Garden. The jury took only a few hours to answer that question: acquittals on all counts.

Gerald Lefcourt, the lead defense lawyer in the Panther case, was just twenty-eight years old—an underdog Brooklyn Law School grad just beginning his career.[9] The verdict instantly made him the go-to lawyer for such notorious criminal cases—a much-deserved reputation that would endure for over five decades to come. In future years, Lefcourt would represent not just the Panthers and Abbie Hoffman, but a slew of other notorious clients, including sex offender Jeffrey Epstein.

Early on, Lefcourt had a knack for publicity that propelled his career. Already, he had a scrapbook of hundreds of clippings in which he was mentioned. Lefcourt worked out of an office on Union Square West—the walls filled with posters and radical slogans, not diplomas—and lived in a one-room apartment uptown strewn with briefs, posters, and buttons with such slogans as: *If you're not part of the solution, you're part of the problem.*

"Youth— that's what it's all about," he said. "In three or four years we're going to turn the legal system upside down."[10]

Sure enough, Lefcourt's defense of the Panthers paid off. Since their arrests almost two years earlier, the Panthers had been in solitary confinement on Rikers Island. The first to walk out of the courtroom as a free man was Curtis Powell, holding both arms up with clenched fists and smiling. Five others followed, one slamming the courtroom door as he went into the hallway. Seven other Panthers were sent back to Rikers, since they still faced other criminal charges.[11]

Bullets were doing the talking because there was little to no dialogue otherwise. An example: It took the Congressional Black Caucus a year to get a meeting on the books with President Nixon, and two more months after that to get a response to their demands, which included more low-income housing, a minimum welfare payment of $6,500 (about $51,000 today), and more federal funding for Black enterprises. When the thirteen Black congressional members finally got their answer from the White House, it was a 112-page response that was mostly a brush-off. One thing the president said he was adamant about: maintaining the police practices of "preventive detention" and "no-knock entry" in the capital city of Washington, DC. Nixon wanted to appear tough on crime, and DC had been tarred by Nixon as the crime capital. For the president, any attack on DC was a reelection tailwind. It played well with his base.[12]

In New York City, cops were under attack, and the summer of '71 was the bloodiest one in the NYPD's history. The last time officers were the subject of such unrelenting fear was four decades earlier, during the post-Prohibition gangland era of the early 1930s.[13] The cause of their fear was different this time: Black revolutionaries had the cops in their gun sights, and they were making a point by targeting and killing them. Before August was over, the 1930 record for cop killings would be tied at ten. By the end of the year, fourteen policemen had been killed on the job.

Even the NYPD, in its documentary history, to this day does not mince words about the dangers of that year. Here's the official police account, as it appears on the department's current website, boldface type and all:

> **1971 was not a good year to be a cop in New York.**
>
> The city was dying, everyone agreed, and not from natural causes. In one precinct in Harlem, one in 500 of its residents would be murdered. Citywide, homicide spiked 30 percent. Child pornography was sold openly in Times Square. Over a million people were on welfare, and destitution and blight were rampant. Slumlords found it more profitable to burn their buildings than to maintain them, and corporations were packing up and heading for the suburbs. Race relations

> were rancorous, as the protest marches of the early '60s gave way to riots, and the rise of Black Power was followed by waves of white flight. You can see the mood of bleary futility in a sampling of *Times* headlines: "In Brownsville, Looting is a Condition of Life; Robbery at Schools Accepted by People as a Necessity," "Trend Seen in Robbery-Killings of Elderly on Lower East Side," "Squalor is a Way of Life at a Welfare Hotel Here." Assaults on police were surging, and bulletproof vests were not yet standard equipment. Fourteen officers would die in the line of duty in 1971, 11 of them shot to death.
>
> At no point in history was the NYPD needed more, and admired less. The Knapp Commission began public hearings on police corruption in October 1970, leading to two years of headlines about shakedowns and bribes. Investigators told of cops responding to a break-in at a warehouse in Greenwich Village and taking whatever was left to steal. Any cop with a new car, or even a cop's wife with a new coat, would be met with knowing smirks by the neighbors. A greater loss in public support came in January 1971, when patrolmen conducted a five-day wildcat strike over a pay dispute, and only a sudden cold snap—along with the round-the-clock conscription of detectives and bosses—kept the city from greater mayhem. For what it was worth, expectations of what even an ideal department might accomplish were low: Mayor Lindsay believed that crime was a fact of the environment in poor neighborhoods, like asthma. Morale was in a tailspin. Not many cops encouraged their sons to follow them on "the job."[14]

In New York City, it would never be more dangerous to be a cop than in the summer of '71.

Wednesday, May 19, 1971, 10:00 p.m.

It was Malcolm X's birthday.

Six days after the verdict in the Black Panther trial, two officers assigned to a patrol car guarding the residence of District Attorney Frank S. Hogan were raked by fire from an automatic weapon—apparently, a machine gun—when they tried to stop a car for a traffic violation on Riverside Drive. They were critically wounded. The gunfire hit one policeman in the face, neck, and chest; the other in the neck, stomach, and arms.[15]

Hogan, the Manhattan DA, had twenty-four-hour police guards because of threats during the Black Panther conspiracy trial. The home of the judge in that case, John M. Murtagh, had been firebombed the previous August.

It was not certain, at first, if the attack was related to the Black Panther trial. But then the answer became clear.

Friday, May 21, 1971, 8:30 p.m.

The police had the license plate numbers for the getaway car in the Wednesday shootings, and the plate numbers were heavily publicized. It turned out to be a stolen car, but still, that was the only clue.

The shooters figured that if the police had the plate numbers, they might as well have the plates, too. So, at 8:30 p.m. that Friday, two days after the shooting, two people delivered one plate each—along with a live .45-caliber cartridge, same as the ones used in the shootings—to the front desks of the *New York Times*, on West Forty-Third Street, and radio station WLIB-FM, at 125th Street and Lenox Avenue in Harlem. A Black woman took the package to WLIB; a Black man to the *Times*. A typewritten note, black capital letters on white paper,[16] came inside each package. On the outside of the parcel, the sender said the contents related to: *the shooting of two NYPD pigs on Malcolm's birthday.*[17] The Black revolutionary, murdered in 1965, would have been forty-six years old.

The killers' note said:

> ALL POWER TO THE PEOPLE,
>
> HERE ARE THE LICENSE PLATES SOUGHT AFTER BY THE FASCIST STATE PIG POLICE. WE SEND THEM IN ORDER TO EXHIBIT THE POTENTIAL POWER OF OPPRESSED PEOPLES TO ACQUIRE REVOLUTIONARY JUSTICE.
>
> THE ARMED GOONS OF THIS RACIST GOVERNMENT WILL AGAIN MEET THE GUNS OF OPPRESSED THIRD WORLD PEOPLES AS LONG AS THEY OCCUPY OUR COMMUNITY AND MURDER OUR BROTHERS AND SISTERS IN THE NAME OF AMERICAN LAW AND ORDER; JUST AS THE FASCIST MARINES AND ARMY OCCUPY VIETNAM IN THE NAME OF DEMOCRACY AND MURDER VIETNAMESE PEOPLE IN THE NAME OF AMERICAN IMPERIALISM ARE CONFRONTED WITH THE GUNS OF THE VIETNAMESE LIBERATION ARMY, THE DOMESTIC ARMED FORCES OF RACISM AND OPPRESSION WILL BE CONFRONTED WITH THE GUNS OF THE BLACK LIBERATION ARMY, WHO WILL METE OUT IN THE TRADITION OF MALCOLM AND ALL TRUE REVOLUTIONARIES REAL JUSTICE. WE ARE REVOLUTIONARY JUSTICE.
>
> ALL POWER TO THE PEOPLE
>
> JUSTICE

When a *Times* guard asked what was in the package, the man who brought it turned and ran from the building.

The typewritten note said the Wednesday shootings had been carried out by "oppressed third world peoples." And it said that there would be more shootings to come. Ninety minutes later, that happened.

Ninety minutes later on May 21, 10:00 p.m.

Two New York City cops—one Black, one white—were ambushed and killed with .45-caliber weapons in a housing development on the northern edge of Harlem. Earlier that evening, two men threw lye into the face of a Transit Authority bus dispatcher standing on a Bronx street corner—because they mistook him for a policeman.[18]

The policemen killed were identified as Waverly M. Jones, thirty-three years old, and Joseph A. Piagentini, twenty-eight. Both were attached to the Thirty-Second Precinct and both had joined the force on August 1, 1966. They were pronounced dead on arrival at Harlem Hospital.

Trembling with emotion, Edward Kiernan, the head of the Police Benevolent Association (PBA), the union representing cops, declared that he was "directing every member assigned to a radio car to purchase a shotgun and keep it loaded and ready to use at all times."[19]

Kiernan said, "If circumstances require a patrolman to use his gun, he will shoot to kill." Kiernan held up a jacket belonging to one of the dead patrolmen and a shirt belonging to the other. The back of the jacket contained at least six bullet holes and the back of the shirt had at least two.

Police Commissioner Patrick Murphy called the shootings "the work of madmen."

Urban warfare had broken out in New York City—right there, right now.

Angela Davis now had a New York connection, too—although by the summer of '71, she was back in California, returned to the scene of the courtroom shooting.

The FBI's search for her had gone on for two months. Her first California jail cell was one floor up from the San Rafael courtroom where the shooting took place the previous August.

Davis faced the death penalty, because under the law in California, a conspirator to murder was as guilty as the murderer.

Davis had gone on the run while police were still tracing the four guns registered to her. She wore a short-hair wig and traded her granny glasses for horn-rims.

Davis made her way first to New York City, arriving there within five days of the 1970 courthouse shooting. She traveled with a friend named David Poindexter, who was from Chicago. That's where they went next. Then to Miami. She was put on the FBI's Ten Most Wanted list.

The FBI was far behind, but the Bureau got a break when an informant in Chicago reported seeing Poindexter with someone resembling Davis.[20] Agents found her fingerprints in the Chicago apartment where they'd holed up. Another informant placed the couple at an apartment in Miami. When agents entered, the couple was already gone, but they'd forgotten to take the registration papers for a new Toyota and a roll of film, which, once the FBI developed it, showed the new, stylish Angela—sans her enormous Afro. So now the FBI had a new description to put out.

There was also a soap wrapper from a Howard Johnson motel. When another informant reported that the couple had returned to New York, agents started visiting various Howard Johnson's. Soon they spotted Poindexter's new Toyota at the Howard Johnson's near Times Square. The two were arrested later that day, on October 13, 1970, as they returned to their room. Davis was held without bail in the Women's House of Detention in Greenwich Village—a dreary redbrick prison.[21] Poindexter was indicted for harboring a criminal federal fugitive; his mother posted the $100,000 bail.

"People want to know why we were found at Howard Johnson's," Poindexter said. "Well, we weren't in the ghetto because the [FBI] search was concentrated in ghettos all across the country. We know that hundreds of Black women resembling Angela were picked up. . . . When Angela asked me to help her, I was damned happy to comply. And it must be pointed out that in fact we did evade the dragnet for two months."[22]

Extradited back to California to stand trial for murder, Davis's case became a cause célèbre. Her co-defendant was Ruchell

Magee, the only survivor of the San Rafael shoot-out. Magee was so violent that, during pretrial hearings, he remained shackled and was chained to his chair, guards standing behind him. Unable to move, he spit at his handlers. The jail setup for Davis was better—although kept away from other prisoners and held in isolation, she nonetheless had two cells and a dayroom available for her use. Davis wrote letters to the outside, incessantly.

And she received visitors, who were successful at reframing the narrative around Davis. With racial tension in America at a peak, Davis's many supporters recast her as a political prisoner, not a murderer. Black activists, such as Jesse Jackson, came calling, as did cultural icons. Aretha Franklin offered to post bail. Nina Simone visited and brought along a red balloon, signifying hope.[23] James Baldwin wrote a lengthy open letter to her,[24] a portion of which starkly described the punishment the state of California was threatening:

> Only a handful of the millions of people in this vast place are aware that the fate intended for you, Sister Angela, and for George Jackson, and for the numberless prisoners in our concentration camps—for that is what they are—is a fate which is about to engulf them, too. . . .
>
> [W]e must fight for your life as though it were our own—which it is—and render impassable with our bodies the corridor to the gas chamber. For, if they take you in the morning, they will be coming for us that night.

By the summer of '71, Davis had been held in solitary confinement for eight months. The immediate question for the judge in her case was whether Davis would be granted bail. A second question was whether she would ever again see George Jackson. Davis longed for a visit with him.

Answers to both questions would come soon.

Friday, June 11, 1971

"The Rock" is a tiny island that sits a little more than a mile off the coast of San Francisco. A notorious federal prison used to be there. But now it was surplus federal property—and a group of Native Americans declared it to be their homeland. They journeyed out to the island and claimed it as their own, in the name of their native heritage, demanding that it be returned to the indigenous peoples who once occupied it. The group set up living quarters and established a radio station, Radio Free Alcatraz, which reached one hundred thousand listeners.[25]

The day the squatters landed, the island's lone federal guard had declared: "Mayday! Mayday! The Indians have landed!"[26] For months, and then more than a year, the government left things alone, until finally Nixon decided they'd had enough and planned a raid to remove the several dozen occupiers. His special adviser, lawyer Leonard Garment, counseled against it. "A mean and petty exercise of power," Garment called it. Bad optics.

Garment's memo began:

> CONFIDENTIAL
> Memorandum for John Ehrlichman
> From Leonard Garment
> Subject: Alcatraz
>
> I have a nagging feeling we would be wise to leave bad enough alone, but I admit I can't marshal convincing, factual arguments for this proposition. My basic concern is that our action now, after all that has transpired, with Alcatraz a symbol (however confused to begin with and tarnished now) of a "new Indian militancy" and a "new Indian identity," will come as something of a depressing anti-climax, and may be seen (or portrayed) as a mean and petty exercise of power.

Nixon didn't buy it. The government had already cut all electric and phone lines to the island. The original four hundred occupiers had dwindled to a hard core of fifteen. Garment thought that "the occupation might wither away completely." But that would have deprived Nixon of the law-and-order statement he wanted to make. One day after Garment sent his memo, armed federal marshals, FBI agents, and police stormed the island, forcibly removing the few remaining occupiers: women, children, and unarmed men.

Nixon had barely eked out a victory in 1968 over Humphrey and Alabama's George Wallace, running as a third-party candidate. And Wallace was showing every sign of readying to be a spoiler again in 1972.

By the summer of '71, Wallace, an avowed segregationist, with a devoted following in the South, had moderated his racist pronouncements somewhat. He announced that he would enter primaries for the Democratic presidential nomination. The Democratic field was getting crowded. Humphrey was seeking a rematch; Muskie, ditto. Also in the race was New York City's mayor, John Lindsay, who'd just switched parties, and the antiwar candidate George McGovern, senator from South Dakota.

Wallace was enjoying the limelight, playing the spoiler—and he enjoyed tweaking Nixon.[27] But when Nixon visited Wallace's home state late in May,[28] his first visit there as president, it was Wallace whom Nixon snubbed as the governor hitched a ride on Air Force One,[29] and then put in his place again during remarks to reporters and editors in Birmingham.

John Osborne, a columnist for the *New Republic,* and an indefatigable Nixon watcher (his weekly column was "The Nixon Watch"), typed up his notes. He was the only reporter traveling with the president who wrote what really happened[30]:

> The President putting George Wallace in his place was something to see and remember. . . .
>
> In both cities, the big crowds along the motorcade routes were naturally more interested in the president

> than they were in familiar little George, and they had to notice that the Governor was not invited to ride with Nixon in either city. At the Mobile airport, it was Wallace who (literally) saluted Nixon, and it was that way throughout the visit.[31]

Osborne also noted how Nixon deftly put down Wallace without explicitly shunning him in front of the home crowd. In Mobile, the first of Nixon's two stops in Alabama on his way home from Texas and Florida, the president remarked that he was more afraid of "Bear" Bryant, Alabama's legendary Crimson Tide football coach, than he was of Governor Wallace—and, by implication, of any effort that Wallace might make in the coming '72 election to deny Nixon the white vote in the Deep South.

Wallace's issue of the moment was the use of forced busing as a means of integrating schools. Wallace called it unconstitutional. But in April, in a decision involving school systems in North Carolina and Alabama, the Supreme Court had already ruled—unanimously—that much more stringent action was needed to eliminate the remnants of racial segregation in public schools than the president thought necessary, or politically expedient.[32] Nixon called Attorney General Mitchell to the White House the next day to discuss how to thread the needle—in other words, how to comply with the Court's order, without really doing so.

The busing issue was a racist trope, a proxy for every segregationist's complaint about judicial overreach.

Over the summer, the Alabama governor said he didn't intend to comply with the Supreme Court's order, or that of another federal appeals court that required busing of students to desegregate schools. Although the second case originally involved only schools in Austin, Texas,[33] a federal appeals court order later applied it, in effect, to every school system in the South's Fifth Circuit—including those in Wallace's state of Alabama.

Nixon had the summer of '71 to decide what to do. As Nixon sought to shore up support among voters on the left for his coming reelection bid, he had to contend with the demands and expectations of Wallace's voters on the right. August came, and Nixon was still waffling. He finally issued a statement that sought to have it both ways, not disavowing the court orders, but expressing his opposition to busing "simply for the sake of busing":

> I am against busing as that term is commonly used in school desegregation cases. I have consistently opposed the busing of our nation's schoolchildren to achieve a racial balance, and I am opposed to the busing of children simply for the sake of busing.[34]

Wallace remained defiant.[35] Reporters pressed Ron Ziegler during the noon press briefing at the White House on Friday, August 13. A reporter asked: "Now that you have had twenty-four hours to find out the details of what Governor Wallace seems to be up to, can you tell us the president's reaction to Wallace's refusal to carry out the court's order?"

Ziegler didn't have anything to add. "We will obviously continue to watch the situation in Alabama and other states."[36]

Wallace kept on challenging Nixon, and fellow Democrats, winning startling 1972 campaign victories in Texas, Florida, Michigan, Maryland, North Carolina, Tennessee, and his own state of Alabama[37]—until he was shot during an assassination attempt at a Laurel, Maryland, political rally on May 15, 1972.[38] That sidelined him for good. Wallace remained paralyzed for the rest of his life.

Meanwhile, presidential adviser Len Garment wasn't done trying to get Nixon to do something, anything, to show some solidarity with disillusioned minorities. He sent a memo to Clement Conger, the White House official who curated the presidential residence's art and furnishings[39]:

> I am interested in considering the possibility of hanging a portrait of a black American in the Residence, if it

> would meet your standards for works in the building and would be compatible with your overall planning and placement of paintings. Attached is a list of portraits of blacks in the National Portrait Gallery collection, one of which might be available. If we do this, I would hope it can be done without any fanfare whatever.

Pat Buchanan, Nixon's thirty-two-year-old adviser, weighed in a few days after that with another "Nixon is pro-Black" idea. Buchanan's memo, written in a breathless, telegraphic style, was titled "Blacks in 1972." With a misspelling placed deep into the memo, Buchanan inadvertently coined a new word that mixed his boss's name with "noxious." Buchanan's new word was "nixious":

> SITUATION: RN got 12 percent of the black vote in 1968, when he was generally portrayed as anti-black by Democrats and Left. Potential exists for raising that to 20 percent at least—which could provide a critical margin in major states in 1972. This, especially true, as Muskie, the most likely nominee now, has far less strength and pull with black voters than EMK [Ted Kennedy] or HHH [Hubert Humphrey]. Also, of interest—42 percent of Southern blacks think RN is doing a good job. So, a try is worth it.
>
> PROPOSAL: That RN emulate the Houston Ministers Meeting of JFK [during Kennedy's 1960 campaign against Nixon][40] by scheduling, spur of the moment, an appearance before a national black group of great size here in Washington. That RN appear, deliver 15 minutes of address, the thrust of which is that "America is not a racist nation," and the new stereotype that all blacks are oppressed and downtrodden is as nixious and silly as the old stereotype that all blacks are shiftless and lazy. Following the 15 minutes, RN throws open the floor to questions for 20 minutes—for which an in-depth briefing book has been prepared—

> then RN closes with 5 minutes of "No Party has a monopoly on Virtue. We can disagree without being disagreeable—in any event, let's work together to make this a better country for our children."

Garment loved the idea. He wrote back: *Right on the money. I can't think of a better way of making clear that RN's anti-busing views and directives are not anti-Negro than to confront this and other racial issues head on before a black audience. It would help reinforce these views (to whites) because it would be calm, direct, visible. It would have all the elements of presidential drama: surprise, guts, timing.*

The proposal didn't go anywhere.

June 15, 1971, 9:25 a.m.

The chief deputy probation officer of Marin County filed a letter with the judge in Angela Davis's case, recommending that she be released on bail. There was the standard recounting of the defendant's assets; in this case, Davis's net worth was zero, and her worldly belongings were nothing other than a stereo and some books. But that wasn't the point, the probation officer wrote: *I have received and perused numerous letters and petitions requesting fairness in Miss Davis' case and that she be released on bail. There were still many more letters and petitions that time did not permit me to read.* His bail recommendation appeared to be nothing short of a home run for Davis and her attorneys:

> There is, in my estimation, a commitment on Miss Davis' part to her family, attorneys and supporters who have given their time, skills, and money to her case. Miss Davis at one time made public statements to the effect that she could not receive a fair trial. However, she now feels that due to the public support and concern which her case has attracted, the opportunity now exists for some measure of fair judicial treatment.

> She cites the recent trial of Bobby Seale and Ericka Huggins (charges against the two Black Panthers had just been dismissed by the judge in the New Haven trial)[41] as an example of this possibility.
>
> In light of the above statements, I feel that for Miss Davis to flee the jurisdiction of the court would be a great disappointment to her family, supporters and attorneys. It would also question her role as a leader for social reforms in the minds of her supporters. If she fled the jurisdiction of the court, she would have to go to a country that did not have an extradition agreement with the United States. I feel that this would limit and isolate her and would not satisfy her professed need to continue with the struggle for her people and vindication for herself. I also feel that if she wanted to flee the jurisdiction of the court, she appeared to have had ample opportunity to do so from August 7th until her arrest in October.[42]

The probation officer recommended "bail in the amount of $100,000" (about $785,000 today).[43] She would have to report to him weekly, in person.

But would the judge buy it?

The answer was a quick no, handed down by Judge Richard Arnason[44] that same morning. "A defendant charged with an offense punishable with death cannot be admitted to bail, when the presumption of her guilt is great."[45]

So that was that.

A group calling itself the San Francisco United Committee to Free Angela Davis immediately issued a fundraising flyer and started compiling a list of people who pledged bail money. The group's leaflet was headlined, in bold capital letters, **BAIL DENIED ANGELA**. Its message blared out in ALL CAPS:

> ONCE AGAIN WE HAVE BEEN DEALT WITH UNJUSTLY BY THE COURTS OF INJUSTICE.

> SO WE MUST TAKE OUR STRUGGLE TO THE STREETS. WE RECOGNIZE THAT THE AMERICAN JUDICIAL SYSTEM IS INCAPABLE OF DEALING OUT JUSTICE TO BLACK, THIRD WORLD, OR ANY OPPRESSED PEOPLE. IT HAS NEVER BEEN GEARED TO DO THIS. WE RECOGNIZE THAT THE ONLY PLACE WE CAN RECEIVE JUSTICE IS IN THE STREETS WITH THE PEOPLE. THE DENIAL OF BAIL TO OUR SISTER WILL ONLY STRENGTHEN OUR DETERMINATION TO EDUCATE AND MOBILIZE ALL PEOPLE AGAINST THE OPPRESSIVE CONDITIONS THAT EXIST HERE TODAY. . . . FREE ANGELA!!! FREE RUCHELL!!! FREE THE SOLEDAD BROTHERS!!! FREE ALL POLITICAL PRISONERS!!![46]

Davis had failed to gain release on bail, but the outside-pressure campaign was having an effect. Later that month, Judge Arnason and the Marin County sheriff relaxed some of Davis's conditions of confinement, allowing daily exercise and the ability to meet with other female inmates. But a big win for Davis came on June 29, 1971, when Arnason ruled that she (along with her lawyer and an investigator) could meet in person with the Soledad Brothers: George Jackson, Fleeta Drumgo, and John Clutchette. The three were accused of killing a Soledad Prison guard. Like Davis, they faced murder charges, and the gas chamber if convicted.

The visits would bring things full circle, back to the scene of the crime. Davis's guns had been used by George Jackson's brother, Jonathan, in his failed hostage-taking courtroom escape, which led to the killings ten months earlier. Davis had been intent on freeing the Soledad Brothers; Jonathan had launched a fatal plan.

George, now twenty-nine years old and having served the last eleven in prison,[47] was to be brought from San Quentin to the Marin County Civic Center, where the gun battle took place.

Davis's attorney asked the judge not to limit the number of visits she could have with Jackson. Although the judge rejected that request, he did allow "at least three separate occasions without further order of the court."

On July 8, Jackson, his hands loosely chained to his waist, was brought to a holding cell beside the courtroom in the Marin County Civic Center.[48] Davis had seen Jackson one other time, when she attended his pretrial hearing a year earlier. This was the first time they'd been face-to-face, in the same room together for an extended period of time.[49]

Davis kept up her correspondence with Jackson, using visitors to smuggle out her letters, which were typewritten, single-spaced, on legal paper. She confessed to depression.

I love you, she wrote to Jackson, *but do you feel the same as before?*[50]

Saturday, August 21, 1971, 1:15 p.m.

The bloodiest day in San Quentin's history was about to unfold.

The murder trial of Soledad Brother George Jackson was scheduled to begin in two days. On this Saturday afternoon, he had a couple of visitors. One was a young civil rights lawyer, Stephen Bingham, who had been talking to Jackson about filing a lawsuit challenging Jackson's confinement conditions at San Quentin.[51] The other visitor was an investigator for the upcoming trial; she was at the prison to go over galleys with Jackson for his second book, to be titled *Blood in My Eye*. Jackson's first, a book of letters titled *Soledad Brother*, had landed big.

"The authorities had been clamping down on George's incredible number of visitors," Bingham recalled many years later, "Sure enough, her visit was denied."

Bingham went in alone. Jackson, held in the prison's solitary-confinement wing known as the Adjustment Center, was strip-searched[52] right before the meeting; then he put his coveralls back on. He wasn't shackled, there was no barrier between him and Bingham that day, and the guards weren't watching.

What followed next has long been the subject of debate and multiple interpretations, but what isn't in doubt is that Soledad Brother George Jackson and five others—three guards and two inmates deemed "snitches"—were killed as Jackson, with a 9mm handgun somehow smuggled in, started a riot and tried to make a bold escape from San Quentin.

Bingham and Jackson met in a small room that had originally been meant for condemned men's visits with their relatives, but that had come to be used for attorney-inmate visits. Once their visit ended, a guard took Jackson back to the Adjustment Center. There, he would be strip-searched once more.

But when a guard reached toward Jackson's hair, prison authorities described a hellish, almost incomprehensible scene: Jackson jumped aside, whipped off a wig from which he took a pistol and two clips of ammunition, and, in one motion, swept a clip of ammunition into the pistol and turned on his unarmed guards. (Guards who mix with the general inmate population never carry guns.)

"This is it!" Jackson said.

Jackson was shot by a prison-tower rifleman as he ran for the San Quentin gate. The guards and prisoners died after twenty other inmates in the prison's most secure cellblock—the Adjustment Center—were either shot with Jackson's gun or had their throats slashed with makeshift knives.

Jackson's supporters called it a planned execution of the Soledad Brother. Bingham, the lawyer who was with Jackson immediately before the mayhem broke out, fled to Europe, where he assumed a false identity and lived using a pseudonym for thirteen years. Bingham voluntarily returned to the United States in 1984, to stand trial on two counts of murder and one of conspiracy. Two years after that, a Marin County jury unanimously acquitted him of all charges.[53]

The twenty-two hundred inmates at New York's maximum-security Attica Prison, a Depression-era relic forty-five minutes due east from Buffalo, were already on edge. Severe overcrowding meant the inmates were in quarters meant to fit about sixteen hundred. The men in the prison were locked in their six-by-nine-foot cells for fourteen to sixteen hours a day and worked five hours a day. They received just one shower a week.[54]

Workers at the prison's metal shop went on strike on July 7. The 450 inmates assigned to the metal shop, where they built steel cabinets and office furniture for state institutions, demanded higher wages. Inmates in the metal shop earned a pittance—from six cents to twenty-nine cents a day, adding up to $1.20 to $5.80 per month. Half of whatever they earned was required to be saved for their release. What remained was not enough to cover their basic personal needs while in prison.[55]

A group of inmate leaders created the Attica Liberation Faction. The ALF put together a manifesto of twenty-eight demands[56] for State Corrections Commissioner Russell Oswald, a reformer new to the job, and Governor Nelson Rockefeller. It went nowhere.[57]

August 22, 1971

When word of George Jackson's killing reached Attica Prison, a hunger strike was called in his honor. The Jackson Day Fast was a memorial to the Soledad Brother, one day after Jackson's death. Seven hundred silent prisoners took seats in the mess hall, sporting matching black armbands and refusing to eat. On August 30, another protest was held at the prison hospital, with prisoners occupying hospital beds to dramatize the inadequate health conditions.[58] There was an expectation that Oswald would be present at the hospital that morning.[59]

Cornell Capa was a famed battlefield photographer for *Life* magazine and the Magnum photo agency, which had been co-founded by his younger brother, Robert—an even more renowned wartime photographer—and Henri Cartier-Bresson, among others.

Cornell Capa had seen and photographed war. Here is how he described what he saw during the summer of '71 at Attica[60]:

> From the outside, Attica, situated in the rolling farmland in western New York, has a Disneyland-like appearance, especially at night.
>
> Attica's inmates are all locked in their individual cells from approximately 5 p.m. until 7 a.m. the next morning. Officers on the night shift make lonely rounds, checking the count six times during the night.
>
> All movement in Attica is limited by locks. At night, the duty officer must carry with him all the keys he will need on his nightly round of inspection.
>
> Confined to their 4x9 cells,[61] inmates may talk to one another across the cell blocks and play musical instruments until 8 p.m.
>
> Locked in a cell, a mirror is an inmate's eyes to the rest of his gallery, and whenever something happens, the mirrors appear as if on cue.
>
> After 8 pm., talking and noise are not permitted. There is little to do until lights out at 11 p.m. except read, write letters or listen to one of the three channels of the prison radio which play music, sports, and the audio portion of TV shows.
>
> Correction officers on the day shift leave homes in the town of Attica and surrounding communities and report for roll calls at 7 a.m., 9:20 a.m., 3 p.m., and 11 p.m. to receive their assignments.
>
> For a few hours each day, inmates are allowed to go into their cell block's yard for outdoor recreation. [Then] it is back to the cells to pass the hours until supper. The site of disembodied hands outside the bars playing cards is not unusual here.
>
> Some play chess but the opponent remains unseen.
>
> There is so much idle time.

Wednesday, September 8, 1971, 3:45 p.m.

What set off the tinder keg was a scuffle between guards and two prisoners that should never have happened—because it was the result of a misunderstanding.

The exercise yard was filling with inmates returning from their work assignments. Some men played cards; others watched television. Off to one side of the yard, a white inmate who was a defensive coach for a prison football team was showing a young Black inmate some linemen's moves and feints.

To a prison guard, it looked like a fight—but it wasn't.

The guard stepped in and put his hand on the Black inmate's shoulder. Instinctively, the Black inmate spun around and struck the guard. This was such a huge breach of prison protocol that activity in the yard stopped. All eyes were on the two inmates and the guard who'd been struck. More guards arrived, and the Black inmate was ordered out of the yard and into "the box"—a solitary-confinement area of the prison officially known as Housing Block Z. That was an area of the prison where inmates were routinely assaulted by guards.

But the Black inmate refused the order, and other inmates encircled him for protection. The guards backed off, deciding not to escalate the situation. At least one inmate yelled a warning: If the guards sought later to punish the "brawling" inmates, "we'll take this prison off you."[62]

Later that evening, after inmates had been locked into their cells for the night, guards took both inmates from their cells. Soon a rumor spread that the two had been beaten.

Thursday, September 9, 1971, 8:50 a.m.

As inmates walked to the prison mess hall for the second breakfast sitting, a seemingly spontaneous riot broke out. The few guards who were mixed into the prison population soon were overpowered. Inmates ran down a narrow corridor and toward the central courtyard. The gate controlling access was manned by a lone guard, twenty-eight-year-old Billy Quinn. He was beaten, his skull fractured in two places. Quinn's death two days later would vastly complicate negotiations to end the Attica standoff.

A group of around twenty prisoners overpowered four guards, locking them in cells and taking control of the various cellblocks. Altogether, forty-two guards and staff were rounded up and taken as hostages.

Inmate leaders from the ALF drafted a list of five demands—later, the list would grow much longer—as preconditions for ending their occupation of the prison:

> 1. We want complete amnesty, meaning freedom from all and any physical, mental and legal reprisals.
> 2. We want immediate speedy and safe transportation out of confinement to a non-imperialistic country.
> 3. We demand that the Federal Government intervene, so that we will be under direct Federal Jurisdiction.
> 4. We want the Governor and the Judiciary, namely Constance B. Motley, to guarantee that there will be no reprisals and we want all factions of the media to articulate this.
> 5. We urgently demand immediate negotiations.[63] We guarantee the safe passage of all people to and from this institution. We invite all the people to come here and witness this degradation so that they can better know how to bring this degradation to an end. This is what we want.[64]

The inmates named eleven people they wanted brought in as negotiators. Their list included Huey Newton, of the Black Panthers; Minister Louis Farrakhan, of the Nation of Islam; attorney William Kunstler; Assemblyman Arthur Eve (Attica was in his assembly district); and Tom Wicker, of the *New York Times*. The list would expand to include other officials.

The wild-haired Kunstler was a radical lawyer known for his flamboyant courtroom style and high-profile defense of controversial activists, including Bobby Seale in the Chicago Seven trial. He could already see what was coming. Kunstler knew the amnesty demand would be a deal breaker for Governor Rockefeller. As Rockefeller later testified, Kunstler told Rockefeller's people that "the key issue would be amnesty, criminal amnesty. That was a flat statement and it was made before he talked to the inmates or before he talked to the rest of the observers."[65]

Friday, September 10, 1971, 12:00 p.m.

Wicker later testified:

> On that Friday, about noon, my office in Washington received a telephone call from the office of Assemblyman Arthur Eve, who said that my name had been included on a list of names that prisoners, who then were in revolt at Attica, had asked to come and observe the proceeding there. And Assemblyman Eve's office had asked if I could possibly come.
>
> I found I could get a flight out almost immediately to Buffalo. I was told that if I could get there, that then either by helicopter or automobile the state troopers would get me to the Attica Prison. So, I did that.

Wicker had never been to Attica, or, for that matter, to any other prison in New York State. A few weeks earlier, he'd written a widely reprinted article about George Jackson's death. Wicker assumed that's why the inmates wanted him.

Wicker soon encountered Oswald, the state corrections commissioner. Oswald feared for his own safety: "[Oswald] was not going back in the prison." But Oswald wanted Wicker to do that, along with the other negotiators who'd been called in. Wicker was surprised. He thought he was there to be an observer. Instead, "we were more and more cast in the role of doing the negotiating ourselves." Wicker had "arrived there in Attica without even so much as a suitcase or toothbrush or a clean shirt, because I thought I was probably going home that night." That certainly wasn't the case.

When Wicker and the other negotiators were escorted into the prison yard on Friday evening, they saw 1,281 inmates—to Wicker, it seemed like more—gathered in what appeared to be a very well-organized rebellion. Hostages were under guard. There was an administrative cadre, with at least one typewriter for messages being sent out. Wicker related what he initially saw:

> As for the [inmates], at that particular stage of the game, more so than any other time I was in there, there was a certain—I don't want to overstate it—but there was a kind of lightheartedness about it. I don't mean to imply that everybody was skylarking or there was a picnic atmosphere. At that particular time I didn't feel what I felt later, which was a gathering sense of despair and frustration, perhaps even fear.[66]

Saturday, September 11, 1971, 7:00 p.m.

Negotiations went on through the weekend. Governor Nelson Rockefeller had been at the White House for a conference on international relations when the riot began. By Saturday evening, he was back in Albany, conferring by phone with Oswald and others. Many of Rockefeller's senior staff had traveled to Attica, but Rockefeller resisted going to the scene.

The original five demands of the inmates had expanded to include everything that the Attica Liberation Front had included in its original July manifesto that protested the prison's conditions. Oswald, the corrections commissioner, was willing to agree to twenty-eight of the demands, but the sticking point was amnesty for the rioters.

Wicker became discouraged when he learned that the prison guard, young Billy Quinn, had died from wounds inflicted on the first day of the riot. "That obviously worsened the whole situation," Wicker recalled, "because after that there clearly existed the possibility of a capital charge against someone."

Billy Quinn's death made any discussion of amnesty impossible.

The inmates asked that Black Panther Bobby Seale be brought into the negotiations. Seale showed up at seven o'clock that evening. Wicker recalled:

> We waited for some time for Seale to arrive there—for his entrance to the prison to be worked out—because it was felt by some members of the group that if we could present our package of 28 points to the prisoners with the approval of Bobby Seale, we felt that his name would carry great weight among the prisoners. Particularly since so many of them were Blacks and Puerto Ricans, we felt that if he would join us in saying to the prisoners, "This is the best you can get," if he would even go so far as to recommend that they accept them. Of course, it was quite dubious that he would do that. But certainly, if he would join with us in the presentation of those points to the prisoners, we thought that might favorably dispose them toward the points; that Bobby Seale's reputation would carry that kind of weight.[67]

But Seale's visit got off to a rocky start. He was kept waiting for so long outside the prison that he left. When Wicker's group found out, they urged the state police to go after him. A state police car was sent out to chase Seale down and escort him back to the prison. Wicker recalled, during his testimony to the Attica Commission, how the observer group then went over the twenty-eight points with Seale:

> We went through the whole thing with him and he, like Kunstler, immediately went to the amnesty point.

The observers hoped that Seale could turn things around for them. But, Wicker explained, "more was being expected of Bobby Seale than he could reasonably deliver."[68] Seale told them he couldn't lend his support to the twenty-eight points without buy-in from the Panther headquarters in Oakland. "He said he had to consult his group."

By now, the inmates had held the prison for three days. Tempers were frayed. The observers had promised they would return that night with Seale. And so, even though Seale had said he couldn't help, the group—Seale included—agreed to return to the prison yard to speak to the more than twelve hundred inmates and their hostages. Wicker recalled Seale's eagerly anticipated speech as a letdown:

> He made a very brief, very cool and certainly non-inflammatory speech to the prisoners, the gist of which was that he stood very solid with them. That he could not as yet associate himself with any of our work. He had to consult his group on the West Coast.
>
> He said that he would try to send word to them of what he thought about these points later that night, and he would try to return the next morning.

Wicker had expected that Seale would arrive in the yard to a "tremendous ovation." There was only silence. "By this time the prisoners had been in that yard about three days, and the whole thing had begun to wear them down. And I think they were just not in a mood to cheer for anybody."

Seale left Attica.

Sunday, September 12, 11:00 a.m.

Although Rockefeller readily conceded he was out of touch with what went on inside the state prison system,[69] he had no intention of finding out now[70]: When Wicker and three other observers got Rockefeller on the phone and urged him to come directly to Attica, Rockefeller was disdainful of the idea. He figured: "[I]f I got there, the first thing they would do was say, 'We demand the governor comes into the yard.'"

Wicker initiated what turned into a ninety-minute phone call.[71] He was the first one to speak to the governor, and he made an impassioned plea for Rockefeller to show up:

> Four of us talked to the governor, and my recollection is that he understood the point that we were making, that the observer group invited him to come to Attica and talk to the observer group. At no point did I say, "Governor, you know, you ought to come up here and go in and talk to the prisoners, or even talk to the prisoners from outside," or anything like that.
>
> In fact, I think one of the things that he felt was that was not a proper thing for him to do, to be in contact with the prisoners. One of the objections that he made to coming to Attica was that he would immediately be under pressure to meet personally with the prisoners.

Rockefeller thought Wicker and the others were simply trying to buy time—political grandstanding, to forestall what the governor increasingly felt was going to be a violent outcome[72]:

> So I said, "Well, what do you think would be accomplished by my presence?" And their answer was, "Well, we don't know. Two things: One, something might happen. And two, we could buy time."
>
> "Well," I said, "who do you want to buy time from? Are you worried that the prisoners are going to move and kill the hostages, or are you worried the state is going to move?" And they said, "We're worried about the state."
>
> Well, I felt we had now moved into what I considered the political phase of this thing. Those who were pushing this were not interested in seeing the settlement,

> or seeing a reform. What they wanted to do was to drag this out, preserve the theater for worldwide coverage relating to revolutionary forces, and get another round.

Rockefeller was done with the negotiations. He turned things back over to his corrections commissioner, Oswald. Around midnight, Oswald and his men told Rockefeller that they wanted to make one last offer to the inmates. Their proposal involved Rockefeller coming to Attica, to personally take charge of negotiating what were now being called "the twenty-eight points."

Now the impetus for Rockefeller's visit was coming from the corrections commissioner and his staff, not Wicker and his cohorts. Rockefeller was incredulous. He feared becoming one of the hostages.[73] If he went to Attica, Rockefeller said, there would be nothing to stop the inmates from asking for President Nixon next[74]:

> I said I thought the 28 points had been turned down flat, so I didn't know what the point of negotiating the details of the 28 points were if they had already been turned down. Russ [Oswald, the corrections commissioner] was the originator of this idea. He felt that, well, that would put me in a better position, that I had offered to come to Attica. But that had no relation. I wasn't trying to posture myself in a good public relations position. I was trying to do the best I could to save the hostages, save the prisoners, restore order, and preserve our system without undertaking actions which could set a precedent which would go across this country like wildfire.

Arthur Liman, thirty-nine years old, served as chief counsel—in practical terms, the principal interlocutor—on the commission that investigated the Attica uprising the following year. Liman was a former Manhattan assistant district attorney and, at the time of the investigation, a young partner at the prestigious white-shoe firm of Paul, Weiss, Rifkind, Wharton & Garrison (now Paul, Weiss).

Liman later wrote a ten-page memo to his files during the Attica investigation, expressing disdain for Rockefeller's failure to show up at the prison. "A sign of continuing indifference," Liman called it. "There was nothing to lose (except recognizing the inmates' right to be heard) and over 1,200 lives—inmates, hostages, and assault personnel—to save."[75]

Monday, September 13, 1971, 7:00 a.m.

Oswald made one final attempt to put the twenty-eight points in front of the inmates and gave them until 9:00 a.m. to reply.

Wicker recalled:

> We felt, most of us, I think, as we could look out the window and see the activities of the prison, catch the atmosphere as we passed through the corridors and through the grounds where we were permitted to go, we felt that the state was getting ready to act very decisively, act forcibly. . . . There were all kinds of indications to us that an attack was coming, and coming soon. And we felt—I think all of us unanimously felt—that the attack was going to result in a great deal of bloodshed.

"You know the rest of the story," Rockefeller told the Attica Commission. "At nine, they started parading some of the hostages with so-called executioners."

The prisoners lined up the hostages on a cellblock catwalk, knives at their throats.

"This was 9:15," Rockefeller continued. "And Oswald said, as you also know, the prisoners had given their answer. He had no choice but to move as quickly as possible."[76]

Oswald made the decision, but he had Rockefeller's full support. At 9:43 a.m., power to the prison was shut off, and state troopers advanced behind fire hoses, tear gas, and shotgun fire. The resultant death toll was staggering: Forty-three people were killed, eleven of them corrections officers.[77] All but three victims were killed by the troopers. Attica quickly became a defining event in the annals of the prisoner rights movement.

Earlier that morning, Rockefeller had tried to phone Nixon at the White House, to tell him what was about to go down. But Nixon had been in a cabinet meeting and hadn't taken the call.[78] Instead, Ehrlichman had spoken to Rockefeller and had sent word to Nixon.[79]

Haldeman was the first to talk to Nixon about the retaking of Attica, around midday.[80]

The president asked, "Is this a Black business?"

"Yes sir," replied the chief of staff.

"We have got to be tough on this," Nixon said. "You know what this is? This is the Angela Davis crowd. These are the Negroes." At this point in the conversation, Nixon lumped in Attica with the shoot-out at the Marin Civic Center the year before. Soon the president would also bring up San Quentin. "You can't temporize," he told Haldeman.

"Which concerns me," added Haldeman. "The word is around now that this is the signal for the Black uprising. It's clear this is what they're doing. The revolution thing is moving to the prisons now, versus the campuses where they couldn't get enough action on."

Later that day, Haldeman and Nixon discussed the bloody San Quentin riot of the prior month, when George Jackson was killed. Haldeman, who was unsure in the moment whether it was a federal or state prison, nonetheless assured Nixon that San Quentin was a "model prison." And yet, even there, the violence couldn't be contained.[81] So, obviously, to Haldeman's mind, they were facing something much bigger. "My guess is, looking at it, that it has nothing to do with anything legitimate," Haldeman concluded. "It has to do with the revolution."

The issue was "permissiveness," Nixon replied. The president was concerned about another antiwar march planned for Washington the following month. "What's brought this on, you know, [is] this whole business of permissiveness on campus—why not permissiveness in prison, permissiveness to the Blacks? It's not—we're not going to fuck[82] around here in this town. If they hit this town again (i.e., come to Washington to protest), we've gotta be tough."[83]

Later that afternoon, when Nixon finally reached Rockefeller by phone, Rockefeller had no idea the call was being captured on the White House recording system. The governor, considered a moderate by his fellow Republicans, who saw Nixon as the more cold-blooded one, confessed that he had expected as many as three hundred prisoners to be killed[84]:

OPERATOR: I have Governor Rockefeller for you, sir.

NIXON: Hello.

OPERATOR: There you are.

ROCKEFELLER: Mr. President.

NIXON: I know you've had a hard day, but I want you to know that I just back you to the hilt. And I was sitting here talking to Bob Haldeman. I didn't get your call because I've had a Cabinet meeting, and then I had a meeting with business leaders right afterwards, and I've been—I just got out. But the courage you showed and the judgment in not granting amnesty, it was right, and I don't care what the hell the papers or anybody else says. I don't care what they say. I think that you had to do it that way, because if you would have granted amnesty in this case, it would have meant that you would have had prisons in an uproar all over this country.

ROCKEFELLER: That's right, absolutely.

NIXON: And you did the right thing. It's a tragedy that these poor fellows were shot, but I just want you to know that's my view, and I've told the troops around here they're to back that right to the hilt.

ROCKEFELLER: Well, aren't you great, Mr. President. I only called you because I wanted to alert you that we were going in.

NIXON: Right.

ROCKEFELLER: And when we went in, we couldn't tell whether all 39 hostages would be killed and maybe two or three hundred prisoners.

NIXON: Tell me this, is this—are these primarily Blacks that you're dealing with?

ROCKEFELLER: Oh, yes, the whole thing was led by the Blacks.

NIXON: I'll be darned. Are all the prisoners that were killed Blacks? Or are there any whites?

ROCKEFELLER: I haven't got that report, but I have to—I would say, just offhand, yes.

NIXON: Yeah.

ROCKEFELLER: We did it, though, only when they were in the process of murdering the guards, or when they were attacking our people as they came in to get the guards.

NIXON: You had to do it.

ROCKEFELLER: And otherwise we recaptured all the cell blocks and so forth without shooting a shot. And no troopers were wounded. One of them—well, one of them was in the leg. But—

NIXON: Only one trooper was wounded?

ROCKEFELLER: That's right.

NIXON: Good, good, good.

ROCKEFELLER: It really was a beautiful operation.

Rockefeller, once Nixon's rival, now sought to flatter him. He told Nixon during the same call[85] that his corrections commissioner, Oswald, a Democrat, now agreed with Attorney General

John Mitchell and Vice President Spiro Agnew that "there is a national conspiracy, and he will be supporting you for reelection."

"Boy, oh boy," Nixon replied. Then the president abruptly jumped to a different question[86]:

> NIXON: What the hell is Tom Wicker doing in this thing?
>
> ROCKEFELLER: Well, you won't believe it, that we had a—we had a committee of citizens, invited by the prisoners, 32 of them. Tom Wicker was one. We had that Kunstler, that lawyer.
>
> NIXON: Yeah, yeah, I know of him.
>
> ROCKEFELLER: We had the head of the Mau Maus (possibly this was a derogatory reference to Bobby Seale). A motley crowd.
>
> NIXON: Yeah.
>
> ROCKEFELLER: And some good people, some legislators. And Tom Wicker was so emotional in this thing—
>
> NIXON: Mm-hmm.
>
> ROCKEFELLER: —that it was unbelievable.
>
> NIXON: Which side?
>
> ROCKEFELLER: Oh, on their side.
>
> NIXON: Always, always. I know, I know.
>
> ROCKEFELLER: You see, I had, at the end—they were putting the pressure yesterday on me all day to go up there. Ended up—because everything else had failed and—
>
> NIXON: Did you go?
>
> ROCKEFELLER: Of course not. I wouldn't go.
>
> NIXON: No, of course not.
>
> ROCKEFELLER: But I had to talk to these guys, Wicker and all these people, on the phone. You know.
>
> NIXON: Yeah, yeah, yeah.
>
> ROCKEFELLER: And I said, "Look, I go up there. We can't give amnesty. The next thing is, 'Well, we'll let them go, if you'll just come into the courtyard.'"

> NIXON: Yeah.
> ROCKEFELLER: You know.
> NIXON: Yeah.
> ROCKEFELLER: With—in front of all the men. Well—
> NIXON: Did Wicker—was he recommending amnesty?
> ROCKEFELLER: Oh, yes.
> NIXON: Oh, God.
> ROCKEFELLER: Oh, you—he—listen, it's a great—this separated the sheep from the goats.[87]

After the call ended, Haldeman asked Nixon, "Were they all Black?"

"Every one," Nixon replied.

The president expressed satisfaction about what he'd heard from Rockefeller.

"This might have one hell of a salutary effect. They can talk all they want about the radicals. You know what stops them? Kill a few. Remember Kent State? Didn't it have one hell of an effect, the Kent State thing?"

"Sure did," replied Haldeman. "Gave them second thoughts."

Buffalo, New York, activist Bill Gaiter, born in Selma, was another of the citizen observers summoned by the prisoners and empowered by the authorities to try to negotiate an end to the standoff. In the immediate aftermath, Gaiter looked at the dead in front of him:

> You know, I was amazed at Kent State; shocked by Jackson State. But this. To see a decision being formulated that leads to so many deaths. I don't believe I'll ever be able to forget this.[88]

CHAPTER 15

Aftermath

DANIEL ELLSBERG REMAINED UNDERGROUND FOR two weeks. He surrendered to authorities in Boston on June 28, 1971, a few days before the Supreme Court affirmed the right of the *New York Times* and the *Washington Post* to continue publishing the Pentagon Papers. Although the Papers were later declassified, the Nixon administration remained determined to go after Ellsberg. In January 1973, Ellsberg and an accomplice, Anthony Russo, were indicted in Los Angeles (the location of the theft from RAND's headquarters) under the Espionage Act on charges of theft and conspiracy. The charges carried a possible 115 years in prison. During Ellsberg's trial on the charges later that spring, the 1971 break-in by Nixon's White House Plumbers into the Los Angeles office of Ellsberg's psychiatrist, Lewis Fielding, finally was revealed. Further evidence of illegal wiretapping against Ellsberg, as well as John Ehrlichman's ex parte contacts with the federal judge in the case, also were revealed in court. The Nixon administration's gross misconduct torpedoed the case. On May 11, 1973, Judge William Matthew Byrne Jr. dismissed all the charges against Ellsberg and Russo, telling the court: "The totality of the circumstances of this case, which I have only briefly sketched, offend a sense of justice. The bizarre events have incurably infected the prosecution of this case." As a result of the revelations involving Ellsberg and, later, the Watergate scandal, numerous officials from the Nixon administration went to prison, including Ehrlichman, H. R. Haldeman,

Attorney General John Mitchell, White House counsel John Dean, Charles Colson, and White House Plumbers G. Gordon Liddy and Egil Krogh. Ellsberg spent the rest of his life writing and lecturing. He was ninety-two years old when he died in 2023.

Neil Sheehan left his redoubt at the New York Hilton and returned to his home in Washington on July 2. His wife, Susan, fashioned a giant WELCOME HOME! banner from the classified-ad section of that day's newspaper, and subtitled it CLASSIFIED. SENSITIVE. TOP SECRET. LIES, LIES, LIES.[1] Sheehan expected to be arrested or indicted any day, but Abe Rosenthal got him out of harm's way by sending Sheehan and his family to Mexico for a month, all expenses paid. The arrest or indictment never happened; Nixon and his men were focused on Ellsberg.

Sheehan expected to be awarded the Pulitzer Prize for his work, but that didn't happen, either. The Pulitzer jury for the Public Service prize unanimously recommended a gold medal for the *Times* and Sheehan for "the remarkable journalistic feat which has come to be known as the Pentagon Papers"—and, at the second step in the process, a Pulitzer advisory board also unanimously agreed. But since the Public Service award could only go to a news organization, and not an individual, Sheehan was out of consideration. The last word went to the trustees of Columbia University, which administers the prizes. Unaccountably, the trustees at first balked; they objected to giving a prize for printing official government secrets. Although the trustees finally relented and awarded the prize to the *Times*, they did so, along with a harsh rebuke of the newspaper: *In the trustees' deliberations on the 1972 Pulitzer Prizes, a majority of them had reservations about the timeliness and suitability of certain of the journalism awards. Had the selections been those of the trustees alone, certain of the recipients would not have been chosen.*[2] Sheehan was stunned and angry, and he received consolations from all over.

He also continued his tempestuous relationship with his *Times* editors. In October, back from Mexico, Sheehan objected to the way in which the newspaper was trying to obfuscate his role in getting the Papers. He wanted full credit, and wrote a long memo to James Greenfield, the foreign editor:

> I really object to that phrase that the desk is using to describe my role in the publication of the Pentagon Papers. That is, the phrase: "whose investigative reporting led to publication of a series of articles on the study in the *New York Times*." . . . I hope I'm not sounding like a prima donna, but it is a matter of professional pride to me that I obtained these papers for the *Times*. I want credit for what I did and I don't want people who read stories to think I'm being investigated for some vague investigative reporting I did. If I'm going to be indicted, I don't want people to think I'm being indicted for "whose investigative reporting led to publication, etc." That's not worth being indicted for.[3]

Greenfield cabled back:

> OCTOBER 18, 1971
> WASHINGTON
> FRANKEL PRO SHEEHAN
> FINE NEIL. WE WILL USE PHRASE "NEIL SHEEHAN, WHO OBTAINED THE PENTAGON PAPERS FOR THE NEW YORK TIMES."
> REGARDS
> GREENFIELD[4]

On June 29, Rosenthal awarded Sheehan a $3,000 bonus for his efforts and raised Sheehan's salary to $500 a week—equivalent to about $200,000 a year in today's dollars. Sheehan remained nominally on the *Times* staff, due to his and the newspaper's belief that this would provide more in the way of legal protection in case of a grand jury investigation or indictment. But he was marginalized at the paper, and soon moved on to another epic project.

Sheehan's 1988 book, *A Bright Shining Lie: John Paul Vann and America in Vietnam*, won the 1988 National Book Award for Nonfiction and the 1989 Pulitzer Prize for General Nonfiction. (Susan Sheehan had earlier won the 1983 Pulitzer Prize for General Nonfiction for her book *Is There No Place on Earth for Me?*) Neil Sheehan died in 2021, at age eighty-four. He refused throughout his life to talk about how he got the Pentagon Papers, although the *Times* published excerpts from an oral history after his death.

The *New York Times* kept count of the letters the newspaper received about the Pentagon Papers during the last two weeks of June. The mail was overwhelmingly in the newspaper's favor. Of the 2,835 letters received, 2,021 favored publication. The paper also tracked its legal expenses. Legal fees for the Pentagon Papers litigation totaled $302,000—about $2.5 million today.

It would take Sarah Weddington two years, and two oral arguments before the Supreme Court, before winning a 6-to-3 victory in 1973 in *Roe* v. *Wade*. Weddington served two terms in the Texas Legislature, representing Austin, before being appointed general counsel of the Agriculture Department in 1977 at the start of President Jimmy Carter's administration. The following year, she moved over to the White House as Carter's adviser on women's issues. Weddington continued teaching and lecturing after that, but nothing she did thereafter eclipsed her achievement in *Roe* v. *Wade*. Years before she died, Weddington designed her own huge granite tombstone and had it installed at the Texas State Cemetery in Austin. It weighed two tons and dwarfed all the grave markers around it. The inscription said: *Winning Attorney, Roe v. Wade, U.S. Supreme Court, 1973*. Weddington died the day after Christmas in 2021, at age seventy-six, as the Supreme

Court was considering *Dobbs* v. *Jackson Women's Health Organization*, the case that ultimately overturned *Roe* v. *Wade*.

Averell and Pamela Harriman were married in New York on September 27, 1971, weeks after they were reunited at a dinner party at Katharine Graham's Georgetown mansion. Averell was seventy-nine; Pamela, fifty-one. Congratulations came in from all over: Kay Graham (of course), Rose and Ethel Kennedy, Katharine Hepburn (a Leland Hayward connection), Richard Avedon, Mia Farrow, Cecil Beaton, and assorted other friends and hangers-on. On the day of the wedding, 150 of their friends gathered at Harriman's Upper East Side townhouse to celebrate. Averell died in 1986, at age ninety-four. Pamela remained a power player in Washington, spending the Harriman fortune freely and eventually being named ambassador to France by President Bill Clinton. She remained in touch with her old flame Frank Sinatra, and with Jackie Kennedy's wealthy Greek husband, Aristotle Onassis. When Frank was on a concert swing to New York in April 1974, he and Ari wound up at Sinatra's favorite Broadway watering hole, Jilly's, on West Fifty-Second Street. The two penned a note to Pamela—Sinatra wisecracking about whether she'd contribute to his "fund for ugly young girls; will you join the committee?"; Ari simply sending his "usual sweet thoughts."[5] (Pamela saved the card with other valued mementos.) She died at age seventy-six in 1997 in Paris after suffering a cerebral hemorrhage while swimming at the Ritz Paris a day earlier. The morning after her death, Jacques Chirac, the French president, placed the Grand Cross of the Légion d'Honneur on her flag-draped coffin, which President Clinton arranged to have flown back to America on Air Force One.

Angela Davis spent sixteen months in jail awaiting trial before finally being freed on $102,500 bail on February 23, 1972.[6] The trial judge who'd previously denied her bail, on the ground that bail wasn't permitted in capital murder cases, said the changed circumstance was a new California Supreme Court decision that effectively eliminated the death penalty in the state. Davis's trial began the following Monday, February 28, and lasted until June 4, when an all-white jury in Santa Clara County (the venue was changed from Marin County) found her not guilty of murder, kidnapping, and criminal conspiracy charges.

Davis never took the stand, but she was allowed to participate in her defense and thus was able to address the jury once it was seated.[7] "Though I cannot say that this is a jury of my peers," she told the jurors in the box, "I can say that, after much discussion, we have reached the conclusion that the women and men sitting on the jury will put forth their best efforts to give me a fair trial."[8] The prosecution's case was entirely circumstantial (any witnesses to the alleged murder conspiracy, if there ever was one, were dead), and the jury found reasonable doubt. When the verdict came in, one juror raised his fist in a Black Power salute;[9] ten jurors later attended a private celebration with Davis and her attorneys, raising a toast to the verdict.[10]

Although Davis later expressed her grief and rage at the courthouse murders she was on trial for, she never evinced a sense of personal culpability. In her 1974 autobiography,[11] she treated the episode as a political persecution based on her race, gender, and activism—not as an admission of guilt. Davis wrote that she wasn't present at the courthouse and didn't know of Jonathan Jackson's plan to seize hostages. She acknowledged that she had purchased the guns that were used, but insisted that she bought them legally for her own protection and had no idea they would be used in an attack. She framed the tragedy as the product of systemic state violence and the unbearable conditions of the prison system that drove Jonathan Jackson's act of desperation.

In 1997, Davis came out as a lesbian during an interview with *Out* magazine.[12] She continued to tackle oppression faced by Blacks, women, and the LGBTQ+ community. After spending time lecturing and traveling (including to Cuba as a guest of Fidel Castro while writing her autobiography), Davis returned to teaching at the University of California, Santa Cruz. She ran for vice president twice in the 1980s on the Communist Party ticket, although she split from the party after the fall of the Soviet Union in 1991 and later described herself as a "small *c*" communist, remaining enthusiastic about the ideology, but not beholden to any single organization.[13] To this day, Davis remains a Black icon and an international symbol of resistance.

Ruchell Magee, the only gunman to survive the San Rafael shootout (and Davis's original co-defendant; their cases were later split), spent most of the rest of his life in prison, until his death at age eighty-four.[14] After the state dropped its murder charge for Judge Haley's death, Magee pleaded guilty to aggravated kidnapping. He was sentenced to life without parole and spent his remaining years as a jailhouse lawyer. Eighty-one days before his 2023 death, Magee was released from Folsom Prison[15] under California's compassionate release law.

Tom Wicker died in 2011 at age eighty-five. He was the prolific author of twenty-one fiction and nonfiction works, including 1975's *A Time to Die: The Attica Prison Revolt.* Wicker never stopped demanding justice for those who were killed in the Attica Prison uprising. Three decades later, he wrote a column in the *Times* that accused state authorities of an ongoing cover-up:

> So far, New York has done nothing remotely adequate to compensate these forgotten victims for what one investigatory commission called "the bloodiest encounter between Americans since the Civil War." In some cases, the state has deceived widows and survivors. And no state administration, Republican or Democratic, has admitted responsibility for the uprising at the overcrowded

> prison, for its poorly planned and brutal repression or for the 43 resulting deaths. . . .
>
> In 1976, Gov. Hugh Carey issued a blanket pardon for everyone involved and sealed the state's records* concerning Attica for 50 years.[16]

Spiro Agnew, Nixon's attack-dog vice president, died in 1996 at age seventy-seven. He turned out to be a crook; during his years as vice president, he'd been receiving bribes for actions taken while he was a local official in Maryland. Agnew resigned as vice president after pleading nolo contendere to federal tax evasion charges (treated as a guilty plea for sentencing purposes). The FBI investigated him for bribery, but he was not prosecuted on that charge.[17] Nixon appointed, and Congress confirmed, Representative Gerald Ford (R-MI) as his new vice president.

Richard Nixon died in 1994, at the age of eighty-one. There was no state funeral. Nixon resigned the presidency on August 9, 1974, after his complicity in the Watergate cover-up and other White House crimes became clear. Nixon's resignation letter was delivered by Chief of Staff Alexander Haig to Henry Kissinger, who by then had become Nixon's secretary of state, on August 9, 1974.[18] Gerald Ford then assumed the presidency—the first and only person to move into the role without having first been elected vice president.

Nixon's wage and price freeze remained in place for ninety days, and was replaced by a series of boards and commissions

*Some records still haven't been released. A partial set of the records was made available online by the New York Attorney General's Office: https://www.archives.nysed.gov/research/oag/attica-project-pathfinder. See also this 2021 article from Spectrum News: "Remembering Attica: Legislation would allow remainder of Attica report to be unsealed," retrieved from https://spectrumlocalnews.com/nys/buffalo/politics/2021/09/10/legislation-would-allow-remainder-of-attica-report-to-be-unsealed

whose job it was to control increases in the cost of living. That plan was a miserable failure; inflation continued unabated. It would be another fourteen years before the Federal Reserve Board, under the strong leadership of Paul Volcker, finally brought prices and interest rates under control.

Nelson Rockefeller was appointed vice president after Gerald Ford assumed the presidency. Rockefeller died in 1979, at age seventy, of a heart attack at his West Fifty-Fourth Street townhouse, off Fifth Avenue.[19] The circumstances were unusual and never fully explained; he was in the presence of a twenty-five-year-old female aide, who initially summoned a friend, rather than an ambulance, to the residence. Rockefeller never apologized for Attica.

Henry Kissinger outlived almost everyone, and, as usual, got the last word. He died at age one hundred in 2023. His legend lives on.

ACKNOWLEDGMENTS

I OWE GREAT THANKS TO many who helped make this book a reality. You all know who you are—and please forgive me if I have failed to mention you here.

My wife, Susan Raleigh Jenkins, a lawyer and editor, has been my sounding board and confidante about this book since Day One, when it was a mere nascent idea.

My longtime agent, Jane Dystel, never gave up on me no matter how many self-imposed deadlines I missed over the past God-knows-how-many years. Jane believed in this book, and made sure it was published well.

My editor, Denise Silvestro, was the very best that an author could ask for—an intermediary when needed, a diplomat when it was called for, and an advocate, always, for authentic storytelling.

The copy editor for this book, Stephanie Finnegan, took the greatest of care to ensure that my voice, and those of the other players in this work, came through clearly. I am grateful for the attention she paid to fact-checking behind me.

New York actor and producer Mary Rose Synek offered wise and honest counsel throughout my research process, particularly as I dug deeply to understand Sarah Weddington's experience and how best to portray it in these pages.

Miriam Goderich was the second set of eyes on my proposal, and the ultimate reality check as my idea for this book took shape.

Readers will see five researchers credited in the opening pages of this book. I could not have written *Summer of '71* without their assistance.

Noah Feiwell, Ben Gilbert, Caitlin Doherty, and Seth Kershner pored over thousands of pages of documents, scanned every one, and, at times, dug for proverbial needles in the haystack in order to nail down facts. Noah and Ben worked alongside me many days at the Library of Congress. Seth answered the call when I needed additional documents from the Ellsberg Papers at UMass/Amherst. Caitlin proved that journalism is in her DNA, locating facts at the New York Public Library and the Library of Congress that I thought might be impossible to find.

Once the manuscript was finished, the process of gathering photographic and textual clearances began. I made a fortuitous connection with Isabella Pietro, courtesy of my good friend Steve Errick. Isabella spent innumerable hours managing text permissions and tracking down and verifying the photos that do much to bring this book to life.

Among the archivists who assisted me, three people, in particular, went far above and beyond the call.

Ryan Reft jumped on the phone with me when I first reached out to the Library of Congress. With an encyclopedic memory of what is in the Library's collections, Ryan guided my early research and pointed me to some of the surprises you have read about in these pages. Tal Nadan, at the New York Public Library, made sure I had access to necessary collections, and then worked patiently behind the scenes to assist with rights and permissions. Jeremy Smith, curator of the Daniel Ellsberg archives at the University of Massachusetts, walked me through that vast collection and spent many hours assisting with photograph and text clearances. This book benefits hugely from the consummate professionalism of Ryan, Tal, and Jeremy.

Early on, David Dunlap, historian at the *New York Times*, welcomed me to the *Times* museum to view and copy artifacts from the Pentagon Papers that are available nowhere else. As I wrapped up the manuscript, he was a helpful go-between with the *Times* legal department.

Among the many people who graciously allowed me to quote from letters and diaries, I owe special thanks to the family of Neil Sheehan—his wife, Susan, and his daughters, Maria and Catherine. The ability to quote directly, and at length, from Neil's private writings—his notebooks, letters, memos, and the like—makes this book special.

To others who also provided assistance and special courtesies as I went about my research and writing, I offer heartfelt thanks: Grace Bichler, Sheila Bickle, Andrew Blauner, Jonathan Broder, Rose Buchanan, Todd Combs, Stacy Davis, Loretta Deaver, Corynthia Dorgan, Ernie Emrich, Pamela Gilbert, Morton Halperin, Kimberly Johnson, Monica Johnson, Lisa London, Ellie Lottero, Meghan-Lee Parker, Ann Pryor, John Rogovin, Wendy Rogovin, Peter Safir, Geoff Shepard, Ellen Tuttle, Gilberto Vargas, and Alex Ward.

SOURCES

When I began research for this book in early 2024, Joe Biden was America's president and his party's presumptive nominee for a second term. But as Donald Trump's reelection became a probability, and then a reality, my thoughts turned to events that I witnessed firsthand as a young journalist more than five decades ago. There are striking parallels to the present day, as readers of this book will see.

History really does rhyme, if not repeat. And if you live long enough, sometimes you get to relive the proof.

The summer of 1971 was the summer *before* the infamous Watergate burglary. Richard Nixon's presidency eventually imploded because of Watergate, but not before he was reelected in a historic 1972 landslide, winning 49 of 50 states. To this day, the Watergate scandal has overshadowed—and defined—almost everything else about the politics and activism of the early 1970s, and certainly Nixon's presidency.

The public's collective memory is very short; only the memory of Watergate is seared in. Largely forgotten are the events that this book covers, from one year earlier, when Nixon and his closest aides wrote a vengeance playbook that is once again in use—secretly plotting revenge on perceived enemies and calling in thousands of federal troops to arrest and imprison protesters. Courageous journalists fought back using the power of the press. The stage was set for the drama that plays out today.

To tell the story of this parallel world of a half century ago, when America faced events and crises strikingly like those of today, I relied on first-person accounts found in the notes, diaries, letters, photographs and ephemera of dozens of archival collections—and, of course, in Nixon's infamous White House tapes.

I wouldn't have been able to tell this story through the lives and words of those who lived it without the help of many researchers and archivists. I am grateful to the professionals at all the institutions listed below who provided invaluable assistance to my researchers and me.

The thirty-six collections that were consulted for this book are listed alphabetically. In the Notes that follow, citations to these collections are given as the last name of the donor, followed, where available, with box numbers or folio numbers (e.g., *Sheehan, B47/F3*). From these and other sources, I amassed and reviewed over 100,000 pages of documents that comprise the foundation of this book. Research in the collections listed below was supplemented by archival materials from the National Archives and Records Administration (the repository of Nixon's minute-by-minute White House Daily Diary and his chief of staff H. R. Haldeman's diaries); the Nixon Library in Yorba Linda, California; and the online news archives of many newspapers, including the *New York Times*, the *Washington Post*, and the *Los Angeles Times*.

There are numerous sites online that provide access to the White House tapes of Richard Nixon. I found two sites to be particularly useful: the Miller Center of Public Affairs, University of Virginia; and NixonTapes.org.

The Library of Congress is the repository of Henry Kissinger's stenographic phone transcripts. They are a historical treasure. Seldom, if ever, have Kissinger's transcripts been mined in the way I've used them here, to augment the White House tapes and triangulate Kissinger's wide-ranging, and mostly secret, wheeling and dealing with politicians, diplomats, journalists, and celebrities during this epic summer.

When Kissinger spoke to someone on his White House line, his secretaries—unbeknownst to those on the other end of the call—listened in using a "dead key" extension and typed up verbatim transcripts for Kissinger from their shorthand notes. They transcribed calls even of a strictly personal nature, including between Kissinger and his most improbable of best buddies, Frank Sinatra.

After Nixon was driven from office by the revelations from the White House tapes confirming the Watergate cover-up, Kissinger made off with what he insisted were his own "personal" phone transcripts and locked them in a vault inside David Rockefeller's estate at Pocantico Hills, New York. When that became known, Nixon's former speechwriter William Safire (by then a columnist for the *New York Times*) pushed to obtain the transcripts under the federal Freedom of Information Act. Kissinger fought this, but Safire ultimately succeeded after years of lawsuits, aided by the Reporters Committee for Freedom of the Press. The Kissinger transcripts are a treasure trove. Because of Safire's doggedness, readers of this book now have another window into the machinations of Nixon and Kissinger, and the others they spoke to. I am grateful to the late Bill Safire for his enormously important posthumous contribution to this book.

Where White House transcripts are quoted, I've provided the date and time so that transcripts and audio can be retrieved either from the Miller Center website (MillerCenter.org) or at NixonTapes.org. Where Kissinger's phone conversations are quoted, my sole source for transcripts was the Library of Congress.

Where someone's age is listed, it is that person's age at the time the events being described were taking place.

Where a person is said to have "thought" or "believed" something, such an attribution is based upon a comment by that person to me or in a document, oral history, or previously in print.

No person who participated in the preparation of this book received any assurances as to how they would be portrayed, or how their comments would be used; and no one who provided assistance reviewed the manuscript before publication.

All significant citations can be found below except when, in deference to a source, I have preserved confidentiality.

Archival Collections

The following archival collections were consulted during the research for this book:

Alsop, Joseph, Papers. Manuscript Division. Library of Congress.

Bagdikian, Ben. Oral history conducted by Lisa Rubens 2010, Regional Oral History Office, The Bancroft Library, University of California, Berkeley.

Berrigan, Daniel and Philip, Collection. Division of Rare and Manuscript Collections. Cornell University Library.

Blackmun, Harry A., Papers. Manuscript Division. Library of Congress.

Broder, David S., Papers. Manuscript Division. Library of Congress.

Carter, Robert L., Papers. Manuscript Division. Library of Congress.

Davis, Angela, Collection. Schlesinger Library on the History of Women in America. Radcliffe Institute for Advanced Study. Harvard University.

Davis, Angela, Legal File. Schomburg Center for Research in Black Culture. Manuscripts, Archives and Rare Books Division. The New York Public Library. Astor, Lenox, and Tilden Foundations.

Ellsberg, Daniel, Collection. Special Collections and University Archives. University of Massachusetts Amherst Libraries.

Fonda, Jane, Collection. Sophia Smith Collection of Women's History. Smith College.

Garment, Leonard, Papers. Manuscript Division. Library of Congress.

Gesell, Gerhard A., Papers. Manuscript Division. Library of Congress.

Harriman, W. Averell, Papers. Manuscript Division. Library of Congress.

Harriman, Pamela, Papers. Manuscript Division. Library of Congress.

Kameny, Frank, Papers. Manuscript Division. Library of Congress.

Kissinger, Henry A., Stenographic Transcripts of Telephone Conversations. Manuscript Division. Library of Congress.

Leventhal, Harold, Papers. Manuscript Division. Library of Congress.

Lewis, Anthony, Papers. Manuscript Division. Library of Congress.

McGrory, Mary, Papers. Manuscript Division. Library of Congress.
Moore, Howard Jr., Papers. Stuart A. Rose Manuscript, Archives, and Rare Book Library. Emory University.
New York Times Company Records. Manuscripts and Archives Division. The New York Public Library. Astor, Lenox, and Tilden Foundations.
Osborne, John, Papers. Manuscript Division. Library of Congress.
Rodwell, Craig, Papers. Manuscripts and Archives Division. The New York Public Library. Astor, Lenox, and Tilden Foundations.
Rosenthal, A. M., Papers. Manuscripts and Archives Division. The New York Public Library. Astor, Lenox, and Tilden Foundations.
Safire, William, Papers. Manuscript Division. Library of Congress.
Schiff, Dorothy, Papers. Manuscripts and Archives Division. The New York Public Library. Astor, Lenox, and Tilden Foundations.
Sheehan, Neil, Papers. Manuscript Division. Library of Congress.
Spivak, Lawrence E., Papers. Manuscript Division. Library of Congress.
Stein, Jean, Papers. Manuscripts and Archives Division. The New York Public Library. Astor, Lenox, and Tilden Foundations.
Thomas, Helen, Papers. Manuscript Division. Library of Congress.
Tigar, Michael, Papers. Briscoe Center for American History. The University of Texas at Austin.
Vann-Sheehan Vietnam War Collection. Manuscript Division. Library of Congress.
Washington Star Photograph Collection, The People's Archive, District of Columbia Public Library, Washington, DC.
Weddington, Sarah, Papers. Woman's Collection. Texas Woman's University Library.
Wicker, Tom, Papers. New York Times Company Records. Manuscripts and Archives Division. The New York Public Library. Astor, Lenox, and Tilden Foundations.
Ziegler, Ronald, Papers. Manuscript Division. Library of Congress.

Text Permissions

This book quotes directly from many diaries, letters, oral histories, and other documentation of the events of the summer of '71. I express appreciation to those listed below, each of whom graciously allowed me to include excerpts from textual material for which they control rights:

American Civil Liberties Union and ACLU of the District of Columbia: For excerpts from the 1972 Report, *May Day 1971: Order without Law—An ACLU Study of the Largest Sweep Arrests in American History*. © 2025 by ACLU/ACLU of the District of Columbia.

Christian G. Appy, Director, The Ellsberg Initiative for Peace and Democracy, and Professor of History, University of Massachusetts, Amherst: For excerpts from his narrative about Daniel Ellsberg's Vietnam days, found at umass.edu/ellsberg/timeline.

Association for Diplomatic Studies and Training: For the oral history excerpts from Ambassador Joseph S. Farland, interviewed by Charles Stuart Kennedy. Foreign Affairs Oral History Collection, Association for Diplomatic Studies and Training, Arlington, VA, adst.org.

Bancroft Library, University of California, Berkeley: For excerpts from the oral history of Ben H. Bagdikian, Journalist, Media Critic, Professor & Dean Emeritus, UC Berkeley's Graduate School of Journalism, conducted by Lisa Rubens 2010, Regional Oral History Office, the Bancroft Library, University of California, Berkeley, 2011.

Todd Combs: For excerpts from the first-person account by his father, Ken Combs, of the Marin Courthouse kidnappings and killings.

Grand Central Publishing: For the first-person account of Malcolm Browne about his reporting in Vietnam, taken from *Reporting America at War* by James Tobin. Copyright © 2003. Reprinted by permission of Grand Central Publishing, an imprint of Hachette Book Group, Inc.

Chuck Lewis, emeritus professor at American University and executive editor of the Investigative Reporting Workshop: For excerpts from the Pentagon Papers oral history of Bill Kovach, found on the *Investigating Power* website at investigatingpower.org/bill-kovach.

Susan Sheehan, Maria Sheehan, and Catherine Sheehan: For excerpts from the letters, notes, and other writings of Neil Sheehan and Susan Sheehan.

John Rogovin: For excerpts from the contemporaneous Pentagon Papers memo prepared by his father, attorney Mitch Rogovin.

Peter Safir: For excerpts from the post-White House writings and letters of his uncle, Bill Safire.

Texas Woman's University: For family photos and excerpts from Sarah Weddington's letters to her parents. Text and images courtesy of TWU Libraries Woman's Collection, Texas Woman's University, Denton, Texas.

PHOTOGRAPHIC CREDITS AND PERMISSIONS

Page 1: Daniel Ellsberg in Vietnam, c. 1966. *Credit: Daniel Ellsberg Papers, Robert S. Cox Special Collections and University Archives Research Center, University of Massachusetts Amherst Libraries. Used with permission.*

Page 2, top: Neil Sheehan in Vietnam, c. 1962. *Credit: Courtesy of the Sheehan family. Used with permission.*

Page 2, bottom: Daniel Ellsberg in Vietnam rice paddy with gun, c. 1966. *Credit: Daniel Ellsberg Papers, Robert S. Cox Special Collections and University Archives Research Center, University of Massachusetts Amherst Libraries. Used with permission.*

Page 3, top: Daniel Ellsberg at lectern, New York City, 1972. *Credit: Library of Congress, Prints & Photographs Division. Photograph by Bernard Gotfryd. Reproduction number LC-DIG-ppmsca-12429.*

Page 3, bottom: Nixon and Kissinger walking on White House grounds, August 10, 1971. *Credit: National Archives and Records Administration (NARA). Photograph by Oliver F. Atkins. NAID 194731; Local ID NLRN-WHPO-6990-18A.*

Page 4, top: John Kerry, spokesman for Vietnam Veterans Against the War, at microphone, Washington, DC, April 21, 1971. *Credit: Library of Congress, Prints & Photographs Division, U.S. News & World Report Photograph Collection. Photograph by Warren K. Leffler. Reproduction number LC-DIG-ppmsca-50415.*

Page 4, bottom: Demonstration by Vietnam Veterans Against the War, U.S. Capitol grounds, April 19, 1971. *Credit: Library of Congress, Prints & Photographs Division, U.S. News & World Report Photograph Collection. Photograph by Marion S. Trikosko. Reproduction number LC-DIG-ppmsca-50413; call number LC-U9-24262-13A [P&P].*

Page 5, top: Marines from Camp Lejeune landing at Washington Monument to reinforce police, May 3, 1971. *Credit: D.C. Public Library, Washington Star Collection, "Marines Land at Washington Monument, Mayday 1971." Courtesy of the DC Public Library Washington Star Collection. Photograph by A. J. Smith.* © The Washington Post. *Used with permission.*

Page 5, middle: Mass incarceration at a makeshift outdoor prison near RFK Stadium, Washington, DC, May 1971. *Credit: DC Public Library, Washington Star Collection, "Protesters Held at RFK," 1971. Courtesy of the DC Public Library Washington Star Collection. Photograph by Pete Copeland.* © The Washington Post. *Used with permission.*

Page 5, bottom: Sarah Weddington, 25-year-old attorney for Jane Roe, moderates Citizens' Hearings on Abortion, Austin, Texas, January 1971. *Credit: TWU Libraries Woman's Collection, Texas Woman's University, Denton, Texas. Used with permission.*

Page 6, top: Angela Davis marches to free the Soledad Brothers, State Building, Los Angeles, June 20, 1970. *Credit: Photograph by Ray Graham,* Los Angeles Times. *Photographic Collection, UCLA Library Special Collections. © The Regents of the University of California. Used with permission.*

Page 6, middle: Civic Center shoot-out, San Rafael, California, August 7, 1970. *Credit: Photograph by Jim Kean, MediaNews Group/*Marin Independent Journal *via Getty Images. Editorial #1392042486. © 2022 MediaNews Group. Used with permission.*

Page 6, bottom: Angela Davis, Wanted Poster, August 18, 1970. *Credit: National Museum of African American History and Culture. Object Number: 2012.146.*

Page 7, top: Nixon, Hoover, Mitchell, and Ehrlichman in the Oval Office, May 26, 1971. *Credit: National Archives and Records Administration (NARA). Photograph by Byron E. Schumaker (White House staff photographer), Washington, DC, May 26, 1971. NAID 194722; Local ID NLRN-WHPO-6397-09A.*

Page 7, bottom: Henry Kissinger and Frank Sinatra at the Tenth Annual Scopus Awards Dinner, Century Plaza Hotel, November 11, 1979. *Credit: Photograph by Ralph Dominguez. © MediaPunch Inc./Alamy. Used with permission.*

Page 8: Attica: Police carrying wounded on stretcher, September 13, 1971. *Credit: Courtesy of the Elizabeth Fink Estate (AtticaBrothersFoundation.org), Michael Hull, executor. Used with permission.*

The following photographs appear on the front cover of the book jacket (in top-to-bottom order):

Women march after eviction from park, May 2, 1971. *Credit: DC Public Library, Washington Star Collection. Used with permission.*

National Guard troops and antiwar protesters, University of Maryland, May 7, 1971. *Credit: © Bettmann. Image ID U1703902. Used with permission.*

Protesters at U.S. Capitol, Washington, DC, May 5, 1971. *Credit: Prints & Photographs Division, Library of Congress, U.S. News & World Report Collection. Photograph by Thomas J. O'Halloran and Marion S. Trikosko. Reproduced courtesy of the Library of Congress.*

Antiwar protesters at Justice Department, Washington, DC, May 1971. *Credit: Prints & Photographs Division, Library of Congress, U.S. News & World Report Collection. Photograph by Warren K. Leffler. Reproduced courtesy of the Library of Congress.*

Police confront protesters at U.S. Capitol, Washington, DC, May 5, 1971. *Credit: Prints & Photographs Division, Library of Congress, U.S. News & World Report Collection. Photograph by Thomas J. O'Halloran and Marion S. Trikosko. Reproduced courtesy of the Library of Congress.*

NOTES

Chapter 1

1. Ellsberg Papers UMass https://www.umass.edu/ellsberg/featured-documents/vietnam-war/ says he was first in Vietnam 1961: "Daniel Ellsberg went to Vietnam for the first time in September 1961 as part of a Pentagon fact-finding task force. He hoped to learn that the South Vietnamese government of Ngo Dinh Diem, with U.S. backing, was defeating the Communist-led insurgency of the Viet Cong. After all, Ellsberg was a dedicated cold warrior, a foreign policy hawk. He discovered, instead, that Saigon was losing the war; a Communist victory seemed virtually inevitable. Returning to his job at the Rand Corporation think tank in Santa Monica, California, he advised colleagues to avoid studying Vietnam–it might taint their careers. Ellsberg himself went back to his work on nuclear war plans."
2. Vietnam Diary, *The Reporter*, January 13, 1966. The diary was unbylined, but other sources have confirmed over the years that the diary was Ellsberg's. Meg Greenfield was Washington editor and bureau chief of the Reporter at the time, and edited Ellsberg's diary for publication. See Meg Greenfield Papers at the Library of Congress, Box 42: "Filed separately is an article submitted by Daniel Ellsberg, titled 'Vietnam Diary,' published in the Reporter in January 1966. Letters from Ellsberg relate how he wrote the article and comment on its editing." https://tile.loc.gov/storage-services/service/gdc/gdcfindingaidpdfs/ms011109/ms011109.pdf
3. Vietnam Diary, *The Reporter*
4. https://www.umass.edu/ellsberg/timeline/UMass timeline 1959–1964
5. This project is also explained by Tom Wells in *Wild Man*, p. 154.
6. "Risk, Ambiguity, and Decision"—Harvard PhD thesis in economics, April 1962 https://archive.org/details/RiskAmbiguityAndDecisionThesis/mode/2up
7. NIH website definition: https://pmc.ncbi.nlm.nih.gov/articles/PMC10352116/
8. JStor: http://www.dklevine.com/archive/refs47605.pdf. Also found here as "Risk, Ambiguity, and the Savage Axioms": https://academic.oup.com/qje/article-abstract/75/4/643/1913802?redirectedFrom=fulltext

9. Timeline, Ellsberg Papers, UMass https://www.umass.edu/ellsberg/timeline/
10. Timeline, Ellsberg Papers, UMass
11. August 4, 1964, according to UMass website
12. USS *Maddox* might have been "attacked," although the United States may have started it. The *Turner Joy*, definitely not. Ambiguity about this incident may remain, but it is clear now that the U.S. pretext was false.
13. https://www.umass.edu/ellsberg/featured-documents/vietnam-war/#:~:text=Yet%20Ellsberg%20remained%20a%20loyal%20official.%20He,justify%20a%20bombing%20campaign%20against%20North%20Vietnam
14. Ellsberg's August 4, 1964, start date at the Pentagon is confirmed in *Wild Man*, p. 199. But at p. 203, author Tom Wells paints a different picture of Ellsberg around this time: "Dan Ellsberg was, without question, a hawk on Vietnam." Quotes others about Ellsberg's hawkishness. Harry Harris is quoted: "We're going to really strike these guys. . . . You can't attack an American ship on the high seas, and anybody that does has to pay for it."
15. *Wild Man*, pp. 188–189 establishes their breakup as 1963. P. 189: After Carol tells him she wants a divorce, Dan goes skydiving . . . "with a girlfriend," Carol Ellsberg recounts.
16. Sheehan Notes, Sheehan Papers LC
17. Sheehan Notes, Sheehan Papers LC
18. Sheehan typewritten notes, Vann-Sheehan Vietnam War Collection, LC
19. https://www.umass.edu/ellsberg/timeline/ The accident occurred July 3, 1946. Ellsberg was fifteen years old. Both he and his father were seriously injured. Clipping is on the UMass website.
20. Sheehan typewritten notes, Vann-Sheehan Vietnam War Collection, LC
21. https://www.umass.edu/ellsberg/featured-documents/vietnam-war/#overview UMASS summary
22. https://www.umass.edu/ellsberg/featured-documents/vietnam-war/
23. Tom Wells, in *Wild Man*, p. 231, is more specific, and calls it September 1965. Ellsberg was certainly back in the country by then. Stays two years.
24. Sheehan typewritten notes, Vann-Sheehan Vietnam War Collection, LC
25. This was from McGeorge Bundy, national security adviser to LBJ, according to Sheehan typescript quoting Ellsberg. Sheehan typewritten notes, Vann-Sheehan Vietnam War Collection, LC.
26. Sheehan typewritten notes quoting Ellsberg in Vann-Sheehan Vietnam War Collection, LC
27. Vann-Sheehan Vietnam War Collection, LC, B28F21.2: 6/1/72 letter from Vincent Davis, University of Kentucky, to Admiral Rectanus: Davis says he introduced Vann and Ellsberg in 1965, "after Dan was terminated in his job" at DoD "and was looking around for a job in Vietnam. He was John's aide during his time in Vietnam, and he did

a good job then, too. It was only later that some of his psychoneurotic tendencies became fairly clearly evident."

28. Vann's shoot-downs and military bravery medals are recounted in Vann-Sheehan Vietnam War Collection, B28F21.2: 6/1/72 letter from Vincent Davis, University of Kentucky, to Admiral Rectanus.
29. Vann CV: https://archive.org/details/CVAndResumeForJohnPaulVann/mode/2up
30. Vann CV: https://archive.org/details/CVAndResumeForJohnPaulVann/mode/2up
31. Vann CV: https://archive.org/details/CVAndResumeForJohnPaulVann/mode/2up
32. Ellsberg's recollections of Vann are in Sheehan's typescript notes, Vann-Sheehan Vietnam War Collection, LC
33. Vann's CV is on Internet Archive: https://archive.org/details/CVAndResumeForJohnPaulVann/mode/2up
34. "Harnessing the Revolution in South Vietnam," by John Paul Vann: https://archive.org/details/HarnessingTheRevolutionInSouthVietnam
35. See https://www.nytimes.com/1988/09/25/books/the-man-who-was-the-war.html (NYTBR of *Bright Shining Lie* provides insight.)
36. Sheehan typescript notes quoting Ellsberg, Vann-Sheehan Vietnam War Collection, LC
37. Vietnam Diary, *The Reporter*, January 13, 1966
38. *Wild Man*, p. 231: "Danger was a main theme of a piece that Ellsberg wrote on the sights and smells of Saigon that September."
39. Vietnam Diary, *The Reporter*
40. According to Tom Wells, in *Wild Man*, p. 231, "Jerry" is Jerry Rose, "an American adviser to the GVN who may have been on the CIA's payroll. Rose's death shook Ellsberg. He had visited Rose's apartment the night before learning of it, hoping to have dinner with him." According to Wells, Ellsberg wrote the diary "while laid up in bed with a case of amoebic dysentery. He drank some water without boiling and filtering it (despite being instructed to do so), so of course he got very sick." Wells says State Department censors cleared the article. Ellsberg didn't like the editing he received from Meg Greenfield, the Washington bureau chief of *The Reporter*. Still, he ordered fifty copies of the article to pass around. See sourcing on p. 630 of *Wild Man*.
41. Vietnam Diary, *The Reporter*
42. https://dreamofacity.com/2012/08/19/a-walk-down-rue-catinat-saigon/
43. https://niemanreports.org/1972-reflections-on-vietnam-the-press-and-america/
44. Peter Arnett 1972 article in *Nieman Reports*, republished 12/15/99 https://niemanreports.org/1972-reflections-on-vietnam-the-press-and-america/
45. https://time.com/3791176/malcolm-browne-the-story-behind-the-burning-monk/

46. https://www.famouspictures.org/burning-monk/
47. https://www.pbs.org/weta/reportingamericaatwar/reporters/browne/protests.html#:~:text=The%20following%20day%2C%20President%20Kennedy%20had%20the,support%20for%20the%20Ngo%20Dinh%20Diem%20regime
48. https://history.state.gov/historicaldocuments/frus1961-63v03/d281. August 24 cable, November 2 assassination of Diem
49. https://history.state.gov/historicaldocuments/frus1961-63v03/d281
50. https://millercenter.org/the-presidency/educational-resources/diem-coup
51. https://nsarchive2.gwu.edu/NSAEBB/NSAEBB101/index.htm. The CIA also provided $42,000 in immediate support money to the plotters the morning of the coup, carried by Lucien Conein, an act prefigured in administration planning (Document 17).
52. https://www.history.army.mil/html/reference/army_flag/vn.html. Exact number is 746.
53. https://www.digitalhistory.uh.edu/disp_textbook.cfm?smtID=11&psid=3844. This is from the University of Houston, "Troop Levels By Year In Vietnam." 1968 is the high point.
54. Vann-Sheehan Vietnam War Collection, LC
55. Susan Sheehan wrote about the tapeworm in a *New York Times Magazine* story, April 15, 1990.
56. Sheehan's notes in Sheehan Papers, LC
57. Sheehan notes, Sheehan Papers, LC

Chapter 2

1. Halperin proposed the study in June 1967, and McNamara approved it that same month.
2. Instead of using existing Defense Department historians, McNamara assigned his close aide and Assistant Secretary of Defense John McNaughton to collect the papers. McNamara wanted the study done in three months. McNaughton died in a plane crash one month after work began in June 1967, but the project continued under the direction of Defense Department official Les Gelb.
3. McNamara was appointed president of the World Bank by LBJ the following February.
4. McNamara told others, such as Dean Rusk, that he only asked for a collection of documents rather than the studies he received. Motives aside, McNamara neglected to inform either President Lyndon Johnson or Secretary of State Dean Rusk about the study.
5. *NYT* story 3/10/68: https://timesmachine.nytimes.com/timesmachine/1968/03/10/90030622.pdf?pdf_redirect=true&ip=0

6. Sheehan notes, Sheehan Papers, LC. Sheehan wrote, "I had done much of the reporting for it."
7. The anger, and the consequences of the story, are recounted numerous places. See Ellsberg, *Secrets*, p. 209, and also *Politico*: https://www.politico.com/story/2018/03/25/this-day-in-politics-march-25-1968-477991. The "Wise Men" discussion on March 25 is recounted both places, and also in works by various historians.
8. Sheehan took the notes after a dinner at Rostow's home in Austin, 4/22/70. Sheehan, in his typewritten notes, refers to the number "206,500" throughout, but the *NYT* story says "206,000" and that number is used here for the sake of clarity.
9. Sheehan notes, 4/22/70, Sheehan Papers, LC
10. *Secrets*, p. 203. "...not I, I regret to say..."
11. *Secrets*, p. 203
12. *Secrets*, p. 204
13. *Secrets*, p. 204
14. *Secrets*, p. 206
15. *Secrets*, p. 206.
16. *Secrets*, p. 206
17. *Secrets*, p. 207
18. https://www.nytimes.com/1968/03/19/archives/us-undervalued-enemys-strength-before-offensive-cia-reports-forces.html
19. *Secrets*, p. 207
20. *Secrets*, p. 207
21. *Secrets*, p. 207. Ellsberg quotes the memo in his memoir, *Secrets*. This wasn't the only time Sheehan's reporting on enemy troop strength perplexed the Defense Department and the CIA. See also https://www.cia.gov/readingroom/docs/CIA-RDP80R01720R000100020002-3.pdf
22. https://timesmachine.nytimes.com/timesmachine/1968/03/20/77094840.pdf?pdf_redirect=true&ip=0
23. https://timesmachine.nytimes.com/timesmachine/1968/03/21/76871318.html?pageNumber=1
24. https://timesmachine.nytimes.com/timesmachine/1968/03/21/76871318.pdf?pdf_redirect=true&ip=0
25. Politico story recounting the fateful March 25, 1968, meeting: https://www.politico.com/story/2018/03/25/this-day-in-politics-march-25-1968-477991
26. This appears to be the case based on the State Department notes found here (confirms meeting at WH began at 3:15 p.m. on March 26, a Tuesday, and Johnson's comments confirm there were briefings the evening before): https://history.state.gov/historicaldocuments/frus1964-68v06/d158
27. https://www.masshist.org/database/viewer.php?item_id=3225&pid=36

28. https://www.history.com/topics/world-war-ii/omar-bradley#later-years-and-honors
29. *Secrets*, p. 209
30. *Secrets*, p. 209, and *U.S. Department of State, Office of the Historian, Foreign Relations of the United States, 1964–1968, Volume VI, "Notes of Meeting," Washington, March 26, 1968 (Document 156)*, available online
31. This and all other comments from the March 26 meeting come from Tom Johnson's contemporaneous notes, found here at the State Department website: https://history.state.gov/historicaldocuments/frus1964-68v06/d158
32. Also see Politico: https://www.politico.com/story/2018/03/25/this-day-in-politics-march-25-1968-477991
33. All the foregoing comes from Tom Johnson's notes, found here at the State Department historian's website: https://history.state.gov/historicaldocuments/frus1964-68v06/d158. There was also an audio recording of the meeting, and some of the comments, particularly from Taylor and LBJ himself, are included verbatim in the historian's later footnotes to Tom Johnson's notes.
34. See fn 7 @ https://history.state.gov/historicaldocuments/frus1964-68v06/d158
35. See fn 7 @ https://history.state.gov/historicaldocuments/frus1964-68v06/d158
36. https://timesmachine.nytimes.com/timesmachine/1968/04/01/77096488.html?pageNumber=1
37. On May 13, 1968, the first session of the Paris peace talks that would go on until 1973 opened. As the peace talks moved slowly, Johnson seriously considered the advice of Rostow and Rusk to start bombing North Vietnam north of the 20th parallel. Alarmed, Harriman sent Vance to Washington on May 28 to tell Johnson that the Vietnamese would break off the talks if the Americans bombed north of the 20th parallel.
38. See Sanford J. Ungar, "The Papers Papers," *Esquire*, May 1972
39. The exchange of letters is found in *NYT* Collection at NYPL.
40. Sheehan made handwritten contemporaneous notes about what he called the "soul session" with Frankel and Phelps. The meeting took place on or about December 3, 1969.
41. Sheehan's final falling-out with Frankel occurred on June 15, 1972, a year after publication of the Pentagon Papers. Sheehan's eight-page memorandum to Frankel is found in the papers of Abe Rosenthal at the NYPL, in a folder marked "Sheehan, Neil (Mr. & Mrs.) (Susan)."
42. Frankel's reply to Sheehan, June 16, 1972, is found in the papers of Abe Rosenthal at the NYPL, in a folder marked "Sheehan, Neil (Mr. & Mrs.) (Susan)."
43. *NYT* Collection at NYPL. Frankel's memo to Abe Rosenthal, dated June 16, 1972, is found in the papers of Abe Rosenthal deposited by

the *New York Times* at the NYPL, in a folder marked "Sheehan, Neil (Mr. & Mrs.) (Susan)."

Chapter 3

1. Tom Wells, in *Wild Man*, p. 126, establishes this date.
2. *Wild Man*, p. 127
3. Reviewed here: https://www.jstor.org/stable/2146196
4. Dissertation is called *A World Restored*. Explainer: https://sais.jhu.edu/kissinger/about/legacy
5. From Kissinger Center paper at JHU SAIS: https://sais.jhu.edu/kissinger/about/legacy
6. https://timesmachine.nytimes.com/timesmachine/1957/10/13/96961293.html?pageNumber=270
7. Transcript of WABC interview 7/13/58 (found at OCLC) is here: https://hrc.contentdm.oclc.org/digital/collection/p15878coll90/id/67/
8. https://www.hollywoodreporter.com/news/general-news/henry-kissinger-hollywood-love-affairs-power-ultimate-aphrodisiac-1235704158/
9. https://www.hollywoodreporter.com/news/general-news/henry-kissinger-hollywood-love-affairs-power-ultimate-aphrodisiac-1235704158/
10. They were called the Three M's: https://www.ephemerasociety.org/the-three-ms/
11. Author interview 2/11/24 with a source who greeted Van Doren at the door
12. This comes from *Time* magazine, 2/7/72.
13. https://www.ocweekly.com/balboa-bay-bombshell-6390437/
14. This is Bill Safire speaking. The comment is in Safire Papers, LC.
15. *Time*, 2/7/72
16. See *Secrets*, p. 345, for more on Lloyd Shearer and Kissinger.
17. Peter Maas, "The City Politic: Nixon's Favorite Wordsmith," *New York* Magazine, p. 7, 1/11/71
18. The memo is found in Safire Papers, LC.
19. This is in the speech typescript by Safire for Kissinger.
20. This quote is legendary, and is used all over. Example in *The Hollywood Reporter*: https://www.hollywoodreporter.com/news/general-news/henry-kissinger-hollywood-love-affairs-power-ultimate-aphrodisiac-1235704158/. It's been used by, among others, the AP and PBS, and I heard the line quoted by Pete Peterson when he was working with Kissinger at the White House.
21. Safire Papers, LC, Box 122, Folder 3. It's likely a memo Safire prepared as he was writing his book, *Before the Fall*, about his years with Nixon.

22. See https://archive.org/stream/InterviewWithHistoryByOrianaFallaciInterviewArtEbook/Interview%20with%20History%20-%20by%20Oriana%20Fallaci%20%28Interview%20Art%20Ebook%29_djvu.txt
23. https://sais.jhu.edu/kissinger/about/legacy
24. https://sais.jhu.edu/kissinger/about/legacy
25. HAK in a 1963 lecture, quoted here: https://sais.jhu.edu/kissinger/about/legacy
26. https://sais.jhu.edu/kissinger/about/legacy
27. https://sais.jhu.edu/kissinger/about/legacy
28. A young Susan Faludi, writing for the *Harvard Crimson* in 1979, broke this: https://www.thecrimson.com/article/1979/11/16/kissinger-harvard-and-the-fbi-phenry/
29. *Wild Man*, p. 127
30. See *Secrets*, p. 344: "It wasn't a tactic I was recommending for the United States, or anyone else, for that matter. Far from it. For someone to imitate Hitler in this respect was to cultivate madness and court disaster."
31. *Wild Man*, p. 128
32. *Wild Man*, p. 127
33. *Secrets*, p. 344
34. *Secrets*, p. 239
35. Described by Ellsberg in *Secrets*, p. 228
36. *Secrets*, p. 228
37. *Secrets*, p. 229
38. *Secrets*, p. 229
39. Vann-Sheehan Vietnam War Collection, LC, B28F21.1: Letter to Vincent Davis, 7/26/68: The stationery says Room 1034, 50 Rockefeller Plaza.
40. Documented in Safire's FOIA litigation and in many articles, including this one: https://thebaffler.com/latest/clintons-emails-kissingers-vault#anchor1
41. July 3, 1968, letter from Walter S. Mack to Neal D. Peterson of Humphrey's staff, found in Vann-Sheehan Vietnam War Collection at LC, B28F21
42. Nixon to Sam Yorty, letter dated October 25, 1968, Vann-Sheehan Collection, B28F21.1: "I found his proposals to be most interesting, and have taken the liberty of referring the newspaper clipping to my research and policy staff." Nixon basically stuck with his stated position that, as he said in the letter, "the de-Americanization of the war must proceed with all deliberate speed."
43. https://pattersonschool.uky.edu/history-leadership
44. B28F21.2, Vann-Sheehan Vietnam War Collection, Letter from Davis to Rectanus, 6/1/72
45. See Peter Kurtz, https://peterkurtz.wordpress.com/2022/02/17/a-bright-shining-lie-john-paul-vann-and-america-in-vietnam-book-review/

46. https://timesmachine.nytimes.com/timesmachine/1968/06/18/issue.html?login=email&auth=login-email
47. According to Sheehan's handwritten notation on the July 6, 1968, letter from Davis to Kissinger: "JPV apparently did not get to see H.K. at this time. He and H.K. apparently only talked on phone at this or some other point. . . ." Vann-Sheehan Collection, B28F21
48. July 26, 1968, Kissinger to Vincent Davis, Vann-Sheehan Collection, B28F21.1: Sheehan's handwritten notation: "H.K. did not actually get JPV's new plan until after Nixon nomination."
49. https://www.politico.com/magazine/story/2014/10/nelson-rockefellers-last-stand-112072/
50. Vincent Davis letter to Kissinger, August 9, 1968, Vann-Sheehan Vietnam War Collection, B28F21
51. Vincent Davis letter to Kissinger, August 9, 1968, Vann-Sheehan Vietnam War Collection, B28F21
52. https://www.nytimes.com/1971/07/14/archives/ellsberg-says-kissinger-knew-about-pentagon-papers-in-70.html
53. Sheehan's handwritten notes, found in Vann-Sheehan Collection, B18F21.2; the notes are titled "Telecon Jan 18, 1980."
54. According to Sheehan's handwritten notes of 1/18/80: "K was asking JPV's advice because JPV had credibility and K was talking [to] him. The back channels may have gone through CIA. . . ." Sheehan's notes, based on his phone call with Hersh, also reflect that the back channel was open by 1969. Vann-Sheehan Collection, B28F21.2
55. August 9, 1968, letter from Davis to Kissinger, Vann-Sheehan Vietnam War Collection, B28F21.1
56. Kissinger letter to Vincent Davis, August 20, 1968, Vann-Sheehan Vietnam War Collection, B28F21
57. *Secrets*, p. 228
58. *Secrets*, p. 228

Chapter 4

1. *NYT* 12/4/68: https://timesmachine.nytimes.com/timesmachine/1968/12/04/77183427.pdf?pdf_redirect=true&ip=0
2. *Secrets*, p. 232
3. *Secrets*, p. 232
4. *Secrets*, p. 233. All that follows is Ellsberg's chronology from his book.
5. *Secrets*, p. 233
6. *Secrets*, p. 234
7. See Karnow, *Vietnam: A History*, p. 582
8. *Secrets*, p. 235
9. https://www.pbs.org/frontlineworld/stories/cambodia/tl02.html

10. https://www.nationalmuseum.af.mil/Visit/Museum-Exhibits/Fact-Sheets/Display/Article/196023/hitting-sanctuaries-cambodia/
11. Karnow, *Vietnam*, p. 582
12. Haldeman (1978), *The Ends of Power*, p. 122
13. https://www.nixonlibrary.gov/sites/default/files/virtuallibrary/documents/haldeman-diaries/37-hrhd-journal-vol01-19690317.pdf
14. https://www.nixonlibrary.gov/sites/default/files/virtuallibrary/documents/haldeman-diaries/37-hrhd-journal-vol01-19690318.pdf
15. https://www.history.com/news/nixon-war-powers-act-vietnam-war-cambodia
16. https://www.bbc.com/culture/article/20240503-kent-state-university-1970-protests-that-shook-the-us
17. https://timesmachine.nytimes.com/timesmachine/1969/05/09/88992642.html?pageNumber=1
18. *Secrets*, p. 260
19. https://www.nytimes.com/2024/02/18/business/media/william-beecher-dead.html
20. Full text and context of Hoover memo to Nixon, May 11, 1970, found at National Security Archives: https://nsarchive.gwu.edu/document/30337-document-77-fbi-j-edgar-hoover-wiretap-surveillance-report-president-nixon-top
21. Full text of letter and context at the GWU National Security Archives: https://nsarchive.gwu.edu/document/30337-document-77-fbi-j-edgar-hoover-wiretap-surveillance-report-president-nixon-top
22. Safire Papers, LC, B22F6
23. Safire Papers, LC, B22F3 (White House Diary, October 4 and 5, 1969)
24. Harriman dictated this to Mark Lincoln Chadwin, his private secretary, on 6/28/70. Harriman Papers at LC, B874F8. The two segments from this lengthy oral history are from pp. 6 and 8 of that document.
25. Sheehan Papers at LC, in folder: "Pentagon Papers Correspondence." Krock's memorandum is dated April 18, 1972.
26. Here is the quote in context: https://libquotes.com/henry-wadsworth-longfellow/quote/lbg7m6j
27. *Secrets*, p. 343
28. https://www.thecrimson.com/article/1970/5/14/kissinger-aide-resigns-in-protest-to/
29. This and following from *Secrets*, p. 344
30. *Secrets*, p. 346
31. This is from Sheehan's handwritten bio, Sheehan Papers, LC. The bio lists 2/1969 as the promotion date.
32. This is the memo in full. Undated. It was found in Sheehan Papers at LC.
33. U.S. bombing had cut off a key supply conduit that went through this key Cambodian port. See fn 15 here: https://en.wikipedia.org/wiki/Cambodian_campaign

34. See "Nixon Speaks" here: https://en.wikipedia.org/wiki/Cambodian_campaign
35. https://www.nixonlibrary.gov/sites/default/files/virtuallibrary/documents/haldeman-diaries/37-hrhd-journal-vol05-19700427.pdf
36. Sheehan memo to Frankel, 5/15/70, Sheehan Papers, LC
37. John M. Dunn obit (3/30/95, age 69): https://www.nytimes.com/1995/03/30/obituaries/maj-gen-john-m-dunn-69-military-aide-to-vice-presidents.html
38. According to Sheehan's handwritten notes, that meeting was to occur on June 11 at 6:00 p.m.
39. Lake's resignation became known to *NYT* on 5/22/70. Story the following morning: https://www.nytimes.com/1970/05/23/archives/4-more-leaving-kissingers-staff-a-5th-member-is-reported-planning.html
40. James Risen interview with Ellsberg, "The Secret History," published 10/7/23 at https://theintercept.com/2023/10/07/pentagon-papers-daniel-ellsberg-neil-sheehan/
41. James Risen interview with Ellsberg
42. Sheehan notes, Sheehan Papers at LC. Cross verification: Safire papers at LC include a Sunday, May 3, "diary" entry that shows Harlow, although by now back at P&G, is involved, along with other strategists. Kissinger, Laird, and Rogers not in the room for this meeting.
43. Lending credence to Harlow's working both sides of the aisle, regardless of administration: Oral History for LBJ Library, link here: https://dev.lbj.freelock.net/object/document/oral-history-transcript-bryce-n-harlow-interview-2-ii-561979-michael-l-gillette. Also full text PDF here: https://bj-new-assets.s3.amazonaws.com/artifacts/files/2021-08/27500879-oh-harlowb-19790506-2-80-27.pdf?VersionId=tBOytxS__lOW.ieJYSpmO01q_Ah8ZVXO. Taped WH call between LBJ and Harlow, 11/14/68 (LBJ and Harlow are well acquainted): https://prde.upress.virginia.edu/conversations/4011253 Bryce Harlow Foundation bio of Harlow: https://bryceharlow.org/about/who-was-bryce-harlow/biography/
44. Sheehan Papers, LC: Notes on his "Interview with H" dated June 19, 1970
45. Osborne Papers, LC. Osborne conducted the interview at 445 Park Avenue, NYC, on 10/27/68.
46. As recounted by David Smith in the *Guardian*, 4/2/22
47. https://time.com/archive/6838367/martha-mitchells-view-from-the-top/
48. https://www.washingtonpost.com/local/obituaries/neil-sheehan-ny-times-reporter-who-obtained-pentagon-papers-and-chronicled-bright-shining-lie-of-vietnam-dies-at-84/2021/01/07/86794382-f943-11e7-ad8c-ecbb62019393_story.html
49. This has also been described in Chapter 2.
50. Frankel memo to Abe Rosenthal, 6/16/72: "As we here feared all along, while also fearing to face it, Neil (and/or Susan) now feel confirmed

and have extended their exaggerated estimate of his talents and of The Times' debt to him/them." Found in Rosenthal's papers at NYPL.

51. https://timesmachine.nytimes.com/timesmachine/1970/05/31/354996382.html?pageNumber=162
52. Susan letter to Neil, 6/6/70, Sheehan Papers, LC
53. https://timesmachine.nytimes.com/timesmachine/1970/11/22/102289848.html?pageNumber=223
54. https://www.nytimes.com/1970/06/30/archives/cambodian-decision-why-president-acted-reconstruction-of-cambodia.html
55. Sheehan Papers, LC, handwritten notes by Sheehan
56. Story of 1958 rejection of Child's book here: https://bloomsite.wordpress.com/2014/11/21/two-years-blooming-bloom-hits-two-and-100/
57. Sheehan Papers, LC. Unpaginated handwritten notes on the *60 Minutes* episode of October 13, 1970
58. Sheehan Papers, LC, B169F5
59. Susan Sheehan letter to Neil Sheehan, undated, Sheehan Papers at LC, B169F5

Chapter 5

1. Crime stats for DC found here (Disaster Center): https://www.disastercenter.com/crime/dccrime.htm
2. Fagan, Zimring & Kim in the *Journal of Criminal Law & Criminology*: https://scholarlycommons.law.northwestern.edu/cgi/viewcontent.cgi?referer=&httpsredir=1&article=6979&context=jclc#:~:text=After%20steady%20to%20declining%20trends%20until%20the,only%20to%20drop%20off%20again%20after%201991
3. Source: Disaster Center: https://www.disastercenter.com/crime/cacrime.htm
4. Gallup polling: https://news.gallup.com/poll/544415/personal-safety-fears-three-decade-high.aspx
5. 5'8", 145 lbs. on the FBI Wanted poster: https://nmaahc.si.edu/object/nmaahc_2012.60.8
6. Egil "Bud" Krogh recalls being told to focus on DC: https://www.pbs.org/wgbh/pages/frontline/shows/drugs/etc/script.html
7. *The Nation* 8/13/08: "Rick Perlstein's 'Nixonland': A Gripping Look at the Nixon Era." https://www.thenation.com/article/archive/rick-perlsteins-nixonland-gripping-look-nixon-era/
8. https://www.thenation.com/article/archive/rick-perlsteins-nixonland-gripping-look-nixon-era/
9. This quote is from American Public Media's "Campaign '68": https://features.apmreports.org/arw/campaign68/b2.html

10. https://www.nixonfoundation.org/1968/10/the-nixon-answer-southern-town-hall/
11. The exchange is quoted verbatim here: https://features.apmreports.org/arw/campaign68/transcript.html
12. Vox article quoting the 1994 interview and 2016 reporting in *Harper's* by Dan Baum: https://www.vox.com/2016/3/22/11278760/war-on-drugs-racism-nixon
13. Vox article quoting the 1994 interview and 2016 reporting in *Harper's* by Dan Baum: https://www.vox.com/2016/3/22/11278760/war-on-drugs-racism-nixon
14. These details are drawn from *LA Times*: https://www.latimes.com/local/lanow/la-me-ln-watts-riots-explainer-20150715-htmlstory.html
15. 2015 *LA Times* editorial: https://www.latimes.com/opinion/editorials/la-ed-watts-lapd-20150812-story.html
16. https://www.latimes.com/opinion/editorials/la-ed-watts-lapd-20150812-story.html
17. 1992 *Los Angeles Times* story on Parker, after the Rodney King riots: https://www.latimes.com/archives/la-xpm-1992-05-25-mn-236-story.html?_gl=1*pabqok*_gcl_au*MTc5MzcoOTg4Ny4xNzM3NDg4ODE5
18. https://www.blackpast.org/african-american-history/hunter-s-point-san-francisco-uprising-1966/
19. Here is Reagan's announcement of his candidacy: https://www.americanrhetoric.com/speeches/ronaldreagancalgovcandidacy.htm
20. https://www.berkeley.edu/free-speech/
21. Jack Weinberg: https://en.wikipedia.org/wiki/Free_Speech_Movement
22. Berkeley Library's oral history Free Speech project uses the 10,000 number: https://www.lib.berkeley.edu/visit/bancroft/oral-history-center/projects/free-speech-movement
23. https://www.berkeley.edu/free-speech/
24. https://steinhardt.nyu.edu/metrocenter/teaching-about-berkeley-free-speech-movement-civil-disobedience-and-mass-protest-0
25. Source: UC Berkeley Library; some sources list less than 800 but I consider UC Berkeley to be authoritative. https://www.lib.berkeley.edu/visit/bancroft/oral-history-center/projects/free-speech-movement
26. https://www.lib.berkeley.edu/visit/bancroft/oral-history-center/projects/free-speech-movement
27. https://steinhardt.nyu.edu/metrocenter/teaching-about-berkeley-free-speech-movement-civil-disobedience-and-mass-protest-0
28. Interestingly, Seymour Martin Lipset cites Gallup polling that shows the majority of college students supported the Vietnam War until the Tet Offensive of 1968, when polling showed 50 percent "against." https://www.jstor.org/stable/20037859. Further context here, from a special 1969 Gallup poll of students: https://news.gallup.com/vault/230501/gallup-vault-1969-college-students-resistance-vietnam.aspx. Also see *NYT*, "Six

Decades of Student Protest": https://www.nytimes.com/2024/05/04/us/college-protests-free-speech.html (Some excellent 1964 Berkeley photos)

29. https://www.nytimes.com/1974/11/30/archives/regents-meet-last-time-with-reagan-a-member.html
30. https://www.pbssocal.org/shows/lost-la/reagans-1966-gubernatorial-campaign-turns-50-california-conservatism-and-donald-trump. Quoting: David Broder, Notes from Ronald Reagan's Speech at the Pacific Telephone Company Public Affairs Forum, May 31, 1966, B59,F7, David S. Broder Papers, Manuscript Division, Library of Congress. Audio of the speech is here: https://www.reaganlibrary.gov/archives/audio/ronald-reagan-campaign-speech-statler-hilton-hotel-town-hall-los-angeles-california
31. 2023 JStor Daily article: https://daily.jstor.org/daily-author/livia-gershon/
32. https://daily.jstor.org/ronald-reagan-v-uc-berkeley/
33. https://daily.jstor.org/ronald-reagan-v-uc-berkeley/
34. https://archives.alabama.gov/research/guidance/fast-facts/officials/governor.aspx
35. https://www.archives.gov/electoral-college/1968
36. Tony Platt, "Interview with Angela Davis," found on JSTOR: *Social Justice*, Vol. 40, No. 1/2 (131-132), 40th Anniversary Issue: Legacies of Radical Criminology in the United States (2013), pp. 37–53 (17 pages) https://www.jstor.org/stable/24361660?read-now=1&seq=1#page_scan_tab_contents
37. Tony Platt, "Interview with Angela Davis," found on JSTOR: *Social Justice*, Vol. 40, No. 1/2 (131-132), 40th Anniversary Issue: Legacies of Radical Criminology in the United States (2013), pp. 37–53 (17 pages) https://www.jstor.org/stable/24361660?read-now=1&seq=1#page_scan_tab_contents
38. Tony Platt, "Interview with Angela Davis," found on JSTOR: *Social Justice*, Vol. 40, No. 1/2 (131-132), 40th Anniversary Issue: Legacies of Radical Criminology in the United States (2013), pp. 37–53 (17 pages) https://www.jstor.org/stable/24361660?read-now=1&seq=1#page_scan_tab_contents
39. New York Historical says she joined Communists in high school. https://wams.nyhistory.org/growth-and-turmoil/feminism-and-the-backlash/angela-davis/
40. Kum-Kum Bhavnani, 1988 interview of Angela Davis in *Feminist Review* No. 31, The Past Before Us: Twenty Years of Feminism (Spring, 1989), pp. 66–81 (16 pages) https://www.jstor.org/stable/24361660?read-now=1&seq=1#page_scan_tab_contents
41. https://plato.stanford.edu/entries/adorno/
42. P. 14: https://www.archives.gov/files/research/jfk/releases/docid-32989676.pdf

43. Tony Platt "Interview of Angela Davis," Ibid. Davis added in that interview: "When I was arrested in 1970, I did not say a single word to the FBI. I am very proud of that."
44. Kum-Kum Bhavnani interview of Angela Davis, Ibid: https://www.jstor.org/stable/1395091?searchText=Angela+Davis+Kum-Kum+Bhavnani&searchUri=%2Faction%2FdoBasicSearch%3FQuery%3DAngela%2BDavis%2BKum-Kum%2BBhavnani%26so%3Drel&ab_segments=0%2Fbasic_search_gsv2%2Fcontrol&refreqid=fastly-default%3A662a2aadc28d42c42db0454c22197f83&seq=4
45. Kum-Kum Bhavnani interview of Angela Davis, Ibid. Che-Lumumba was an all-Black arm of the Los Angeles Communist Party. https://www.jstor.org/stable/1395091?searchText=Angela+Davis+Kum-Kum+Bhavnani&searchUri=%2Faction%2FdoBasicSearch%3FQuery%3DAngela%2BDavis%2BKum-Kum%2BBhavnani%26so%3Drel&ab_segments=0%2Fbasic_search_gsv2%2Fcontrol&refreqid=fastly-default%3A662a2aadc28d42c42db0454c22197f83&seq=3
46. "The AAUP and the Angela Davis Case," https://www.aaup.org/article/aaup-and-angela-davis-case#15
47. *Encyclopedia of Alabama*: https://web.archive.org/web/20140313145214/, http://www.encyclopediaofalabama.org/face/Article.jsp?id=h-1427. Note: The offer from Swarthmore was confirmed in the *LA Times* story of 9/19/69 cited elsewhere in this work. However, the *Encyclopedia of Alabama*, also cited in this fn, incorrectly reported the offer from Princeton. When the *LA Times* contacted Princeton, the university confirmed she'd been considered for a teaching position, but "was not far enough along in her work to be hired." See also "The AAUP and the Angela Davis Case," which further documents that Davis wasn't able to complete her dissertation while at UCLA due to all the controversy surrounding her appointment. https://www.aaup.org/article/aaup-and-angela-davis-case#15
48. *LA Times*, 9/21/69: "Admitted Red Will Test Firing from UCLA in Courts." The article lists this amount as her annual salary.
49. "The AAUP and the Angela Davis Case," https://www.aaup.org/article/aaup-and-angela-davis-case#15
50. *NY Times*, January 18, 1969: "Two Negroes Slain at UCLA Meeting of Black Students." This article cites the 150 figure.
51. https://dailybruin.com/2019/01/17/throwback-thursday-fifty-year-anniversary-of-bunchy-carter-john-huggins-shooting
52. *LA Times*, "2 Black Panther Students Slain in UCLA Hall," 1/18/69. This story mentions the bomb. Other arms are also described. The more comprehensive listing of weapons is from "2 Slayings at UCLA Investigated," *Washington Post* (UPI), 1/19/69.
53. *LA Times*, 1/19/69: "Black Panther Aide Lauds 2 Who Were Slain in UCLA Hall"

54. *LA Sentinel*, January 30, 1969, https://www.proquest.com/hnplasentinel1/docview/564936057/59DC2D6A98004FB5PQ/4?accountid=35635&sourcetype=Historical%20Newspapers, and *LA Times*, January 25, 1969, "Hundreds Attend Rites," https://www.proquest.com/hnplatimes/docview/156126656/AFC10ACBF764B61PQ/12?accountid=35635&sourcetype=Historical%20Newspapers
55. Supplementary Detailed Staff Reports on Intelligence Activities and the Rights of Americans, Book III, Final Report of the Select Committee to Study Governmental Operations with Respect to Intelligence Activities, United States Senate, p. 187; https://www.intelligence.senate.gov/sites/default/files/94755_III.pdf26
56. US founder Ron Karenga offered his perspective on the shoot-outs in a 1995 *Washington Post* interview: https://www.washingtonpost.com/archive/lifestyle/1995/12/30/the-kwanzaa-conundrum/3492b385-8abd-496f-9296-c33ee15fe25c/. "The police provoked the shootouts. The state imposed the violence. And you've got to stop calling them murders, because both groups were shooting at each other. The liberal media always wants to make out that the Panthers were totally innocent victims. . . . It was a question of police infiltration." Karenga went on to become a professor at Cal State Long Beach and is credited as the founder of Kwanzaa.
57. Mitchell's March 20, 1969, approval of the wiretaps: https://www.archives.gov/files/research/jfk/releases/docid-32989583.pdf
58. *Daily Bruin* 4/7/69, "Curriculum Committee Appointed," found at p. n386: https://archive.org/details/ucladailybruin50losa/page/n385/mode/2up?q=%22Angela+Davis%22
59. *Daily Bruin*, February 20, 1969, "Regents Meeting," p. n294 at: https://archive.org/details/ucladailybruin50losa/page/n293/mode/2up?q=Marcuse
60. Rabble Rouser Index documented here: https://downloads.paperless-archives.com/p/fbi-rabble-rouser-index-documents-download/. Davis was not on the Rabble Rouser Index, which was created in 1967 and was limited to the Top 100 most dangerous agitators. In 1968, it was renamed the Agitator Index.
61. P. 12: https://www.archives.gov/files/research/jfk/releases/docid-32989676.pdf
62. *Daily Bruin*, June 24, 1969, "UCLA History Grad Divale Becomes Paid FBI Informer," p. n135: https://archive.org/details/ucladailybruin51losa/page/n135/mode/2up?q=Divale
63. More about Lumumba here: https://news.un.org/en/spotlight/patrice-lumumba-brian-urquhart
64. P. 20: https://www.archives.gov/files/research/jfk/releases/docid-32989676.pdf
65. See p. 16 in Rabble Rouser files here: https://www.archives.gov/files/research/jfk/releases/docid-32989676.pdf

66. Blow-by-blow of the vitriolic Senate campaign against Helen Gahagan Douglas: https://en.wikipedia.org/wiki/1950_United_States_Senate_election_in_California
67. Lawyer for the "defendants" was John Abt. https://www.nytimes.com/1991/08/13/nyregion/john-j-abt-lawyer-dies-at-87-communist-party-counsel-in-us.html
68. "Student Undercover Agent for FBI Testifies at SDS Hearing," *Los Angeles Times*, June 18, 1969
69. *Daily Bruin*, July 1, 1969, "FBI Student Spy Answers Criticism," p. 164: https://archive.org/details/ucladailybruin51losa/page/n163/mode/2up
70. *LA Times*, September 21, 1969, "Admitted Red Will Test Firing from UCLA in Courts"
71. *NY Times*, 9/20/69, "UCLA Teacher Is Ousted As Red"
72. Chancellor Charles E. Young, see *NYT* story 9/20/69
73. *NYT* 9/20/69, see url elsewhere
74. "The AAUP and the Angela Davis Case," https://www.aaup.org/article/aaup-and-angela-davis-case#15
75. *New York Times*, 9/20/69: "UCLA Teacher Is Ousted As Red" https://www.nytimes.com/1969/09/20/archives/ucla-teacher-is-ousted-as-red-a-battle-in-court-predicted-on-action.html
76. *Daily Bruin*, 5/8/14: "For my generation, there was no one more radical than Angela Davis," said Robin Kelley, a UCLA history professor and acting chair of the African American studies department. "What I mean by that is not just her experience as an incarcerated person. . . . It had nothing do with 'afros' and the FBI—it had to do with what she wrote." https://dailybruin.com/2014/05/08/activist-former-ucla-professor-angela-davis-to-give-lecture

Chapter 6

1. *LA Times*, 3/26/06: "As Dynasty Evolved, So Did Power in L.A." This is an excellent history of the rise and fall of the Chandlers, as told in their newspaper at the time of the fall. https://www.latimes.com/news/la-me-power26mar26-story.html#:~:text=This%20is%20a%20story%20about%20power%20in,was%20extraordinarily%20intertwined%20with%20the%20city%20itself
2. https://www.latimes.com/local/california/la-me-los-angeles-times-history-20180617-story.html
3. This Halberstam quote is legendary in and of itself. Here is his April 1979 *Atlantic* cover story: https://www.theatlantic.com/magazine/archive/1979/04/the-california-dynasty/665643/
4. https://www.theatlantic.com/magazine/archive/1979/04/the-california-dynasty/665643/

5. *LA Times*, 9/19/69, "Explosive Academic Freedom Case Confronts UC Regents"
6. *LA Times*, 9/20/69, "Admitted Red Fired from UCLA Faculty"
7. *NY Times*, 9/20/69, "UCLA Teacher Is Ousted As Red"
8. *LA Times*, 9/25/69, "The Case of Angela Davis"
9. *LA Times*, 9/21/69, "Admitted Red Will Test Firing From UCLA in Courts"
10. *NY Times*, 10/21/69, "UCLA Barred from Pressing Red's Ouster" The U.S. Supreme Court later denied cert. See: https://go.gale.com/ps/i.do?id=GALE%7CA650747595&sid=googleScholar&v=2.1&it=r&linkaccess=abs&issn=01472011&p=AONE&sw=w&userGroupName=anon%7Eb3062715&aty=open-web-entry
11. *LA Times*, 9/27/69, "UCLA Schedule Changed; Red to Teach This Term"
12. *NY Times*, 10/7/69, "UCLA Students Are Urged to Resist Regents"
13. *Reader's Digest*, March 1971, "Angela Davis: The Making of a Martyr," p. 110
14. *Reader's Digest* says this pistol was automatic; *Road to Hell*, p. 82, says semiautomatic .380. The gun was licensed, and it would be unlikely that authorities would register an automatic.
15. *Reader's Digest*, March 1971, "Angela Davis: The Making of a Martyr," p. 110
16. *NY Times*, April 3, 1969, "Bomb Plot Is Laid to 21 Panthers" https://timesmachine.nytimes.com/timesmachine/1969/04/03/90083782.pdf?pdf_redirect=true&ip=0
17. https://leonardbernstein.com/about/humanitarian/radical-chic-flap
18. https://leonardbernstein.com/about/humanitarian/radical-chic-flap
19. Wolfe is quoted in Charlotte Curtis's obituary in the *Times*: https://www.nytimes.com/1987/04/17/obituaries/charlotte-curtis-a-columnist-for-the-times-is-dead-at-58.html?pagewanted=all&src=pm
20. https://nymag.com/docs/07/05/070529radical_chic.pdf
21. Angela Davis Legal Defense Collection, 1970–1972. Manuscripts, Archives, and Rare Books Division, Schomburg Center for Research in Black Culture, The New York Public Library. Jackson letter 3/24/70, reprinted in a Soledad Brothers Defense Committee flyer
22. "Soledad Prison Wracked By Violence," *Deseret News*, 9/29/70: https://news.google.com/newspapers?id=ikYKAAAAIBAJ&sjid=fooDAAAAIBAJ&pg=5681,6964144&dq. This is an excellent quick rundown of the case, with a photo of the warden pointing to the prison yard where three prisoners were shot to death.
23. *Reader's Digest*, March 1971, "Angela Davis: The Making of a Martyr," retrieved from Harvard Schlesinger Library
24. Angela Davis Legal Collection, NYPL. Soledad Brothers Defense Committee flyer, undated, with a letter from George Jackson dated March 24, 1970

25. *Road to Hell*, p. 84
26. Angela Davis interview, on video, found here: https://www.instagram.com/law4blacklives/reel/CwQS2i9AP7w/
27. Letter introduced by DA during Davis's trial: https://www.nytimes.com/1972/05/16/archives/state-rests-case-of-angela-davis-prosecutor-reads-portions.html
28. Found at Angela Davis Legal Collection, NYPL, B4F2
29. Found at Angela Davis Legal Collection, NYPL, B4F2. Note: Davis incorrectly listed the date as May 9. It is corrected here to May 8.
30. Found at Angela Davis Legal Collection, NYPL, B4F2
31. See "Who Killed Melvin X?" https://www.reddit.com/r/UnresolvedMysteries/comments/cievwz/who_killed_melvin_x_on_06061970/?rdt=63504
32. Angela Davis Legal Collection, NYPL. Davis letter to George Jackson, undated but approximately June 7, 1970.
33. *LA Times*, 6/9/70, "Regents Reported in Agreement on Firing Angela Davis"
34. *LA Times*, 6/19/70, "Panel Will Help Prison Trio in Guard Slaying"
35. *LA Times*, 6/20/70, "Regents Refuse to Renew Miss Davis' UCLA Contract." Applies also to the continued quote in the paragraph that follows.
36. *LA Times*, 6/20/70, "Regents Refuse to Renew Miss Davis' UCLA Contract"
37. Spring 2024, *The AAUP and the Angela Davis Case: Revisiting the AAUP's 1971 UCLA Investigation* by Emily Houh: https://www.aaup.org/article/aaup-and-angela-davis-case#15
38. All of the following in this chronology comes from court reporter Ken Combs in the *Marin Independent Journal*, 8/7/05, "The untold story—court reporter recalls horrific day at the Hall of Justice in 1970," unless otherwise indicated. https://www.marinij.com/2005/08/07/aug-7-2005-the-untold-story-court-reporter-recalls-horrific-day-at-the-hall-of-justice-in-1970/
39. Contemporaneous news reports and court records indicate that there were other inmates present in the holding area, waiting for unrelated court proceedings. Some were reportedly witnesses or defendants in unrelated cases. However, they were not involved in the takeover, nor were they taken as hostages.
40. "The untold story—court reporter recalls horrific day at the Hall of Justice in 1970," *Marin Independent Journal*, August 7, 2007, by Ken Combs. https://www.marinij.com/2005/08/07/aug-7-2005-the-untold-story-court-reporter-recalls-horrific-day-at-the-hall-of-justice-in-1970/
41. *Road to Hell*, p. 90
42. This is according to the *Reader's Digest* story, p. 111.
43. This is from *NY Times* 4/6/72: https://www.nytimes.com/1972/04/06/archives/davis-jury-hears-of-events-in-van-crippled-hostage-testifies-he.html

44. Judge Haley was hit by a .357 Magnum round, although it was the shotgun blast that killed him. Ballistics testimony: https://news.google.com/newspapers?id=OrEiAAAAIBAJ&sjid=OrMFAAAAIBAJ&pg=703%2C371771
45. Ballistics testimony: https://news.google.com/newspapers?id=OrEiAAAAIBAJ&sjid=OrMFAAAAIBAJ&pg=703%2C371771

Chapter 7

1. Speech to nation 4/30/70: https://www.vassar.edu/vietnam/documents/doc15.html
2. https://www.kent.edu/may4visitorscenter#:~:text=On%20Monday%2C%20May%204%2C%201970,four%20students%20and%20wounding%20nine
3. https://www.zinnedproject.org/news/tdih/jackson-state-killings/#:~:text=On%20May%2015%2C%201970%2C%20the%20police%20opened,school%20student%20James%20Earl%20Green)%20were%20killed
4. https://www.pbs.org/wgbh/americanexperience/features/my-lai-selected-men-involved-my-lai/
5. https://www.famous-trials.com/mylaicourts/1634-myl-uscma
6. https://www.famous-trials.com/mylaicourts/1634-myl-uscma
7. https://magazine.richmond.edu/article/-/16573/capt.-daniel-vs.-the-president.html
8. By Colonel Henderson: https://www.pbs.org/wgbh/americanexperience/features/my-lai-selected-men-involved-my-lai/
9. https://magazine.richmond.edu/article/-/16573/capt.-daniel-vs.-the-president.html
10. https://enewspaper.latimes.com/infinity/article_share.aspx?guid=6534720d-c274-408b-a00a-fb7019ad66b5
11. https://magazine.richmond.edu/article/-/16573/capt.-daniel-vs.-the-president.html
12. https://www.washingtonpost.com/history/2019/08/08/how-charles-manson-almost-won-mistrial-courtesy-richard-nixon/
13. See Outline/Headline Synopsis *NYT* for May 1, 1971
14. https://firstamendment.mtsu.edu/article/students-for-a-democratic-society/
15. https://archive.org/details/PrairieFire_20170422/mode/2up
16. https://www.fbi.gov/history/famous-cases/weather-underground-bombings
17. https://www.fbi.gov/history/famous-cases/weather-underground-bombings

18. https://library.cqpress.com/cqalmanac/document.php?id=cqal71-1254546#_=_
19. https://vva.org/books-in-review/invasion-of-laos-1971-by-robert-d-sander/
20. https://library.cqpress.com/cqalmanac/document.php?id=cqal71-1254546#_=_
21. https://www.nytimes.com/1971/03/21/archives/its-not-just-fonda-and-company-its-not-just-fonda-and-company.html
22. This is a direct transcription by the FBI and is part of Fonda's FBI file, which is archived at Smith College. The speech was on February 17, 1971. The FBI titled the speech "Security Matter—Anarchist."
23. https://www.nytimes.com/1970/12/27/archives/conversations-with-americans-conversations-with-americans.html
24. The most authoritative reporting on the FBI files about VVAW and Winter Soldier Investigation is by Gerald Nicosia, *LAT*, and I'm summarizing that here. https://www.latimes.com/style/la-tm-kerry21amay23-story.html
25. DOB 12/11/43 https://en.wikipedia.org/wiki/John_Kerry
26. Mary McGrory writing in the *Washington Star*, 6/6/71
27. Various pamphlets for Mayday and Gay Mayday found in the Frank Kameny Papers, LC: https://findingaids.loc.gov/exist_collections/ead3pdf/mss/2009/ms009068.pdf and the Craig Rodwell Papers, NYPL, Box 5.
28. Pamphlet from "Gay Mayday Tribe," Author Unknown, Frank Kameny Papers, LC, B107F3.
29. Mayday Target Map: Craig Rodwell Papers, NYPL, Box 5. Rodwell was a gay rights activist who participated in the Stonewall riots in 1969 and figured prominently in the gay liberation movement of the 1970s and 1980s.
30. Safire Papers, LC
31. Safire Papers, LC
32. Safire Papers, LC
33. The narrative about how Spivak and Dukert recruited Kerry and Hubbard is found in the Lawrence Spivak Papers, LC. The summary was prepared by Spivak—most likely for the higher-ups at NBC since at one point it refers to Spivak in the third person ("Mr. Spivak").
34. This part of the chronology is from Gerald Nicosia's *LAT* story, 5/23/04.
35. Transcript, *Meet the Press*/Sunday, April 18, 1971
36. As reported by Gerald Nicosia in the *LAT*. See previous notes.
37. This narrative timeline is from my previous book, *The Partisan*, pp. 86 and 87.
38. Peter Applebome, 2/3/21, writing Davis's obituary in the *New York Times*
39. Unless otherwise noted, this chronology comes from the ACLU Report "Mayday 1971, Order Without Law."

40. Haldeman Diary, May 1, 1971 https://www.nixonlibrary.gov/sites/default/files/virtuallibrary/documents/haldeman-diaries/37-hrhd-audiotape-ac07b-19710501-pa.pdf
41. Based on the author's previous reporting for *The Partisan*, p. 86. Although federal troops clearly were in the city, exact numbers vary in news reports. The troop numbers cited in the ACLU report, likely obtained through legal discovery, are used here.
42. Ellsberg's old division; he reports this in *Secrets*, p. 378.
43. *The Partisan*, p. 86
44. American Civil Liberties Union, *May Day 1971: Order without Law—An ACLU Study of the Largest Sweep Arrests in American History*. New York: American Civil Liberties Union, 1972. https://assets.aclu.org/live/uploads/publications/5256_ri.pdf
45. ACLU Report, p. 2
46. ACLU Report, p. 7
47. ACLU Report, p. 1
48. May Day 1971, ACLU study, July 1972, p. 14
49. Politico has an account of this incident: https://www.politico.com/magazine/story/2018/10/28/nixon-protest-law-and-order-221920/
50. https://timesmachine.nytimes.com/timesmachine/1975/01/17/98372187.html?login=email&auth=login-email&pageNumber=1
51. "Mayday and Playboy," *New York Times*, 1/27/75
52. Anthony Lewis Papers, LC Box II-111 Folder 5
53. Mayday maps are in the Frank Kameny Collection, LC.
54. Martha Mitchell's diary notes are found in the Helen Thomas Papers at LC, B4F6.
55. The two had married the previous year, 1970: https://www.nytimes.com/1970/08/09/archives/daniel-ellsberg-of-mit-marries-patricia-marx.html
56. Ellsberg's side of this story is told in *Secrets*, pp. 376–381. Ellsberg's quotes are from the book unless otherwise indicated. *Wild Man*, pp. 384–385, also covers this episode, and some material—mainly the recollections of others—is also used from that.
57. *Secrets*, p. 377
58. *Secrets*, pp. 377–378
59. Chomsky's account is from *Wild Man*, pp. 384–385.
60. *Secrets*, p. 385
61. *Secrets*, p. 381
62. NPR Democracy Now interview with Ellsberg, 5/3/2021: https://www.democracynow.org/2021/5/3/amy_goodman_daniel_ellsberg_edward_snowden
63. Sheehan's notes on this conversation with Ellsberg about Bundy and Mayday are in Sheehan Papers, LC.

Chapter 8

1. *Oxford Companion to the Supreme Court*, p. 740; also see *The Brethren*, p. 168
2. *Oxford Companion to the Supreme Court*, p. 3; also see *The Brethren*, p. 168
3. https://en.wikipedia.org/wiki/Griswold_v._Connecticut. This entry shows just how splintered the opinions were, with justices going off in all directions. Douglas wrote for the majority.
4. Unless otherwise noted, the narrative about Rehnquist's involvement in sabotaging Abe Fortas as a replacement for Chief Justice Earl Warren comes from John Dean's 2001 book, *The Rehnquist Choice*, and from the author's later reporting for the 2012 biography of Rehnquist, *The Partisan: The Life of William Rehnquist.*
5. The fact that only 77 senators cast a vote was not unusual for the time.
6. Nixon remarks to reporters, April 9, 1970: https://www.presidency.ucsb.edu/documents/remarks-reporters-about-nominations-the-supreme-court
7. The full statement here: https://www.nytimes.com/1971/04/04/archives/nixon-abortion-statement.html?smid=nytcore-android-share
8. https://www.nytimes.com/1971/04/22/archives/high-court-upholds-dc-abortion-law-supreme-court-rules-5-to-2-that.html
9. *NY Times*, Roy Lucas, 61, "Legal Theorist Who Helped Shape Roe Suit" 11/7/03
10. https://a860-collectionguides.nyc.gov/repositories/2/archival_objects/929137
11. *Vanity Fair*, "A Woman's Choice," by Leslie Bennetts, September 1992
12. https://coachellavalleyweekly.com/sarah-weddington/
13. *Vanity Fair*, "A Woman's Choice," by Leslie Bennetts, September 1992
14. https://coachellavalleyweekly.com/sarah-weddington/
15. *Vanity Fair*, "A Woman's Choice," by Leslie Bennetts, September 1992
16. Forty-eight states out of fifty had restrictions. Only NY and Hawaii left the matter solely to pregnant women and their physicians. https://www.nytimes.com/1971/05/04/archives/justices-to-hear-2-abortion-suits-put-appeals-on-georgia-and-texas.html
17. *Vanity Fair,* "Roe v. Wade's Secret Heroine," by Joshua Prager, January 19, 2017
18. https://case-law.vlex.com/vid/buchanan-v-batchelor-civ-887633830. However, the Supreme Court later vacated and remanded on other grounds. Buchanan ultimately lost his case: https://law.justia.com/cases/texas/court-of-criminal-appeals/1971/44010-3.html
19. *Vanity Fair*, "The Accidental Activist," February 2013
20. *Vanity Fair*, "The Accidental Activist," February 2013

21. Foregoing is from *Vanity Fair*, "The Accident Activist," by Joshua Prager.
22. McCluskey's body was found on July 9, 1973, according to the death certificate.
23. https://coachellavalleyweekly.com/sarah-weddington/. The fact of two earlier births (and adoptions) by McCorvey is confirmed in *Vanity Fair*, "The Accidental Activist," by Joshua Prager, February 2013.
24. *Vanity Fair*, January 19, 2017, by Joshua Prager
25. Weddington Papers, Texas Women's University
26. *Vanity Fair*, January 17, 2013, by Josh Prager
27. Weddington Papers, TWU
28. https://www.nytimes.com/2003/11/07/us/roy-lucas-61-legal-theorist-who-helped-shape-roe-suit.html. From the obit (DOB 11/27/41): "Mr. Lucas continued to argue abortion rights cases after Roe, but remained deeply disappointed at having been passed over as lead counsel before the Supreme Court, said David Garrow, a legal historian at Emory University and the author of *Liberty and Sexuality: The Right to Privacy and the Making of Roe v. Wade* (University of California Press, 1998)."
29. *Texas Monthly*, "Supreme Moment," February 2003, by Pamela Colloff
30. *The Brethren*, p. 165
31. Linda Coffee was born on Christmas Day, 12/25/42, so she's 28 years old at this point. Weddington DOB is 2/5/45, so she's just 26 years old when SCOTUS takes up the case.
32. Also useful context, this *Atlantic* article, more for bibliography than source notes: https://www.theatlantic.com/ideas/archive/2022/01/sarah-weddington-obituary-roe-v-wade/621160/
33. Again, *The Brethren* provides helpful context, p. 165.
34. *Roe* v. *Wade* Tr., p. 3
35. *Roe* v. *Wade* Tr., p. 5
36. *Roe* v. *Wade* Tr., p. 15
37. *ABA Journal*: https://www.abajournal.com/news/article/was_comment_in_roe_v._wade_the_worst_courtroom_humor_of_all_time
38. *Salon*, 7/26/13: https://www.salon.com/2013/07/26/8_horrible_courtroom_jokes_and_their_ensuing_legal_calamity/

Chapter 9

1. Sheehan Papers, LC, B169F5
2. All notes and telexes in this section are from LC Sheehan Papers, LC, B169F5.
3. Review by John Leonard in *NY Times* on Thursday, 10/15/70: https://archive.nytimes.com/www.nytimes.com/books/97/06/01/reviews/wills-nixon.html

4. https://www.nytimes.com/1979/01/11/archives/dr-william-y-elliott-82-dies-a-harvard-professor-emeritus-hissed-by.html
5. Sheehan handwritten note to self, November 3, 1970, on reverse of a phone message slip from Harvey Shapiro. Found in Sheehan Papers at LC, B169F5
6. As first mentioned in Chapter 5: Sheehan had caused a furor with a scathing review of Lane's book about Vietnam atrocities, *Conversations with Americans*. Sheehan's review accused Lane of fabricating interviews—the worst journalistic crime. Lane ended up getting dropped from the Winter Soldier program, and Sheehan avoided covering it.
7. The description of how Sheehan came to the project, and his thoughts about it, comes from *Newsweek*, January 11, 1971, "Rush to Judgment?" found in Sheehan Papers at LC, B198F3.
8. All quotes from Sheehan's review are taken from here: https://www.nytimes.com/1970/12/27/archives/conversations-with-americans-conversations-with-americans.html
9. For an excellent description of John Leonard's aspirations for the *Review*, see this article in Slate: https://slate.com/news-and-politics/2008/11/remembering-john-leonard-the-great-new-york-times-book-review-editor.html
10. John Leonard obit *NYT*: https://www.nytimes.com/2008/11/07/arts/07leonard.html
11. https://www.nytimes.com/2008/11/07/arts/07leonard.html
12. https://en.wikipedia.org/wiki/Elizabeth_Peer
13. Sheehan Papers, LC, B198F3
14. Various kudos are from Sheehan Papers, LC B198F3.
15. Found in NY Times Collection, Rosenthal Papers, NYPL
16. https://timesmachine.nytimes.com/timesmachine/1971/03/28/91277111.html?pageNumber=127
17. https://theintercept.com/2023/10/07/pentagon-papers-daniel-ellsberg-neil-sheehan/
18. Memo 6/16/71 from AMR to Jimmy Greenfield, NYPL *NYT* Collection, Rosenthal Papers, Box 100
19. From The Intercept, p. 13 (the online version): https://theintercept.com/2023/10/07/pentagon-papers-daniel-ellsberg-neil-sheehan/
20. February date comes from Rogovin memo, p. 1.
21. As quoted by Risen in The Intercept
22. As quoted by Risen in The Intercept
23. As described and quoted by Risen in The Intercept
24. As described by Risen in The Intercept: "Decades later, Marcus Raskin finally told Ellsberg what had happened."
25. Callout that follows is from Risen, The Intercept: https://theintercept.com/2023/10/07/pentagon-papers-daniel-ellsberg-neil-sheehan/

26. This and the chronology following is from undated Mitch Rogovin (Arnold & Porter) memo, as first published in The Intercept. Here is the memo, via DocumentCloud: https://www.documentcloud.org/documents/24019173-rogovin-sheehan-memo/
27. Later renamed the Capitol Hilton, but in 1971 it's the Statler Hilton: https://www.nytimes.com/1971/03/14/archives/35-women-picket-gridiron-dinner-protest-club-policy-excluding-them.html
28. Gridiron Dinner background from *WP* 3/22/85: https://www.washingtonpost.com/archive/lifestyle/1985/03/23/the-grand-old-gridiron/acef6b6b-0b91-45b8-b25d-a9e6b62c928d/
29. https://www.nytimes.com/1971/03/14/archives/35-women-picket-gridiron-dinner-protest-club-policy-excluding-them.html
30. https://www.washingtonpost.com/wp-srv/style/longterm/books/reviews/nixons.htm
31. https://www.loc.gov/exhibits/hope-for-america/political-speech.html?__cf_chl_tk=GTIXPTL7PIhhQsMtlJzLladwUIYt_Psh5hq9Fl.mufo-1741898291-1.0.1.1-z1OHBWxUUzsmbUG526.ixiZ5nSLVN.wl536Oyu6lFRk
32. Rogovin Memo, p. 3. https://www.documentcloud.org/documents/24019173-rogovin-sheehan-memo/
33. Sheehan FBI File, p. 271. When, as here, the FBI files on Sheehan are used, all page numbers refer to the FBI's 2023 Freedom of Information Act release: Request No. 1600884-000, Subject: Sheehan, Cornelius Mahoney. The FBI released 357 pages of documents, sequentially paginated. The page numbers refer to the FBI's pagination.
34. Key fob "Harvard Square" verified on eBay here: https://www.ebay.com/itm/274816062948
35. FBI, p. 277
36. FBI, p. 192
37. FBI, p. 270
38. https://www.nytimes.com/2021/01/07/us/pentagon-papers-neil-sheehan.html
39. FBI, p. 236
40. March 20: This is from Rogovin Memo, p. 3.
41. FBI, p. 177
42. FBI, p. 141
43. FBI, p. 32. FBI places the Ellsbergs' time away as Tuesday, March 23, through the following Monday, March 29. Rogovin memo says Neil finished copying on March 23 and returned to DC on March 24.
44. The timing of all this requires further context, but settling upon a single set of facts is possible by understanding that the Ellsbergs first went to Patricia's Sutton Place apartment before leaving for the Islands. If the FBI timeline is to be believed—and I consider it highly credible—Neil and Susan Sheehan and their confederates were doing the copying

while the Ellsbergs were away, in New York. As the *Times* revealed in a story after Sheehan's death, "Sheehan smuggled the papers out of the apartment in Cambridge, Mass., where Mr. Ellsberg had stashed them; then he copied them illicitly, just as Mr. Ellsberg had done, and took them to the *Times*." This, of course, is true. The FBI documents are definitive as to the timing of Sheehan's copying; it is clear from the FBI files that Sheehan was doing his copying very quickly, March 21 through March 23, while the Ellsbergs (according to the FBI) had not yet departed for the Islands. I believe that Sheehan got the entire seven thousand pages that weekend—the first of two full sets he would obtain through Ellsberg (the second from Sutton Place, May 27). According to handwritten notes that Sheehan later made, the Ellsbergs were in NYC that March weekend. The FBI chronology says they left for the Islands on Tuesday, March 23. Author's transcription of Sheehan's handwritten notes that Sheehan made on or about November 23, 1978: [p. 14] "Ask Ehrlichman if he got the impression I'd committed a burglary from the circumstances under which the FBI reported Susan & I copying PP's—my going in & out of apartment w/ key, report I double-crossed DE & DE & Patricia [being?] in NY & then leaving for Barbados [?—this is a ? noted by Sheehan] the night Susan & I completed copying the papers & flew back to D.C. See my FBI file. Susan said to look up mention of key in file."

45. The year 1969 is confirmed in the FBI files, p. 62.
46. https://www.nytimes.com/2021/01/07/us/pentagon-papers-neil-sheehan.html
47. Sheehan handwritten notes, c. 12/2/78, found in Sheehan Papers, LC.
48. Sheehan's handwritten notes also reveal that Dun said he hadn't paid Miller's bill, and was "proud now of all the resistance he gave the Nixon Administration at the time": *Dun said he is proud now of all the resistance he gave the Nixon Administration at the time, and sees its effects post-Watergate, and would have been less annoyed at having to do it and willing to do more had he been able at the time to see the extent of the changes to our liberties the executive branch and the presidency were posing, and what the effect of the publication of the PPs would be, leading to Watergate and the pushing out [of Nixon]. (It would be nice to get the grand jury minutes and the FBI interview reports to see just how much he did resist.) Dun is an "operator," as Mitch [Rogovin] said at the time. . . . Pebble also advised him not to talk. She is also afraid it might have negative effects on a political future. Dun is convinced that DE is still very angry at him.*
49. In the interview, she refers to Neil as "Dan" here, but I am fixing this for the sake of accuracy.
50. WBUR/NPR "Here and Now" interview with Pebble Gifford, 6/19/23: https://www.wbur.org/hereandnow/2023/06/19/daniel-ellsberg-pentagon-papers

51. According to the *Times* account of Sheehan's oral history: "Mr. Sheehan duplicated the apartment key in case he lost the original. Then he began copying the seven thousand pages—first in a real estate office where an acquaintance worked, then, with Ms. Sheehan's help, in the suburban copy shop. He was ferrying piles of pages by taxi between the apartment and the copy shop, then to a locker in the Boston bus terminal and later to a locker at Logan airport. When the machines in the copy shop crashed under the strain, the Sheehans relocated to a copy shop in Boston run by a Navy veteran." See https://www.nytimes.com/2021/01/07/us/pentagon-papers-neil-sheehan.html
52. Transcript is here: https://investigatingpower.org/tag/pentagon-papers/
53. Note: Kovach, in this interview with Chuck Lewis, refers to a "Mr. Thompson." I am using "Johnson" because that, clearly, is the alias that Sheehan was using, according to the FBI files.
54. Kovach says "late Friday," but that is not possible, given the FBI timeline and also the timeline in Rogovin's memo. Sunday is more likely, since Rogovin's memo places Neil in DC at the *Times* on Saturday morning, the FBI has Neil at the Treadway on Saturday afternoon, and Neil's oral history says he went first to the Cabot offices, and if Neil was calling Dun Gifford in the morning, while Gifford was still in bed, that would be Sunday morning.
55. Note: Sheehan tells a different story, see it here: https://www.nytimes.com/2021/01/07/us/pentagon-papers-neil-sheehan.html: "From the *Times* bureau chief in Boston, he got the name of a copy shop that could handle thousands of pages. He asked the bureau chief to get him several hundred dollars in expense money for a secret project he declined to explain. When the bureau chief called the *Times* newsroom and reached the editors on duty that night, they declined the request. So he called the national editor at home. 'Give it to him,' the editor said, according to Mr. Sheehan. No questions asked." Given the conflicts between the story told by Kovach, on the record and during Kovach's lifetime, and Sheehan, whose account was released posthumously, Kovach's account is used here.
56. FBI, p. 8. The FBI report says the copying at Victor was done on Sunday, 3/21/71.
57. From Sheehan oral history: https://www.nytimes.com/2021/01/07/us/pentagon-papers-neil-sheehan.html
58. From *NYT* account of Sheehan oral history: https://www.nytimes.com/2021/01/07/us/pentagon-papers-neil-sheehan.html
59. FBI, pp. 206–207
60. FBI, p. 100: Neil and Susan took taxis to Liberty Square Press downtown, then to Western Union. FBI pp. 270 and 280: $600 wired to Sheehan, which he picked up at Congress St. downtown, but there wasn't enough in the till to cash it, so Sheehan took $100 in cash and

got a money order for the $500, which FBI, p. 280, says he cashed at a different Western Union office in Cambridge. Then Sheehan returned to the Hotel Continental, and then to Victor Publishers, the Bedford print shop. This chronology shows that Sheehan received some money wired up by the *Times* on Tuesday morning. He and Susan then began picking up all the copies that they'd left at various places, using the money from the *Times* wire to pay for the copies.

61. Rogovin memo, p. 4
62. The entire essay linked here, from the ProQuest collection at NYPL: https://timesmachine.nytimes.com/timesmachine/1971/03/28/91277111.pdf?pdf_redirect=true&ip=0
63. Van Woerkom Studio today: https://www.vanwoerkomstudio.com/home
64. See Sanford J. Ungar, "The Papers Papers," *Esquire*, May 1972, p. 99. Ungar describes the newsroom controversy. Sheehan's notes, among his papers at LC, reflect that both Susan and Neil Sheehan may have written letters to *Esquire*, opposing some aspects of Ungar's reporting, see Sheehan Papers, LC B162F4.
65. Tom Wicker, "The Greening of the Press," *Columbia Journalism Review*, May 1, 1971, p. 7.
66. NYPL, A.M. Rosenthal Collection, undated journal entry, approximately May 24, 1971, based on others proximate to it.
67. Gruson, originally a reporter and foreign correspondent for the *Times*, at this point had moved over to the publisher's office with the title of vice president and special assistant to Publisher A. O. Sulzberger. He was a newsroom troubleshooter and intermediary between Rosenthal and Sulzberger, when the situation demanded.
68. A.M. Rosenthal Papers, NYPL, undated journal entry, most likely on or proximate to May 24, 1971
69. Originals at NYPL, *NYT* Collection, Rosenthal Papers, Box 39
70. William M. Hammond, *Public Affairs: The Military and the Media, 1968–1973*, U.S. Army in Vietnam. Washington, DC: Center of Military History, U.S. Army, 1996, pp. 493–494
71. Rosenthal kept the journals from 1971 through 1986, seventeen volumes in all. See https://archives.nypl.org/mss/17930
72. A.M. Rosenthal Papers, NYPL
73. Emanuel R. Freedman obit: https://www.nytimes.com/1971/01/28/archives/emanue-i-r-freedman-6-o-dies-editor-on-the-times-since-1948-an.html
74. Sheehan Papers, LC
75. Rogovin memo, p. 5
76. Rogovin memo, p. 6
77. Rogovin memo, p. 7
78. NYPL Pentagon Papers Collection, NYT General files, 1971, Box 100

79. https://theintercept.com/2023/10/07/pentagon-papers-daniel-ellsberg-neil-sheehan/
80. NYPL A.M. Rosenthal Collection, Rosenthal Journal, Volume One
81. Neil Sheehan Papers at LC, "Office Files, Chronological Correspondence"

Chapter 10

1. https://www.nytimes.com/1994/09/22/obituaries/arthur-b-krim-89-ex-chief-of-movie-studios.html
2. Averell Harriman Papers, LC. Harriman sent the cable on 5/4/71.
3. See Larson, *The Splendid and the Vile*
4. Pamela Harriman Papers at LC, Personal and Family Papers, Frank Sinatra
5. Harriman Papers, LC. The memo from Harriman is dated December 6.
6. Harriman Papers, LC. Memo is dated June 24, 1971.
7. Averell Harriman memo of telephone conversation, June 24, 1971, found in Averell Harriman Papers, LC, B604, F3, Chronological File.
8. Harriman Papers, LC, June 30, 1971
9. Safire Papers, LC, B125F6, Typescript notes for "Before the Fall"
10. The chronology of events is described on the UVA site (White House telephone recording, https://prde.upress.virginia.edu/conversations/4001822) accompanied by this narrative: "On this day (27 April 1971), the Pakistani ambassador had delivered a note to Nixon from Chinese premier Zhou Enlai, responding to a December 1970 message from the President that had been delivered to Beijing through the Pakistani government." Also see https://nsarchive2.gwu.edu/NSAEBB/NSAEBB145/index.htm from the GWU National Security Archives, which provides a more nuanced description but keeps to the basics of the December-to-April chronology.
11. Transcript has been edited, condensed, and cleaned up for grammar and style.
12. White House transcript here: https://prde.upress.virginia.edu/conversations/4001822
13. Safire Papers, LC, B125F6. Safire likely made this note in preparation for his 1975 book about Nixon, *Before the Fall.*
14. As late as 6/21/71, Rogers was still in the dark, assuming Kissinger was stopping in Pakistan to snub the Indians, and not understanding the logic. See Haldeman Diary entry: https://www.nixonlibrary.gov/sites/default/files/virtuallibrary/documents/haldeman-diaries/37-hrhd-audiocassette-ac09b-19710621-pa.pdf. "He [Rogers] had kept thinking up all the reasons for his reservations, saying that it would look as if Henry has a major mission rather than just going out on a first-hand appraisal

deal in Vietnam and Thailand. He feels the India-Pakistan thing is so sensitive that it would look like we were setting up a private channel to Yahya in some way, and that the President should really consider what the point of this is and whether he wants to go ahead with it. This was exactly the reaction that Henry was expecting to get from Rogers, and he was quite amused when it came through that way. I reported to the President and he felt we should let Henry and Rogers work it out from here on."

15. Kissinger phone transcript, LC Papers, 3:25 p.m., on 6/21/71. Call is with Haldeman.
16. Transcript: https://www.presidency.ucsb.edu/documents/the-presidents-news-conference-135
17. Oral History by Farland: https://tile.loc.gov/storage-services/service/mss/mfdip/2004/2004far02/2004far02.pdf
18. For context on this punchline from Nixon's 1968 presidential campaign, see, for example, "When It's Gross, and Not At All Funny," *WP* 7/19/00, by Bob Levey: https://www.washingtonpost.com/archive/lifestyle/2000/07/19/when-its-gross-and-not-at-all-funny/870f4e3b-38a7-4f53-b761-131b779c1e15/
19. Kissinger memorial remarks for Peterson: https://www.henryakissinger.com/remembrances/pete-peterson/
20. Safire witnessed this. Safire Papers, LC, B121F1

Chapter 11

1. Sheehan handwritten notes, Sheehan Papers at LC
2. Sheehan letter to Craig Whitney, Sheehan Papers, LC, Professional File. Letter to Whitney is 11/18/71: ". . . that submarine in the Hilton Hotel . . ."
3. This is p. 3 of the full document that is in the *NYT* Museum, as provided by historian David Dunlap.
4. Sheehan Papers at LC, Vann-Sheehan Vietnam War Collection B107F1
5. Memorandum from Nona Brown, *NYT Magazine*, Washington Bureau, dated 6/2/71 in Sheehan Papers at LC, "Professional File, New York Times"
6. President Richard Nixon's Daily Diary, June 12, 1971, White House Central Files, National Archives and Records Administration, Nixon Presidential Materials, Yorba Linda, CA. The complete White House wedding guest list: https://www.nixonlibrary.gov/sites/default/files/virtuallibrary/documents/PDD/1971/053%20June%201-15%201971.pdf
7. This entry, and the foregoing description of Nixon at the wedding, are from Haldeman Diary for June 12, 1971: https://www.nixonlibrary.gov/sites/default/files/virtuallibrary/documents/haldeman-diaries/37-hrhd-audiocassette-ac09a-19710612-pa.pdf

8. As described by Ellsberg, in *Secrets*. Note: It is unclear, from Ellsberg's account, whether this call took place on Saturday night, or Sunday morning. Sheehan's oral history, however, makes clear that someone had tipped Ellsberg off by Saturday night. That tip likely came from Austin.
9. Excerpt from *Secrets*, as published on the UMass website
10. As described in the *NYT* article accompanying Sheehan's oral history
11. All direct quotes here and on succeeding pages are from Bagdikian Oral History (UC Berkeley), p. 92 et seq. https://digitalassets.lib.berkeley.edu/roho/ucb/text/bagdikian_ben.pdf. Full citation from the Bancroft Library: Ben Bagdikian, "Ben H. Bagdikian: Journalist, Media Critic, Professor & Dean Emeritus, UC Berkeley's Graduate School of Journalism," conducted by Lisa Rubens 2010, Regional Oral History Office, the Bancroft Library, University of California, Berkeley, 2011.
12. Rowen obituary: https://www.nytimes.com/2015/11/20/us/henry-s-rowen-professor-economist-and-ex-president-of-rand-dies-at-90.html. "The leaking of the Pentagon Papers was the final straw. In November 1971, Mr. Rowen announced his resignation. In a terse statement, he said, 'Maintaining vitality in institutions and in people is brought about by change—RAND and I are no exception.'"
13. President's Daily Diary: https://www.nixonlibrary.gov/sites/default/files/virtuallibrary/documents/PDD/1971/053%20June%201-15%201971.pdf
14. Rosenthal to Greenfield, 6/16/71. NYPL *NYT* Collection, Rosenthal Papers, Box 100, Pentagon Papers General Folder
15. All forty-seven volumes linked here, full text: https://www.archives.gov/research/pentagon-papers
16. Rosenthal memo to Greenfield, 6/16/71, NYPL, *NYT* Company Records, A.M. Rosenthal Papers, Box 100
17. Bagdikian Oral History (UC Berkeley), p. 92 et seq. https://digitalassets.lib.berkeley.edu/roho/ucb/text/bagdikian_ben.pdf
18. The quotes from Nixon and Haig that follow are from White House Tapes, White House Telephone Conversation 005-050 (Richard M. Nixon and Alexander M. Haig, Jr.), June 13, 1971, 12:18–12:42 p.m. https://prde.upress.virginia.edu/conversations/4002135
19. Conversation 471–2, 19 March 1971, 7:03 a.m. to 7:27 p.m., Oval Office. See https://millercenter.org/the-presidency/educational-resources/a-rough-guide-to-richard-nixon-s-conspiracy-theories#fn1_26
20. https://www.nytimes.com/2018/01/20/reader-center/history-of-pentagon-papers.html
21. Cf. GWU National Security Archive analysis, https://nsarchive2.gwu.edu/NSAEBB/NSAEBB48/nixon.html
22. Described at https://nsarchive2.gwu.edu/NSAEBB/NSAEBB48/nixon.html

23. Nixon ordered the Brookings Institution burglary on June 17, 1971, although it was never carried out. See: https://revealnews.org/article/caught-on-tape-the-presidential-edition/
24. Sanford J. Ungar, writing in *Esquire*, "The Papers Papers," May 1972, p. 107
25. Laird Schedule 6/13/71 from Gerald Ford Library, not yet catalogued but provided by archivist Stacy Davis
26. Finney doesn't appear in any of the Pentagon Papers memos leading up to publication.
27. *Face the Nation* transcript from 6/13/71 from the bound volume in LC Reading Room, Week 24, p. 170
28. The newscaster was NBC's David Brinkley. There are letters to/from Brinkley in Sheehan's and/or Rosenthal's papers.
29. WH tape transcript, https://nsarchive2.gwu.edu/NSAEBB/NSAEBB48/transcript.pdf
30. Sinatra phone call with Kissinger before the performance, discussing travel and other logistics. Found in Kissinger phone transcripts at LC.
31. It's clear from the context of Kissinger's phone transcripts that Sinatra had made private jet arrangements, both to and from Los Angeles for Kissinger.
32. Kissinger phone transcripts at LC. As related by HAK in a phone call with Laird, 6/15/71, Kissinger says he arrived 2:00 p.m.
33. Sourcing for all Kissinger phone calls: stenographic transcripts available at the Library of Congress
34. All forty-seven volumes of the Papers are linked here: https://www.archives.gov/research/pentagon-papers
35. In his March 31, 1968, speech withdrawing as a candidate for reelection, LBJ announced that the United States would suspend bombing of North Vietnam north of the 19th parallel on April 1. He invited North Vietnam to agree to negotiations to end the conflict. With this speech, Johnson signaled the end of his administration's willingness to support the demands of field commanders in Vietnam for additional troops. Johnson then surprised the nation by announcing that he would not seek a second term as president of the United States. Details: https://www.vietnamwar50th.com/1968_tet_and_shifting_views/President-Johnson-Suspends-Bombing-and-Invites-Peace-Negotiations/#:~:text=Drea%2C%20McNamara%2C%20Clifford%2C%20and,altogether%20on%20November%201%2C%201968
36. The quote is from p. 202 of the final Pentagon Papers volume. https://nara-media-001.s3.amazonaws.com/arcmedia/research/pentagon-papers/Pentagon-Papers-Part-VI-C-4.pdf
37. Kissinger stenographic phone transcripts at LC, Kissinger/Rostow, 6/14/71, 7 p.m.

38. Cerf died that August. He left his friend Sinatra $1,000 as a token of esteem. https://www.nytimes.com/1971/09/03/archives/cerf-left-estate-of-over-1million-some-small-bequests-made-to.html
39. Kissinger stenographic phone transcripts at LC, Kissinger/Sinatra, 6/14/71, 7:12 p.m.
40. Kissinger stenographic phone call transcripts, LC
41. President's Daily Diary for 6/14/71: https://www.nixonlibrary.gov/sites/default/files/virtuallibrary/documents/PDD/1971/053%20June%201-15%201971.pdf
42. Full White House transcript here: https://prde.upress.virginia.edu/conversations/4002139
43. Two lanes in the EOB basement: https://time.com/2970061/white-house-bowling-alley/. Also see https://www.whitehousehistory.org/photos/president-richard-nixon-bowling-at-the-white-house-in-1970

Chapter 12

1. A copy of the original provided by David Dunlap, *NYT* historian.
2. https://www.nytimes.com/1971/06/15/archives/court-step-likely-return-of-documents-asked-in-telegram-to.html
3. Rosenthal Journal, June 1971, p. 1 et seq. Rosenthal also recounted the comments of Jimmy Greenfield, Sydney Gruson, and Harding Bancroft in his office that evening, as well as the back-and-forth between the NYT and DOJ telex operators.
4. [*Sic*] This is how Sheehan took down the warning, on a Hilton notepad.
5. Sheehan's transcription of call with Rogovin, Sheehan Papers, LC
6. "Blow the Safe" transcript: https://prde.upress.virginia.edu/conversations/4006738
7. Halt was effective November 1, 1968: https://en.wikipedia.org/wiki/October_1968#:~:text=October%2031%2C%201968%20(Thursday),-Citing%20progress%20in&text=Johnson%20announced%20in%20a%20nationwide,local%20time%20on%20November%201
8. June 17, 5:15 pm transcript here: https://prde.upress.virginia.edu/conversations/4006738
9. In a later phone call, soon after the Oval Office meeting, same day, Nixon told Kissinger to call Rostow and tell LBJ to hold a news conference. Kissinger said he didn't think Johnson would do it, but agreed to phone Rostow immediately. Nixon: "Well, you ought to tell Rostow this: That unless he has a press conference, I'm not prepared to defend him. Now, just as cold as that. They've just got to know. I'm not going to defend him. Why should I?" https://prde.upress.virginia.edu/conversations/4002148

10. The colleague was Jeb Stuart Magruder. Liddy also described the incident in his book, *Will*, at p. 292: "Jeb, if you don't take your arm off my shoulder, I'm going to tear it off and beat you to death with it."
11. *LAT* 3/1/03: "Brookings Guard Who Foiled Burglary Dies": https://www.latimes.com/archives/la-xpm-2003-mar-01-na-warrick1-story.html. Verification: Liddy tells this story on pp. 171–172 of his memoir, *Will.*
12. Bradlee, p. 314
13. Bradlee, p. 316
14. Verification: Williams isn't listed in the index to *Bright Shining Lie.*
15. Sheehan Papers, LC, Vann-Sheehan Vietnam War Collection, B107F1
16. DuPont, a psychiatrist, had recently left office as White House Drug Czar under President Gerald Ford.
17. Haldeman Diary for 6/21/71: https://www.nixonlibrary.gov/sites/default/files/virtuallibrary/documents/haldeman-diaries/37-hrhd-audiocassette-ac09b-19710621-pa.pdf
18. Haldeman Diary for 6/21/71: https://www.nixonlibrary.gov/sites/default/files/virtuallibrary/documents/haldeman-diaries/37-hrhd-audiocassette-ac09b-19710621-pa.pdf
19. [*Sic*] It's "demonstration," singular in the transcript.
20. Kissinger stenographic phone transcript, LC Papers, 6/21/71
21. Benefit was 5/27/71: https://www.nytimes.com/1971/05/28/archives/front-page-1-no-title-scores-of-notables-attend-preview-of-kennedy.html?searchResultPosition=4
22. *NYT* 5/28/71: https://www.nytimes.com/1971/05/28/archives/front-page-1-no-title-scores-of-notables-attend-preview-of-kennedy.html?searchResultPosition=4
23. Wife of Henry Ford (her second husband) at the time. *NYT* confirms she was present at the 5/27/71 Kennedy Center gala, escorted by Bill vanden Heuvel.
24. Funeral was 11/12/70. Confirming Ted Kennedy was there: https://www.artnet.com/artists/marc-riboud/edward-kennedy-at-charles-de-gaulles-funeral-zt7GZa80il-VZshvDnv9sg2
25. Kissinger had dated Candice Bergen. See https://www.washingtonpost.com/history/2023/11/29/henry-kissinger-dies-dating-life-playboy/
26. Haldeman Diary for June 23, 1971: https://www.nixonlibrary.gov/sites/default/files/virtuallibrary/documents/haldeman-diaries/37-hrhd-audiocassette-ac09b-19710623-pa.pdf
27. Argued 6/26/71 and decided 6/30/71: https://www.oyez.org/cases/1970/1873
28. From the Nixon Foundation: The burglars were looking for information to discredit Ellsberg. Operatives of the group broke into the Los Angeles office of his psychiatrist, Dr. Lewis Fielding, looking for his motivation, intentions, and possible co-conspirators. https://www.nixonlibrary.gov/news/fielding-break-50th-anniversary#:~:text=Looking

%20for%20information%20to%20discredit,%2C%20and%20possible%20co%2Dconspirators

Chapter 13

1. 10/9/70, meeting with editors in New Orleans: http://transascity.org/files/news/1970_10_09_Boston_Record_American_27.jpg
2. Safire Papers, B123F4, folder is titled "Writings/Books/Before the Fall." Safire describes the January 5, 1971, meeting.
3. https://en.wikipedia.org/wiki/John_Lindsay
4. Safire Papers, LC, as above. Safire typescript, p. 1
5. Safire Papers, LC, as above. Safire typescript, p. 2
6. Safire Papers, LC, as above. Safire typescript, p. 2. This colloquy has been edited and condensed for clarity (Nixon interrupted Rockefeller between his two statements).
7. More about Pringle: https://www.peterpringleauthor.com/bio.htm
8. Pringle's obituary of Connally: 6/16/93: https://www.the-independent.com/news/people/obituary-john-connally-1492170.html
9. McNamara Oral History 4/4/64, p. 17 https://static.jfklibrary.org/7g7x881l536l521700marl73dv014xa.pdf?odc=20231115180846-0500
10. 6/18/64: LBJ and Connally at the White House, on the phone to McNamara: https://millercenter.org/the-presidency/secret-white-house-tapes/conversation-robert-mcnamara-and-john-connally-july-18-1964
11. "JFK and McNamara," Part Three, by Peter Osnos. Linked here: https://peterosnos.substack.com/p/jfk-and-mcnamara
12. Connally in office as Navy secretary at Pentagon: January 25 to Dec 20, 1961. Oswald's letter is dated January 30.
13. Getty Image of the letter is here; it has a Minsk, USSR, return address: https://www.gettyimages.com/detail/news-photo/letter-dated-january-30-from-former-us-marine-lee-harvey-news-photo/576877770
14. https://www.maryferrell.org/showDoc.html?docId=1136#relPageId=729
15. "Letters: Did Lee Harvey Oswald actually target Texas Gov. Connally?" 11/22/23, by David Fleshman. Fleshman's account is linked here: https://www.postandcourier.com/opinion/letters_to_editor/did-lee-harvey-oswald-actually-target-texas-gov-connally/article_cc76b342-7f11-11ee-a7fb-0f7cff3150de.html
16. First-person account from person who was told by Connally: "I do not, for one second, believe the conclusions of the Warren Commission." So, why not speak out? "Because I love this country and we needed closure at the time. I will never speak out publicly about what I believe." https://educationforum.ipbhost.com/topic/12956-john-connally-and-doug-thompson/
17. The bill passed in August 1970.

18. 1/4/71 transcript: https://www.presidency.ucsb.edu/documents/conversation-with-the-president-interview-with-four-representatives-the-television
19. Safire Papers, LC, B123F4, "Nixon Style: The Big Play"
20. Safire Papers, LC, B123F4, "Nixon Style: The Big Play"
21. Zachary Taylor (Whig), 1849, prior to Nixon
22. Safire Papers, LC, B123F4, p. 3 of Safire memo of conversation
23. Safire memo of conversation, LC Files, 1/5/71, B125F4
24. *Newsweek*, April 19, 1971: "The Shafting of Mr. Average," by Stewart Alsop, p. 132
25. https://www.nytimes.com/1971/05/05/archives/currency-trading-buffets-europe-dollar-is-target-mark-in-demand.html
26. https://timesmachine.nytimes.com/timesmachine/1971/05/05/issue.html
27. https://www.nytimes.com/1971/05/18/archives/connally-is-firm-on-dollar-policy-stresses-curbs-on-inflation.html
28. *NYT* 6/22/71, Ed Dale reporting on Stans's 6/21 speech in Washington: https://www.nytimes.com/1971/06/22/archives/may-prices-rose-at-twice-the-rate-of-first-4-months-inflation.html
29. New contract, August 1, 1971: 30 percent increase over three years: https://www.nytimes.com/1971/08/02/archives/3year-steel-agreement-averts-strike-wage-increase-is-30-price-rise.html#:~:text=August%202%2C%201971%2C%20Page%201Buy%20Reprints.%20New%20York%20Times%20subscribers&text=The%20steelworkers%20will%20be%20given%20a%201%E2%80%90cent%20increase%20for%20each%20rise%20of
30. https://www.nixonlibrary.gov/sites/default/files/virtuallibrary/documents/haldeman-diaries/37-hrhd-audiocassette-ac09b10a-19710627-pa.pdf
31. Safire describes this: White House File, B22F4. The meeting is 6/29/71, 10:00 a.m.
32. Cont'd: Safire describes this: White House File, B22F4. The meeting is 6/29/71, 10:00 a.m.
33. The official law here: https://www.congressionalinstitute.org/2022/08/13/the-august-recess-a-congressional-reform-that-will-last/. Layman's explanation from *Time* magazine 8/4/14: https://time.com/3060041/congress-summer/
34. President's Daily Diary shows the meeting underway by 10:00 a.m., Shultz in attendance until 10:28 a.m., and then Connally alone with Nixon until 11:25 a.m. when Haldeman joins. Connally leaves at 11:53 a.m. and returns at 1:24 p.m. https://www.nixonlibrary.gov/sites/default/files/virtuallibrary/documents/PDD/1971/057%20August%201-15%201971.pdf
35. All foregoing from the official State Department historian: https://history.state.gov/historicaldocuments/frus1969-76v03/d164
36. This is from the State Department historian: https://history.state.gov/historicaldocuments/frus1969-76v03/d164

37. All foregoing from the official State Department historian: https://history.state.gov/historicaldocuments/frus1969-76v03/d164
38. President's Daily Diary: https://www.nixonlibrary.gov/sites/default/files/virtuallibrary/documents/PDD/1971/057%20August%201-15%201971.pdf
39. President's daily schedule, p. 16 at this link: https://www.nixonlibrary.gov/sites/default/files/virtuallibrary/documents/PDD/1971/057%20August%201-15%201971.pdf
40. Nixon tape for Aug 5: https://www.easynixon.org/tapes/555-001
41. DJIA one-hundred-year interactive chart: https://www.macrotrends.net/1319/dow-jones-100-year-historical-chart
42. Also of note: On this day, August 6, William McChesney Martin, the former chair of the Fed, proposes drastic reform for the securities industry: one central market, so investors will get the same price for stock everywhere. There will be huge implications for markets in the years ahead as this proposal slowly gains traction.
43. Nixon Daily Diary links: https://www.nixonlibrary.gov/sites/default/files/virtuallibrary/documents/PDD/1971/057%20August%201-15%201971.pdf
44. Haldeman Diary for 8/13/71: https://www.nixonlibrary.gov/sites/default/files/virtuallibrary/documents/haldeman-diaries/37-hrhd-audiotape-ac12ab-19710813-pa.pdf
45. Haldeman Diary: https://www.nixonlibrary.gov/sites/default/files/virtuallibrary/documents/haldeman-diaries/37-hrhd-audiotape-ac12ab-19710813-pa.pdf. President's Daily Diary for 8/13, p. 81: https://www.nixonlibrary.gov/sites/default/files/virtuallibrary/documents/PDD/1971/057%20August%201-15%201971.pdf
46. Safire Diary
47. Safire Diary
48. Safire Diary
49. This is quoted verbatim in Haldeman Diary of 8/15/71: https://www.nixonlibrary.gov/sites/default/files/virtuallibrary/documents/haldeman-diaries/37-hrhd-audiotape-ac12b-19710815-add-pa.pdf
50. President's Daily Diary for 8/15/71: https://www.nixonlibrary.gov/sites/default/files/virtuallibrary/documents/PDD/1971/057%20August%201-15%201971.pdf
51. Total federal spending in 1971: In fiscal year 1971, the total federal budget outlays were $211.6 billion, with receipts at $188.3 billion, resulting in a near-record deficit of $23.2 billion. Full text Of Nixon's speech here, including 10 percent cut in foreign aid: https://www.cvce.eu/content/publication/1999/1/1/168eed17-f28b-487b-9cd2-6d668e42e63a/publishable_en.pdf. Relevant text: "Looking to the future, I have directed the Secretary of the Treasury to recommend to the Congress in January new tax proposals for stimulating research and development

of new industries and new techniques to help provide the 20 million new jobs that America needs for the young people who will be coming into the job market in the next decade. To offset the loss of revenue from these tax cuts which directly stimulate new jobs, I have ordered today a $4.7 billion cut in Federal spending. Tax cuts to stimulate employment must be matched by spending cuts to restrain inflation. To check the rise in the cost of Government, I have ordered a postponement of pay raises and a 5 percent cut in Government personnel. I have ordered a 10 percent cut in foreign economic aid."

52. President's Daily Diary shows at least twenty-four phone calls: https://www.nixonlibrary.gov/sites/default/files/virtuallibrary/documents/PDD/1971/057%20August%201-15%201971.pdf
53. Nixon's address to the joint session of Congress was Thursday, September 9, 1971.
54. Full text of memo: https://commons.wikimedia.org/wiki/File%3ADean-enemies-1.jpg. Dean testified on 6/27/73 before the Senate Watergate Committee that "I was asked to prepare a strategy for dealing with political enemies that involved the entire White House staff, and [the memo] was sent forward, to the best of my recollection, to Mr. Haldeman and Mr. Ehrlichman for approval, disapproval, or comment." See pp. 97–101 in the hearing record, found here: https://archive.org/details/statementofinforo8unit/page/96/mode/2up

Chapter 14

1. Torres was accused in the Harlem murders, hung jury; later, in prison for bank robbery. Still later, more police murders in San Francisco, revealed by DNA: https://www.nytimes.com/2007/01/29/nyregion/29torres.html
2. Two cops murdered: https://www.nytimes.com/1971/05/22/archives/2-policemen-slain-by-shots-in-back-2-men-are-sought-patrolmen.html
3. "Leslie Bacon, who is being held as a material witness in the March 1 bombing of the Capitol in Washington, has admitted having been a member of the group plotting the bombings": https://www.nytimes.com/1971/05/08/archives/5-in-bomb-plot-here-sentenced-3-get-maximum-4year-terms-5-in-bomb.html
4. Wiretaps rose from 302 in 1969 to 597 in 1970. Reporting was required by Omnibus Crime Act of 1969. https://www.nytimes.com/1971/05/03/archives/courtapproved-wiretaps-by-police-doubled-in-1970-police-wiretaps.html
5. *NYT* 5/4/71 front page, lead headline: https://www.proquest.com/hnpnewyorktimes/docview/119352514/fulltextPDF/71F3DFBE4DFE4571PQ/2?accountid=35635&sourcetype=Newspapers

6. Anti-riot charges announced by AG Mitchell: https://www.nytimes.com/1971/05/14/archives/abbie-hoffman-is-indicted-on-us-antiriot-charges.html
7. Wallace began his second term as governor in January 1971. https://en.wikipedia.org/wiki/George_Wallace#:~:text=George%20Corley%20Wallace%20Jr.,finally%20from%201983%20to%201987
8. *NYT* 5/14/71: https://www.nytimes.com/1971/05/14/archives/black-panther-party-members-freed-after-being-cleared-of-charges-13.html
9. Lefcourt was born on June 1, 1942, so he was indeed just 28 when the Panther verdict came in: https://www.nytimes.com/1970/02/17/archives/activist-lawyer-with-a-cause-gerald-bernard-lefcourt.html
10. *NYT* 2/17/70 profile of Lefcourt: https://www.nytimes.com/1970/02/17/archives/activist-lawyer-with-a-cause-gerald-bernard-lefcourt.html
11. Not guilty verdicts: https://www.nytimes.com/1971/05/14/archives/black-panther-party-members-freed-after-being-cleared-of-charges-13.html
12. https://www.nytimes.com/1971/05/19/archives/nixon-answers-black-proposals-refuses-a-bid-by-caucus-for-higher.html
13. *NYT* 8/27/71: "Not in four decades have so many New York City police men been killed in such a way. Ten were killed in 1930 and nine in 1931, more than any other years in the department's history." By August 1971, already ten police officers had been killed in the line of duty. https://www.nytimes.com/1971/08/27/archives/wide-hunt-begun-in-police-killing-slain-detective-worked-in.html
14. The year 1971 was the deadliest in NYC's history, with fourteen officers killed in the line of duty: Official NYPD history, by Edward Conlon: https://www.nyc.gov/site/nypd/news/f0719/the-war-home-remembering-foster-laurie#/0
15. https://www.nytimes.com/1971/05/20/archives/machinegun-fire-hits-2-policemen-machinegun-fire-hits-2-policemen.html
16. https://www.nytimes.com/1971/05/22/archives/2-policemen-slain-by-shots-in-back-2-men-are-sought-patrolmen.html
17. https://www.nytimes.com/1971/05/22/archives/2-policemen-slain-by-shots-in-back-2-men-are-sought-patrolmen.html
18. https://www.nytimes.com/1971/05/22/archives/2-policemen-slain-by-shots-in-back-2-men-are-sought-patrolmen.html
19. Kiernan's comment quoted here: https://www.nytimes.com/1971/05/22/archives/2-policemen-slain-by-shots-in-back-2-men-are-sought-patrolmen.html
20. This chronology is from *Reader's Digest*, "Angela Davis: The Making of a Martyr."
21. See Jacobin.com
22. Michael Myerson Memoir, 6/29/21: https://jacobin.com/2021/06/michael-myerson-memoirs-angela-davis-david-poindexter-trial-prosecution

23. Simone brings red balloon: https://www.theguardian.com/us-news/2022/mar/05/angela-davis-on-the-power-of-protest-we-cant-do-anything-without-optimism#:~:text=Davis's%20became%20the%20public%20face,offered%20to%20pay%20her%20bail
24. Published in the *NY Review of Books*, 1/7/71; Baldwin's letter is dated 11/19/70: https://www.nybooks.com/articles/1971/01/07/an-open-letter-to-my-sister-miss-angela-davis/
25. Pacifica Radio archives: https://web.archive.org/web/20151215000753/http://pacificaradioarchives.org/recording/bb545701-bb545740
26. From PBS: https://web.archive.org/web/20021222102053/http://www.pbs.org/itvs/alcatrazisnotanisland/occupation.html
27. The Air Force One story is eloquently told by John Osborne. See Osborne typescript in Osborne Papers, LC, B68F4
28. The date was May 25, 1971.
29. Passenger manifest of Air Force One, Mobile to Birmingham, 1:11 p.m. departure
30. Osborne Papers, LC, B68F4
31. Here is how the *NYT* covered it: https://www.nytimes.com/1971/05/26/archives/crowds-in-alabama-give-nixon-warm-welcome-nixon-gets-warm-welcome.html
32. SCOTUS Decision on Busing: *Swann* v. *Charlotte-Mecklenburg* https://www.history.com/this-day-in-history/supreme-court-declares-desegregation-busing-constitutional-swann-v-charlotte-mecklenburg. On April 20, 1971, the U.S. Supreme Court unanimously declared busing for the purposes of desegregation to be constitutional. The decision in *Swann* v. *Charlotte-Mecklenburg Board of Education* settled the constitutional question and allowed the widespread implementation of busing, which remained controversial over the next decade.
33. *U.S.* v. *Austin Independent School District* (1971): https://law.justia.com/cases/federal/appellate-courts/F2/532/380/98960/
34. https://www.nytimes.com/1971/08/04/archives/text-of-nixon-statement.html
35. MTP courted Wallace, booking him for a live 1:00 p.m. broadcast on Sunday, August 22. Lawrence Spivak later invited Wallace and his wife, Cornelia, to visit Spivak at a Key Biscayne resort.
36. WH Press Briefing, 8/13/71
37. Primary map here: https://en.wikipedia.org/wiki/1972_Democratic_Party_presidential_primaries
38. *WP* 5/16/71, by William Grieder: https://www.washingtonpost.com/wp-srv/politics/daily/sept98/wallace051672.htm
39. Garment's memo was dated 8/3/71. Buchanan's memo was dated 8/7/71. Garment Papers at LC.
40. JFK's speech was on 9/12/60. https://www.jfklibrary.org/learn/about-jfk/historic-speeches/address-to-the-greater-houston-ministerial-association

41. https://en.wikipedia.org/wiki/New_Haven_Black_Panther_trials
42. Letter from James B. Soetaert, chief deputy probation officer, to Judge Richard E. Arnason, June 15, 1971, found at Harvard Schlesinger Library, Angela Davis collection.
43. https://www.in2013dollars.com/us/inflation/1971?amount=100000
44. Judge Richard E. Arnason Papers: https://oac.cdlib.org/findaid/ark:/13030/c8z3258n/
45. NYPL Schomburg Library, Angela Davis Collection, Angela Davis/Minutes & Bail Report
46. Flyer, S.F. United Committee to Free Angela Davis, unattributed authorship, undated but with context indicating it was distributed on June 15, 1971. Found at Harvard Schlesinger Library, Angela Davis Collection, Bail, probation report, bail pledges
47. *NYT* 8/22/71, "The Soledad Story Opened in Death," by Steven R. Weisman
48. UPI story, *NYT* 7/9/71, "Angela Davis Meets a Soledad Brother"
49. The Love Letters of Angela Davis & George Jackson: https://www.usprisonculture.com/2012/09/14/the-love-letters-of-angela-davis-george-jackson/
50. According to the cited article, this letter was introduced at Davis's trial: https://www.usprisonculture.com/2012/09/14/the-love-letters-of-angela-davis-george-jackson/
51. Bingham's account here and in succeeding paragraphs is from an interview dated 3/10/24: https://truthout.org/articles/once-a-fugitive-attorney-for-black-panther-member-recounts-his-life-underground/#:~:text=On%20August%2021%2C%201971%2C%20I,go%20over%20the%20final%20galleys
52. *NYT* 9/3/71 by Wallace Turner: https://www.nytimes.com/1971/09/03/archives/two-desperate-hours-how-george-jackson-died-two-desperate-hours-how.html#:~:text=Part%20way%20through%20the%20visit,they%20had%20finished%20the%20visit
53. Exact dates: Bingham fled to Europe, where he assumed a false identity and lived using a pseudonym for thirteen years. Bingham voluntarily returned to the United States on July 9, 1984, to stand trial on two counts of murder and one of conspiracy. On June 28, 1986, a Marin County jury unanimously acquitted Bingham of all charges.
54. American Friends Service Committee report: https://afsc.org/newsroom/history-attica-uprising#:~:text=In%20the%201970s%2C%20during%20the%20onset%20of,in%20the%20Attica%20Correctional%20Facility%20were%20abysmal.&text=The%20men%20in%20the%20prison%20were%20locked,20%20cents%20to%20one%20dollar%20an%20hour
55. Testimony before NY State Special Commission on Attica, 4/17/72, pp. 91–92, found in Robert Carter LC Papers

56. Based on the full set of demands from July, the correct number is twenty-eight—the mimeographed set of demands was misnumbered in the original.
57. American Friends Committee timeline (9/10/21)
58. American Friends Committee timeline (9/10/21): https://afsc.org/newsroom/history-attica-uprising#:~:text=In%20the%201970s%2C%20during%20the%20onset%20of,in%20the%20Attica%20Correctional%20Facility%20were%20abysmal.&text=The%20men%20in%20the%20prison%20were%20locked,20%20cents%20to%20one%20dollar%20an%20hour
59. Testimony before NY State Special Commission on Attica, 4/17/72, pp. 91–92
60. This was Capa's sworn testimony to the Attica Commission.
61. [*Sic*] The transcript of Capa's April 17, 1972 testimony to the Attica Commission contains this description, which is at odds with other descriptions of the cells as measuring approximately six feet by nine feet.
62. This portion of the chronology comes from *NYT* 10/4/71—Attica Hour by Hour: https://www.nytimes.com/1971/10/04/archives/the-attica-revolt-hour-by-hour-a-misunderstanding-sparked-uprising.html
63. The inmates listed eleven people they wanted as negotiators. Here is the list, as released by the inmates: "William M. Kunstler, Attorney at Law, 588 9th Avenue, New York, New York; Assemblyman Arthur O. Eve of Buffalo; the Prisoner Solidarity Committee of New York; Minister Farrakhan of the Muslims. We want Huey P. Newton from the Black Panther Party and we want the Chairman of the Young Lords Party. We want Clarence B. Jones of the *Amsterdam News*. We want Tom Wicker of the *New York Times*. We want Richard Roth from the *Courier Express*. We want the Fortune Society; Dave Anderson of the Urban League of Rochester; Brine Eva Barnes. We want Jim Hendling of the *Democratic Late Chronicle* of Detroit, Michigan." (Note: "Jim Hendling" and "Democratic Late Chronicle" appear to be garbled or misprints; neither is mentioned in Heather Ann Thompson's Pulitzer Prize–winning 2016 account of the Attica uprising, *Blood in the Water.*)
64. As documented by the American Friends Service Committee timeline: American Friends Committee timeline (9/10/21): https://afsc.org/newsroom/history-attica-uprising#:~:text=In%20the%201970s%2C%20during%20the%20onset%20of,in%20the%20Attica%20Correctional%20Facility%20were%20abysmal.&text=The%20men%20in%20the%20prison%20were%20locked,20%20cents%20to%20one%20dollar%20an%20hour
65. Rockefeller testimony to Attica Commission, p. 21, in Robert Carter papers at LC
66. Wicker testimony to Attica Commission
67. Wicker testimony

68. Wicker testimony
69. See Rockefeller testimony to Attica Commission, Tr at 78, referencing "my own lack of perception..." Source: Rockefeller testimony to Attica Commission, in Robert Carter papers at LC
70. Also of interest: This was the very last exchange between Liman and Rockefeller during the governor's testimony to the Attica Commission: LIMAN: Have you ever visited a state prison? ROCKEFELLER: Sure. Did you ever, before you came into this? LIMAN: Never, governor. Source: Rockefeller testimony to Attica Commission, Tr p. 83, in Robert Carter papers at LC
71. Rockefeller called it an hour and a half. See Rockefeller Testimony to the Attica Commission, original transcript, April 5, 1972, pp. 23–46.
72. Rockefeller feared being taken hostage. See Rockefeller Testimony to the Attica Commission, original transcript, April 5, 1972, pp. 23–46.
73. This is clear from his Monday afternoon call (the first one) with Nixon, in which he quotes the next request as likely to "come into the courtyard."
74. The Nixon comment is referenced in Arthur Liman private memo to the files, May 10, 1972. Robert L. Carter Papers, LC, Box II–14, Folder 4. The entire document was mailed to the full commission on April 6. It excoriates Rockefeller.
75. See generally, the above-referenced Arthur Liman private memo to the files, May 10, 1972. Robert L. Carter Papers, LC, Box II–14, Folder 4
76. Rockefeller testimony
77. This is based on the official history of the NY State Police website: https://troopers.ny.gov/attica-prison-riots#:~:text=Governor%20Nelson%20Rockefeller%20ordered%20the,uprising%2C%20including%2011%20Corrections%20Officers
78. President's Daily Diary shows that Nixon and Haldeman (with others coming in and out) discussed Attica first, likely around 12:30 p.m. on Monday, with Nixon phoning Rockefeller around 1:30 p.m. that day. https://www.nixonlibrary.gov/sites/default/files/forresearchers/find/tapes/finding_aids/tapesubjectlogs/oval571.pdf
79. President's Daily Diary, p. 14. This shows the interaction between Ehrlichman and Rockefeller, when Rockefeller didn't get through to Nixon. https://www.nixonlibrary.gov/sites/default/files/forresearchers/find/tapes/finding_aids/tapesubjectlogs/oval571.pdf
80. This is based on the Miller Center chronology. https://millercenter.org/the-presidency/educational-resources/kill-few
81. This comes at 3:04 on Tape 4 that day. https://millercenter.org/the-presidency/educational-resources/kill-few
82. Although some transcripts may omit the "f" word, Nixon definitely said it here.

83. 3:13: https://soundcloud.com/the-miller-center-at-uva/attica-13-september-1971-nixon-and-haldeman-discuss-police-raid
84. The call was not revealed until forty years later, in 2011. Transcript here: https://www.democracynow.org/2011/9/16/40_years_after_attica_rebellion_new
85. This occurs at 4:02 on the second of the four calls found here: https://millercenter.org/the-presidency/educational-resources/kill-few
86. This occurs at 4:39, same conversation: https://millercenter.org/the-presidency/educational-resources/kill-few
87. Here is the *NYT* report on this conversation: https://www.nytimes.com/2011/09/13/nyregion/rockefeller-initially-boasted-to-nixon-about-attica-raid.html
88. "Four Days of Attica Talks End in Failure," by Tom Wicker, *NYT*, 9/14/71, p. 29. https://timesmachine.nytimes.com/timesmachine/1971/09/14/issue.html

Chapter 15

1. The banner is found in Sheehan Papers, LC, B187F2.
2. David Dunlap, *Times* historian: https://www.nytimes.com/2016/04/18/insider/1972-a-pulitzer-for-the-pentagon-papers-not-so-fast.html
3. Sheehan Papers, LC, B187F2. Sheehan's typewritten memo to Greenfield is dated in cursive script "Oct. 1971."
4. Greenfield memo to Sheehan, 10/18/71, Sheehan Papers, LC, B187F2
5. Pamela Harriman Papers, LC, Frank Sinatra file
6. https://www.nytimes.com/1972/02/24/archives/miss-davis-freed-on-102500-bail-judge-in-california-releases-her.html
7. Angela Davis autobiography available on Internet Archive: https://ia802303.us.archive.org/8/items/angela-davis-an-autobiography-pdfdrive/Angela%20Davis%20An%20Autobiography%20%28%20PDFDrive%20%29.pdf
8. https://www.nytimes.com/1972/03/15/archives/allwhite-jury-with-8-women-seated-for-angela-davis-trial.html
9. http://www.documentcloud.org/documents/693589-angela-davis-aquittal.html
10. http://www.documentcloud.org/documents/693589-angela-davis-aquittal.html
11. In the acknowledgments, Davis thanked Fidel Castro: "I am deeply grateful to the Cuban Communist Party and its First Secretary Fidel Castro for having invited me to spend several months in Cuba to work full time on the manuscript." https://ia802303.us.archive.org/8/items/angela-davis-an-autobiography-pdfdrive/Angela%20Davis%20An%20Autobiography%20%28%20PDFDrive%20%29.pdf

12. https://www.glbthistory.org/angela-davis-info
13. https://www.nytimes.com/interactive/2020/10/19/t-magazine/angela-davis.html
14. Magee dates: 3/17/39 to 10/17/23
15. Documents Folsom, also photo of Magee on the pavement after the gunfight: https://sfbayview.com/2023/08/ruchell-cinque-magee-was-just-released-from-prison-after-67-years-of-being-caged/
16. https://www.nytimes.com/2000/09/23/opinion/attica-s-forgotten-victims.html
17. FBI records on Agnew: https://vault.fbi.gov/Spiro%20Agnew
18. Kissinger initialed it at 11:35 a.m. https://archivesfoundation.org/documents/richard-nixon-resignation-letter-gerald-ford-pardon/
19. https://www.nytimes.com/1979/01/29/archives/new-details-are-reported-on-how-rockefeller-died-time-of-death.html

BIBLIOGRAPHY

The works below served as references and sources for key dates and background for *Summer of '71*. A listing of other works that readers may find of interest is also provided.

Bradlee, Ben. *A Good Life: Newspapering and Other Adventures.* New York, Simon & Schuster, 1995.

Davis, Angela Y., ed. *If They Come in the Morning: Voices of Resistance.* New York, Third Press, 1971.

Ellsberg, Daniel. *Secrets: A Memoir of Vietnam and the Pentagon Papers.* New York, Viking, 2002.

Fallaci, Oriana. *Interview with History.* Boston, Houghton Mifflin, 1977.

Gage, Beverly. *G-Man: J. Edgar Hoover and the Making of the American Century.* New York, Viking, 2022.

Goulden, Joseph C. *Fit to Print: A. M. Rosenthal and His Times.* Washington, DC, Regnery Gateway, 1988.

Graham, Katharine. *Personal History.* New York, Alfred A. Knopf, 1997.

Hall, Kermit L., James W. Ely Jr., and Joel B. Grossman, eds. *The Oxford Companion to the Supreme Court of the United States,* 2nd ed. New York: Oxford University Press, 2005.

Jenkins, John A. *The Partisan: The Life of William Rehnquist.* New York, Public Affairs, 2012.

Karnow, Stanley. *Vietnam: A History.* New York, Viking, 1983.

Larson, Erik. *The Splendid and the Vile: A Saga of Churchill, Family, and Defiance During the Blitz.* New York, Crown, 2020.

Lenzner, Terry F. *The Investigator: Fifty Years of Uncovering the Truth.* New York, Penguin Press, 2013.

Liberatore, Paul. *The Road to Hell: The True Story of George Jackson, Stephen Bingham, and the San Quentin Massacre.* New York, Atlantic Monthly Press, 1996.

Liddy, G. Gordon. *Will: The Autobiography of G. Gordon Liddy.* New York, St. Martin's Press, 1980.

McCorvey, Norma, with Andy Meisler. *I Am Roe: My Life, Roe v. Wade, and Freedom of Choice.* New York, HarperCollins, 1994.

New York State Special Commission on Attica. *Attica: The Official Report of the New York State Special Commission on Attica.* New York, Bantam Books, 1972.

Purnell, Sonia. *Kingmaker: Pamela Harriman's Astonishing Life of Power, Seduction, and Intrigue.* New York, Viking, 2024.

Rudenstine, David. *The Day the Presses Stopped: A History of the Pentagon Papers Case.* Berkeley, University of California Press, 1996.

Safire, William. *Before the Fall: An Inside View of the Pre-Watergate White House.* Garden City, NY, Doubleday, 1975.

Thompson, Heather Ann. *Blood in the Water: The Attica Prison Uprising of 1971 and Its Legacy.* New York, Pantheon, 2016.

Wells, Tom. *Wild Man: The Life and Times of Daniel Ellsberg.* New York, Palgrave Macmillan, 2001.

Wicker, Tom. *A Time to Die: The Attica Prison Revolt.* New York, Quadrangle/The New York Times Book Co., 1975.

Wills, Garry. *Nixon Agonistes: The Crisis of the Self-Made Man.* Boston, Houghton Mifflin, 1970.

Woodward, Bob, and Scott Armstrong. *The Brethren: Inside the Supreme Court.* New York: Simon & Schuster, 1979.

Books by or about the Principal Players in *Summer of '71*

Davis, Angela Y. *Angela Davis: An Autobiography.* New York, Random House, 1974.

Dean, John. *Blind Ambition: The White House Years.* New York, Simon & Schuster, 1976.

———. *The Rehnquist Choice: The Untold Story of the Nixon Appointment that Redefined the Supreme Court.* New York, Free Press, 2001.

Ehrlichman, John. *Witness to Power: The Nixon Years.* New York, Simon & Schuster, 1982.

Garment, Leonard. *Crazy Rhythm: My Journey from Brooklyn, Jazz, and Wall Street to Nixon's White House, Watergate, and Beyond.* New York, Times Books, 1997.

Haldeman, H. R., with Joseph DiMona. *The Ends of Power.* New York, Times Books, 1978.

Haldeman, H. R. *The Haldeman Diaries: Inside the Nixon White House.* New York, G. P. Putnam's Sons, 1994.

Harriman, W. Averell. *America and Russia in a Changing World: A Half Century of Personal Observation.* Garden City, NY, Doubleday, 1971.

Harriman, W. Averell, and Elie Abel. *Special Envoy to Churchill and Stalin, 1941–1946.* New York, Random House, 1975.

Jackson, George. *Soledad Brother: The Prison Letters of George Jackson.* New York, Coward-McCann, 1970.

———. *Blood in My Eye.* New York, Random House, 1972.

Johnson, Lyndon Baines. *The Vantage Point: Perspectives of the Presidency, 1963–1969.* New York, Holt, Rinehart and Winston, 1971.

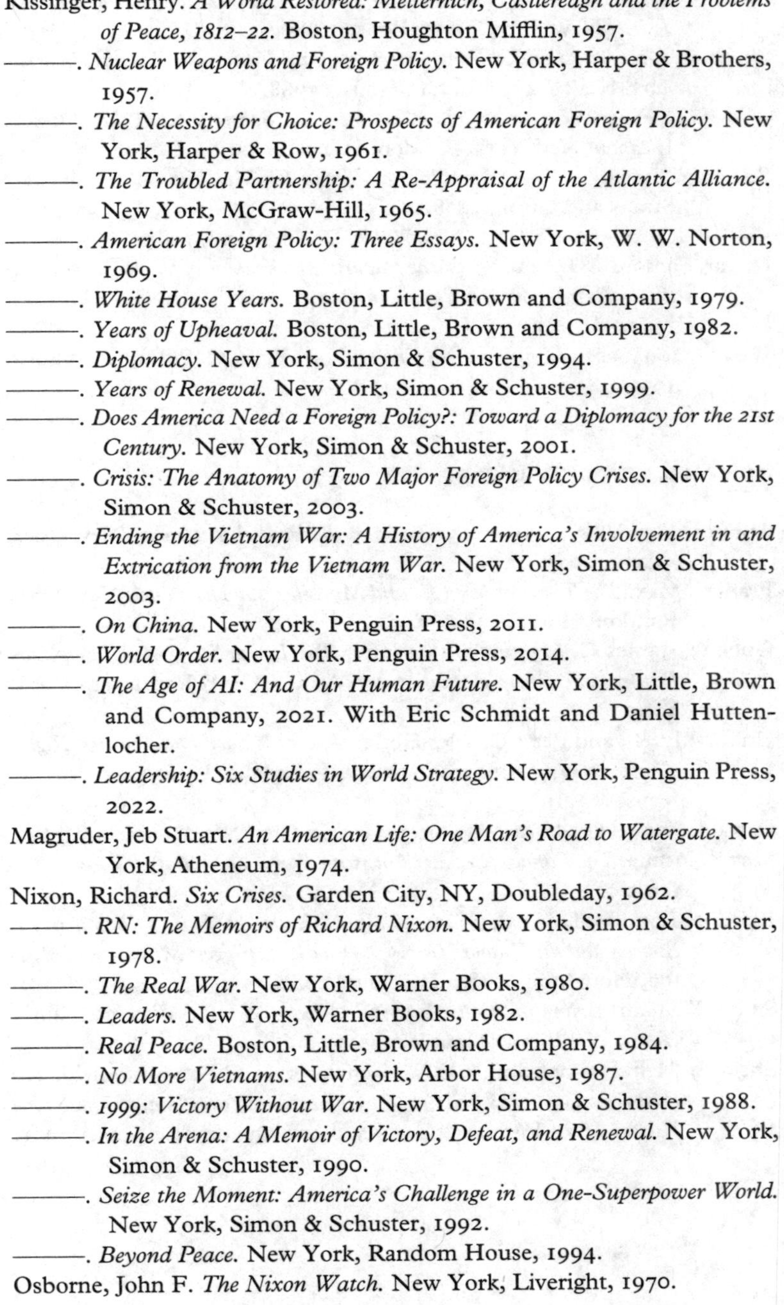

Kissinger, Henry. *A World Restored: Metternich, Castlereagh and the Problems of Peace, 1812–22*. Boston, Houghton Mifflin, 1957.

———. *Nuclear Weapons and Foreign Policy*. New York, Harper & Brothers, 1957.

———. *The Necessity for Choice: Prospects of American Foreign Policy*. New York, Harper & Row, 1961.

———. *The Troubled Partnership: A Re-Appraisal of the Atlantic Alliance*. New York, McGraw-Hill, 1965.

———. *American Foreign Policy: Three Essays*. New York, W. W. Norton, 1969.

———. *White House Years*. Boston, Little, Brown and Company, 1979.

———. *Years of Upheaval*. Boston, Little, Brown and Company, 1982.

———. *Diplomacy*. New York, Simon & Schuster, 1994.

———. *Years of Renewal*. New York, Simon & Schuster, 1999.

———. *Does America Need a Foreign Policy?: Toward a Diplomacy for the 21st Century*. New York, Simon & Schuster, 2001.

———. *Crisis: The Anatomy of Two Major Foreign Policy Crises*. New York, Simon & Schuster, 2003.

———. *Ending the Vietnam War: A History of America's Involvement in and Extrication from the Vietnam War*. New York, Simon & Schuster, 2003.

———. *On China*. New York, Penguin Press, 2011.

———. *World Order*. New York, Penguin Press, 2014.

———. *The Age of AI: And Our Human Future*. New York, Little, Brown and Company, 2021. With Eric Schmidt and Daniel Huttenlocher.

———. *Leadership: Six Studies in World Strategy*. New York, Penguin Press, 2022.

Magruder, Jeb Stuart. *An American Life: One Man's Road to Watergate*. New York, Atheneum, 1974.

Nixon, Richard. *Six Crises*. Garden City, NY, Doubleday, 1962.

———. *RN: The Memoirs of Richard Nixon*. New York, Simon & Schuster, 1978.

———. *The Real War*. New York, Warner Books, 1980.

———. *Leaders*. New York, Warner Books, 1982.

———. *Real Peace*. Boston, Little, Brown and Company, 1984.

———. *No More Vietnams*. New York, Arbor House, 1987.

———. *1999: Victory Without War*. New York, Simon & Schuster, 1988.

———. *In the Arena: A Memoir of Victory, Defeat, and Renewal*. New York, Simon & Schuster, 1990.

———. *Seize the Moment: America's Challenge in a One-Superpower World*. New York, Simon & Schuster, 1992.

———. *Beyond Peace*. New York, Random House, 1994.

Osborne, John F. *The Nixon Watch*. New York, Liveright, 1970.

Salisbury, Harrison E. *Without Fear or Favor: The New York Times and Its Times.* New York, Times Books, 1980.

Sheehan, Neil. *A Bright Shining Lie: John Paul Vann and America in Vietnam.* New York, Random House, 1988.

———. *A Fiery Peace in a Cold War: Bernard Schriever and the Ultimate Weapon.* New York, Random House, 2009.

Sheehan, Susan. *Is There No Place on Earth for Me?* New York, Farrar, Straus and Giroux, 1982.

———. *Kate Quinton's Days.* New York, Dodd, Mead, 1984.

Ungar, Sanford J. *The Papers & the Papers: An Account of the Legal and Political Battle over the Pentagon Papers.* New York, E. P. Dutton, 1972.

Weddington, Sarah. *A Question of Choice.* New York, G. P. Putnam's Sons, 1992.

Selected Other Works

Abrams, Floyd. *Speaking Freely: Trials of the First Amendment.* New York, Viking, 2005.

Frankel, Max. *The Times of My Life and My Life with The Times.* New York, Random House, 1999.

Goodale, James C. *Fighting for the Press: The Inside Story of the Pentagon Papers and Other Battles.* New York, CUNY Journalism Press, 2013.

Hull, N. E. H., and Peter Charles Hoffer. *Roe v. Wade: The Abortion Rights Controversy in American History.* Lawrence, University Press of Kansas, 2010.

Oswald, Russell G. *Attica—My Story.* Garden City, NY, Doubleday, 1972.

Prager, Joshua. *The Family Roe: An American Story.* New York, W. W. Norton, 2021.

Roberts, Lawrence. *Mayday 1971: A White House at War, a Revolt in the Streets, and the Untold History of America's Biggest Mass Arrest.* Boston, Houghton Mifflin Harcourt, 2020.

Safire, William. *Before the Fall: An Inside View of the Pre-Watergate White House.* New York, Doubleday, 1975.

Sheehan, Neil, Hedrick Smith, E. W. Kenworthy, and Fox Butterfield. *The Pentagon Papers as Published by The New York Times: The Secret History of the Vietnam War.* New York, Quadrangle Books, 1971.

INDEX

ABC-TV, 41, 289
abortion, 157–58, 166–75, 349–50
  Nixon on, 166–67
  Roe v. *Wade,* xv, 157–58, 169, 170–75, 349–50
  U.S. v. *Vuitch,* 157–58, 167, 170, 174
  Weddington's role, xvi, 168–70, 171–75, 349–50
Acheson, Dean, 26, 29–31
Adorno, Theodor, 95
AFL-CIO, 294
Agger, Carolyn, 163
Agnew, Judy, 238
Agnew, Spiro
  death of, 353
  election of 1968, 58–59, 78
  election of 1970, 283–84
  election of 1972, 344
  Gridiron Club Dinner speech, 190–92
  Tricia Nixon's wedding, 238
  Vietnam War and, 75
Ailes, Roger, 86–87
Air Force One, 321, 350
Alabama Crimson Tide, 322
Alaska, abortion law, 157
Albert, Carl, 277–78
Alcatraz Island, occupation of, 311, 320–21
Alexander, Deacon, 101
Alsop, Stewart, 140, 292–93
American Civil Liberties Union (ACLU), 146–49, 150
American Friends Service Committee, 94
American Legion, 99
American Medical Association, 290
American University Law School, 160
Amos 'n' Andy (radio show), 238
Andrews Air Force Base, 301
antiwar protests, 127–56. *See also* Mayday
  Cambodia operation and, 65, 75, 127
  Fonda and, 131–34
  Jackson State killings, 127, 345
  Johnson and, 217
  Kent State shootings, 65, 127, 345
  Kerry and, 134–37, 140–44
  Martha Mitchell on, 79
  Nixon and, 86, 138–40, 145–46, 149–52, 237–38, 342
  the Weathermen, 127, 130–34
Arbatov, Georgy, 216
Arlington Cemetery, 136
Armies of the Night, The (Mailer), 144
arms control, 54
Arnason, Richard, 326–27
Arnett, Peter, 12
Arnheiter Affair, The (Sheehan), 71
Arnold & Porter, 209
"Art of Coercion, The" (Ellsberg), 53–54
Associated Press, xii, 12, 262
Atlantic Monthly, 105–6, 107–8
atomic bombing of Hiroshima, 54
atomic weapons, 4, 30–31, 54
  Kissinger's "small war" theory, 38–44, 51, 84
Attica Commission, 336–37, 340
Attica Liberation Faction (ALF), 330, 333, 335
Attica Prison riot, 330–45
  aftermath of, 352–53
  background, 330–31
  initial uprising, 332–34
  negotiations, 333–37
  Nixon and, 341–45

Attica Prison riot, *cont.*
retaking of prison and retaliation, 337–41
Austin, Anthony, 241–42
Avedon, Richard, 350

Baez, Joan, 92
Bagdikian, Ben, 242–43, 246, 265–68, 272
Baker, Russell, 39–41
Baldwin, James, 97, 319
Ball, George, 26, 29
Baltimore Sun, 39
Bancroft, Harding, 262, 263
Bañuelos, Romana Acosta, 228*n*
Barnet, Richard, 187–89, 230
Baylor Law School, 168
Bay of Pigs invasion, 27, 219, 271
Beaton, Cecil, 350
Beebe, Fritz, 273–74
Beecher, William, 65
Bell & Howell, 229
Bergen, Candice, 45, 280–81
Bergen, Edgar, 280
Bergman, Lewis, 177–78, 213, 214
Bernstein, Felicia, 109–11
Bernstein, Jamie, 110
Bernstein, Leonard, 108–11
Bill of Rights, 158, 167–68
Bingham, Stephen, 118, 328–29
Birmingham, Alabama, 93–94, 95
Black, Hugo, 161
Black Liberation Army, 310, 316
Black Lives Matter, 85
blackmail, 44, 51, 53–54, 63, 269, 270, 280
Blackmun, Harry, 165–66, 173
Black Panther Party, 123, 168
Bernstein fundraiser, 108–11
Davis and, 95–99, 351
New York City and Panther 21, 108–9, 310–11, 315
Blood in My Eye (Jackson), 328
Boeing B-52s, 9
Bond, Julian, 116
Boston Public Library, 53–54
Bradlee, Ben, xiii, 242–43, 246, 272–74
Bradley, Omar, 26–30
Brandeis University, 95, 153
Brando, Marlon, 116
Brandt, Willy, 215–16
Bretton Woods Agreement, 293–94, 306
Bright Shining Lie, A (Sheehan), 349
Brinkley, Douglas, xvii
Bronze Star, 134, 287
Brookings Institution, 66, 268–70, 271, 281, 282
Brooklyn Law School, 312
Brown, Edmund "Pat," 91–93
Browne, Malcolm, 12–14
Brown, Nona, 176–77
Brownsville riots, 314
Bryant, Paul "Bear," 322
Buchanan, Alvin Leon, 169
Buchanan, Pat, 324–25
Buckley, James, 283–84
Buckley, William F., 182, 283
Bui Diem, 216
Bundy, McGeorge
Ellsberg and, 155–56
at Ford Foundation, 74, 155, 216
Vietnam War and, 26–27, 29–30, 74, 155, 213, 216
Bunker, Ellsworth, 67
Burger, Warren, 163, 165–66, 190, 292
Burns, Arthur, 288–91, 294, 299, 302, 303, 304, 306–7
Butch Cassidy and the Sundance Kid (film), 241
Byrne, William Matthew, Jr., 346

Cabot, Cabot & Forbes, 194, 196, 206–7
California, abortion law, 157
California Board of Regents, 101–4, 106–8, 113–17
California gubernatorial election of 1966, 88, 91–93
California Highway Patrol, 91
California Supreme Court, 351
Calley, William, 127–29, 292–94
Cambodian campaign, 46, 63–84, 127, 176
Sheehan's investigation and story, 70–84
Camp David, 239, 259, 294–96, 303–7

Canadian Broadcasting Corporation, 183
Capa, Cornell, 330–31
Capa, Robert, 330–31
Capitol bombing of 1971, 130–31
Carey, Hugh, 353
Carlyle Hotel, 280
Carson, Johnny, 307
Carswell, G. Harrold, 164–65
Carter, Alprentice "Bunchy," 96–97
Carter, Jimmy, 349
Cartier-Bresson, Henri, 330–31
Castro, Fidel, 352
Catledge, Turner, 210
CBS-TV, 191, 202, 250–51, 289
Census Bureau, 292
Cerf, Bennett, 256
Chandler family, 105–6, 107
Chappaquiddick, 195
Che-Lumumba Club, 96, 100–101
Chicago Seven, 138, 144, 334
Child, Julia, 83
China, xv, xvi–xvii, 217–29
  Harriman and Ronning and, 217–18, 219–21
  Kissinger's secret trip to, 47, 221–25, 226–29, 256, 295
  Nixon and, 221–24, 226, 228
Chirac, Jacques, 350
Chomsky, Noam, 116, 153–55
Christmas, William Arthur, 120, 123
Churchill, Randolph, 218
CIA (Central Intelligence Agency), 6, 15, 23–25, 26, 59, 271
civil liberties, 146–49
Cleaver, Eldridge, 97
Cleaver, Kathleen, 97
Clifford, Clark
  Pentagon Papers and, 195, 213, 249, 280
  Vietnam War and, 20, 24–25, 26, 245, 253
Clinton, Bill, 75, 350
Clutchette, John, 327
Coffee, Linda, 168–70, 173–74
"cognitive bias," 4–5
COINTELPRO, 98
Cold War, 4, 26, 27, 43, 56–57
  "linkage" theory, 47, 229
Colorado, abortion law, 157
Colson, Charles, 275, 280–81, 347
Columbia Journalism Review, 200
Columbia University, 200, 347
Combs, Ken, 121–22
Communist Party, 94–95, 96, 100, 101–2, 105, 106–8, 116–17, 352
Conein, Lucien, 6, 15
Conger, Clement, 323–24
Congressional Black Caucus, 312–13
Congressional Medal of Honor, 8
Connally, John, 286–88
  background of, 286–87
  Haldeman and, 228–29, 302–3
  inflation and economic reforms, 228, 291–92, 294–96, 298–305
  Oswald and, 287–88
  threatening to resign, 228–29
  treasury secretary, xii, 228–29, 291–92, 294–96, 298–305
conservatism, 103, 158, 163–64, 182, 283
conspiracy theories, 134, 179, 180, 195, 219
Consumer Price Index, 294
Conversations with Americans (Lane), 134, 179–84, 199
Cost of Living Council, 288
Council of Economic Advisers, 302
Council on Foreign Relations, 155
Cox, Edward, 237–41, 243, 259, 301
Cox, Tricia Nixon, 259, 301
  White House wedding, 237–41, 243–44
crime, 85–93, 313–14
  Nixon and election of 1968, 86–88, 313
  Reagan and, 88–92
Cronkite, Walter, 191
Cuba, 34, 96, 271, 352
  Bay of Pigs invasion, 27, 219, 271
Cuban Missile Crisis, 27
Cullen, George, xii
Cummings, Theodore, 224–25
currency arbitrage, 293–94
Curtis, Charlotte, 109–10
Cuyahoga River, xvii

Daily Bruin, 97, 99, 101, 102, 103, 108

Davis, Angela, xiii, xvi, 85, 93–104
aftermath of summer of 1971, 351–52
arrest and trial of, 171, 311, 317–19, 325–28, 350–51
background of, 93–95
FBI surveillance of, 100–103, 317–18
Jackson and Soledad Brothers, 112–23, 327–29
at UCLA, 96–106
firing, 106–8, 111, 113, 115, 116
Davis, Rennie, 138, 144–45
Davis, Vincent, 57–60
Dean, Arthur, 26, 29
Dean, John W., 159, 165, 308–9, 347
Democratic National Committee, Watergate break-in, 282
Democratic National Convention (1956), 69
Democratic National Convention (1968), 144
Diamonds Are Forever (film), 49
Dillon, Douglas, 26, 29
District of Columbia, abortion law, 157
District of Columbia Fire Department, 271
Divale, William Tulio, 101–3
Dobbs v. *Jackson Women's Health Organization,* 350
Dobrynin, Anatoly, 216
Doe v. *Bolton,* 173
Don Tran Von, 216
Don van Sung, 216
"double secret probation," 148–49, 149*n*
Douglas, William O., 158, 161, 173
Dow Jones Industrial Average, 301–2
Dragnet (TV series), 90
Drumgo, Fleeta, 327
Dukert, Betty Cole, 141–42
Dulles, John Foster, 252
Dunlap, David, 248–49
Dunn, John M., 75
Durdin, Tillman, 221
Dylan, Bob, 130

Economic Stabilization Act of 1970, 288–91, 295–96
Ehrlichman, John
Alcatraz occupation and, 320
Attica Prison riot and, 341
Fortas and Supreme Court, 161
Johnson and election of 1968, 268–70
Nixon and economic policy, xii, 304, 308
Nixon and war on crime, 88
Pentagon Papers and, 257, 278, 279, 346
82nd Airborne Division, 146
Eisenhower, Dwight D., 26, 30, 39–40, 42, 77, 287, 296
Eisenhower, Julie Nixon, 237, 240, 243
Eisenhower, Mamie, 238, 240
election of 1948, 287
election of 1956, 69
election of 1960, 287, 324
election of 1964, 58
election of 1968, 56–60, 78–79, 86–88, 94, 160, 161, 179, 228*n*, 311, 321
election of 1970, 283–84, 291
election of 1972, 159, 215, 247, 286, 288–91, 311, 313, 321–23
Elisabeth Irwin High School, 94–95
Elliott, William Yandell, 178
Ellsberg, Daniel, xiii, xvi
aftermath of summer of 1971, 347
FBI wiretaps of, 66–67
fortieth birthday party of, 205–6
at Harvard, 4–5, 38, 53–54, 155
Kissinger and, 38–39, 40, 53–64, 69–70
Mayday protests, 153–56
at Pentagon, 5–6, 18
Pentagon Papers and, 184–90, 205–14, 230–37, 281, 346–47
fallout, 260, 265–68, 271, 272, 282, 346–47
IPS leaks, 187–89, 192–93, 230–31
"moral release," 231, 232, 234–36
"official approval," 232–34, 236–37
publication, 241–42, 244–45
terms of agreement, 192–94, 207–8, 230–31

at RAND, 4–5, 60, 61–62, 186, 194
at State Department, 7–8, 54–55
"The Theory and Practice of Blackmail," 53–54, 63
trial of, 346–47
Vietnam War and, 3–4, 5–11, 15–25, 54–60
leaks, 22–30, 31, 65–67
Westmoreland's request for additional troops, 19–22
Ellsberg, Patricia Marx, 153, 155
Pentagon Papers and, 193–94, 231–32, 241, 267–68
Ellsberg's Paradox, 5
Epstein, Jeffrey, 312
Espionage Act, 346
Esquire, 80
Eve, Arthur, 333, 334

Face the Nation (TV series), 250–51
Farland, Joseph, 224–25, 226–27
Farrakhan, Louis, 333
Farrow, Mia, 218, 247, 350
FBI (Federal Bureau of Investigation)
Agnew and, 353
antiwar protests and, 131–32, 135, 141–42, 143
Black Panthers and, 97–99, 100–103, 110
Carswell and, 164
Davis and, 311, 317, 318
Pentagon Papers and, 192–93, 194–95, 197, 198, 242, 262, 263, 265, 271, 272
Ten Most Wanted list, 318
wiretaps and surveillance, 65–67, 75–76, 98–99, 100–101, 135, 141–42, 215–16, 346
Federal Reserve Board, 288, 294, 354
Feiffer, Jules, 132
feminist movement, 49, 95–96, 172
Ferguson, Niall, 52–53
Ferlinghetti, Lawrence, 116
Fielding, Lewis, 282, 346
Finney, John, 250
First Amendment, 104, 277, 281
Floyd, Jay, 174–75
Folsom Prison, 352
Fonda, Jane, 116, 131–34, 135
Ford, Cristina, 280–81
Ford Foundation, 74, 155, 216
Ford, Gerald, 353
Ford, Henry, II, 280
foreign aid, 307–8
Fortas, Abe, 217
Supreme Court and, 159–65
Vietnam War and, 26, 30–31
Fort Benning, 129
Fort Bragg, 132
Fort Holabird, 133
Fort Leavenworth, 129
Forty Carats (film), 46
Fourteenth Amendment, 158
Fox News, 86
Frankel, Max, 187
Gridiron Club Dinner, 190–92
Sheehan and Cambodia investigation, 70–71, 75, 79, 80, 82, 83, 176
Sheehan and Pentagon Papers, 187, 190, 207–8, 209–13
Sheehan and Vietnam War, 32–37, 198
Franklin, Aretha, 319
Freedman, Manny, 204
Free Speech Movement, 92, 103
Friedan, Betty, 172
FTA ("Fuck the Army"), 131–32
Fulbright, J. William, 136–37
Furman v. *Georgia,* 310

Gabor, Zsa Zsa, 46
Gaiter, Bill, 345
Gallup, 79, 85, 129
game theory, 4–5, 44, 53–54, 55, 62–63
Garment, Leonard, 320–21, 323–25
Gay Mayday, 137–39
gay rights, 127, 137–38
Gelb, Leslie, 62, 253, 268, 270
General Revenue Sharing Act of 1972, 284
Gershon, Livia, 93
Gesell, Gerhard A., 157
Gideon v. *Wainwright,* 160
Gifford, Dun, 194–97, 206–7, 207*n*

Gilded Age, 215
Ginsberg, Allen, 116
Golden Gate Bridge, 119
Gold, Gerald, 209–12, 213, 235, 236
gold standard, 293–94, 298–300, 302–3, 306, 307–8
Goodale, James, 190–92, 210–11
Goodell, Charles, 283–84
Goodell, Roger, 283–84
Good Life, A (Bradlee), 272–73
Goodrow, Garry, 132
Gosden, Freeman, 238, 252
Graham, Billy, 238
Graham, Katharine, 273–74, 350
Gravel, Mike, 242
Great Depression, xii
Greenfield, James, 187, 208, 210–11, 231, 245–47, 261–62, 263, 348
"Greening of the Press, The" (Wicker), 200–201
Gregory, Dick, 131–32, 179
Gridiron Club Dinner, 190–92
Griswold v. *Connecticut,* 158, 167–73
Gruson, Sydney, 201, 202, 210, 262, 393*n*
Gulf of Tonkin incident, 5–6, 241, 265
Gurfein, Murray, 265–66
Gwertzman, Bernard, 264–65

Haig, Alexander
  Ellsberg and, 69–70
  Kissinger and China visit, 223, 227
  Nixon's resignation, 353
  Pentagon Papers and, 247–49, 251, 252
Halberstam, David, 12, 105–6
Haldeman, H. R. "Bob," xii, 346–47
  antiwar protests and, 138–40, 145–46
  Attica Prison riot and, 341–42
  background of, 47
  Cambodian campaign, 64–65, 74–75
  Connally and, 228–29, 295–96
  economic policy, 295–96, 302–3, 308
  Johnson and election of 1968, 268–70
  Pentagon Papers and, 275, 277–81
  Safire and, 47, 138–40
  Tricia Nixon's wedding, 238–39, 240–41
Haley, Harold, 119–23, 352
Halperin, Morton, 59, 62, 65–67, 69, 268, 270
Harlem Hospital, 317
Harlow, Bryce, 77–78, 83
Harriman, Pamela Digby, 218–19, 350
Harriman, W. Averell, 215–21
  aftermath of summer of 1971, 350
  ambassador at large, 14–15, 26
  background of, 26, 27, 215, 218
  Cambodian campaign and, 67–69, 74
  China and Ronning and, 217–18, 219–21
  election of 1968, 56–57
  FBI surveillance of, 34, 215–16
  Johnson and, 216–17, 218–19, 254, 269
  Kerry and antiwar protests, 144
  Paris peace negotiations, 31, 68, 74, 215–18, 220, 254, 269, 278, 279, 280
  Vietnamese coup d'état and, 14–15
Harvard Crimson, 155
Harvard Law School, 237, 238
Harvard University, 4–5, 38–39, 52–53
Hatfield, Mark, 141–42
Hawaii, abortion law, 157
Hayden, Tom, 116, 144
Haynsworth, Clement, 163–64
Hayward, Leland, 218
health care, 290
Hepburn, Katharine, 350
Herman, George, 250
heroin, 88, 225–26
Hersh, Seymour, 59, 129, 199
Hilliard, David, 97
Hiss, Alger, 276, 282
Hitler, Adolf, 52, 54, 70, 199
Ho Chi Minh, 64, 135
Hoffman, Abbie, 310–11, 312
Hoffman, Dustin, 153
Hogan, Frank S., 315

Hoopes, Townsend, 19–21, 23
Hoover, J. Edgar, 191
  antiwar protests and, 131–32, 143
  Black Panthers and, 97–99, 100–101
  Harriman and, 215–16
  Haynsworth and Supreme Court, 164
  Pentagon Papers and, 193, 238, 271
  Sheehan and, 33
  wiretaps, 65–67, 75–76, 98–99, 100–101, 215–16
Hope, Bob, 191–92
Hopkins, Harry, 69
Houghton Mifflin, 83
House Ways and Means Committee, 285–86, 290
Howar, Barbara, 45–46
Hubbard, Al, 141, 142, 143
Hubert, Claude "Chuchessa," 97
Huggins, Ericka, 326
Huggins, John, 96–97
Hughes, Howard, 47–48
Hughes, Sarah, 170, 171
Humphrey, Hubert, 57, 94, 217, 246, 268, 321, 324
Hunt, E. Howard, 271
Huston, Tom Charles (Huston Plan), 269–70, 271, 275, 281–82, 308–9

income taxes, xvii, 284–86, 290
inflation, 283, 288–91, 292–93, 294–95, 298–99, 354
Institute for Policy Studies (IPS), 187–89, 192–93, 230–31
Intercept, The, 185–88
interest rates, 294, 354
Internal Revenue Service (IRS), 279–80
International Monetary Fund, 299–301
Isaacson, Walter, 45
Is There No Place on Earth for Me? (Sheehan), 349

Jackson Day Fast, 330–31
Jackson, George
  Davis and Soledad Brothers, 112–19, 319, 327–28
  Marin County Courthouse incident, 119–23, 327
  prison escape attempt and death of, 327–29, 330–31, 341
Jackson, Georgia, 113, 117
Jackson, Jesse, 319
Jackson, Jonathan, 113–16, 117–23, 351
Jackson, Lester, 118
Jackson State killings, 127, 345
James Madison Constitutional Law Institute, 167–68, 171–72
Jennings, Jay, 153
Jim Crow, 93–94
John F. Kennedy Center for the Performing Arts, 280
Johnson, Claudia Alta "Lady Bird," 217
Johnson, J. Daniel, 97
Johnson, Lyndon B., xvii, 244
  Connally and, 286–87
  election of 1968, 268–70
  Harriman and, 215–19, 254, 269
  JFK assassination, 219, 288
  LBJ Library, 216–17
  Supreme Court and, 158, 159–61
  Vietnam War and, 5–6, 8, 15, 18–23, 26–32, 54–60, 215, 244, 254, 255–56, 268, 397*n*
    Operation 34A, 205–7
    Pentagon Papers, 254, 255–56, 268–69
    Westmoreland's request for additional troops, 19–22
    Wise Men and, 26–32
Johnson, Tom, 28–29
Jones, Harold "Tuwala," 97
Jones, Waverly M., 317
Jorgensen, Christine, 284
J. Walter Thompson, 47

Kalish, Donald, 99
Kennedy Center for the Performing Arts, 280
Kennedy, Edward "Ted"
  election of 1972, 324
  Gridiron Club Dinner, 190
  health care coverage, 290
  Pentagon Papers and, 194–95, 206–7, 276, 280–81
  Vietnam War and, 27–28, 60

Kennedy, Ethel, 350
Kennedy, John F.
assassination of, 27, 85, 169, 170, 179, 219, 288
Bay of Pigs invasion, 27, 219, 271
Connally and, 287
election of 1960, 287, 324
Vietnam War and, 12, 14, 18, 251
Kennedy, Robert F., 28, 85, 194, 283
Kennedy, Rose Fitzgerald, 350
Kent State University shootings, 65, 127, 345
Kerry, John, 134–37, 140–44
Keystone Kops, 154–55
Khoi Dang Duc, 215–16
King, Martin Luther, Jr., 85, 110
Kissinger, Henry, xiii, 38–60
aftermath of summer of 1971, 354
background of, 52–53
Baker and, 39–41
China secret trip of, xvi, 47, 221–29, 256, 295
election of 1968, 56–60
Johnson and, 268–70
Ellsberg and, 38–39, 40, 53–64, 69–70
FBI and wiretaps, 65
Gridiron Club Dinner, 190–92
Harriman and, 67, 68, 215–16
at Harvard, 38–39, 41, 42, 52–53
Kennedy and, 280–81
national security adviser, 47, 61–62, 63, 65, 74–75
Pentagon Papers and, 246–47, 250, 251–59, 269, 274–77
reputation and power of, 49–51
secretary of state, 353
Sheehan and, 71–76, 82–84, 176–78, 184, 213–14
Sinatra and, 44, 225, 246–47, 251, 252, 256–57
"small war" theory of, 38–44, 50–53, 54
Vietnam War and, 40, 54–60, 215–16, 268, 278
Cambodian campaign, 46, 63–65, 71–75, 82–84, 224
Wallace interview, 41–44, 51
women and starlets, 44–49
Women's Press Club speech, 47–49
Kissinger, Nancy Maginnes, 56
Kleindienst, Richard, 163
Klute (film), 131
Knapp Commission, 314
Kopechne, Mary Jo, 195
Kovach, Bill, 196–98
Krim, Arthur, 217
Krock, Arthur, 68–69
Krogh, Egil, 195, 347
Ku Klux Klan, 87, 93–94
Kunstler, William, 333–34, 336, 344

Lafayette Park, 238
Laird, Melvin R., 77–78, 250, 253–55
Lake, Anthony, 75–76, 188
Lambert, William, 161
Lane, Mark, 134, 179–84, 199, 389*n*
Laos, 73–74, 130, 223–24
Lasky, Victor, 140
Last of the Southern Girls, The (Morris), 45
Latimer, George, 129
Latino voters, 228*n*
Lefcourt, Gerald, 312
Legislative Reorganization Act, 298
Leonard, John, 182–83, 200, 201–2
"lesser evil," 39, 53
Lewis, Anthony, 151–52
Liberatore, Paul, 117
Liberty Square Press, 198
Liddy, G. Gordon, 270–71, 280, 281–82, 308–9, 347
Life (magazine), 161–63, 330
Liman, Arthur, 339–40
Lincoln Memorial, 138–39
Lindsay, John, 284–86, 314, 321
"linkage" theory, 47, 229
Linkletter, Art, 238
Little Big Man (film), 153
Lodge, Henry Cabot, Jr., 8, 14–15, 26, 55
Loeb, Louis, 231
Logan Airport, 192
Lord Day & Lord, 263
Los Angeles Police Department (LAPD), 89–90, 97, 101, 118
Los Angeles Times, 89–90, 97, 105–6, 107, 236–37
Los Angeles, Watts riots, 89–90
Lucas, Roy, 167–68, 171, 172–73

Lunar New Year, 19

McAdoo, Richard, 83
McCarthy, Eugene, 28
McCarthy, Joseph (McCarthyism), 94–95, 102, 107, 181
McClain, James, 119–20, 123
McCloskey, Pete, 186, 230–31, 232, 236–37
McCluskey, Henry, 168–70
McCorvey, Norma, 169–70
McCracken, Paul, 302, 303, 304
Mace, 154–55
McGinniss, Joe, 86
McGovern, George, 131, 137, 141–42, 186, 190, 321
McGovern-Hatfield Amendment, 141–42
MacLaine, Shirley, 45
McNamara, Robert
  Connally and, 287
  Operational Plan for General Nuclear War, 4–5
  Vietnam Study (Pentagon Papers), 18–19, 22–23, 59, 62, 65, 156, 186, 193, 213, 244–45, 248–50, 253, 254–55
  Vietnam War and, 4–5, 15, 18–19, 55–56
McNaughton, John, 368*n*
McTernan, John T., 107–8
Madman Theory, 63, 64, 70, 72–73, 78
Magee, Ruchell, 119–20, 318–19, 352
Mailer, Norman, 144
Malcolm X, 315–16
Mansfeld, Jayne, 45
Mansfield, Mike, 190, 277–81
Manson, Charles, 129, 171, 282, 282*n*
Mao Tse-tung, 98, 219
Marcuse, Herbert, 95, 99, 101, 106
Mardian, Robert, 260–63, 274–75
marijuana, 88, 93, 226
Marin County Civic Center and Courthouse, 119–23, 327–28, 329
Marine One, 228, 301, 303
Marshall Plan, 26
martial law, 149
Marx, Groucho, 229
Marx, Louis, 231
Mayday, 127, 144–56
  Cambodian campaign and, 65
  Ellsberg and, 153–56
  Kent State University shootings, 65, 127, 345
  mass arrests and civil liberties, 144–52
  Nixon and, 138–40, 145–46, 149–52, 237–38
  planning, 136–40
  the protests, 144–56
May Day Tribe, 144–45, 151, 155
Mayflower Hotel, 139
Meadlo, Paul D., 128
Means, Cyril, 172
Meany, George, 294
Meet the Press (TV series), 140–43
Melvin X, 115
Metternich, Klemens von, 41, 55, 84
military draft, 22, 130, 131–32
Miller, Herbert J., 194–95
Millones, Peter, 210–11
Mills, Wilbur, 285–86
Minnelli, Liza, 45
Minnesota Twins, 165
Miranda v. *Arizona,* 160
MIT (Massachusetts Institute of Technology), 67
Mitchell, John N.
  Attica Prison riot and, 343–44
  Back Panthers and, 98–99, 102
  election of 1968, 78–79
  election of 1972, 322, 343–44
  Fortas and Supreme Court, 162–63
  Mayday protests and, 145–46, 149–50, 152–53
  Pentagon Papers and, 250, 251–52, 257–59, 260–63, 265–68, 347
Mitchell, Martha, 78–79, 152–53
Mitford, Jessica, 116
Mohr, Charles, 25
Monroe, Marilyn, 45
Mooney, Richard E., 208
Morris, Willie, 45
Murphy, Patrick, 317
Murphy, Robert, 26–30

Murrow, Edward R., 202
Murtagh, John M., 315
Muskie, Edmund, 81–82, 190, 321, 324
My Lai massacre, 127–29, 132–33, 199, 276, 292–93

Nader, Ralph, 238, 240
Nader's Raiders, 238, 238*n*, 240
Napoleonic Wars, 41
National Airport, 155
National Book Award, 38–39
National Guard, 65, 91, 127, 345
National Lampoon's Animal House (film), 149, 149*n*
National Mall, 145
National Peace Action Coalition, 137
National Press Club, 47
National Review, 182, 283
National Security Council, 61–62, 63
National Welfare Rights Organization, 137
Nation of Islam, 333
Native Americans, and occupation of Alcatraz Island, 311, 320–21
NATO (North Atlantic Treaty Organization), 26
Nazi Germany, 52, 54, 70
NBC-TV, 140–41, 143, 228, 239, 240–41, 289
"new federalism," 284
Newman, Edwin, 239
New Republic, 78–79, 321–22
Newsweek, 140, 183, 201, 292–93
Newton, Huey, 97, 311, 333
New York (magazine), 111
New York, abortion law, 157
New York Botanical Garden, 312
New York City, 294, 310–17
  bankruptcy, 284–86
  murder rate, 85, 294
  Panther 21 trial, 108–9, 310–12, 315–17
New Yorker, 80
New York Hilton, 231, 232, 235, 242, 347
New York Police Department (NYPD), 108–9, 310–17
  Intelligence Unit (Red Squad), 168
New York Times, xi–xii, 176–90. *See also specific persons*
  antiwar protests and, 134, 141, 150–52
  Black Panthers and, 109–10, 111, 315–16
  Cambodia investigation, 70–84
  Kissinger and, 39–41, 57, 61
  Pentagon Papers and, xvi, 185–90, 347–49
    background to publication, 193, 196–97, 207–14, 230–37
    legal battle and fallout, 230–31, 257–59, 260–63, 275, 281, 346
    publication, 241–59
    Salisbury's account, 207*n*, 233–36
  Vietnam War and, 11–12, 17, 18, 19, 32–37, 57, 179–84
    Ellsberg's leaks, 22–30, 31
New York Times Book Review, 41, 178, 179–84, 198–205
New York Times Co. v. *United States*, 281, 346
New York Times Magazine, 80–82, 178–79, 213–14
Ngo Dinh Diem, 13–14, 365*n*
"nixious," 324–25
Nixon Agonistes (Wills), 178
Nixonland (Perlstein), 87
Nixon, Pat, 132, 237, 240, 243, 259, 301
Nixon, Richard
  abortion issue, 166–67
  aftermath of summer of 1971, 353–54
  Alcatraz occupation and, 320–21
  antiwar protests and, 86, 132, 138–40, 145–46, 149–52, 237–38, 342
  Attica Prison riot and, 341–45
  Connally and, 228, 286–87, 291–92, 299, 301–3
  economic policy of, xvii, 284–86, 288–308, 353–54
    address to the nation, 307–8, 402–3*n*
    Camp David meetings, 294–97, 303–7

criticisms, 289–90, 292–93
gold standard decision, 293–94, 298–301, 302–3, 306, 307–8
inflation and, 288–91, 292–93, 294–95, 298–99, 354
legislation, 284, 288–91, 295–96, 298
VAT, xvii, 285–86, 290
wage and price controls, 228, 289, 290, 294, 296, 307, 353–54
election of 1968, 56–60, 78–79, 86–88, 160, 161, 228*n*, 268–70, 311, 321
election of 1972, 159, 215, 247, 286, 288–91, 302, 311, 313, 321–23
Gridiron Club Dinner, 190–92
Hoover and wiretaps, 65–67, 75–76, 98–99, 100–101
Huston Plan and Brookings, 269–70, 271, 275, 281–82, 308–9
Kissinger and, 44–45, 60–61, 246–47, 250, 251–53, 269–70, 275–77, 280, 301, 353
China secret trip, 221–24, 226, 228
Kissinger's disdain for Nixon, 60, 61
Madman Theory, 63, 64, 70, 72–73, 78
"new federalism" of, 284
New York City and, 285–86
Pentagon Papers and, 194, 237–38, 275–82, 346–47
legal battle, 257–59, 260–63, 268–70
publication, 243–59
the Plumbers and Watergate, xii, xvii–xviii, 250, 271, 275, 282, 308–9, 346–47
race and segregation and, 312–13, 322–25
resignation of, 353
Supreme Court and, 158–66
tapes, xvi–xvii, 305
Tricia's wedding, 237–41
Vietnam War and, 40, 127, 129–30, 215–16
Cambodian campaign, 63–65, 70–75, 127, 176
death toll, 247–48
news conference on drug problem, 225–26
Western White House, 46, 69–70, 166–67
Nobel Prize, 63
Nol, Lon, 72
No, No, Nanette (musical), 301
Normandy landings (D-Day), 27
North Carolina Law Review, 167
North Vietnamese Army, 3–4, 19, 20, 23–24, 31–32, 67–68, 130
nuclear weapons. *See* atomic weapons
Nuclear Weapons and Foreign Policy (Kissinger), 38–39, 40, 84
Nunn, Louie, 284, 291

occupation of Alcatraz, 311, 320–21
Odessa Group, 271
Office of Legal Counsel, 148
Office of Management and Budget (OMB), 296, 299, 302, 304
Onassis, Aristotle, 80–81, 350
Onassis, Jacqueline Kennedy, 79, 80–81, 350
101st Airborne Division, 133
Operation Breakfast, 64–65
Operation Dewey Canyon III, 136
Operation Torch, 27
Operation 34A, 205–7
Osborne, John, 78–79, 321–22
Osnos, Peter, 287
Oswald, Lee Harvey, 169, 179, 219, 287–88
Oswald, Russell, 330, 334–35, 339, 340–41, 343–44
Ottinger, Richard, 284

Pacific Southwest Airlines, 123
Paine, Thomas, 133–34
Pakistan, 221–22, 224–26, 394–95*n*
Pakula, Alan J., 131
Panther 21, 108–9, 310–11, 315
Parade (magazine), 46
Paris peace talks, 64, 68, 74, 215–18, 220, 244, 245, 250, 254, 268, 278, 279, 280, 370*n*

Parker, William, 90
Paul, Weiss, Rifkind, Wharton & Garrison, 340
Peace and Freedom Party, 179
Peale, Norman Vincent, 238
Peer, Elizabeth "Liz," 183
Pentagon Papers, xvii–xviii, 186–90, 192–98, 203, 205–14, 227, 230–37. *See also specific persons*
  aftermath, 346–47
  background on McNamara Vietnam Study, 18–19, 22–23, 59, 62, 65, 156, 186, 193, 213, 253
  IPS leaks, 187–89, 192–93, 230–31
  legal battle and fallout, 230–31, 256–59, 260–63, 274, 281
  Operation 34A, 205–7
  Post publication, 272–74
  Risen's story on, 185–88, 209
  Rogovin's role, 209–13, 230–31, 232, 236, 265
  Times publication, 241–59
People's Coalition for Peace and Justice, 137
Perlstein, Rick, 87
Peterson, Pete, 229, 301
Phelps, Bob, 34, 183, 189, 207, 209–10, 236
Piagentini, Joseph A., 317
Piedras Negras, 168
Pierre Hotel, 62
Planned Parenthood, 172
Playboy Bunnies, 49
Plumbers, the, xvii–xviii, 250, 271, 275, 282, 308–9, 346–47
Poindexter, David, 318
Police Benevolent Association (PBA), 317
"Political Uses of Madness, The" (Ellsberg), 54
Poor People's Mule Train, 137
Porter, Paul, 160, 163
Powell, Curtis, 312
Prager, Joshua, 173
Prairie Fire (manifesto), 130
President's War, The (Austin), 241–42
price controls, 228, 289, 290, 294, 296, 353–54
Princeton University, 238, 379*n*
Pringle, Peter, 286
Procter & Gamble, 77
Pulitzer Prize, 80, 151, 161, 189, 241, 347, 349
Purple Hearts, 134, 142

Quadriad, 299, 302, 303–7
Quinn, Billy, 333, 336

race and racism, 85–86, 88, 93–96, 137, 321–25
"Radical Chic: That Party at Lenny's" (Wolfe), 111
Radio Free Alcatraz, 320
RAND Corporation, 4–5, 44–45, 60, 61–62, 67, 186, 194, 243, 258–59
Random House, 256, 287
Raskin, Jamie, 187
Raskin, Marcus, 187–89, 230
Rayburn, Sam, 287
Reagan, Ronald
  California gubernatorial election of 1966, 88, 91–93
  Communist Party and, 105, 106–8, 116–17
  crime issue, 85, 88–93
  Davis and, 102, 103, 105
Rebozo, Bebe, 34, 238, 243, 259
"red baiting," 102
Red Scare, 94–95
Rehnquist Choice, The (Dean), 159
Rehnquist, William, 148–49, 162–65
Republican National Convention (1968), 56, 58–59, 86–87
Republic F-105 Thunderbirds, 3–4
Reston, James "Scotty," 61, 189–90, 208–11, 232
revenue sharing, 284–86, 290
RFK Stadium, 147
Richard M. Nixon Library, 217
Ridgway, Matthew, 26–27
Rikers Island, 312
Risen, James, 185–88, 209
RKO Pictures, 47
Road to Hell, The (Liberatore), 117
Robb, Lynda, 240–41
Rock Creek Park, 45

Rockefeller, Nelson
aftermath of summer of 1971, 354
Attica Prison riot and, 330, 334–45
election of 1968, 56–59
election of 1970, 283, 291
election of 1972, 286
Kissinger and China secret mission, 221–23
Nixon and New York City, 284–86, 291
Roe v. *Wade,* xv, 157–58, 169, 170–75, 349–50
Rogers, William P.
Kissinger's China visit and, 221, 222, 224, 226, 229
Pentagon Papers and, 249–50, 252–53, 257, 273–74
Sheehan and, 77–78, 214
Rogovin, Mitch, 209–13, 230–31, 232, 236, 265
Ronning, Chester, 217–21
Roosevelt, Franklin D., xvii, 26, 69, 306–7
Roosevelt, Theodore, xvii
Rose, Jerry, 367*n*
Rosenthal, Abe
Sheehan and Cambodia investigation, 70
Sheehan and Pentagon Papers, 196–97, 203–5, 207–13, 231, 232–33, 244, 245–47, 261–63, 347, 348–49
Sheehan and Vietnam War, 32–37, 183–84, 200–203
Rostow, Walt, 19–23, 21*n,* 255–56, 258
Ruby, Jack, 169
Rush to Judgment (Lane), 179
Russell, Jane, 48
Russell, Richard, 28
Russo, Anthony, 346

Sacharoff, Mark, 199
Safire, William
antiwar protests and, 138–40, 150–52
Kissinger and, 46–50, 224
Nixon and economic policy, 290–91, 303, 304, 305–6
Saigon, 9–11, 13–14, 247
St. John, Jill, 49, 227–28
Salinger, Pierre, 216
Salisbury, Harrison, 207*n,* 233–36
Sanchez, Manolo, 139
San Francisco International Airport, 123
San Francisco Police Department, 91
San Francisco riots, 90–91
San Francisco Superior Court, 118
San Francisco United Committee to Free Angela Davis, 326–27
San Quentin Prison, 112, 113, 118–19, 120, 171, 327, 328–29, 341
Santa Barbara oil spill, xvii
Santa Rita Jail, 92
Santillana, Dorothy de, 83–84
Saturday Night Live (TV series), 132
Savio, Mario, 92
Schelling, Tom, 62–63
Schieffer, Bob, 250
Schoenbrun, David, 202
Schwarz, Daniel, 200, 201
Screen Actors Guild, 107
Seale, Bobby, 97, 116, 311, 326, 334, 336–37, 344
2nd Marine Division, 146
"Secret History, The" (Risen), 185–88, 209
Securities and Exchange Commission (SEC), 161
Seeger, Pete, 116
segregation, 93–94, 164, 302, 321–23
Selling of the President, The (McGinniss), 86
Senate Finance Committee, 290
Senate Foreign Relations Committee, 136–37, 143, 210
Senate Judiciary Committee, 164
Sevareid, Eric, 289–90
sexism, 95–96
Shafer, Raymond, 284, 291
Shapiro, Harvey, 178
Shearer, Lloyd, 46, 69–70
Sheehan, Neil, 176–90
aftermath of summer of 1971, 347–49
The Arnheiter Affair, 71
Ellsberg and, 11–12, 15–17, 18–25, 76, 156, 184–90, 192–98, 207–14, 230–37
leaks, 22–30, 31

Sheehan, Neil, *cont.*
  Kerry and *Meet the Press*, 141, 142–43
  Kissinger and, 71–75, 82–84, 176–78, 184, 213–14
  Pentagon Papers and, xvi, 185–90, 192–98, 203, 206–14, 230–37
    copying, 193–94, 196–98, 206–7, 208, 390–93*n*
    fallout, 265, 272, 273–74, 347–49
    Gifford's role, 194–97, 206–7
    IPS leaks, 187–89, 192–93, 230–31
    "moral release," 231, 232, 234–36
    "official approval," 232–34, 236–37
    publication, 241–42, 244, 246
    Rogovin's role, 209–13, 230–31, 232, 236, 265
    terms of agreement, 192–94, 207–8, 230–31
  Rosenthal and Frankel and role in newsroom, 32–37
  Vietnam War and, 11–12, 15–17, 18–25
    Cambodia investigation, 70–84, 176
    Lane's book review, 134, 179–84
    war crimes essay, 180, 184–85, 188, 198–205
    Westmoreland's request for additional troops, 19–22, 23–24
Sheehan, Susan, 80–82, 84, 177, 184, 347, 349, 350
  Pentagon Papers and, 192, 194, 197, 198, 231
"Should We Have War Crime Trials?" (Sheehan), 184–85, 188, 198–205
Shultz, George, 296, 299–305
Sidle, Winant, 203
Siegal, Allan, 183–84, 213
Sihanouk, Norodom, 72–73
Simone, Nina, 319
Simon & Schuster, 180–81
Sinatra, Frank, 44, 218, 225, 246–47, 251, 252, 256–57, 350
Sixteenth Street Baptist Church bombing, 95
60 Minutes (TV series), 41
Skelton, Red, 238
Smith, Hedrick "Rick," 19, 244–45
  Cambodia investigation, 70–74, 82–83
Smith, Howard K., 289
Smith, William French, 115
Soledad Brother (Jackson), 328
Soledad Brothers, 112–23, 327–29
Soledad Brothers Defense Committee, 113–16, 117
Southern Christian Leadership Conference, 137
Southern Colorado State College, 132–33
South Vietnamese Army (ARVN), 4, 8–9, 16, 27–28, 55, 130
Soviet Union. *See also* Cold War
  Ellsberg on, 53–54
  Kissinger on, 42–43, 44, 51
  Oswald and, 287–88
  Pentagon Papers and, 264–65
Spivak, Lawrence E., 141–42, 143
Stans, Maurice, 294–95
Statler Hilton, 190–91
Stavins, Ralph, 187–89, 230
Steadman, Richard, 24–25
Steinem, Gloria, 49
Stevenson, Adlai, 69
Stokes, Muriel, 231
Stone, I. F., 155
strict constructionism, 163–64, 165
Student Nonviolent Coordinating Committee (SNCC), 95, 100
Students for a Democratic Society (SDS), 102, 130, 138, 144
"Subterranean Homesick Blues" (song), 130
Subversive Activities Control Board, 102–3
Sullivan, Bill, 67
Sulzberger, Arthur Ochs "Punch," 200, 201, 208, 232–33, 265
"summer soldiers," 133–34
Supreme Court. *See also individual cases*
  Nixon and, 158–66
Sutherland, Donald, 131–32, 135
Swann v. *Charlotte-Mecklenburg*, 322, 405*n*

Swarthmore College, 96, 379*n*
Swift Boat, 134

Taiwan, 217, 220, 227
Talese, Gay, 80
tariffs, xii, 296–97, 298–99, 307
Tate, Sharon, 129, 282*n*
tax policy, xvii, 284–86, 290
Taylor, Elizabeth, 45
Taylor, Maxwell, 26–29, 30, 76–77
Temple University, 199
Tet Offensive, 19–25, 60
Texas Medical Association, 172
"Theory and Practice of Blackmail, The" (Ellsberg), 53–54, 63
Thich Quang Duc, 13–15, 27
"thin blue line," 90
Thomas, Gary, 120, 122–23
Thomas, Helen, 239
Thomas, Marlo, 45
Thornberry, Homer, 159
Time (magazine), 79
Time to Die, A (Wicker), 352–53
Tolson, Clyde, 238
Tonkin Gulf incident, 5–6, 241–42, 265
Tonkin Gulf Resolution, 28
Topping, Seymour, 208–13, 221
Treadway Inn, 192, 193, 194, 196–97
Trudeau, Pierre, xii
Truman, Harry, 26, 69, 248

Ullmann, Liv, 45
unemployment, 289, 294, 295, 306
United Nations, 26, 167, 220, 226
University of California, Berkeley, 89, 92–93, 103, 115
University of California, Los Angeles (UCLA), 96–106, 115
  Davis's firing, 106–8, 111, 113, 115, 116
University of California, San Diego, 95, 96
University of California, Santa Cruz, 352
University of Texas, 168, 216–17, 287
UPI (United Press International), 33, 70, 80, 239
U.S. Agency for International Development (USAID), 8
U.S. News & World Report, xi
U.S. v. *Vuitch,* 157–58, 167, 170, 174

Vance, Cyrus, 26, 27, 29, 31, 68, 74
Van Doren, Mamie, 45
Vanity Fair (magazine), 173
Vann, John Paul, 8–9, 11–12, 15–17, 55, 57–60, 185, 366–67*n*
VAT (value-added tax), xvii, 285–86, 290
Victor Publishers, 197–98
Viet Cong, 4, 7–9, 16, 19, 135
Vietnamese coup d'état, 14–15
Vietnam Veterans Against the War (VVAW), 132–34, 135–38, 140–41, 143, 144–45
Vietnam War, xvi, 3–32
  Browne's reporting, 12–14
  Cambodia campaign, 46, 64–84, 127, 176, 224
  death toll, 247–48
  Ellsberg's leaks, 22–30
  Halberstam's reporting, 12, 105–6
  Johnson and Wise Men, 26–32
  McNamara Study (Pentagon Papers), 18–19, 22–23, 59, 62, 65, 156, 186, 193, 213, 244–45, 248–50, 253, 254–55
  My Lai massacre, 127–29, 132–33, 199, 292–93
  Operation 34A, 205–7
  Nixon's news conference on drug problem, 225–26
  protests against. *See* antiwar protests
  Tet Offensive, 19–22, 23–24
  Tonkin Gulf incident, 5–6, 241–42, 265
  Westmoreland's request for additional troops, 19–22, 29–31
Voege, Ray, 307–8
Volcker, Paul, xii, 302–5, 354
Vung Tau, 15–17

Wade, Henry, 169, 170–75
wage and price controls, 228, 289, 290, 294, 296, 353–54

Wallace, George, 94, 302, 311, 321–23
Wallace, Mike, 41–44, 51
Walters, Barbara, 239
War on Drugs, 86
Warren Commission, 179, 180, 219
Warren, Earl, 159–60, 161, 163
Washington, abortion law, 157
Washington, George, 135
Washington Post, xi–xii, xvi, 163, 239
  Pentagon Papers and, 240, 242–43, 246, 265–66, 281, 346
    publication, 272–74
Washington Redskins, 147
Washington, Walter, 190
Watergate, xii, xvii–xviii, 282, 346–47
Watts riots, 89–90
Wayne, John, 132
Weather Underground, 127, 130–34
Weddington, Sarah Ragle, xiii, xvi, 168–70, 171–75, 349–50
Welch, Raquel, 45
welfare, 286, 290, 292, 294, 312–13
Wellesley College, 80
Wells, Tom, 53–54
Western Surplus Store, 117–18
Westmoreland, William, 8, 19–29
  Pentagon Papers and, 203
  request for additional troops, 19–22, 29–31
  Tet Offensive, 19–25
West Potomac Park, 145
White House Rose Garden, 237–38, 244
"Why Cambodia?" (Sheehan), 75, 77, 82–84
Wicker, Tom
  Attica Prison riots and, 333–40, 344–45, 352–53
  criticism of mainstream press, 200–201
  Pentagon Papers and, 189, 200–201
Wild Man (Wells), 53–54
Williams, Edward Bennett, xiii, 272–74
Wills, Garry, 178
Wilson, Jerry, 150
Winter Soldier Investigation, 132–34
"winter soldiers," 133–34, 135
Without Fear or Favor (Salisbury), 233–34
WLIB-FM, 315
Woerkom, Fons van, 198–99
Wolfe, Tom, 111, 204
Wolfson, Louis, 161, 162
Women's March on the Pentagon, 136
Women's Press Club, 47–49
Woodlawn Cemetery, 97
Woods, Rose, 305
Woodstock, 123
World Bank, 24, 26, 299–301
World Restored, A (Kissinger), 38–39, 41
World War II, 27, 52, 244, 287

Yale University, 134, 141, 292
Yorty, Sam, 57

Zhou Enlai, 218, 219, 221–22, 226, 227
Ziegler, Ron, 227–28, 239, 268–69, 323
Zinn, Howard, 153–55, 241
Zinn, Roz, 241
"zone of privacy," 158